ENGLISH DRAMA

BY

FELIX E. SCHELLING

PROFESSOR IN THE UNIVERSITY OF PENNSYLVANIA
MEMBER OF THE AMERICAN NATIONAL INSTITUTE OF ARTS
AND LETTERS

NEW YORK
E. P. DUTTON & COMPANY
681 FIFTH AVENUE

14907

PREFACE

In the following pages, an endeavour is made to tell, in scale and with a due regard to proportion, the story of English drama from its beginnings in the miracle play and morality to the performance of Sheridan's *Critic,* in the year 1779. A concluding chapter presents a sketch of the course of the drama since that time, in outline and by way of suggestion, and no more. To have completed the book on the same scale would have demanded another volume. But a better reason for the course here pursued is to be found in the circumstance that, by the time of Sheridan, almost the last vestige of the original dramatic impulse had been lost, the impulse that begot Marlowe and Shakespeare and carried the great traditions of their art over the Restoration and into the next century; and when the modern revival came, inspired by a renewed appreciation of the great Elizabethans, it was manifestly not a revival on the stage, but in a new species of literature, the drama of the study, as different from the original parent stock as the novel is different from it or from the drama capable of successful presentation on the stage.

English drama may be likened to a strand in which two threads, among many, are conspicuous: the thread which designates the actable play and the thread which designates that quality to which we give the indefinable term literature. In the days of Elizabeth, these two threads were, for the most part, so interwoven and twisted together that they gave to the cord that strength and unity that we recognise in the great dramas of that time. So complete, we may well believe, was their adaptation to their own stage — which, be it remembered, was not our stage — that, in reading them merely or seeing them reproduced under different conditions, we feel that they have inevitably lost something of their original charm. But the thread of literature and that of actability (shall we call it?) tended, from the first, to fall apart. There are plays of Shakespeare's own time that are inconceivable acted; there are also plays of his time which only the curious student now reads — and that only for discipline. The split became greater and greater as the gentleman writer turned his attention to play-making or as the allurements or profits of the craft attracted those whose cultivation and power of expression in words was inferior to their opportunities of becoming practically conversant with the stage. Until, by the beginning of the last century, the two threads have been torn hopelessly apart, that of the theatre to be represented by Knowles, Robertson or Boucicault, the literary and poetic, by Byron, Shelley and Tennyson, even more completely in severance, by Browning and Swinburne. There is need for a history of this great schism; but it belongs not to a book of this size or plan. For a history of the drama in the England of the nineteenth century must take into consideration political and social developments, changes of attitude in reader and auditor as well as the ideals of literature and cosmopolitan influences of which the happy little world, ruled by Pope and Voltaire, could have had no premonitions.

In presenting the material of this book in as orderly a succession as possible, the wealth of the Elizabethan age has led to a treatment of the drama, there, in its successive varieties rather than in a strict chronological array of the authors and their works. A steady progress forward is, none the less, maintained. While the stage, as well as the literary nature of the works considered, has been constantly kept in view, a history of the stage as such forms no part of the plan of this book. That work has been well done more than once. On the other hand, the attention of the reader is by no means limited to the literary drama, as the progress of the type could in no wise be made clear without a consciousness of the background against which the greater figures stand and a recognition of the conditions that make their work comprehensible. In any inquiry such as this, the author is torn between the two extremes to which the late Mr. Lang once happily alluded in a review: the danger of telling over again what everybody knows, and the peril of calling attention to what nobody cares anything about. The progress of scholarship should alone be a sufficient answer to this embarrassing dilemma, the logical consequence of which would be the reduction of all who write to silence. With new material accumulating daily to modify " what everybody knows," " the peril of calling attention to what nobody cares to hear anything about " sensibly diminishes. The ordering of minor things in a truer relation is a process in which a large part of the function of the historian consists, and out of which major results may issue. Even those most stubbornly content with "the present state of polite learning in Europe" may be constrained to readjust this facile division of all things ascertainable.

The present writer regrets that the plan of this series does not include either as complete an apparatus of notes or such bibliographies as are coming — possibly somewhat pedantically — more and more into vogue. In lieu of the first, he wishes to make his general acknowledgments to his predecessors of whom, among so many, to mention a few would be invidious. An exception, however, must be made in the case of Professor C. W. Wallace, whose indefatigable researches in the Public Records' Office have been so richly and astonishingly rewarded. The documentary material which Professor Wallace has published concerning Shakespeare, the Elizabethan theatres and kindred matters, has been used in this book materially to revise many accepted ideas on these subjects. The writer has not always been able to accept Professor Wallace's inferences, and submits that possibly he may modify his views when he can speak with greater fulness of knowledge as to the many "finds" of Professor Wallace that still await publication. The writer accepts the responsibilities of his own studies for the Elizabethan age and the Restoration period to the death of Dryden; beyond, he confesses frankly that he has trodden more circumspectly in the paths which those have made who preceded him. As to texts and authorities, the student reader is referred to the admirably full and useful bibliographies in the successive volumes of *The Cambridge History of English Literature,* to the excellent lists of authorities in A. H. Thorndike's *Tragedy,* 1907, and to the bibliographical Essay of the present writer's *Elizabethan Drama,* 1908.

CONTENTS

ENGLISH DRAMA

CHAPTER I

THE DRAMA, ITS NATURE, ORIGINS AND RELATIONS

As this book is one of a series of volumes dealing with the major channels of English literature, a statement of the nature and limitations of the subject here in hand can not be out of place. To the modern man a definition of drama might seem simple enough. A drama is " a thing made to be acted ": surely this is sufficient; and, indeed, acting touches the vital point of all drama. But the Senecan tragedies of Neronian Rome were not things "made to be acted "; neither is much of the literary drama of Victorian England, Shelley's *Cenci* for example or Swinburne's splendid trilogy devoted to Mary Stuart. While an historical inquiry into any subject must consider that out of which it arises, its cogeners and its outcomes, this book must be from the nature of the case, concerned, in the main, with that form and variety of written speech which details a connected story by means of dialogue and the attendant action involved in histrionic representation. Mediæval *débat, estrif* and pageant; *ballet,* masque and pantomime, modern closet play, prose conversation, poetic fantasy or rhapsody "writ dialogue wise," each has its place and partakes in its measure of dramatic qualities; but none is strictly drama nor need call for more than a subsidiary mention for the contribution of its tributary stream to the current of the main dramatic channel. Again, this book is of English drama, that is, a history of the growth and development of the drama in one country and in one tongue. There is an interesting chapter on Latin drama in modern western Europe; and foreign influences, in ebb and flow, have always been especially strong in literature of the dramatic type. Neither the examples of the ancients nor borrowings from the moderns can be neglected in an inquiry such as this; but it is easy to make too much of them. They, too, must keep their place for the necessary light which they can throw upon our major subject, and they must be permitted no more. As to one other limitation this book will be found less strict, and this is best suggested in the rejection of the titles, "a history of dramatic poetry," or "a history of dramatic literature." This last word popularly involves an æsthetic appraisement with an exclusion of the inferior and unliterary, a process foreign to rational historical inquiry. Indubitably we care less for productions that live their brief day and perish with the age that begot them than we care for those accredited works which have made their authors immortal. But the history of literature can no more be written in a neglect of the writings of lesser men than we can hope to write the history of a country solely on the basis of the biographies of its kings and princes. There is much admirable drama that is not poetry, whatever definition may be attached to that much abused word. And there are many plays that we read with interest for their place in the history of literature which could never move that detached and extraordinary person, the reader whose standard is the hypothetical absolute.

As a point of departure, Aristotle's simple definition of drama as "imitated human action" has not been bettered. The limitation, "human," is not less pertinent than the much debated term "imitation." For, however an Aristophanes or a Rostand may take us off to Cloudland or to Birdland, it is the human traits, even in these departures, that make such personages as theirs possible. Man cannot escape man even in the drama, and it is the ways of our kind, so dear to us, that constitute the essentials of dramatic subject matter. From another well known definition we may gain another point of view. "A drama is an epic told in lyric parts." But here we must apprehend the components if we are to be sure of the compound. An epic, in large, is a narrative poem, a story of deeds, told outwardly and objectively by some one who has heard them. A lyrical poem (the song element aside for the nonce) is the expression of an inner or subjective emotion by one who has felt what he expresses. Drama, in common with the epic, is concerned in the telling of a story. But the story is not told objectively and in the third person, but in the very speech, action and emotions of the participants, thus involving lyrical expression. It is obvious that we have here less a definition than an illustration, for there are other elements in both epic and lyrical poetry which might readily confuse; and, besides, the range of drama, as we have seen, is broader than that of poetry, however its heights may fall short of the loftier flights of the inspired rhapsodic lyrist. If we combine what we have thus far discussed, we have for a drama a picture or representation of human life in that succession and change of events that we call story, told by means of dialogue and presenting in action the successive emotions involved.

But it is far from true that every story is dramatic, even though it fulfil in presentation the conditions already rehearsed. Every drama involves — so the philosopher would have us know — a conflict between what he calls the universal and the particular, with the triumph in the end of one or the other. In tragedy the universal is some law of general acceptance among men, whether ethical and of man's making or founded on religious sanction. The struggle is therefore of a serious nature as it involves rebellion against Fate, against God or, at the least, against accepted human code. Hence tragedy deals with the deep and turbulent passions, those that lead to violence and crime. In comedy, contrastedly, the universal is some convention of men, a concatenation of circumstances which common experience tells us are likely to lead to certain results, and the struggle of the individual is against such things, the process of his struggle, cleverness, ingenuity, wit against wit, in which the lighter traits of mankind, their manners, follies, peccadilloes, play a diverting part. Hence comedy leads to laughter as irresistibly as tragedy begets tears. And in an ultimate analysis, the philosopher once more tells us, the essential difference between tragedy and comedy lies in the nature of the universal.

To illustrate the nature of dramatic conflict, in the familiar tragedy of *Macbeth,* a struggle is involved between the universal law expressed in the command, " Thou shalt do no murder," and the individual will of Macbeth. The law declares " Thou shalt not slay thy fellow man and thrive thereafter." Macbeth, in his mad infatuation to attain a crown, dares to commit murder; but finds that barely to maintain his crown, he must wade ever deeper in crime. And in the end, even crime will not save him. Macbeth has put his will against eternal law, and he goes down to destruction the consequent victim of his own folly and wickedness. Moreover, we are satisfied artistically as well as ethically with the result. On the other hand, the conflict of *The Taming of the Shrew* lies between the will of Petruchio who has determined to tame Katharine, and the common experience of men that women of Katharine's temper are inconvertible into submissive and amiable wives. Our pleasure lies in the process of the comedy, and especially in the unexpectedness of the triumph of the intrepid bridegroom. The statement of the conflict is not always so simple as in these typical cases. The plot of most plays is involved in minor particulars concerning minor personages. To take the two Shakespearean plays just contrasted: in *Macbeth* we have the subsidiary story of Macduff whose failure to credit the depravity of Macbeth or neglect to provide for so bloody a contingency loses him his wife and children under circumstances of hideously wanton cruelty. Insufficient enough must have been the victory of Macduff's sword on the usurper who died like a man sword in hand. But Macduff is not the hero of *Macbeth*. His story is necessary, like that of the unfortunate Banquo, not for itself but as an essential feature of Macbeth's struggle with fate. So, too, *The Shrew* involves a second story, that of Katharine's sister, Bianca, and her suitors. Bianca is the sweet average young woman, pretty, but wanting Katharine's personality and charm. Her story is an excellent foil for that of the more forceful and entertaining " shrew." You can always tell what will happen to Bianca; in her unexpectedness lies the effective comedy of " Kate the curst."

Dare a man defy the laws of God and make his way by means of murder to a crown? The answer is definitively " no." Dare a man take the life of a friend whom he loves, believing him to be a tyrant and that thus he is preserving the liberties of his country? Again we answer " no," although enormously different is the case of Brutus as contrasted with Macbeth. More, can we justify the folly of an aged king who divides his kingdom among his children before his death and disinherits his only faithful daughter because she is not glib of tongue in the expression of her filial affection? And are we able to extenuate so as to forgive the violent act that caused an honourable soldier to kill his beloved under mistake that she was untrue, when that mistake was the result of the most diabolical practice by means of which an honourable man has ever been duped? For neither King Lear nor for Othello can we conceive a further life in this world, shriven and measurably forgetful of past sorrow. And this leads us to a recognition of the ethical quality of tragedy which demands expiation in full measure no matter what the ultimate cause or justification of crime. Where great tragedy has flourished in the world this rigour of the universal law has been unrelentingly upheld, whether we express our ideas in the religious symbols of Æschylan mythology, in terms of the God of Christian creeds or in Ibsenesque phantoms of heredity and human depravity.

Recurring to comedy, we may ask other questions than that which concerns the temerity of Petruchio. Can a young woman who serves the prince whom she loves in the capacity and disguise of a page, hope to win him by honestly acting as his messenger to another lady whom he affects? Viola accomplishes this in *Twelfth Night;* and Helena in *All's Well that Ends Well,* contrives against lowly birth, her husband's vow and desertion equally to attain her object. But in comedy, unlike tragedy, the outcome of the struggle is not always certain and a triumph for the protagonist. We may query once more: may four young gentlemen lock themselves away from converse with womankind for study and hope to remain undisturbed and undistracted? The answer of *Love's Labour's Lost* is pleasantly " no." And may a young man and a young woman determine each to himself and contrary to the time of the heyday of life that neither will marry, and succeed in keeping this vow? " Not if their own hearts with the help of knavish friends contrive to defeat them " is the answer of the *Much Ado About Nothing.* Obviously if the universal is only relatively such, the outcome may be divertingly uncertain. There is as much delight, from a comedy point of view, in effort disconcerted as in effort successful, in character disproportionate as proportionate to profession. Comedy is more variable than tragedy, as it is dependent on more transient conditions. The triumph of individual effort over fortuitous circumstances still defines a large class of comedies, but pathos, character and laughter all are subserved equally well by the inverse method.

It has of course not escaped the ingenious reader that the foregoing examples have been wholly Shakespearean and he will neither forget that there are many other dramatists both before and after, nor that there are many other methods in the dramatic art. Not yet to leave Shakespeare, there are queries that arise in the solution of the dramatic struggle in his plays which we should not answer as he answered them. Are we satisfied with the fate of Shylock or the forgiveness of Leontes in *The Winter's Tale?* To the query dare a man make the question of his wife's virtue the subject of a common wager and hope for reconciliation and happiness after, we are astonished to find Shakespeare answering "yes" in *Cymbeline,* and the dramatist's source alone will not explain this complaisance. More comprehensible to the contemporary mind is the condoning of incorrigible knavery which we meet in Jonson and Middleton and which had an honest lineal descent from Plautus and the Greek comedians. But these matters are ephemeral and may well be left to the historical part of our subject.

For the conduct of this representation of man in conflict with his environment which we call drama many rules have been devised and many precepts determined. In these matters it is always worth while to ascertain whether the principles of dramatic structure which we find laid down so convincingly in books are the result of an actual examination of the field of the drama entire, even of any one group of plays, or if they are based, as they often are, merely on scholarly ratiocination. Aristotle was an observer of the greatest possible acuteness; but the mere sanction of his name has long since ceased to carry laws to the barbarians. Aristotle wrote,— or was rather reported — with Greek tragedy almost alone in view; Freytag with the German masterpieces of a century ago for his chief illustrations. Many people write books on this topic who forget that the drama has changed since Shakespeare, and more appear to suffer under the superstition that there is a superior merit in a play which is structurally "correct"; as if the growing forms of literary or other organisms could be determined *a priori,* and the process of time and genius, which again and again justifies in success the transgressions of all such laws, were not to be reckoned with.

With such a conception of the relations of the technicalities of any art to the art in its vital development, the reader must not be surprised to find little store set in this book on questions that concern the position of the climax and the advantages of postponed catastrophe. He who wishes to know the differences between "action-dramas and passion-dramas," the subtle distinctions that explain plot and counter-plot, sub-plot and enveloping action, the kinds and varieties of nemesis, and "the moment of tragic suspense," may find all of these things set down in the books that treat them. Obviously, a play, like any other story, is governed by certain principles of construction. It must begin and close at the proper place in the narrative, taking nothing for granted if, as in English drama usually, the plot may be supposed to be unknown to the auditor. The action must admit nothing dramatically irrelevant and the play is less a unified organism if a subsidiary plot is admitted which is not germain to the chief story. The conflict of which we have heard so much, must be presented as an actual conflict, the outcome of which is really in doubt, and naturally there must arise, at some place, a turn in this struggle that marks coming victory or defeat. If it bring any illumination to call the presentations of the relations of the personages in a play the "exposition," the procedure to the turning point of conflict the "rise" and the recedure therefrom the "decline," there can really be no objection to such nomenclature or any other, provided it be remembered that such mechanical matters have very little to do with a veritable appreciation of any dramatist's art. It is related that an excellent university poet, John Watson of St. John's College, Cambridge, in late humanist times, suffered not his Latin tragedy of *Absalom* to come into print or to performance because in a certain passage thereof "anapestus is twice or thrice used instead of iambus." A contemporary professor of literature, applying rigorously the standards of a "correct" construction to the modern novel, is reported to have found only one work that reached his jealous scale of perfection: and that was *The Hound of the Baskervilles!* In the historical consideration of a type such as drama it becomes more than ever important to judge each product by the traits of its own being and to eschew standards and preconceptions.

Many practices of the English drama have been conveniently borrowed from the classics. The soliloquy, the chorus, the aside are such, together with such extraneous parts as the prologue and the epilogue, and the formalities of division into act and scene. None of these things are vital to the drama, for drama may exist without them. On the other hand, no genuinely great work is ever impaired by the stage conventions accepted in its time. A prevalent vulgar error identifies art with life, the representation with the thing represented. Now no art really reproduces life, for first art selects from the abundance of material offered by life, taking only that part of a character, that number of events in a series, those relations of person and place, which are suited to its purposes. This is why it is often said that the logic of art is severer than the logic of life, why a closer causal relation is to be sought in a play than in an historical occurrence. Again, each art has its own conventions and may be likened to a foreign language with all its idioms and peculiar characteristics into which the story taken from life has been translated. It is quite as irrational to quarrel with conventions of dramatic stage representation as it would be to quarrel with a Greek second aorist or with the dual gender in Sanskrit. The grammar and idiom of languages change, and so, too, do the grammar and idiom of the stage. Certain things can be done with colour on canvas, other things with bronze or plaster. The highest art is that which speaks idiomatically in its own dialect, the art that translates life frankly into the terms of its own acceptance.

And now let us turn from these generalities as to the nature of drama to consider why the English drama is what it is. At the outset it may be affirmed that modern drama can in no sense be traced back to any direct literary contact with ancient drama, Greek or Roman. On the supposition that some such touch may once have existed, it has been customary to cite as examples the *Suffering Christ* (Χριστὸς πασχων), once attributed to St. Gregory the Nazianzene, who lived in the fourth century, and the Terentian comedies of the Abbess Hrotswitha of Gandersheim in Saxony. But the first, however suggestive of an acquaintance with Greek tragedy, turns out to belong not to St. Gregory of the fourth century, but to a Byzantine writer of the twelfth. It has been described as "a religious exercise in the garb of Euripidean diction" and as doubtless unknown to Western readers until the sixteenth century. The comedies of Hrotswitha, which belong to the twelfth century, were an honest attempt, by a high-minded and talented woman of culture and rank, to apply the dialogue and situations of Latin comedy to moral and religious teaching. This was precisely what the humanists attempted on a greater scale and more originally two or three hundred years later; but whether any connection really existed between such sporadic efforts and the famous mention by William Fitzstephen, in the later twelfth century, of "miracles of saints and passions of holy martyrs" may well be doubted. These lost saints' plays, like the extant drama of Hilarius who was supposed to have been born in England, seem rather to link on to the sacred drama, however indirectly they may have been effected by literary examples. As one of the northern, outlying provinces of the Roman em-

pire and as a part of that empire which reverted more completely to earlier barbarian conditions than some of the provinces
closer to Rome, we must expect to find little or no influence
of Roman conditions on anything that survived in the nature of
drama in England. This was substantially the history of the
other countries of western Europe, however the successors of
the *scenici* and the degenerate *mime* of Roman origin may have
become confused, in the earlier middle ages, with the tumblers,
buffoons and wandering rimesters who added their rude humour and revelry to the even ruder humour of the folk. The
scop of Saxon times, in contrast to the *mime,* was a personage
of dignity and importance, and his successor in mediæval days,
the minstrel, often maintained much of both. Both of these
old English entertainers could have included little that was
dramatic among their songs and stately recitals, save where the
direct touch of narrated dialogue or mimicry in impersonation
may have added to them verve and life-likeness. But English
minstrelsy was soon to learn many things from the vivacious
trouvères and *jongleurs* of the Norman conqueror, and among
them were the quasi-dramatic disputations, *jeux-partis* and
estrifs among which *The Harrowing of Hell,* an *estrif* on the
beautiful legend of Christ's descent into hell, may be reckoned
as one of the sources of the morality. Among the humble
strollers whose entertainment was of a lighter and more comic
sort, dialogue was certainly early in vogue and the use of
marionettes, which is well authenticated, " implies not only
dialogue but plot." [1] Farce became prevalent enough on the
continent to form a distinct and recognised species of mediæval
drama; but, in England, save for a single mention of " other
japis " in the *Tretise of miracles pleyinge* and the fragment of
the text of the *Interludium de Clerico et Puella,* a dialogue
founded on the popular story of Dame Siriz, we have nothing
to correspond to the considerable repertoire of this kind in
France until we reach the days of John Heywood. Nor do
occasional indications of the performance of satirical attacks in
dramatic form give us the right to reconstruct for England
more than an hypothetical existence of any such dramatic organ-
isations as the *Enfants san souci* or the *Basoche* of Paris. However, that both such actors and such a lighter drama did exist
throughout the mediæval centuries in England is certain in

[1] See *Secular Influences on the Early English Drama,* by H. H.
Child, *Cambridge History of English Literature,* vi, 25.

view of what came after. It is always to be remembered that little of a literary character inheres in popular drama such as this. The art of writing was an unusual accomplishment even among the clergy, and records such as these, which often called down the criticism and the enmity of the church, were little preserved except where, as in the case of the miracle play, they received the church's sanction.

A root of English drama, earlier and deeper than long possible survivals from the classical ages has been uncovered in the study of folk-lore.[2] The festivals and observances of Pagan times, with their set ritual often involving procession, combat, dance, song and disguise, had much in common with the spirit that makes for drama. Festivals such as those that survived in the observances of Christmas, May-day, and harvest time create the holiday mood and induce the exercise of activity for play which has in it the elements of feigning. On the literary side, while the *cantilenae,* or songs celebrating the deeds of the heroes of the folk, may have had in them little of the dramatic elements, traditional festival songs were commonly accompanied by a burden or " chorus " and many were framed by way of query and response amounting at times to set dialogue. In short, while the material connected with early English customs among the folk exhibits no such certain steps as those which can be traced in early Hellenic times, the analogue of a development from folk-song and festival to folk-drama in both cases involves no uncertain process of reasoning. Nor is England without example, in mention and survival, pointing to what this folk-drama may have been. A gossipy attendant at court, Robert Laneham, describes for us a performance of the Hock Tuesday play at Coventry in 1575, one of the many entertainments in honour of Queen Elizabeth's visit to the Earl of Leicester at Kenilworth. This " old storial show " as our informant calls it, was " for pastime wont to be played yearly," and he describes the argument: how the English under Huna defeated the Danes and rid the kingdom of them in the reign of Ethelred on Saint Brice's night, November, 1002. John Rous, Laneham's predecessor, in a mention of the Hock Tuesday play by over a hundred years, assigns the story to a commemoration of the driving out of the Danes which preceded the accession of Edward the Confessor to the throne in

[2] An authoritative book on this subject is that of E. K. Chambers, *Mediæval Drama,* 2 vols., 1903.

1042.[3] In all likelihood the origin harks back to an immemorial folk-custom in the process of which a victim was obtained for the sacrifice by simulated force, women playing an
important part in the struggle. This last feature remained
conspicuous, according to Laneham, in the Hock Tuesday plays.
There are many other examples of the general custom; the performance which Elizabeth saw at Coventry is the only instance
of this folk-custom transformed into the dialogue and action
of a connected play.

Of the Hock Tuesday play we hear no more after Laneham; the sword-dance remained fruitful later. Such a custom
may obviously date, among a warlike people, from exceedingly
early, even savage, times. Writers on folk-lore associate its ritual with primitive customs having to do with the expulsion of
Death and Winter and the resurrection of Summer, and it is
the source of many an extant *débat* and *estrif* on the topic.
The sword-dance soon became mimetic and certain definite
personages developed, such as the fool and the " Bessy," a man
dressed in woman's clothes. Some have held the morris-dance
(in which appear Maid Marian and Robin Hood himself very
often) merely an offshoot of the sword-dance. A development
of more interest to us dramatically is the mummers or St.
George play which has by no means as yet disappeared from
many outlying rural parts of England. Here the central idea
is the killing of one of the personages and his restoration to
life. The chief character is always a saint, a king or a prince
George, there is a spoken introduction of the characters besides
the dialogue, much action, dancing and often a number of subsidiary personages among whom, " the hobby-horse is not forgot." It has been justly remarked that the " king " and " prince
George " are " Hanoverian improvements," as " saint George "
must have been mediæval with its suggestion of the contemporary influences of saints' play and miracle. The Robin Hood
play is still another of these survivals of the customs of the
folk; but here the modifying contemporary influence was
mediæval balladry, itself a lineal descendant from early com-
munal song. The Robin Hood play is regarded a development
of the May-game in which the coming of spring is celebrated
with dance and song, and a king and queen appointed to lead
in the revels. The pastoral form of this play was universal in
France, and Robin became the type-name of the shepherd lover,

[3] *Historia Regum Angliæ* (printed 1716), pp. 105, 106.

Marion that of his mistress. In England, all this was confused
with the ballad story of Robin Hood, Marion became Maid
Marian and the pastoral features were lost in those of free
forest life and fight with dishonest constituted authority, represented in the Sheriff of Nottingham and the delightful out-
lawry of Robin and his friends, Friar Tuck, Little John and
the rest. *The Paston Letters* disclose an interesting mention
of a servant with whom his master was loath to part because
he played Robin Hood and the Sheriff of Nottingham so well.[4]
This familiar mention points to a popularity of such performances in the fifteenth century. Moreover, a fragment of such
a play of much the date of the allusion just mentioned is extant
and " a merry geste " of Robin Hood, " with a new play for
to be played in May Games," was printed about the year 1561.
The story of Robin Hood was later to prove dramatically
fruitful in many plays of the Shakespearean age, but it may be
doubtful if this was so much a survival of any influence from
the old folk-plays as it was referable to the awakened national
spirit that found in this popular hero of old English balladry,
whose ancestry extended to the Teutonic god Wodin (though
little they knew it), a personage peculiarly typical of the new
age. When all has been said for these influences of the immemorial rituals of the folk, their games and festivities, little
can be proved except that such customs preserved among the
people a temper of mind favourable to the dramatic way of
presenting things. This the mediæval Christian clergy were
quick to discern; and the cleverness, that turned the Saturnalia
into Christmas and the pagan licenses of May-day into the re-
joicings of Easter, converted the love of fiction, the impulse
for play and disguise and mumming into a potent means wherewith to spread a knowledge of bible story and an acceptance of
Christian doctrine. That a learned Byzantine priest should
have remembered Euripides when he wrote his *suffering Christ*
and a cultivated German princess her Terence, whom she imitated crudely enough with like pious intent, seem matters in
no wise remarkable. But we may feel more than assured that
these were exceptional cases, academic and to some extent im-
practical. The age needed a translation of the great truths of
Christianity in familiar terms of the present, and mediæval art
accomplished this in its own way. Thus it developed a drama
that employed, of what went before, all that was vital and

[4] *Paston Letters,* ed. Gairdner, iii, 89.

significant, all that it could understand, neglecting as non-existent or declaring active war on all else. The drama in mediæval times was like one of those wonderful and incongruous cathedrals, built out of the ruins of Roman temple and Druid altar alike, in which angels, saints and demons combine with the human hands that framed them, in an ornamentation bizarre and absurd, to produce, none the less, a total result that is sincere, imposing and lasting. Into that stately edifice let us now enter, remembering that it was dedicated singly to the service of God.

CHAPTER II

MEDIÆVAL DRAMA IN ENGLAND

THE drama of England, like that of all other countries of western Europe, had its ultimate origin in the services of the church, though other influences came in time to shape and deflect it from its major purpose, the representations of portions of the scriptures for religious and moral edification. The beginnings of modern drama lie at the heart of the ritual of the church. Technically described, modern drama takes its rise in an antiphonal mimetic development of certain tropes of the mass. Translated, this signifies that in the process of elaboration to which the services of the church were submitted during the ninth and tenth centuries, the choral parts of the mass were extended and supplemented by the insertion of new melodies to which in time new words were written. The inserted melodies were called *neumae,* the words of these amplifications, *tropes.* Some tropes in later metrical developments gave rise to famous mediæval hymns. Other tropes, which were attached to alternating songs, took a dialogue form, and among them a few proved dramatically potential and came in time to be accompanied by a species of stage representation. Such a trope was the *Quem quaeritis,* as it is called from its first two words, an amplification of the *Officium* or *Introit,* the alternating song, " sung by the choir at the beginning of the mass as the celebrant approaches the altar." In its earliest and simplest form the *Quem quaeritis* is little more than a paraphrase of *Matthew* (xxviii, 1-7) or the corresponding passage in *Mark* (xvi, 1-6). This trope was first written at St. Gallen about the year 900. Transferred to the celebration of Easter, it became at once dramatically capable of extension. The earliest scrap of anything like an acted scene that has come down to us in England, is a brief transcript of this dialogue between the angel at the sepulchre of Christ and the two Maries and Salome. It is still preserved in an old manuscript entitled the

Concordia Regularis Monachorum, an appendix to the rule of St. Benedict, in Winchester Cathedral, and dates from the end of the tenth century (959-975), when King Edgar reigned in Wessex and long before William and his Normans had come over to England to disturb Saxon rule. We can imagine, in this case, the rude representation of a cave, beneath one of the arches of the church, beside the entrance to which lay a great stone, apparently just rolled away. Three of the younger clergy, dressed in long garments, betokening womanhood, approach the opening and meet there another figure, arrayed in white, bearing wings and holding a palm in his hand. As he sits beside the tomb, he asks, " Whom seek ye? " and they reply " Jesus of Nazareth, which was crucified." And the angel tells them " He is risen, he is not here; behold the place where they laid him." With these words he lifts the veil, showing the place bare of the cross and only the clothes remaining in which the cross was shrouded. Then the three, taking the cloth, hold it up and sing, *Surrexit Dominus de supulchro,* and the *Te Deum* follows with joy and ringing of bells. As Chambers puts it, here " dialogued chant and mimetic action have come together and the first liturgical drama is, in all its essentials, complete." [1]

But Easter was not the only point about which gathered the nucleus of the drama to be. The *Officium Pastorum* is based on a Christmas dialogue that formed itself about the *praesepe,* or cradle, precisely as the *Quem quaeritis* was formed about the sepulchre. The *praesepe* was arranged near to the altar. To it certain of the clergy, arrayed as shepherds, advanced singing a hymn; while a boy, in the likeness of an angel, sang in reply the good tidings, from a position above. As the shepherds neared the cradle, they were met by two priests, attendants at the divine birth, a dialogue ensued, beginning: " *Quem quaeritis in praesepe, pastores dicite?* " This was followed by another hymn, while the shepherds knelt in adoration, and so the embryonic " play of the shepherds " ends. The *Pastores* as it is called, followed the *Quem quaeritis* in the eleventh and twelfth centuries, beginning in a trope of the third or great mass, but undergoing a similar transfer to the celebration of Christmas. It is somewhat unfortunate that these " choral services for special occasions " should be called

[1] *The Mediæval Stage,* ii, p. 15.

"liturgical plays." With their formal responses and Latin texts they were full of suggestion; but theirs was the efficacy of the symbol. In no true sense do they represent histrionically the events of Bible story. The liturgical plays are interesting to the historian of the drama only in view of what in time was to develop from them.

The dramatic development of the liturgy belongs especially to the twelfth century with half a century added before and after. The dramatic motive involved in the doctrine of the real presence, with its vivid and poignant sense of the human suffering of Christ for mankind, was soon to lift the symbolism of liturgical ceremony into the realism of actual drama. Before the beginning of the eleventh century the process of amplification had set in. The simple colloquy between the angel and the Maries at the tomb was developed at times to embrace the purchase of ointments of the spice merchant by one of the Maries, their communication of the news of the resurrection to the apostles, a like visit of two of them to the sepulchre, and the apparition of the Saviour to Mary Magdalene. Similarly, to the *Pastores* were added the lamentation of Rachel and the *Stella,* a trope of different origin, wherein the three kings of the east are represented as guided by a star, set glittering over the altar, to the cradle that lay beneath. Other tropes of the service also developed, as for example, the *Prophetae,* which originated not in a chant but in an early narrative sermon against the Jews. But, for our purposes, we need not be further concerned with these liturgical beginnings. This incipient drama was early recognised for its value as Creizenach has put it, furnishing " a species of living picture-book " of sacred story wherewith " to fortify the unlearned people in their faith."

The next step towards actual drama is obviously the detachment of these " plays " from their place in the service. They continued long in their original positions even after they had come likewise to be otherwise employed. But once detached, the invention of like episodes dramatic and their use for divers religious purposes were certain to follow. We hear very early of plays on the lives and miracles of saints. Such must have been the *Play of St. Catherine,* prepared by a Norman, Godefroy of Le Mana, head-master of the monastery school at Dunstable, dating 1119, but now lost. And such are the three dramas of Hilarius, a pupil of Abélard on the *Resurrection of Lazarus,* on *Daniel* and *St. Nicholas,* 1125, still to be read in

their monkish Latin and interspersed French with directions
that show their adaptability to matins or vespers. These plays
of Hilarius belong not to England although their author has
been thought by some to have been of English birth. Even
the well known allusion of William Fitzstephen, in his *Life
of Thomas à Becket* (c. 1180), to "the representations of
miracles wrought by holy confessors, or of the tribulations and
constancy of martyrs," all enacted in London, leave us in
doubt as to the language in which they were written and as to
whether they could have been more than performances, at most
Anglo-Norman, if not actually imported from France. Indeed
no such body of saints' plays, as is well known for example in
France, exists for mediæval England; and we are compelled to
reconstruct from rare mention and by analogy a literature which
we have reason to believe must once have been.[2] When we
consider how thoroughly under the dominion of the Normans
both political and clerical life remained from the conquest of
William almost to the time of Edward III, how the language
of learning and the Church was Latin, the language of culture
and of the courts of law Norman-French, and how the vernacular was despised and neglected by the governing classes, we
can hardly wonder that traces of this particular kind are so
few. But there seem, too, to have been other reasons. The
English taste appears less to have delighted in those extensions
of Scripture, the Apocrypha and the legends of the saints. English preference was for the simple bible story; and while the
English distinguished no more than their mediæval brethren
in other lands the facts of history from its fictions, the concreteness of the material of accepted bible story as compared
with the allegory and vagueness of sacred legend may go far
to account for this.

In England, above all other mediæval countries, do we
find the growth and enlargement of the bible story, scene by
scene, carried to its logical conclusion, until from a scene or
two, illustrative and forming a part of the service, this drama
developed to an enormous cycle of sacred history, beginning

[2] Beside the scattered mentions of lost plays of St. George, St.
Laurence, St. Botolph, and others, see the account of *Mary Magdalen*
of the *Digby MS* below and Creizenach's mention of the fragment of
a miracle play on Duke Moraud, belonging to the fifteenth century.
Cambridge History of English Literature, v. 40.

with the creation of man, his fall and banishment from the garden of Eden, and extending through the more important matters of the *Old Testament* and the life of Christ in the *New* to the summoning of the quick and the dead on the day of final judgment. This kind of drama is called the miracle play — sometimes less correctly the mystery play — and it flourished throughout England from the reign of Henry II to that of Elizabeth and became the parent of a large progeny of religious, moral and allegorical productions which in turn formed the soil out of which modern drama was later to spring. Apparently the earliest miracle plays to be performed in England belong to the Eastern Midlands and to a date not far removed from 1250. Singly or in cycle, records declare their existence at scores of places, London, the great sees of Canterbury, York and Winchester, at the universities, and especially at the larger market towns of Kent, Essex, Norfolk and other counties. Indeed miracle plays became in time a feature of the periodical fairs, those well known mediæval resorts of barter and pleasure; and they were employed on secular occasions to celebrate a royal visit, for example, or to signalize some memorable event. Obviously many things attended this extension of the drama, and the most notable was its secularization. From representations on stationary platforms in church, by the clergy, at first in Latin, the miracles were transferred to movable pageants, or platforms set on wheels, drawn from place to place with appropriate decorations and music, acted by tradesmen's guilds — sometimes by professional actors — and in the English language. There is an interesting old manuscript (now often reproduced), showing the arrangement of twenty-two platforms in the church at Donauschingen in the sixteenth century, arranged for the performance of a drama dealing with the passion. Here the pageants were ordered to correspond with the three main divisions of the church, the nave, the body of the church and the sanctuary. Hell was placed nearest the outer doors, heaven, the cross and the sepulchre in the sanctuary itself.[3] Plainly here was much to stage in a single building, however large; and it is clear that the pressure of the crowd had much to do with taking the miracle play out of the churches. But there were other reasons. Early in the history of the mediæval stage certain practices arose even among

[3] This plan is reproduced in Chambers' *Mediæval Stage*, ii, 84.

the clergy, confused in part with the privileges and license accorded to periods of public rejoicing and traceable back to pagan times. The Feast of Fools was a New Year's revel in which the minor clergy parodied the service and carried on loutish tricks. A similar revel, more common in England, was the mock election of a Boy Bishop. These and other like abuses set the more serious clergy against stage acting, and the prohibition of *ludi theatrales* by Pope Innocent III in 1207, was sometimes interpreted by the more zealous — notably by Robert Grosteste the reforming Bishop of Lincoln, in 1244 — as directed against all dramas. This helped, too, to secularize the drama. On the other hand the institution of the feast of Corpus Christi by Pope Urban, in 1214, gave a marked impulse to the lay performance of religious plays. For the trade-guilds in England adopted the miracle play as a feature of the solemn procession of the triumphal church with which they were accustomed to celebrate their chief holiday of the year. It was thus under the fostering hand of the guilds — out of whose body, be it remembered, the civic officers of the mediæval town were recruited — that the miracle play developed into the sumptuous and elaborate spectacle that it became; and it is owing to the pains with which, in certain cases, the civic records were kept and preserved that we owe our first hand knowledge of these interesting avocations of our mediæval forefathers.

Four cycles of collective miracle plays remain extant and all have been carefully reprinted and edited from the original manuscripts and studied in themselves and in their relations. The earliest manuscript is that of the *York Plays* and dates between 1430 and 1440. The *Towneley Plays* are not much later, and those of Chester and the *Ludus Coventriae,* as the fourth is inaccurately called, follow after in the same century, though practically all show signs in certain places of later revisions and the performance of some of the scenes must date far earlier than the manuscripts. All of these cycles begin with the creation or the fall of Lucifer and extend to the day of doom; and all deal with comparative brevity of *Old Testament* subjects to centre interest in the birth, the passion and the resurrection of Christ. The *York Cycle* was acted yearly by the craft-guilds of that town and is mentioned as long in progress, as early as 1378. It consists of forty-eight scenes or plays, each acted by a separate guild. It is written in a variety of styles and stanzas and may be regarded as a compilation rather than the revision of a single author. The *York Cycle* represents most fully the life and work of Christ. The *Towneley Plays,* it is now believed, were acted by the craft-guilds of Wakefield in Yorkshire at the important fairs held at Woodkirk. They consist of a composite, made up of three groups, and show relation in part to an earlier form of the *York Plays*. But other parts of the work stand out as the anonymous composition of a single author whose qualities of humour, effective satire and homely realism have earned for him the title of " our first great comic dramatist, the playwright of Wakefield." The *Chester Cycle* was acted by craft-guilds at Whitsuntide and shows close relations to the French *Mystère du Viel Testament*. It is of somewhat unequal excellence and sophisticated in its effort to achieve dramatic effect. Unlike the cycles of York and Wakefield, it draws on the legends of saints for material, and on the *Apocrypha*. Lastly, the so-called *Ludus Coventriae* is not really of Coventry at all. It may possibly have been of Norfolk. Its scenes fall into several groups, separated by " conclusions " and introduced and explained by a personage, called Contemplacio. Other abstractions figure among its persons, and it draws on matter without the bounds of scriptural story. It is not altogether clear that the *Ludus Coventriae* — better called from a sometime owner the *Hegge Plays* — was acted under clerical supervision and its scenes appear to have been presented not on movable pageants but in " a pleyn place " on scaffolds.

The four cycles with the scattered scenes and parts of scenes, once parts of now lost cycles or existing apart, from a considerable body of material. Not unlike the mediæval ballad, we have here less the collected work of many individual writers than the results of repeated revision and workings over of material, successively adapted to gradually changing conditions. Save for the bond that makes all before and after, the promise and fulfilment of the life of Christ, no unity knits the loose succession of scenes. The sanctity of their biblical sources and a becoming awe for them contrived to keep the more important personages — Jesus, the Maries, Joseph, and the disciples — figures of dignity and measurably faithful to their scriptural models. Neither clumsiness of hand nor dramatic inefficiency could destroy their human and often pathetic appeal; while, in some of the finer scenes of *York* and *Towneley,* we

meet with homely but genuine dramatic quality and success.
As to less important matters, the authors of the old miracles
drew from their own experience and imagination, giving us,
again and again, little glimpses into mediæval character and
touches of the life that existed about them. The most famous
example of the last is *The Second Shepherds' Play* of the
Towneley Cycle, in which is told the story of a thievish rascal,
named Mak, with his theft of a sheep from the shepherds, who
are awaiting for a sign of the coming of Christ on downs,
unmistakably of Yorkshire and amid the rigours of a Yorkshire winter. In the upshot, Mak gets away with a sheep and
conceals it in the cradle in his hovel, where it is at last found
by the shepherds who toss the rogue in a blanket, despite the
asseverations of Tib, his wife, that the sheep is really a changeling, left unbeknown to her and her honest husband by fairies
who had spirited her own child away. Here is a bit of actual
life, cut free from all intent save that of diversion. In such
scenes English comedy was born.

From the manuscripts of these old cycles many interesting
particulars may be gleaned. The pageant at Chester is described as " a high place made like a house with two rooms, being open on the top: in the lower room they appareled and
dressed themselves; and in the higher room they played: and
they stood upon six wheels." The decorations were of the
simplest and apparently the auditors stood on all sides of the
wagon. However, imaginative realism was not wanting: the
ark in the pageant of the flood was shaped like a ship, and hell-
mouth with its flames of fire, its rattling chains and instruments
of torture, and the grim and hideous semblance of its devils,
served its purpose, as a deterrent from sin, doubtless as well as
our bogey, fear of public reprobation. The actors, though amateurs and trades people, members of the various crafts, received
each his fee for acting and other services; and long lists of payments remain in the records, some of them amusing enough
to us. One series of entries begins solemnly, " Imprimis to
God, two shillings," with later entries to Caiaphas and " Pilate
his wife " netting each four pence more. There are items for
five sheepskins for " God's coat," for " a slop for Herod," and
for painting and repairing the devil's head. Among payments
for theatrical services, one Fawnston is allowed four pence
" for hanging Judas," to the same artist is paid as much more

for " cock-crowing." [4] Apparently the strolling minstrel, familiar and engaging figure of mediæval revelry, took his part
in lightening the didactic gravity of these serious representations of bible story, for we hear of the professional Vice (traditional comedy figure, with the devil, of the miracle plays),
as employed " for his pastime before the play and after." Doubtless occasionally a young priest or tradesman of histrionic aptitude developed a reputation for his acting above his fellows.
Such a one must have been the minor devil whom Heywood's
Pardoner met in his infernal journey, one who in life was
famous for " playing the devil at Coventry." As to the settings
and costumes of these old plays, both preserved an ingenuous
contemporaneousness in which the variegated and brilliantly
coloured garments of the different classes of the time, lay, clerical and official, must have served admirably well. Where these
did not answer, the devices were simple. The suit of a knight's
old armour clad St. Paul before the miracle at Damascus, a
bishop's canonicals thereafter, a turban, a crooked sword and
a bearded face made up for the ranting part of Herod; and
the nakedness of our first parents in the Garden of Eden was
clothed rather than suggested in suits of leather or white linen.
Devils were obviously clad in black; " black," says the King
of Navarre, in Love's Labour's Lost, " is the badge of hell."
And correspondingly the saints and angels were robed in white
and their wigs were flaxen. And yet rude, even shocking to
our more delicate sensibilities, as these old dramas are in places,
they are neither irreverent nor do they confuse, as did some
later plays, the elemental laws of right and wrong or sophisticate
a plain morality. It is ever to be kept in mind that the miracle
play took its part along side of the picturesque ritual of the
mediæval church in convicting the wayward of a consciousness
of sin, in bringing the guilty to repentance and in uplifting
men to a truer appreciation of religion and right living. Can
we wonder that dreamers and those that see visions have hoped
that we might some day restore to the stage its important function as a guide in religion and morals?

But, as we have seen, the miracle play was not always acted
in cycles. Single plays exist which could not have formed parts

[4] For these and many other like particulars see, Thomas Sharp, On
the Pageants or Dramatic Mysteries anciently performed at Coventry,
1825, passim.

of a cycle.   Such for example are two plays of the *Digby Manu-script,* which may be dated about 1485.   In the one, *Mary Magdalene,* this touching bible story is treated in much the manner of its second source, *The Golden Legend,* and expanded with inventive freedom and no mean dramatic aptitude to em- brace Mary's earlier life as the sister of Lazarus and Martha, with her later conversion of the " King of Marcylle " and final apotheosis.   The other important play of the *Digby Manu- script, The Conversion of St. Paul,* is scarcely inferior.   In this substitution of an individual theme in the single miracle play for the universal one of the cycle, more was gained from a dramatic point of view than was lost.   The sanctity of the momentous subject, the story of the Saviour, forbade inventive freedom to the writers and revisers of the cycles who therefore expended their ingenuity on unimportant personages and details. It does not seem too much to say that the breaking off of the single miracle play from the cycle had the effect of humanizing the subjects of these plays and bringing them nearer to the un- derstandings and sympathies of their auditors.

Other influences, however, were ready further to disintegrate the old sacred drama.   It is one thing to tell, histrionically or otherwise, a story and let it convey its own impression; it is another to provide an expositor, as in the *Chester Plays,* to make clear the application.   No part of the old sacred drama is free from a didactic intention; for that drama existed that it might teach, first by symbol and secondly, by actual representation, on the stage.   This involved very early a new departure.   It has recently been contended that the actual source of the moral- ity play is the homily or illustrative sermon, an important part of the services from the earliest times and a part not less readily capable of development into dialogue and drama.[5]   The middle ages furnish many examples of compilations intended to guide the clergy in the preparation of sermons and furnish them espe- cially with illustrative material.   These *sermonaires* were fol- lowed by collections of *exempla,* such as *The Alphabet of Tales,* and they shade off into mere collections of legends of the saints, and anecdotes, often involving the allegorical way of present- ing things.   Without here pursuing this subject into its many in- teresting details, we may agree that " The determination to carry

the teachings of the church directly to all classes of men and
women in the most effective and the most interesting way, a
determination that forced the clergy to make the sermon, both
in matter and form, something other than a religious treatise,
led directly to the recognition of the drama as a legitimate and
useful aid."

In the moral play, or morality, the uniform theme is the
struggle between the powers of good and evil for the mastery
of the soul of man. The personages are abstract virtues or
vices, each acting and speaking in accordance with his name;
and the plot, often of extreme ingenuity, is built upon their
contrasts and influences on human nature, with the intent to
teach right living and uphold religion. In a word, allegory
(so dear to the mediæval mind) is the distinguishing mark of
the moral plays. These plays were no less international than
the miracles. It is customary specifically to refer the origin
of the morality to the famous allegorical Latin poem,
Psychomachia, written by the poetical churchman Prudentius,
about the year 400 and devoted to a description of the warfare between virtues and vices after the Homeric example, as
his less known poem *Hamatigenia* describes the siege of man's
soul. But Prudentius by no means originated these similitudes,
however he may have amplified the vivid figurative language of
certain passages of St. Paul, Tertullian and Cyprian. It is,
however, impossible to overestimate the influence of the
Psychomachia on mediæval literature at large, and therefore
specifically on the morality; although we may agree, none the
less, on the intervening influences of the homiletic and like
writings in which allegorical illustrations abounded and where
doubtless a larger number of suggestions for moral plays will
be found than have yet been acknowledged.

The morality appears to have taken its position along side
of the older miracle plays not much before the latter part of the
fourteenth century. Such a production was clearly the *Play
of the Pater Noster* which Wycliff reports as "setting forth
the goodness of our Lord's Prayer, in which play all manner
of vices and sins were held up to scorn and the virtues were
held up to praise." The *Play of the Creed,* acted also at York
from 1446 onward, seems to have been likewise a species of
morality. Earliest and most typical among extant moralities
may be named *The Castle of Perseverance* in which Humanum
Genus is led away in youth by Temptation and the Seven

Deadly Sins, but takes refuge, after absolution, in the Castle
where he withstands the assaults of the Vices, led by the Belial,
while ecclesiastical exposition and argument are carried on by
the Virtues. Led once more into sin by Avarice, Death appears to call Man to judgment and there ensues a further argument between Mercy, Justice, Truth and Peace before the
throne of God, with the result of Man's final salvation by
grace. Obviously all this is of the universal stuff of the sermons and homilies contemporary with it. The staging of the
Castle of Perseverance, set forth by diagram in the old manuscripts is exceedingly interesting.[6] The castle, appropriately
battlemented, was set in the centre of a circular field surrounded
by a ditch. Beneath the castle was a couch for Humanum Genus;
and there were five outlying pageants or scaffolds for Caro,
Mundus, Belial, Coveytyse (covetousness) and Deus. Apparently the action took place not only on the pageants but on the
field between them. In this same manuscript are contained
two other moralities; *Mind, Will, and Understanding,* a production involving little more than the amplification in costume
of a scholastic debate, and *Mankind* which introduces some gross
and vulgar comedy in the form of a merry devil, named Tutivil-
lus, a personage well known under other names to the miracle
plays. *Mankind* is not otherwise memorable.

In these earliest moral plays it is to be noted that the protagonist is always an abstraction; he is Mankind, the Human
Race, the Pride of Life (as an old fragment is entitled), and
there is an attempt to compass the whole scope of man's experience and temptations in life, as there had been a corresponding effort in the miracle plays to embrace the complete
range of sacred history, the life of Christ and the redemption
of the world. The most notable play of the class is *Everyman,*
the earliest printed edition of which belongs to a period between
1509 and 1530. The existence of a Dutch version, in print
by 1495, has led to a nice question of priority; but there seems
now but little doubt that the English play was in writing the
earlier. In its larger relations *Everyman* belongs to that considerable class of the devotional literature of the later middle
ages best represented by the *Ars moriendi,* published in English by Caxton in 1491. In itself it is an attempt to give a
lively dramatic form to a parable, told in the legend of Barlaam

[6] This is reproduced in T. Sharp's *Dissertation,* as above, p. 23.

and Josaphat. The play details how Everyman, in the midst
of a careless life, is suddenly summoned by a dread and hollow-
eyed messenger to prepare for a journey into a distant land
whence there is no return. Everyman seeks out Fellowship and
Kindred, but they offer empty words and refuse him company.
His hoarded Wealth reviles him for his folly in thinking that
he, the universal servant, could now serve him. Good Deeds,
alone, whom Everyman's forgetfulness had suffered to lie
neglected, offers assistance and helps him to the aid of Knowledge. As he nears his end, even the Senses must leave him;
at last Everyman goes down into his grave, penitent and fully
prepared for the world to come by confession. *Everyman* is a
beautiful and touching drama, sustained by a forceable and
unctuous inculcation of the spirit of England's older faith. As
seen on the stage in its recent, effective revivals, it was surprising to what a degree the abstractions disappeared as such in the
efficient concreteness of their representation and in the powerful
enforcement of their underlying spiritual truth. Great must
have been the effect of this old drama on an age in which it
spoke directly to its auditors in the language, the faith, and the
feeling of the day. In our own time the example of *Everyman* has begotten a progeny of contemporary plays, English and
other, and created, even on the popular stage of England and
America, a wholesome diversion from the dismal problems and
trivial improbabilities that for the most part rule there.

Everyman, however, was an exceptional play, especially in the
singleness of purpose with which it inculcated religious ideas.
With the uprise of humanism, in the latter half of the fifteenth
century, and with the filtering into England of Protestant ideas,
the morality was at once seized upon to fulfil new functions,
chiefly ethical and educational and, before long, controversial
as well. Earlier than *Everyman* and certainly before 1500,
Henry Medwell sought, in his moral play called *Nature,* to show
" how Sensuality drives away Reason from man's side "; but
how, in his old age, man must return to Reason. In *The
Nature of the Four Elements,* about 1530, John Rastell, if he
be the author, frankly assumes the pedagogue and treats wearily
and at length of the knowledge of the day. He is not unaware
of the awakening of a new spirit of inquiry, adverting with
animation to the discovery " within these twenty year " of new
lands beyond the sea. Equally close in their alliance to the
arguments of the schools, are the several plays that deal with

the respective merits of Wit, Wisdom and Science, and link
on to the wide literature of the dialogue, a favourite form of
expression for the didacticism of the age.   A more vital group
of pedagogical moralities are made up of those that treat of
the temptations of youth, *Lusty Juventus, Hickscorner* and *The
Interlude of Youth* for example.   And closely allied to these,
though it marks, as has been pointed out, the beginning of the
breaking up of the allegorical drama, is Skelton's *Magnificence*.
This is the only surviving play of that redoubtable old satirist,
and it is not devoid of much plain and vigorous speaking.
In moral plays such as these — all of them, in point of date,
before the Reformation — we have an attempt freely to
dramatize contemporary life, however the figures represented
remain abstractions and partake, on their serious side at least,
of the moralising and allegory of their predecessors.   In moralities of this type, too, the comic element emerges into greater
prominence in the roistering youth (a figure ever dear to the
stage) and the dissolute group of vices and revellers that surround him.   The names of Henry Medwell, who died in 1500,
and John Skelton (1460-1529), thus stand first in our list of
known English dramatists.   Both of these men were of the
humanist clergy and both of them display the zeal for learning,
the reforming spirit and the satirical attitude toward abuses
that brand so unmistakably the Protestant controversialists in
the drama to come.

Before taking up the actual humanist drama which links
on naturally to such moralities as those just enumerated, we
must turn to the controversial morality, which came to involve not only matters of doctrine but politics as well.   The
influence of Luther and his quarrel with the church, the questions that divided men like Cranmer and Gardiner, that kept
Sir Thomas More and Erasmus in the mother church and carried Henry and Cromwell out of it, those violent oscillations
of opinion and faith that made and unmade England, Protestant and Roman Catholic, backward and forward, several times
in a couple of generations — these things need only to be named
to be remembered.   In the midst of such conditions the drama
was naturally resorted to, that powerful medium of public
instruction, hallowed by the usages of two hundred years, and,
the favourite form of the moment being the morality, the
morality was at once turned to controversial uses.   As is always
the case, the attacking party was more violent and fertile in

its choice of weapons than its opponents; and the Protestant plays outnumbered, as they exceeded in violence, the few rejoinders which their triumph suffered to remain extant. The earliest play which touched the Reformation was an attack upon Luther, acted in Latin, in 1528, before Cardinal Wolsey. This is no longer extant, and it seems not to have been speedily followed by similar productions. On Henry VIII's break with Rome, however, and especially when Cromwell and Cranmer advanced the English Reformation more speedily than the King's original intention had seemed to warrant, the Protestant play suddenly arose to embitter, if not always to enliven, the spirit of contention. By 1543 so great had this abuse become that a royal decree was promulgated forbidding the publication, in songs, plays or interludes, of any exposition of Holy Writ, opposed to the teachings of the Church as established by his majesty. The foremost dramatic controversialist of the age was the theologian John Bale, who lived between 1495 and 1563, and was sometime Bishop of Ossory in Ireland. Bale was a zealous and abusively outspoken champion of the new faith and an irreconcilable hater of priests and of popery. He has left us a catalogue of twenty-two plays, almost all of them, from their titles, clearly controversial in character. Of these several, no longer extant, appear to have formed together a species of condensed collective miracle play in a dozen scenes, beginning with the childhood of Christ and extending to the Resurrection. Among the existing plays of Bale is one the lengthy title of which may be condensed into *God's Promises,* a species of *Prophetae;* two others are modelled on scenes of the old cycles and treat of *John the Baptist* and of the *Temptation in the Wilderness.* Of morality type are *The Three Laws of Nature* and *King Johan,* as well as Bale's translation, in 1545, of Kirchmayer's *Pammachius.* All of these plays are filled with abuse of Rome as coarse as voluble and incessant; for Bale forgot his enemies neither in the pulpit, in his dramas nor in his prayers.

King Johan is the most important of Bale's plays, for with it new elements enter into the drama. Although the figure of the king is absurdly misrepresented as a Protestant hero valiantly withstanding the encroachments of Rome, the informing spirit of the whole production is polemic, not political, much less historical. Yet among the abstractions by which he is surrounded — England, Sedition, Clergy and the rest — King

Johan himself stands forth, with Cardinal Pandolphus beside
him, in interest at least actual historical figures. *King Johan*
is the earliest dramatic production to draw on the story of the
English chronicles, later to prove so fruitful in the drama.
However, *King Johan* was not the first morality to cloak political
allusion and satire. As far back as 1527 Cardinal Wolsey
had taken umbrage at a " moral," entitled *Lord Governance,*
acted by students of Gray's Inn, wherein the " misgovernance "
of " Dissipation and Negligence had like to have ruined Public
Weal." Indeed, only the plea that the play was twenty years
old saved the venturesome students from serious pains and
penalties. In *A Satire of the Three Estates,* the most elaborate moral play extant in an English tongue, the Scottish poet,
Sir David Lyndsay, satirized, with bold effectiveness and directness, the abuses, political and clerical, of his own realm, and
created for the nonce a reforming reaction in the heart and
in the court of his master, King James V. *A Satire of the
Three Estates* was acted before the king at Linlithgow and,
for the first time, most likely in 1540. Its studied elaboration
and the completeness of the allegory, its genuine satirical power
and cutting effectiveness mark the play as the very crown of its
species. The morality could go no further and it may be suspected that this famous piece, with its notorious performance
before the notabilities of the realm of Scotland, served again
and again as a model for later and lesser moralities of similar
type.[7] Among other later moralities of political intent, may
be named *Respublica* acted in the first year of Mary's reign
and the only extant polemical morality on the Roman Catholic
side. The two independent investigators have of late attributed
this morality to Nicholas Udall.[8] There is also the interesting
fragment, *Albion Knight,* printed probably in 1566, in which
England in abstraction is represented a prey to the contending
factions of good and evil.

The popularity of the miracle play was great and its vogue
spread throughout England. A similar diffusion, as to place,
and an even greater diversity of occasion, as to presentation, appears to have been true of the morality. Moralities were acted

[7] See A. Brandl, *Quellen des weltlichen Dramas in England vor
Shakespeare,* 1898.

[8] L. A. Magnus in his ed. of *Respublica, E. E. T. S.,* 1905; and C. W.
Wallace, *The Evolution of the English Drama,* 1912.

before princes, Lyndsay's *Satire,* as we have just seen, before King James, Skelton's lost *Nigromansir* at Woodstock before King Henry VII, several like moralities and interludes before his son and successor. Bale's moralities were variously acted in England, at Kilkenny in Ireland, *King John* in revival at Ipswich as late as 1561; and neither the universities nor the Inns of Court disdained the dramatic form which was characteristic of its age. In a word the morality was a diversion alike the favourite of the court and approved by the people.

We have now reached a period in the history of our subject at which the true drama emerges out of these chaotic, mediæval conditions; and that emergence was not single and confined to an individual species, but multiform; for the roots of the chief species of drama, later to flourish, strike back deep into these earlier times and nearly every kind of play that flourished during the reign of Queen Elizabeth may be found already presaged in interlude or morality form. The lineal descendant, so to speak, of the miracle play was the bible play, a drama, as we understand that term as to unity and constructiveness, founded on bible story. Obviously the intermediary between this outcome and the cycle of miracle plays is the single scene of this last, cut off from the sequence and developed, as it came to be before long, into a single play. Such productions are the *Conversion of St. Paul* and the *Mary Magdalen* of the *Digby Manuscript;* and such other transition plays are some of Bale's, already mentioned. It was the finer literary spirit of the Scotch humanist and historian George Buchanan, albeit he wrote his tragedies in Latin, that realised for the island of his birth the possibilities of a modern drama modelled on that of the ancients. Buchanan appreciated the admirable qualities of biblical subjects in their simplicity as well as themes drawn from the story of ancient Greece and Rome. His classical tragedies are little more than Latin transcripts of the *Alcestis* and the *Medea* of Euripides; his *Jephtha* and *Baptistes* are original plays though constructed in obedient observance of Euripidean rules. These tragedies belong to a date close to 1540 when Buchanan was a teacher in the college at Bordeaux; and it adds to our interest in them to know that they were written with a plain pedagogical intent and acted by Buchanan's own students there. In a large sense Buchanan is only one of the generation of European humanists who were busy in Germany, France and Italy rewriting biblical story and devising new allegories with a zealous

educational purpose. Buchanan was, however, above most of
these in his appreciation of the literature of the ancients, and
is memorable as the first man north of the Alps to recognise the
artistic functions of dramatic art.

The story of the bible play is not long. We hear of one
Ralph Radclif, a schoolmaster of Hitchen in Hertfordshire,
whose zeal for the drama caused him to convert the refectory of
an old monastery into a theatre wherein were acted many plays
of his own. Many were biblical in subject, none have escaped the ravages of time. Nicholas Grimald, too, better
known as the editor of *Tottel's Miscellany,* the earliest printed
collection of English lyrical poetry, was the author of two
later plays of the type, and John Foxe the martyrologist contributed one. All of these are extant.[9] But even the humanist
drama was now emerging out of Latin into the vernacular
tongues. In *Godly Queen Hester,* printed in 1561, the Vice
and the abstractions still linger as they do in *King Darius,*
1565, and to a lesser degree in Wager's abler *Repentance of
Mary Magdalene,* 1567. All of these plays, and more that
might be named their contemporaries, are more or less Protestant in their bias. But the last was acted by a company
of itinerant players and in the history of *Jacob and Esau,* 1568,
we leave the morality behind us and in a measure the miracle
play as well. For despite its didactic intention, the unknown
author of this play contrives a " sort of dramatic justification
of the success of Rebecca's ingenuity " however he turns it " to
account for the doctrine of predestination and election."
While little intervening remains, we find the immediate contemporaries of Shakespeare attempting to convert biblical subjects to performance on the stage. Thus Lodge and Greene
wrote, between 1587 and 1591, *A Looking Glass for London*
in which the wicked life of Rasni, King of Nineveh, and his
remarkable repentance wrought by Jonah is turned to present
satirical and moral applications; and, in 1589, Peele's by no
means ineffective *David and Bethsabe* was on the stage. This
was little else than a chronicle play applied to biblical history
and was in no sense a product of the sacred drama. The same
is true of later scattered examples some of which we shall meet
elsewhere.

[9] Grimald's plays are *Christus Redivivus,* 1549, and *Archipropheta,*
1547; Foxe's is *Christus Triumphans,* 1550; all are strictly humanist
dramas.

Returning backward to the drama of the humanists, we have already noted that a favourite subject for one class of the morality was that which dealt with the temptations of youth. The biblical prototype, to be sure, of all of these elaborations, especially the contrast of the ordered and the evil life of the young, is the parable of the prodigal son, a common subject for continental humanists. Among these plays an important one was *Acolastus* of the Dutch classical scholar, William de Volder, first acted by schoolboys at the Hague in 1528 and so popular in England, some dozen years later, that it was made into a text book by John Palsgrave for the teaching of Latin. Three " moral interludes " in English are modelled, more or less, immediately on *Acolastus* or on work that *Acolastus* inspired. These are *The Nice Wanton, The Disobedient Child* and *Misogonus,* ranging in point of date from the close of the reign of Henry VIII to within a year or so of the birth of Shakespeare. A more important production, from the literary point of view, and one marking the culmination of this school drama, as it has been called, is *The Glass of Government,* the work of the notable court poet George Gascoigne, published in 1575. Here the effect of the story is heightened by the contrast of two pairs of brothers especially in their students' life at a modern university, and Terentian situation is employed, after the manner of the elder humanists, to illustrate Christian morals. *The Glass of Government* is a play of merit, regular in construction, light of touch on occasion and couched in ready dialogue, even if the intent to teach remains ever present in the author's mind. It would be interesting to know to what extent some unrecorded visit of its courtier author to one of the Dutch schools, while he was a soldier in Holland, may have inspired this effort. Save for a few later university plays this was the last humanist drama in England. The recurrence of the theme of the prodigal son in subsequent comedies of manners will claim later attention.

We have already met with the term " interlude " in the connotation of moral interlude; and the word was loosely employed to designate almost any form of play from very early times. Whether we accept the older explanation which makes the interlude a dramatic intermezzo between more serious scenes or intervening elsewhere between the parts of some extended entertainment, or whether we define the word with Chambers as simply a dramatic dialogue, it is well to recognise that the in-

terlude emphasises the element of diversion for its own sake
as contrasted with the didactic character of all varieties of
sacred and moral plays. The history of the earlier interlude is
wrapped up with that of disguising and mumming; and this in
turn takes us back to the festivals of the folk. Lydgate in the
fifteenth century gave a literary bias to certain of the mummings
at court; and pageantry there, following the analogy of that long
invoked for religious plays, developed quite early into considerable elaboration.[10] So far as the interlude is concerned, there
are only scant indications of the existence in mediæval England
of a light secular drama, such as we know to have flourished
in contemporary France. And yet the fragments of plays on
Robin Hood, dramatized from the ballads, the many mentions
of plays of St. George, which may have been only partially religious, together with what we can gleam as to the repertory of
the minstrels, all point towards a drama of this type, largely
extemporaneous and perhaps little of it written down for pres-
ervation. Examples of the interlude in the sense of a scene of
diversion are to be found in the miracle plays and moralities
themselves. Such is the scene of Mak and the Shepherds in
the *Towneley Cycle,* and such an interlude is that of Pauper
between the first and second parts of Lyndsay's *Satire of the
Three Estates* in which that unhappy victim of greed and im-
position makes clear his wrongs in a ludicrous recital of them.
But the credit of raising the interlude to an independent place
among dramatic forms I can not but feel, still belongs to John
Heywood, the epigrammatist, poet and privileged wit of the
household of Henry VIII.[11] The dialogues and interludes usu-

[10] On the mumming of Lydgate, see Brotanek, *Die englischen
Maskenspiele,* p. 305, and *Anglia* xxii, 364. Wallace finds the chil-
dren of the Chapel first employed "in a pageant and song" in 1490.
Evolution of the English Drama, p. 13.

[11] In repeating this statement, I am not unaware of a recent effort
by my friend, Professor Wallace, to overturn our accepted notions
concerning the beginnings of the regular drama and to deprive Heywood of the better part of his work. See his *The Evolution of the
English Drama,* 1913, especially pp. 33-60. This attempt involves the
raising up of William Cornish into what Mr. Wallace calls an "Oc-
tavian Shakespeare" and the interpretation of the pageants, disguisings and entertainments in which Cornish figured as actor, deviser
and lyrist into successive steps of momentous import in the evolution

ally ascribed to Heywood lie, in point of date, between 1520 and 1540 and cover some little variety in subject. *Love* and *Wit and Witless* are little more than *débats* of which the earlier annals of France and England alike exhibit many similar examples. In *The Play of the Weather* the dialogue is extended with reminiscences of the methods of the morality into a more original production. Jupiter, in consequence of a disagreement among the gods ruling the weather, summons before him people of various degrees to learn their wants and thereby determine the question. Merry Report, who acts as usher, is a clever adaptation of the Vice and the fun consists in the conflict of wishes and arguments presented by personages such as the Ranger, the Wind and the Water-miller and the Fair Dame. But it is in the other three interludes of Heywood that we find his most characteristic contributions to the drama. "A Merry Play," as it is called, "between the Pardoner and the Frere, the Curate and the Neighbour Pratt " sets its scene in a church and develops an amusing but exceedingly scandalous altercation; a second equally "Merry Play," vivaciously sets forth how Tyb, a shrewish wife, and Sir Jhan, the priest, make a victim of a timid though by no means complaisant husband and force him to fetch and carry; while the last, the famous *Four P's,* ends in a match at lying. In the figure, just named, and in the Pardoner, the Palmer, the Pedler and the "Poticary" of *The Four P's,* the drafts from copy of the miracle play and the abstractions of the morality are left once and for all behind us; for whatever the suggestions of source for these inter-

of the drama. Cornish was master of the Chapel from 1509 to 1523 and we have actual proof that he was the author of one "play," *The Triumph of Love and Beauty,* cited by Collier as far back as 1833. Mr. Wallace hands over to Cornish a story of *Troilus and Pandor* (lost but cited in *The Household Books of Henry VIII,* i, 169, not however as by Cornish). He hands over to Cornish likewise Heywood's *Four P's, Johan Johan* and *Gentleness and Nobility,* in one case because Heywood's name is not on the title page, in another, questioning the contemporary title and Bale's equally contemporary ascription of the work to Heywood. He further assigns the morality of the *Four Elements* and *Calista and Meliboea,* productions amazingly diverse, also to Cornish, because, he says "no other dramatist was then living who had either the opportunity or impetus or skill to work in the manner of his new style drama."

ludes from France, Heywood sketched his figures from the English life that he saw about him and found, in fidelity to that life and in a humorous appreciation of its personages, his real success. Henceforward English vernacular comedy had at least an example, and the step through such an interlude as the anonymous *Tom Tyler and his Wife,* about 1560, in which a shrewish wife maintains her ascendency despite an attempted marital revolt, to *Gammer Gurton's Needle* (earliest regular comedy of the realistic type), becomes a measurable one.

With semi-moralities like *The Disobedient Child* of Thomas Ingeland referred to Ravisius Textor, the French humanist, with Henry Cheke, translating the Italian Bassano's tragedy of *Freewill,* in 1546, and *Everyman* and *Acolastus* touching Dutch humanism, it is clear that the forebears of English drama were not without many foreign examples. But there were influences deeper than this, derived from the classics and breathed in with the education of the day. Humanism was founded on a study of the ancients and on the application of that study to the problems educational and other of the day; and the drama of the humanists seized at once on the plays of Terence and Plautus especially as its guides and examples for comedy. Not only were these authors commonly read and frequently acted in the schools, but they were translated and imitated in adaptation to the condition of the time. The interlude of *Thersites,* 1537, goes back, with the intervention once more of Textor, to the *Miles Gloriosus* of Plautus, and *Jack Juggler,* 1553, is similarly modelled on the *Amphitruo.* Even earlier, in 1530, *Terens in English* had appeared, though Terence was not so often imitated. Thus when Nicholas Udall, sometime master of Westminster School as earlier of Eton, wrote and staged his *Ralph Roister Doister,* he was really doing in itself no novel thing, though the step that he took was momentous in the English drama. This famous comedy tells how the boastful and thick-witted hero of the title name considers it certain, in Benedick's phrase, that he " is beloved of all ladies," and how, abetted by a rascally flatterer, Matthew Merrigreke, Ralph persists in courting Dame Custance against her will and proceeds through a series of amusing rebuffs to his final discomfiture. Udall's comedy is an adaptation of the *Miles Gloriosus* to English manners and conditions; and it is cleverly constructed and well and cleanly written. It was probably prepared for Eton boys who acted it between 1534 and 1541, and it thus preceded many productions that remained more or less affected by imitations of the older drama.[12]

Several plays, however, may be named which have been held for various reasons to dispute with *Ralph Roister Doister* and *Gammer Gurton's Needle* the claims of these plays to the position of the first regular English comedy. *Misogonus* and *Jacob and Esau* have both been already mentioned. Aside from their affiliations with the biblical humanist drama, neither can be dated with certainty earlier than *Gammer Gurton's Needle,* 1552-53. With *Thersites,* 1537, and *Calisto and Meliboea,* 1530, the questions that arise are of another kind. *Thersites* is an exceedingly lively little burlesque in which is set forth the vaunts of a childish boaster and their ludicrous consequences to him, an enormous snail putting him to flight and to the protection of his mother's apron in one scene. The play is an adaptation from a Latin original by Textor, somewhat improved and abbreviated in the process. The merit of *Thersites* lies in its freedom from any ulterior motive; it exists solely for the laughter it may raise and conceals neither bearings on man's conduct in life nor side lights of moral suasion. But all this was equally true of the interludes of Heywood; moreover, *Thersites* is a slight affair of a few scenes and, besides lacking the structure of a complete drama, is little more than a translation. The interlude of *Thersites* stands in the same relation to *Ralph Roister Doister* that the interludes of Heywood or *Tom Tyler and his Wife* hold with respect to *Gammer Gurton. Calisto and Meliboea,* on the other hand, is a carefully considered play, worked out at length and in detail, setting forth a romantic love story, the first important example of its kind in the drama. A young gallant, Calisto, has a passion for Meliboea, a fair lady who dislikes him. Through the endeavours of an old crone, Celestina, however, Meliboea is at length won to consent to lend Calisto her girdle — figurative of a less innocent concession — to recover him from a pretended illness; but repenting, confesses her indiscretion to her father and is by him forgiven. We have here the earliest serious play to rid itself of allegory and abstraction, besides a

[12] See the excellent summary of the whole discussion by C. G. Child in his edition of *Ralph Roister Doister,* 1912, pp. 31-42; I can not but feel that Hale's date, 1553, accepted by Wallace, is quite untenable.

diction and quality of style decidedly beyond its age. But *Calisto and Meliboea* is even more closely a translation than *Thersites,* its original being the famous Spanish tale in dramatic form, *Celestina,* attributed to the authorship of Rojas and first published in 1499. Besides, the unknown English translator in his version departs from his source to convert a tragedy, the logical outcome of the story, into a "moral interlude," ending in an "exhortacyon to vertew." The claims of *Calisto and Meliboea* with all its merits are damaged alike by this moral intrusion, inevitable in its age and even yet the bane of British drama, and by the circumstance that the play is merely a translation.

As between *Ralph Roister Doister* and *Gammer Gurton,* priority in time belongs to the former, and only the degree of Udall's debt to Plautus, which is easily exaggerated, can impair his claim. *Gammer Gurton's Needle* is a coarse but exceedingly vigorous comedy of daily English village life; its figures are as real as Heywood's, its structure as a complete drama away and beyond him. The comedy appears to have been first acted at Cambridge in 1552-53 and has been variously assigned as to authorship to Bishop Still, Dr. John Brydges and to William Stevenson, the last in the early fifties fellow of Christ Church. The whole action turns on the loss of a needle, conceivably a more valuable implement in that day than now, and the manner in which knavish Diccon of Bedlam sets the village by the ears about it. A conclusion is reached by excellent Gammer Gurton who finds the needle at last exactly where she had left it. If freedom from dependence on foreign sources or any intention to teach, a due consideration of structure and amplitude of design be taken into account, together with direct sketching from contemporary life, then *Gammer Gurton's Needle* is our earliest regular English comedy. Perhaps, however, when all has been said, it is best to observe that our English drama emerged out of the didactic state of the moralities and from the trivialities of the interlude all but simultaneously in several forms. *Jacob and Esau* marks the way from the old sacred drama to the bible play; *The Disobedient Child* or *Misogonus,* the growth from morality, through the humanist college drama to a comedy measurably free from the intent to teach. In *Calisto* and *Meliboea* (as in the earlier tragical *Freewill*) romantic material of foreign origin is broached, although the intent to point a moral still rules.

While in *Thersites* and *Ralph Roister Doister* the influence of classical comedy appears in transition from interlude to comedy form; and in *Tom Tyler* and *Gammer Gurton's Needle* the same transition with the realistic present in place of the bookish past its inspiration. Lastly, to turn from comedy, *King Johan* equally marks the emergence of the morality into a recognition of national history as a theme for drama, precisely as the Euripidean tragedies of Buchanan call into requisition the finest models of the past for tragedy.

Tragedy in regular form and in English was later to emerge from the past than comedy; and the influence here, soon substituted for that of Euripides, was Seneca, the tragic writer of Neronian Rome. The first regular English tragedy is the well known *Gorboduc or Ferrex and Porrex,* the work of Thomas Sackville and Thomas Norton, students of the Inner Temple where their play was acted before the queen on New Year's day 1562. Much in the way of like classical imitations had gone before, but these were mostly college dramas and all were in Latin. *Gorboduc* tells the story of an unwise king of England who, like Lear, divided his kingdom with his children, two sons, who fought to the death for supremacy. It is a stately and well constructed tragedy. To its distinction as the earliest tragedy in the English language of anything like regular structure, *Gorboduc* adds the circumstance that it is the first play to be written throughout in blank-verse and one of the earliest to draw on English chronicle history for a subject. This with its Senecan relations will claim a later consideration.

CHAPTER III

LYLY, MARLOWE AND OTHER IMMEDIATE PRE-DECESSORS OF SHAKESPEARE

WHEN *Gorboduc* was staged, three years were yet to elapse before the birth of Marlowe and Shakespeare; and John Lyly, first important literary name in the annals of English drama, was a boy not yet ready for school. But much was to pass before the drama came into the hands of these greater men. *Gorboduc* was first written and acted by students of the Inns of Court in the presence of the queen; *Gammer Gurton* was a college play; *Ralph Roister Doister* was the work of a school-master, written for his scholars and acted by them. Even the earlier plays at court, performed by the gentlemen and children of the Chapel Royal, were matters of the king's house-hold. Clearly we are dealing with an amateur drama as yet, and one as apart from the bourgeois civic character of the old sacred drama as it long remained distinguishable from the pro-fessional drama soon to spring into celebrity.

It would be difficult to overestimate the influence of the court and the queen on the early pre-Shakespearean drama. Elizabeth was pleasure-loving by nature and fond of elaborate and stately ceremonies and sumptuous display. She was like-wise in her way a patron of learning and an encourager of poetry and art; in a word, Elizabeth was a true daughter of the Renaissance. As to the drama, she found all the forms for its encouragement made ready to her hand. In employing them she was only continuing a long established usage. The beginnings of pageantry and disguisings at court are lost in an immemorial past; and the royal records and account books, even the chronicle histories, are full of recitals of the devices of poets, of pageantry, music and other entertainments in which figure Lords of Misrule, masters, gentlemen and children of the Royal Chapel and occasionally other entertainers, both English and foreign. Moralities and interludes were among these entertainments and those concerned in them acquired, as time went on, a more or less professional standing.

The Office of the Revels, originally perhaps no more than a temporary appointment, had become since the days of Sir Thomas Cawarden in Henry VIII's reign, a place of importance, charged with the supervision of the entertainments at court. Elizabeth further developed and enlarged its functions until, by the advent of Shakespeare in London, the Office consisted of a master, a clerk controller, a clerk and a yeoman of the wardrobe and properties. The mastership soon came to guide and control the histrionic activity of the age, and, from its power to license plays and to suppress even at need recalcitrant players and their playhouses, rose before long to an office of dignity. Sir Edmund Tylney, master from 1579 to 1610, thus covering the whole important period of Elizabethan drama, administered this office to the satisfaction of the queen and King James after her, and with no small emolument to himself. It was this office that Lyly sought in the seventies and the reversion of which in the reign of King Charles, Ben Jonson did not live to enjoy. We shall meet with its intervention in the affairs of the drama more than once in the following pages.

We have already found Nicholas Udall preparing his *Ralph Roister Doister* for boys to act, and have recognised that the custom of acting plays by the students of schools extends back to very early times. With an increasing demand for plays at court and the exaction of a higher grade of histrionic ability, these boy troupes, trained and drilled in acting under the ferrules of their schoolmasters, were gradually called upon to take their place beside the children of the Chapel Royal as entertainers of the queen. Thus it was that school boys and choir boys became our first professional actors and that schoolmasters like John Taylor and William Elderton, Udall's successors at Westminster School, and Thomas Gyles, Richard Farrant, and Richard Bower, masters respectively of St. Paul's choir, the Chapel Royal at Windsor and the Queen's Chapel, were the first professional managers and playwrights. The actual contributions of the men just named to the drama are for the most part conjectural and based on entries in the records of the Office of the Revels and the like.[1] With Richard Edwards

[1] See the valuable "Table of Plays and Masques before Queen Elizabeth," 1558-85, by C. W. Wallace, *Evolution of the Drama*, pp. 199-209.

(who died in 1566), and William Hunnis (active up to 1583), both of them successors of Bower as masters of the Queen's Chapel, we are on somewhat sounder ground. *Damon and Pithias* by Edwards, acted at Whitehall at Christmas, 1564, is extant to show that its author was neither without theories concerning the comedian's art nor devoid of ideas as to the dignity of the drama. Two years later, at Oxford, his dramatic version of Chaucer's *Knight's Tale,* entitled *Palaemon and Arcyte,* was acted before the queen, greatly to her majesty's satisfaction. But this play has been lost. Edwards has been thought the author of other plays; while the list ascribed to Hunnis has been enlarged to formidable proportions, though really nothing remains to us to be referred with certainty to his hand.[2] Hunnis retained his position up to 1597 when he was succeeded by Nathaniel Gyles who abused the royal patent to take up children who could sing for the royal choir by actually kidnapping schoolboys and training them by force to act plays for his own emolument.

Turning back to another phase of the drama in earlier Elizabethan days, the studies of young gentlemen were based on the classics and this, with a growing interest in tragedy, resulted in an enthusiastic cultivation of Seneca. Moreover, in Italy and France alike, tragedy in the manner of Seneca was the literary affectation of the moment. Between 1559 and 1581 the *Tenne Tragedies,* that then went under the name of the Roman poet, were translated into English by various hands; and the plays were acted and imitated again and again in Latin dramas at college. Reasons for the choice of Seneca for a model are not far to seek. Seneca is the most modern of the ancients and the most romantic of the classics. His heightened style, his moralising, his lofty commonplaces unctuously expressed, even his sensationalism, his blood and terror, all fell in naturally with the temper of the young romantic age. While his professional manner, show of technique, his conventional verse and rhetoric, equally suited the time. Besides, Seneca was the most available model; his vehicle was Latin, the universal language of scholarship, and neither so remote as the Greek tragedians nor lacking in sanction as were most of the moderns. One of the distinctions of *Gorboduc* was its choice

---

[2] For surmises on the subject, see Mrs. C. M. Stopes: *Shakespeare Jahrbuch,* xxvii and elsewhere.

of an English myth. But this particular myth, the dissensions of two princes, brothers, for a kingdom, to the destruction of both, was prompted by its similarity to the well known Greek story of the Theban Eteocles and Polynices, also treated by Seneca. The next Senecan tragedy of note in English was Gascoigne's *Jocasta*. Gascoigne's was also an Inns of Court play, acted at Gray's Inn before the queen in 1566. The plot returns to a classical subject and is really not much more than an adaptation of Dolce's Italian tragedy, *Giocasta*. Of George Gascoigne's contribution to the school drama, *The Glass of Government* we have already heard. He was less a scholar than a courtier and while his satire, fiction and general poetry do not concern us here, he touched the drama at two other points, in comedy and in pageantry in which he was " a prime contriver." In the year 1576, Queen Elizabeth went on one of her periodical progresses among her loving subjects, journeying to Kenilworth Castle, the seat of the famous Earl of Leicester, whom rumour said at the moment she was likely to marry. In the splendid welcome which the earl accorded her majesty and which Sir Walter Scott immortalised in *Kenilworth,* Gascoigne was one of the several poets employed to frame speeches of welcome and allegorical scenes — one among them setting forth the advantages of matrimony on the recommendation of Juno to the confusion of Minerva. While space will not permit here a specification of Gascoigne's contributions with those of his fellows to what afterwards developed into the masque, it may be remarked that the pageantry of the progress is not to be neglected in the earlier annals of the drama. At court the custom of giving plays to signalise occasions of social importance became before long the thing obvious and expected. Gascoigne marks the step from sheer amateurs like Sackville, Norton or Hughes, to the playwright and professional deviser of entertainments. Legge, in his Latin *Richardus Tertius,* 1579, first employed later English chronicles for the subject of a Senecan play; and Peele, in *Locrine,* 1586 (if it be his), and Thomas Hughes and others in their joint tragedy, *The Misfortunes of Arthur,* 1587, continued the working of English myth in this kind. With the last two plays and others of like type we are on the threshold of the new romantic drama, for *The Spanish Tragedy* was on the stage in the latter year.

The repertory of the early semi-professional companies of boy actors included plays on ancient history and fable; plays founded, to judge by their titles, on modern history or recent occurrence; romantic stories, comedies, and mere farces. Among many titles the following are typical: *Pompey, Narcissus; The King of Scots,* like *Narcissus* ascribed to Hunnis; *Murderous Michael,* possibly an earlier version of the notable murder play, *Arden of Feversham; Jack and Gill* and *The History of the Collier,* in all likelihood the extant *Grim, the Collier of Croydon.* Most of the types of plays just mentioned are illustrated in extant specimens of the period. Among them may be named *Godly Queen Hester,* 1561, *Appius and Virginia,* 1563, *King Darius,* 1565, Pickering's *Orestes,* 1567, and most popular for its day, Preston's *Cambyses.* Thomas Preston was a Cambridge man who rose in time to the dignity of Master of Trinity. His abilities in disputation and cleverness in acting a part in Gager's Latin tragedy, *Dido,* on the occasion of the queen's visit to the university in 1566, had called him to Elizabeth's attention and doubtless for the moment determined his career. *Cambyses, King of Persia,* acted about 1569, smacks of the old allegorical drama and is not a little morally weighted; but its grandiloquence and bombast of tone was long appreciated, at first seriously, later as a theme for ridicule, especially by Shakespeare. In truth, allegory and a moral purpose, forced on the understanding, remained general qualities of this pre-Lylian drama save for a very few exceptions. But these exceptions mark the vital stock of what was to come. In the preface to a narrative poem by Arthur Brooke, entitled *The Tragical History of Romeus and Juliet,* we read: " I saw the same argument lately set forth on stage with more commendation than I can look for." This was two years before the birth of Shakespeare. Several years later, in 1579, we hear of another Shakespearean subject in a play mentioned by Stephen Gosson as expressing " the greediness of worldly choosers (Portia's unsuccessful suitors), and the bloody minds of usurers (Shylock's implacable pursuit of the pound of flesh.) [3] To turn from what is lost to what we have, Gascoigne's *Supposes* is a lively comedy constructed on a series of suppositions (" supposes ") that turn out — like the comedy of " errors "— contrariwise. Acted in 1566, this is the first successful adaptation of an Italian comedy and the

[3] *The Cruel Debtor,* 1566, supposed formerly to be on this subject turns out otherwise. See *The Malone Society's Publications,* " Collections IV and V," 1911, pp. 313 ff.

earliest example of a play written throughout in English prose.
Two years later *Gismond of Salern,* from an Italian *novella*
of that title was staged, the work of five young gentlemen of
the Inner Temple, chief among them Robert Wilmot who later,
in 1591, rewrote and published the entire drama as his own.
Tancred and Gismunda, as it was called in revision, is a Senecan
tragedy in manner; but, as the earliest English play to lay under
contribution that storehouse of Italian fiction, Painter's *Palace
of Pleasure,* it partook of the new romantic spirit which was so
soon to rule the serious drama of the age. *Gismond* is declamatory but its tragic love story, the clandestine meetings of
the lovers, the father's revenge and presentation of her dead
lover's heart to his daughter in an urn, with her tragic death
— all this, crude though it be, is in long advance of the correct
morality that spoiled the story of *Calisto and Meliboea.* More
in touch after all with older methods is George Whetstone's
formidable drama in two parts, *Promos and Cassandra,* 1578.
The subject, referable to a novel of the *Hecatommithi* of Cinthio, is memorable for its after treatment by Shakespeare in his
Measure for Measure. Whetstone was a small poet and friend
of Gascoigne whose memory he celebrated in dull elegiac lines.
He is full of theory as to dramatic writing and says more than
is needful on the subject in his dedication. However, though
free from the bonds of Seneca, which Wilmot and his confreres
were certainly not, Whetstone has left but an awkward, gross
and verbose original for the art of his great successor to fashion.

Supposes, Gismond of Salern, and *Promos and Cassandra*
mark, in drama, a new impulse derived from Italy direct. The
immediate models and inspiration of Lyly, however, were not
these. John Lyly was born in Kent, about 1554, and was
therefore of an age with Spenser. It has recently been shown
that Lyly came of excellent family, his grandfather being no
less a person than the distinguished scholar and grammarian,
William Lyly; John Lyly's father was Registrar of his native
Canterbury. Lyly received his education at Oxford, with a
later sojourn at Cambridge, and enjoyed the patronage of Bur-
leigh and especially of Lord Oxford to whose service he was
for years attached. Oxford was known to his age as a writer
of comedies now lost and he maintained at least one company
of actors, so Lyly's induction as an entertainer at Court was a
natural one. In 1579 Lyly leaped to instant literary repute

by the publication of his famous prose romance, *Euphues, the Anatomy of Wit,* followed in the next year by *Euphues and his England.* His plays seem to have begun with *Campaspe,* staged first, it has been supposed, about 1580 at Blackfriars and, later, by a combination of the Children of Pauls with those of the Royal Chapel at court.

Recent researches inform us that Farrant, master of the children at Windsor, obtaining a lease of certain properties that had belonged to the Revels' Office in Carwarden's time, converted them into " a regular theatre," in 1576, about the time at which Burbage was opening his new Theatre in Shoreditch; that under Farrant's management up to 1580, the drama, acted by the boy companies, thrived in his hands, and that he used his theatre to train not only his own children of Windsor for performances before the queen, but those of the Chapel Royal of whom Hunnis was master, the two masters thus "pooling" their theatrical interests. The children of Blackfriars play a very important part in the early history of the drama, although the increasing vogue of the adult companies, as disclosed by the records of performances at court, created a rivalry, happy for the development of the histrionic art. Farrant died towards the end of 1880, and his widow assigned his lease to Hunnis, who as master of the Chapel Royal was able to continue the double function of his playhouse as a public theatre and a training house for performances before the queen. But before long trouble arose between the owner, Farrant's widow, Hunnis and an associate of his in the conduct of the theatre named John Newman. Into these details we cannot go. By a contemporary letter recently discovered and printed, it appears that in the spring of 1583, the Earl of Oxford acquired the lease of the playhouse in Blackfriars. This interest, according to the same letter, the earl " gave " to Lyly with other houses adjacent. It is not clear that this transfer was more than a part of the vexatious defence, put up by the widow of Farrant, to prevent the owner from re-entering the premises. At any rate Lyly did not enjoy his lease a full year, for the owner won his suit. *Campaspe* and *Sapho and Phao* were acted, according to their title pages, by a conjunction of the Chapel Children with the Paul's Boys and payments were made, according to the accounts of the Audit Office, to the Earl of Oxford his servants for "two plays" on New

Year's night and Shrove Tuesday, 1583-84.[4] But this does not
"prove" these plays to have been *Campaspe* and *Sapho and
Phao,* or that the Earl of Oxford's servants were the children
of the chapel and the boys of Paul's organised into one company under the leadership of Lyly.

Leaving these mooted questions, it is to be remarked that
Lyly was a born courtier and that all of his literary work was
prompted by the moment and calculated alone to the end of his
own advancement. He was constantly in attendance at court
and became in due time one of the queen's "esquires of the
body." He served in parliament and married well, considering
his want of any stable fortune; and he appears to have been for
years an applicant for a post in the Office of the Revels. This
he was never able to procure, though it may be doubted if there
was a fitter man for the mastership in all England. However,
his plays met with a deserved success from the first for their
courtliness, their choice euphuistic prose diction and their nicety
of expression; perhaps even more for their allegory and covert
allusions to matters of passing political interest in the inner
court circle which Lyly made one of their features almost from
the first. For example, *Sapho and Phao* dared allusions in
allegory to the royal flirtation with her majesty's French suitor,
the homely and insignificant D'Alençon; Midas, the ancient
king at whose touch and by whose greed all things were turned
to gold, figured forth in a drama of that title, the master of the
Indies and arch enemy of England, King Philip of Spain; and
Endimion, 1585, among the complications and contradictions
of recent interpretations, long supposed to refer somehow to the
only serious affair of the heart which the Virgin Queen seems
ever to have had, (her preference, if not her "infatuation" for
the Earl of Leicester), must now be interpreted into the wider
political significance that leaves Elizabeth Cythia (the unattainable moon), but makes Tellus (the earth) the captive Mary of
Scots and Endimion no less a personage than her canny, unstable, intriguing son, King James.[5] Dramas of this type are
dependent for their success as much on their happy power of
topical allusion, addressed to the limited and understanding

[4] On this whole subject, see Wallace, as above (especially pp. 174
and 224 ff.), whose researches now clear up a matter long doubtful.

[5] See on this topic A. Feuillerat, *John Lyly,* 1910, pp. 141-190 where
the previous theories are likewise discussed.

audience of the moment, as they are on their inventiveness and literary merit. The former we can no more recover than we can restore the colours of a tropical fish, once removed from its native element. It may be inferred that these comedies of Lyly in their natural court environment must have had an effectiveness which it is difficult for us to imagine. From these model and carefully written comedies all coarseness and vulgarity was banished, the ribaldry of the common folk, and with it the rude practical jests of the old comedy. The figures of Lyly's plays realised the manners and the precious euphuistic speech that the fashionable courtier and lady were striving to attain. It is no wonder that on the basis of his successful *Anatomy of Wit,* its continuance in *Euphues and his England* and these taking court plays, Lyly was, up to the year of the Armada, the literary man of the moment.

However, not quite all of Lyly's comedies were so heavily freighted with matter of purely contemporary moment. *Campaspe* itself is not much more than a " fanciful rendering of a classical legend "; *Mother Bombie,* 1590, is a comedy of every day life in the manner of Terence, but cleverly original; while *Gallathea, Love's Metamorphosis* and *The Woman in the Moon* are pastoral comedies cast in mythological mould and employing little more allegory than was useful to carry a strain of compliment to the queen. As to Lyly's art in general, it is interesting to notice how effectively he developed what he found ready at hand. The old allegory of mere abstraction turned in his hands (as in Spenser's) to a reflex reference to persons and things concrete with the result of an enormous gain in interest. The classical apparatus of the humanists, with its display of ponderous learning, became the winged shaft of mythological allusion or the utilisation, for picturesque subject-matter, of material from that admirable body of classical story which the combined ingenuity of modern ages has never approached. True, only a Renaissance audience could appreciate to the full an art so dependent on a specific kind of culture; but Lyly's audience was just such a one, made up of high born, cultivated, finely tempered folk, alive to every allusion and as keen of wit and ready at repartee almost as the dramatist's own clever figures. To the several things already mentioned as going to make up Lyly's art of court comedy, must be added his effective employment of the pastoral motive in the three comedies mentioned above in this connection. Lyly may have found his suggestion in some of the entertainments of Gascoigne, or more effectively in Sir Philip Sidney's little pastoral interlude, *The Lady of May,* produced for the entertainment of Elizabeth at Wansted, in 1578. But if we would understand by what steps Lyly advanced the drama we should compare this pretty trifle with Lyly's *Gallathea* or such a play as *Endimion* with the anonymous *Rare Triumphs of Love and Fortune,* acted perhaps about 1582, and one of several plays in which the earlier abstractions, translated into the terms of classical mythology, are represented as concerned with the doings of mortals whose story, none the less, constitutes the main interest. Whether this was suggested by the shades and furies of Seneca and his imitators, certain it is that by the time it reached Lyly it was transformed into a thing new and fanciful. Lyly gave to English drama a sense of unity and models of artistic form. He adopted Gascoigne's innovation, the writing of comedy in prose, and developed a medium of much ease, lightness and elegance. He employed dramatic disguise for the first time with effect and supplied his auditors with an idealised transcript of their own court manners and dialogue, giving to his work an immediate effectiveness by its allusiveness to affairs of the moment. Lyly took hand in the Marprelate controversy, the notorious pamphlet war between the extreme Puritans and the upholders of the bishops and of bishops' rights and pretensions. Aside from a prose tract or two, ascribed to him, Lyly's work of this kind included several popular satirical plays.[6] These we may congratulate ourselves have perished; they could have added nothing to his fame. Lyly survived the queen who neglected him, dying in 1606, late enough to see his old " court plays " succeeded by wave upon wave of the new popular drama of his successors; but when he died, at just the age of Shakespeare, he could not but have known that he had borne his part in laying foundations on which were reared the successes of greater as of lesser men.

Among writers of drama for the court in the early eighties, none could be named beside Lyly; and of those who imitated him one man only rivalled him in the thing that he did so well, and this only in one effort. George Peele, son of a clerk of Christ's Hospital, was born in 1558 and was therefore four years the junior of Lyly. At Oxford young Peele

---

[6] On the whole topic, see Feuillerat, as above, pp. 211 ff.

became interested in the drama through a kinsman, William Gager, the author of several Latin plays. Peele himself translated one of the *Iphigenias* of Euripides, whether into Latin or English is not known. Attaining his master's degree in 1597, Peele turned his attention as a playwright from the college to the court and, with Lyly in the first bloom of his repute, at once set about to rival him. Peele's *Arraignment of Paris* has been dated as early as 1581; it was in print by 1584. Borrowing the idea from a poem of Gascoigne, Peele dramatized the story of Paris and Œnone and the discord of the goddesses wrought by the apple of Até, but diverted the award from Venus in the end to a votress of Diana, the gracious and royal nymph, " whose name Eliza is." But Peele's *Arraignment* is not merely compliment and a following of Lyly. Lyly's mastery was that of prose and his power is rhetorical. Peele is a poet and his graceful and fanciful dramatic poem depends for its success, not alone on its theme, but on its poetical quality and happy metrical facility. Of a second court play of Peele's, *The Hunting of Cupid,* only fragments have come down to us; and soon we find Peele transferring his talents to the popular stage, whither we shall now follow him.

It is impossible to fix a date for the earliest performance of secular plays in London. Acting in the yards of inns and other public places by strolling players must have been old when parliament adopted, in 1543, stringent measures against " common players " for their intermeddling in matters religious; and almost as early, the phraseology of such acts habitually classified players, who were not specifically licensed, with vagabonds and masterless men. Adult professional companies of actors, made up of men with boys playing the female parts, date also very early, as does the Elizabethan practice of placing such companies under the protection of noble or royal patrons. Indeed Elizabeth's early statute of 1572, declaring all able-bodied, unemployed men (players among them), not under patronage of some nobleman to be vagabonds, was only regulating an old and established usage. This practice, though later little more than a legal fiction, was continued throughout the reign of Elizabeth largely because of the hostility of the London Council towards all actors. James on his accession placed the companies under royal patronage and ended the old system.[7]

[7] On this subject, see V. C. Gildersleeve, *Government Regulations of the Elizabethan Drama,* 1908, pp. 29, 30, and elsewhere.

The history of Elizabethan theatrical companies is full of difficulties. The evidence concerning them is now, thanks to the researches of Professor Wallace, abundant, though scholars will have to be more than mortal if they do not find themselves at times at variance as to the interpretation of some of it. Companies passed from patron to patron; coalitions, divisions and reorganisations were constantly taking place. For example, we hear of a group of players under the patronage of Lord Robert Dudley, later the great favourite, the Earl of Leicester, not infrequently between 1560 and 1582. This company obtained the earliest royal patent ever granted to a company of players, in 1574. It acted at the Bull, an inn-yard in Bishopsgate Street, and later at the Theatre which James Burbage built, in 1576, in Shoreditch. It appears to have been broken up in 1582-83 by the withdrawal from it of Wilson, Tarlton and other prominent actors. Though some of its sometime members are found still under the patronage of the earl abroad in 1585, acting in Denmark and in Germany and, on their return, visiting several provincial towns, among them Stratford.[8] In London, in consequence of this disruption, a new company was formed called the Queen's servants who played variously at the Bull in Bishopsgate Street and the Bell in Gracious Street under the leadership of Robert Wilson and until about 1591. Their rivals at that time were the Admiral's men playing at the Curtain, and the Chamberlain's men playing at the Theatre. Burbage was not connected, it now appears, at any time with the Queen's men, but succeeded in reorganising the disrupted company of the Earl of Leicester under the patronage of Lord Hunsdon who, as cousin of the queen, brought him a certain amount of court patronage. Without here going into particulars, by 1585 Burbage had so improved his property in the Theatre, despite the innumerable law suits in which he was constantly involved, that he was able to make an agreement with his rival and neighbour, Laneman, manager of the neighbouring Curtain, by which the two companies pooled their interests and divided the profits of the two playhouses. In 1589,

[8] For the foreign visits of Elizabethan theatrical companies abroad, see E. Herz, *Englische Schauspieler in Deutschland,* 1903; for their visits to English provincial towns, see J. T. Murray, *English Dramatic Companies,* 1910.

on the payment of a mortgage long held against the Theatre, Cuthbert Burbage became the legal owner of the property although his father, James Burbage, still remained the leader of the company. A year later, as a result of one of their incessant quarrels, the Alleyns, John and Edward, of the Curtain, severed their alliance with Burbage, and took themselves across the river where they joined hands with Henslowe who controlled the Rose and the playhouse at Newington Butts. Edward Alleyn was now at the head of the Admiral's men and we hear of these theatres as variously occupied by them in the ensuing years, by the Earl of Pembroke's players, those of the Earl of Sussex and by a company known as Lord Strange's, in 1593-94 called Lord Derby's. Some of the earlier plays of Shakespeare were acted by these companies controlled by Henslowe and Alleyn; it does not appear that there is any evidence of Shakespeare's association with Burbage before 1594. Lord Strange, Earl of Derby, died in April of that year and, in the reorganisation that followed, several of those who had constituted that company, William Kempe, Thomas Pope, John Heming, Augustine Philips and George Bryan, combined with Richard Burbage and William Shakespeare in the organisation of a new company under the patronage of Lord Hunsdon, Burbage's old patron, which, under his name, that of his office of Lord Chamberlain and as the King's players after 1603, became permanently Shakespeare's company. As servants to the Lord Chamberlain, Shakespeare and Burbage received the first payment for a performance at court in December of that year, 1594. They were then acting at the Cross Keys in Gracious Street, but their principal houses were the Theatre and the Curtain where *Romeo and Juliet* was acted in 1598. In this year, difficulties arising concerning the renewal of the term of the lease of the ground in Shoreditch on which the Theatre stood, the Burbages pulled down the building in spite of the lessor's protest and re-erected it, with some improvements, on a piece of dumping ground, the only site available, near to the Rose on the Bankside in Southwark. This piece of ground was situated, as the deeds that Professor Wallace has unearthed, make undeniable, " just north of Maiden Lane, on the same side of the street as the Rose," and across the street from the site commemorated by the present tablet. A lease for twenty-one years was granted by the owner, Sir Nicholas Brend, a

neighbour of Shakespeare's in the parish of St. Mary Alderman-
bury, and before the year 1599, the famous Globe had begun
its long and prosperous career.[9]

Of the character and constitution of these earlier companies
we know comparatively little; and it is by no means certain
that all were constituted alike. The company to which Shakespeare was attached was a sharing company. It held a lease
for the Globe theatre and for the theatre in Blackfriars, which
latter is sublet for a time. The number of sharers varied from
five to seven, and while the original cost of the shares was no
more than the rent of the ground and the obligations attending
building and management, in time the shares became quite
valuable. On the other hand, from *Henslowe's Diary,* an
account book kept by Philip Henslowe concerning his transactions as part owner, financier and backer of several theatres,
the organisation of these appears to have been much less democratic.

In considering the theatre of Marlowe and Shakespeare, we
must keep in mind the conditions of Elizabethan London, a
mediæval town of less than 200,000 inhabitants, unlighted, un-
drained, crowded and threaded with narrow streets in which
the upper stories of the timbered houses almost met in places.
There was little of the town beyond the Tower, Bishopsgate
and Temple Bar respectively, though houses extended beyond
the several gates — Bishopsgate, leading to Shoreditch, Lud-
gate, Cripplegate, and the rest — on the main roads leading out
of the city. The Thames was the main thoroughfare from one
part of the city to another as well as to Westminster. Its swift
and unpolluted waters flowed through many a park and its
banks were embellished with handsome houses of nobles and
wealthy tradespeople. The river was crossed but once, by London Bridge, which united the city with Southwark on the
Surrey side where was situated the Bankside. London was
ruled by a Lord Mayor and a council of Aldermen, men
prominent in the various trade-guilds of the city. With the
welfare of the city at heart quite as much as because some were
of Puritan leanings, the city council mistrusted the theatre from
the first; and reasons for this mistrust were not far to seek.
Assemblies of unpoliced crowds led to disorder and occasionally

[9] See especially the valuable paper of Professor Wallace on "The
First London Theatre," *University Studies,* 1913, xiii.

to riot, and in time of plague — a very real danger in the old age — to the spread of pestilence. Moreover, the contents of many of the plays were ungodly, or at the least vain and trifling. Laws were therefore passed restricting theatrical performances and closing all playhouses when the plague became prevalent; and the erection of playhouses within the precincts of the city was forbidden. However, the jurisdiction of the mayor stopped at the several gates and at the middle point of London Bridge, and hence the evil was only transplanted to the suburbs. The earliest playhouses were built beyond the walls; for example, in Shoreditch, Bishopsgate without, where the Theatre, first structure of its kind in England, dating 1576, and the Curtain, near it in Moorfields, 1577, were erected; or across the river along the Bankside where, in the nineties, there arose the Globe, the Rose, the Hope and the Swan. There were other theatres, however, besides these and the earlier inn-yards. Such were the playhouse at Newington Butts, back from the river in Southwark, and the Fortune, a large and fine theatre, built on a new plan, in 1600, by Edward Alleyn, the famous actor, son-in-law of Henslowe, in St. Giles, Cripplegate.

The public playhouses of Elizabeth's day undoubtedly differed in size and structure as do ours of to-day, but some general features may be accepted as characteristic of them all. They were ordinarily circular or octagonal in form, and built about an open space, a feature derived from their probable original, the inn yard. This yard was open to the sky and supplied standing places to the "groundlings" as they were called. It was surrounded on three sides by galleries, two or even three, and in the lowest of these were placed the most desirable seats. On the fourth side of the yard and opposite to the entrance door was situated the stage, a platform jutting far out into the middle of the yard so that the audience there might stand on three sides of it. There was a roof partially covering the stage, supported by two pillars or "pilasters." Their precise position is somewhat doubtful, though it seems not unlikely that they were placed rather close together to produce the effect of a structure near the middle of the stage, leaving a space on either side and in front for free action on the stage around them. Certain it is that they were not placed far at the side to produce the effect of the modern stage, a framing for a picture. Whether a curtain was stretched between them is a moot question. If so, as seems not unreasonable, or if hung, as some think, underneath a balcony further back, or elsewhere, it was drawn, not dropped, for the drop-curtain came in only after the Restoration. Mention has been made of a balcony; this was an important feature of the Elizabethan stage, and the stage directions of old plays show a constant recourse to it. We have thus a stage of three divisions, the forward stage in front of the curtains, really a platform for declamation; secondly, a back or inner stage, before which a curtain might at need be drawn; and third, a balcony or gallery — best conceived as running across the whole diameter of the stage — so arranged as to be visible and practicable whether the curtain dividing the two parts of the stage was drawn or not. Abundance of evidence declares that there were ordinarily at least three stage doors on the Elizabethan stage; and it is likely that the two side doors were obliquely placed.

No assumption of former scholarship is more gratuitous than that which denies scenery to either the private or the public theatres of Elizabeth's time. Scenery in the modern sense was assuredly not in use, and several total changes of it were noted as a novelty as late as 1636; [10] but this is quite a different thing from a statement to the effect that scenery was unknown to the Elizabethan stage.[11] Doubtless the humbler theatres were as bare and preposterous in their attempt at stage illusion as some provincial houses are to-day. But from extant lists of properties, and more especially from the stage directions of contemporary editions of our old drama, we are able to affirm the existence of much to help the imagination to a realisation of place. In a list of Henslowe's properties occur such items as a rock, a cage, a wooden canopy, a tree with golden apples, and two steeples with a chime of bells; while " the cloth of the sun and moon," Belendon's stable, and " the city of Rome," suggest structures and painted canvases of some dimension. On the other hand, it seems not improbable that the Elizabethans were often content with suggestion on the stage where we demand minute realism. A bed, a hanging and a chest, in which Iachimo might hide, may have sufficed for Imogen's chamber; and Juliet's tomb and the Castle of Inverness may have been alike simply suggested. But houses, two or three at a time, trees practicable for climbing or uprooting, caves, groves, a hill, to say nothing of furniture, all must have been, upon occasion,

10 *The Royal Slave,* by William Cartwright.
11 See Lee, *Life of Shakespeare,* p. 38.

the common garnishings of the popular stage. It seems reasonable to regard Elizabethan as the logical outgrowth of mediæval staging, precisely as its modification to conform to certain new ideas introduced from abroad (especially in the masques) finally led to modern conditions. Mediæval staging, it will be remembered, frequently assembled on one large platform the settings of several scenes. It has been held by some that the Elizabethans often did much the same, placing incongruous objects — a throne in a wood, a hearse in a lady's chamber — upon the stage side by side. In some ruder plays the stage was actually set off into localities, so that action in the centre meant (as in one case) Colchester, to the right Malvern, to the left Hardwick. It was this species of " simultaneous scenery " that Sidney criticised in his " Asia of the one side, Africa of the other "; and Sidney was not alone among those of his time in such criticisms. Of late, too, the preposterousness of such extremes has led the orderly critical mind of some investigators to theorise an explanation wherein they assume that heavy properties were invariably placed on the inner stage. The outer stage, a mere platform before the curtain, might stand then by convention for anything, a street, an outer room, or indeed remain indeterminable. On the drawing of the curtain, however, a chair of state, suggestive of the presence chamber, the counter and goods marking a shop, an arbour denoting a garden and so forth, could be disclosed to help the illusion, and, the action of the scene concluded, the curtains were redrawn. From the more or less regular alternation of outer and inner scenes resulting from the supposed necessity of moving in and out these suggestive properties, this has been called " the alternation theory "; and some have even endeavoured to show in Shakespeare a dramaturgy conformable to this state of things. So strict an alternation of scene as this theory demands can neither be proved for Shakespeare nor for the old drama at large; although neither the scene of indeterminable locality nor the suggestiveness of certain properties on occasion is for a moment to be denied.[12]

[12] For further discussion and bibliography of this subject, see the present writer's, " The Elizabethan Playhouse," *Proceedings of the Numismatic Society of Philadelphia*, 1910; and the interesting paper of A. H. Thorndike, " From Outdoors to Indoors on the Elizabethan Stage," *Kittredge Anniversary Papers*, 1913, p. 273.

Popular staging was affected by the devices and maskings at court; to affirm anything else is to deny the most certain of man's simian inheritances, imitation. Therefore if we know (as we do), that canvas was painted, spread on frames and shifted on and off the stage in grooved boards at court, we may feel sure that such things were not unheard of in London. While we must be careful to remember that chronology counts for much in an age of such rapid development, we may cite none the less with confidence an allusion by one of the characters of Jonson, to " a piece of perspective," on the stage, in 1600, an allusion that would not have been made concerning a novelty, unheard of until that date. So, too, Dekker's off-hand remark as to one who " may stand at the helm and steer the passage of scenes," throws light on the subject, though made in 1609 and possibly referable, like Jonson's allusion, to a private theatre.[13] One thing is certain, the costuming of Elizabethan plays, even on the popular stage, was often rich and expensive, though little governed by that sense of fitness as to things past that distinguishes our efforts after we have laboured with history and archæology. To those who know the Elizabethan drama at large, the sea-coast of Bohemia, the pistol of *Pericles* and the striking clock of Brutus seem venial offences. Anachronism was a misdemeanour little recognised as such; and it is likely that Jonson was the only dramatist of the age who would have thought of criticising the acting of Macbeth, Tamburlaine and Cæsar all in the contemporary doublet and hose, and with contemporary accessories of war and court attendance. Even Sidney and Whetstone who recognised, in their earlier time, the incongruities of contemporary staging, were talking of *Gorboduc* and the like, with classical ideals in mind; the age soon became accustomed to the aberrations of romantic art.

Before we turn to the remaining members of the group of playwrights known par excellence as " the predecessors of Shakespeare " let us glance at the popular drama immediately contemporary with the earlier efforts of Lyly. Two shadowy figures stand first in point of time; these are Richard Tarlton and Robert Wilson. Tarlton was the most celebrated clown of his day and furnished many anecdotes to the rude humours of the jest-books. He died in 1588 and has been supposed the

---

[13] See *Cynthia's Revels,* Induction, Gifford-Cunningham, *Jonson,* ii, 210, and Dekker's *The Gulls' Hornbook,* Grosart, *Dekker,* ii, 248.

author of two plays, *The Famous Victories of Henry V,* earliest
and rudest of the chronicle plays, and *The Seven Deadly Sins
of London,* evidently a great effort involving a series of well
known subjects.   From the sketch or plot whence information
of this latter play is derived, it seems that the scenes in their
general content were merely indicated and the actual dialogue
supplied extemporaneously.   It was this sort of thing, especially
the extemporal clown, such as Tarlton, that Shakespeare later
so reprobated in *Hamlet.*[14]   Wilson has been identified with
the player who introduced Greene to a dramatic career, if we
are to believe the vivid account of the matter in that romancer's
Groatsworth of Wit.   Wilson was an actor of note and left
behind him no less than four plays, quasi-moral in character,
printed in the eighties and earlier nineties, most important
among them *The Three Ladies of London.*   Another play, by
some attributed to Wilson, is *Fair Em, the Miller's Daughter
of Manchester.*   Here an absurd pseudo-romance about William
the Conqueror (and his quest of a wife in Sweden to correspond
with a picture emblazoned on a shield) is tied up with the
underplot which gives title to the play wherein, under guise of
the affairs of Fair Em and her sisters, there seem figured forth,
allegorical wise, particulars of the stage history of the day.

It is a mistake to suppose the romantic element in literature
the specific introduction of any age or time.   The art that lays
stress on novelty and seeks to produce its effects by means of
strangeness belongs to all time, though it may not always rule;
the variety of its manifestations is infinite, *Calisto and Meliboea,*
Spanish in origin, *Promos and Cassandra,* Italian, each was
possessed of this quality and so was *Fair Em,* the major plot
of which belongs to a type of story that strikes its roots far
back into the fiction of the middle ages.   The *Accounts of
the Revels* contain several titles that suggest material of this
kind: *The Irish Knight, Herpetulus, The Blue Knight, The
Solitary Knight, The Knight in the Burning Rock.*   Other
subjects, such as *Paris and Vienna,* are well known in their
prose form, or, like *Palaemon and Arcyte* of Edwards, are
stories already treated by Chaucer.   To dramas of this type we
may give the title heroical romances in dramatic form, as the
term " heroic play " has long since been applied to a more
specific and a far later variety of a not dissimilar species.   The

[14] III. ii. 42.

step from the morality to the heroic play, for example, is represented in *The Marriage of Wit and Science,* 1569. Here Wit has been metamorphosed into a knightly lover, passionately enamoured of his lady, Science. *Common Conditions,* of much the same date, is a "romance" of the class run wild in which a Duke of Phrygia, an Arabian knight and a French lady, all figure, turbulently in love and plotting through three continents, besides "the Isle of Marofus." Of the same type are *Sir Clyomon and Sir Clamydes,* variously placed between 1570 and 1584 and ascribed perhaps hastily to the authorship of Peele, and Greene's *Orlando Furioso,* different though its literary origin, yet little less absurd in its romantic extravagance of personage and plot. When we add that it was out of such productions that the conqueror play of *Tamburlaine* type was evolved, we establish still another line of growth from early times into the period of regular drama.

We left George Peele, an imitator of Lyly at court, as he had been an imitator of Gager at Oxford. It seems likely that, finding little prospect of success such as Lyly's at court, Peele turned, about 1586, to the popular stage to write plays alone and with others for a living. Peele was one of those men of Bohemian disposition to whom careless revelry and unregulated conduct are matters of second nature. He died early, in 1597, it is said worn out by his excesses. The range of his authorship must be surmised rather than determined, and the conditions of the moment account for this state of things with Peele as with others. It was the prevalent custom to regard a play, once accepted, absolutely the property of the company; and publication, in earlier times (other things being equal), usually meant that the company had done with it. The professional actor was held in little esteem; it was worse with the professional playwright, for he was not even recognised as existent. Mention of the poet, that mere contriver of the devices, would have struck an early Elizabethan, we may believe, as quite preposterous; as preposterous, indeed, as our printed mention of the wig-maker and the stage upholsterer. Once more, the habit of collaboration in the writing of plays was general and the outgrowth of the immediate and constant demand for new plays. When a play was thus written, nobody claimed it and the incessant revision of old plays, revised, as often as not, by another hand than that of the original author, further complicated the question. Peele was a playwright for seventeen or

eighteen years and he seems not to have been "a slow writer."
Therefore when we find less than half a dozen plays assigned
to his pen in his collected works, and some of these even doubtfully, we wonder what has become of the rest of his work.
Besides *The Arraignment of Paris* and *Sir Clyomon,* which is
probably Preston's, four other dramas are usually printed as
Peele's: these are *The Old Wives' Tale,* a pleasing extravaganza, apparently a burlesque of the heroical romances just
described, *David and Bethsabe,* a bible story revived and treated
chronicle-wise, *Edward I,* a chronicle play far from conspicuously able, and *The Battle of Alcazar,* a conqueror drama of
the class of Marlowe's *Tamburlaine.* All these plays have been
clustered, in point of date of writing, about the year 1590; and,
while they are diverse enough in subject matter, all exhibit the
metrical facility, lyrical readiness, careless, easy conglomeration
of plot, together with certain mannerisms of diction and style
recognised as Peele's. In addition to this, Peele has long been
thought to be one of the several poets that appear to have
worked together on our earlier English chronicle plays; those
on Henry VI (in their later revised state included in editions
of Shakespeare), *The Troublesome Reign of King John,* the
older *Richard III.* And now a share in *Jack Straw,* Marlowe's
Edward II and the older *King Leir* is added to his list, together with two more or less romantic comedies, *Wily Beguiled* and *The Wisdom of Doctor Doddypoll,* the last an imitation, in part at least, of *A Midsummer-Night's Dream,* and
an earlier draft of the satirical medley, *Histriomastix.*

Recent criticism, too, has been incidentally busy with Peele;
and three plays of importance in the history of tragedy are involved, *Alphonsus of Germany, Locrine,* and *Titus Andronicus.*
The first is a revenge play, remarkable for the idiomatic German which it contains; it was thus attributed long ago by
Anthony à Wood, and the notion is now revived despite long
association with the name of Chapman. If *Locrine* is Peele's,
it must have been early work, as it shows close touch with
Seneca at court, even if relieved by comic scenes in a very contrasted vernacular manner. Most important is the serious
ascription of *Titus Andronicus,* so long and disturbingly accepted as Shakespeare's, to the part authorship of Peele.[15] While
it is impossible in the space here at command to enter into the
intricacies and nice weighing of Mr. Robertson's arguments, it

[15] J. M. Robertson, *Did Shakespeare Write Titus Andronicus,* 1905.

must be frankly confessed that he makes out a very strong case. *Titus* was first published in the recently discovered quarto of 1594, and thereafter several times, never as Shakespeare's until its inclusion in the folio. It is mentioned contemporaneously as Shakespeare's only by Meres, and this is explainable. Jonson refers to it contemptuously and in connection with work older than any of Shakespeare's could possibly have been. Moreover, *Titus* was originally in the possession of a theatrical company, the Sussex men, with which Shakespeare was never associated, however it may have been subsequently claimed by reason of revision. The subject of *Titus* was old to the stage and had been repeatedly recast. If the *Titus Andronicus* that we have is the work of Shakespeare, it must be dated early to account for its difference from his later works and its extraordinary crudity; but plot, diction, and metre point to a date not much before that of publication; and at that date Shakespeare was writing in no such manner. On the other hand, internal evidence, elicited by a comparison of the plotting, diction, versification and vocabulary of *Titus,* discloses many of the qualities and mannerisms of Peele in particular and of Greene in lesser degree. Wherefore the conclusion that "between 1590 and 1592, Greene revised and expanded an older play in which Peele had already a large share"; with "the alternative possibility that Peele revised an old play by Greene and Kyd." Before the reader of Mr. Robertson's acute brochure pooh-poohs the idea of depriving Shakespeare of the authorship of this tragedy, let him carefully reread *Titus Andronicus* and ask himself if it were not a genuine service to the greatest name in English literature, could we relieve Shakespeare of the onus and the odium involved in the callousness to human suffering and the accumulation of gruesome and nauseating details that distinguish this tasteless example of the horrible overdone. As to Peele dramatically, it is obvious that he tried to do everything, court drama, biblical play, masque, Senecan tragedy, chronicle play, comedy, burlesque, and what not. Possibly after *The Arraignment of Paris,* Peele's most characteristic contribution to the drama is to be found in the fantastic irony of *The Old Wives' Tale* in which he daintily turns the absurdities of the old historical plays and romances to ridicule in a series of burlesque scenes capitally conceived and executed. Does it seem altogether preposterous, considering this and the extravagant bombast and overdone classical allusions of *Locrine,* to believe that Peele (if *Titus Andronicus* be his) was doing much the same for Senecan tragedy in this case?

And now the newly awakened popular stage was more and more attracting men of education. Thomas Lodge was the son of a Lord Mayor of London and received his education at Oxford and Lincoln's Inn. Almost before he left college Lodge threw himself with zeal into criticism and general pamphleteering, although he published no poetry until 1589. Lodge's voyages by sea and adventures concern us even less than his rather voluminous prose, translations and poetical plunderings especially of the French lyrists. In general he gave interest for the things that he used, for Lodge had the stuff of poetry in him. His early life in London seems to have been of much the Bohemian nature of Peele's and Greene's; but unlike these, his associates, he recovered himself to become, in the reign of James, a reputable physician and to outlive almost all his literary contemporaries. Lodge's contact with the drama is difficult to trace; for he was clearly ashamed of it — perhaps not without reason. We know that he had a share with Greene in the absurd hodge-podge of biblical story, modern farce and moral application, called *A Looking Glass for London and England,* acted in 1589, and that his name occurs as the sole author of *The Wounds of Civil War,* a classical chronicle history of no unusual merit, concerning Marius and Sulla, published in 1594. The rest is surmise. If Lodge's renunciation of the stage is to be taken seriously, he may none the less have had a hand in the older *King John* and in *King Leir,* in *A Larum for London,* a dramatization of the all but contemporary siege of Antwerp, and in the murder play, *A Warning for Fair Women,* all of which has been alleged. Two comedies have also been assigned to Lodge, the enormously popular, if trivial, *Mucedorus,* first printed in 1598, and the older *Taming of a Shrew,* which we know that Shakespeare revised to make it *The Taming of the Shrew.* If it be possible to reconstruct a dramatic Lodge out of these scanty traces, we can find him taking the part of a collaborator in earlier chronicle plays, dramatizing items of contemporary interest, mere hack work, and showing his best talent in lighter romantic comedy such as naïve *Mucedorus* and the comedy scenes of *King Leir.* At best Thomas Lodge is but a shadowy figure among " the predecessors of Shakespeare."

We proceed on firmer ground with Robert Greene, notorious for his grudging slur at Shakespeare, the first unmistakable allu-

sion to the great poet's activity as a dramatist. Greene was the
son of a minister and born at Norwich, in 1558. He studied
both at Oxford and Cambridge, a matter that he was never
weary of boasting. Travel abroad and an early acquaintance
with the low life of London little bettered his disposition to
self-indulgence. On the contrary he fell away from his friends,
patrons and family, and at last deserted his wife to live disso-
lutely among his inferiors. Greene was famous in his day for
his pamphlets and stories, many of them more or less autobiographical. His *Groatsworth of Wit Purchased with a Mil-
lion of Repentance,* 1592, is best known for the allusion to
Shakespeare; in it Greene tells, too, a circumstantial story of
his own induction into the craft of playmaker by a portentous
personage who has been identified with Robert Wilson, mentioned above. Greene's career was short at best. He could
have written little before 1580; and was dead of his own excesses in September, 1592. Though constantly deploring his
evil ways and, in moments of misfortune, sincerely repentant,
little can be said in extenuation of his life which he threw away
in his folly to the unhappiness of those who loved him and to
the impoverishment of his genius.

Greene in his work, like Peele, was imitative yet little bound
by precept or example. The list of his plays includes *The
Looking Glass for London,* as we have seen, showing the influence of Wilson; *Orlando Furioso,* 1592, an heroical drama,
a slight advance on the absurdities of *Common Conditions;
Alphonsus of Aragon,* an unsuccessful effort to out-bombast the
Tamburlaine of Marlowe; *Friar Bacon,* 1590, a charming
comedy of " white magic," matched against the " black magic "
of *Faustus;* and *The Scottish History of King James IV,* 1591,
an effort to play upon the popularity of chronicle history in a
comedy of romantic interest. Haste, carelessness and a want of
constructive forethought, all are characteristic more or less of
these acknowledged works of Greene; and yet they are not
without their merits. Again and again we meet in them with
passages of poetic quality, with personages, especially in comedy,
that live and breathe naturally, with delicacy and beauty of
sentiment, and a power to give reality to picturesque or romantic
situations. *Friar Bacon* and *King James* afford us, too, in
Margaret of Fressingfield, Lady Ida, and the Queen, three of
the most genuine and charming women in the drama preceding
Shakespeare; while above all we have in Greene a fine fidelity

to English scene and English life. In the last named play we find, too, a constructive excellence, an ability to seize the dramatic moment and use it that suggest unfulfilled possibilities in the genius of Greene, could his life have been less disordered. Perhaps it was the recognition of this and the contrasted image of his successful younger rival, Shakespeare, that so embittered Greene. The dying man must have felt, with that instinct that is the poet's, that in Shakespeare's benignity and silent, artistic thrift lay the inevitability of an achievement that was never to be his own.

Conjecture has been no less busy increasing the limits of the authorship of Greene than in the other like cases. There seems little reason to doubt that his hand was engaged in some of the earlier chronicle plays, especially in the plays on Henry VI with the lifting of a line from one of which he specifically charges Shakespeare. *Selimus,* a tragedy on Turkish history in the vein of *Tamburlaine,* was confidently ascribed to Greene, and edited as his by the late Dr. Grosart. Robertson believes Greene a collaborator with Peele in *Titus* and *Locrine,* with Kyd in *The Spanish Tragedy* and *Soliman and Perseda,* finding " Greenish " traces too in *Sir Clyomon, Alphonsus of Germany* and the older *Leir.* And on the score of similarities in action, vocabulary, and figure, he would ascribe all of *Edward III,* the finest parts of which are often assigned Shakespeare, to Greene's authorship as well. Whatever the merits of these investigations — and there can be no question of their scholarly seriousness — one other play, *George-a-Greene or the Pinner of Wakefield,* which is now more doubted than believed to be Greene's, the present writer would like to be able to preserve for him, so characteristic it seems of the man. In it is told the story of the simple-hearted service and prowess of the excellent young yeoman whose name and office of under-sheriff give title to the comedy; while in the dénouement, George refuses knighthood at the hands of his sovereign, preferring to be first in his father's class rather than abjure it. Here was an appeal of a popular tone, eminently at variance with that of the court drama of which we have heard. Nor is this the only case among the plays of these elders of Shakespeare in which we find the drama reaching out for the approval of him whom we should now call " the man in the street." It is essential that we should recognise that however aristocratic may have been many of its tendencies and ideals, the London drama of the heyday of Eliza-

beth truly deserves the designation popular. Shakespeare wrote
emphatically for the many, not, as did Jonson at times, for " the
judicious few "; and, however the select taste of the court may
have determined the drama of Lyly, writing for the choir boys
of Blackfriars, the plays of Greene, Peele, Kyd and Marlowe,
delivered at the Theatre, the Curtain, the Globe and the Rose,
constituted a great, popular, national utterance.

In Thomas Kyd we meet with a man of somewhat different
type from the gentlemen and schoolmaster playwrights, from
illiterate actors turned makers of plays, or the " university
wits" as Professor Saintsbury somewhat unhappily dubbed
Peele, Greene, Lodge, and Marlowe, a sobriquet that appears
to stick. Kyd was born in London in 1558, the son of a
scrivener. He attended the Merchant Tailors' school while
Richard Mulcaster was master, and may have caught under that
encourager of the drama the taste that made him a playwright.
Investigation has not shown that Kyd was ever of either university; but he knew his classics well, if somewhat carelessly,
and was not unacquainted with the three important modern
Latin tongues. The career of Kyd as a dramatist probably
lay between 1585 and 1590 at the latest, and his authorship
and collaboration is even less certain than that of other members of his group. It must have been close to the earlier date
just mentioned that Kyd made his leap to immediate fame with
The Spanish Tragedy. This play shared for years with *Tamburlaine* the greatest popularity of any tragedy outside of
Shakespeare; and became the parent of a considerable group of
successors, known as the tragedies of revenge. In *The Spanish
Tragedy* is set forth the pathetic situation of a father who has
lost his son by murder at the hands of assassins unknown. In
his endeavours to learn the authors of the crime, Hieronimo, the
father, totters on the verge of madness and in the end, finding
his prince the instigator and redress by ordinary form and
process of law therefore impossible, he attains his revenge by
means of a play arranged within a play. *The Spanish Tragedy*
came at a time when *Gorboduc* and *Tancred and Gismunda*
represented the height of English tragic achievement. It would
be too much to expect any tragedy at such a moment to have
been unaffected by the prevalent Senecan ideals. And Kyd's
master work is Seneca in bone and sinew, if clothed with
Renaissance romantic flesh. *The Spanish Tragedy* is well
planned and constructed, even in view of what was to come;

its figures are vital and the dramatic moments are seized with appreciation and effectively handled.   Even the verse and style, if somewhat stiff and inflated, mark a long stride forward.   In short, the popularity of this famous tragedy was thoroughly well deserved.

If we recur to the story of *The Spanish Tragedy,* for which, by the way, the ingenuity of scholarship has as yet failed to find a source, we are struck at once by its likeness to the well known story of Hamlet.   In *Hamlet,* to be sure, it is the father that has proved the victim and the son is left to avenge him; but the situation, a secret crime, the perpetrator above the law, the burden on the avenger suggesting insanity, the discovery (in Kyd's play the revenge) arranged by a play within a play: here are striking parallels.   As far back as the year 1589 there are allusions to a tragedy by name *Hamlet;* the play of Shakespeare that we know belongs at earliest to the very last years of Elizabeth's reign.   Moreover, a German version of the drama of early date differs materially in certain particulars, and the two quartos of Shakespeare's *Hamlet,* with certain differences in the folio, disclose the likelihood of a revision from an older play.   We are not left then wholly to a certain famous passage by Nash in his prefatory epistle to Greene's *Menaphon,* 1589, in which the title *Hamlet* is coupled darkly with " Kidde in Æsop," for the inference that Kyd was the author of this earlier version of the master tragedy of Shakespeare.   This revision, save for traces in the German version and in the Shakespeare texts (if indeed there be such traces?), is now totally lost.   But it is of interest to note, looking forward for a moment, that about the time that Shakespeare was submitting the old *Hamlet* of Kyd to a thorough rewriting for the Chamberlain's men, Ben Jonson was engaged by Henslowe to add scenes to *The Spanish Tragedy* and further to develop the character of Marshal Hieronimo for the Admiral's men, their rivals.

Two other plays that have been assigned to Kyd are less memorable.   They are the *First Part of Ieronimo,* printed in 1605 and purporting to be a fore-piece to *The Spanish Tragedy,* and *Soliman and Perseda.   Ieronimo* is probably the work of an imitator, anxious to profit by the popularity of Kyd.   *Soliman and Perseda* is more like *The Spanish Tragedy* in conduct and style, though distinctly inferior.   It, too, utilises the subject of the more popular *Tragedy,* dramatizing at length the play in the fifth act by the means of which Hieronimo reaches his revenge. Although the evidence on the subject is slender enough, it seems reasonable to regard *Soliman and Perseda* as the work of Kyd, written soon after *The Spanish Tragedy* and in consequence of the success of that greater effort. Among the several other plays with which the name of Kyd has been more or less ingeniously associated, may be named *Titus Andronicus* (if Shakespeare is to gain by the loss of it); *The Taming of a Shrew* (if Kyd's, his only essay in the realm of comedy); and *Arden of Feversham*. Kyd is likewise the certain author of an able translation, in 1594, of the *Cornelie* of Robert Garnier, the contemporary French Senecan. This is dedicated to Lady Sussex, an aunt of Lady Pembroke, who presided over a literary circle especially interested in French tragedy. A more important association of Kyd's was that with Marlowe. In 1593, Kyd was arrested on the charge of sedition, being supposedly implicated in certain libels against foreigners, found affixed to the wall of the Dutch churchyard. The unfortunate dramatist was tortured without eliciting a confession; but, as a disputation of " atheistical " contents was found among his papers, he was remanded for further examination. The documents in this case, especially the defence of Kyd, inform us that, at one time, Kyd and Marlowe occupied the same chamber where, according to the affirmation of the former, their papers became mixed on the same table. We do not know the outcome of the matter. It appears to have been confused with the accusations against Marlowe. Nor does Kyd's own conduct, judged by his words, seem either ingenuous or fair to his associate. Doubtless through this affair, Kyd lost any chance that he may have had for advancement by his patrons. He was dead in December 1594, when his parents significantly renounced their right to administer what must have been the exceedingly slender estate of their deceased son.[16]

Christopher Marlowe was born in Canterbury in March 1564; and was thus a month older than Shakespeare. Marlowe's father was a shoemaker, his mother a clergyman's daughter. He was about as well born as Shakespeare; but he had the good fortune, living in a larger community, to attract attention by his precocity (we may infer) while a student at the King's School, Canterbury, and he was accordingly sent up to Cam-

[16] On the whole topic see F. S. Boas, *The Works of Thomas Kyd*, 1901. This renunciation was discovered by Schick.

bridge. There he remained until 1587, taking his bachelor's and master's degrees in course and perhaps falling into disfavour towards the end. There has been much " mystification," to call it no worse, as to the life of Marlowe; criticism now turns to the agnostic attitude. Francis Kett, Fellow of Corpus Christi, was convicted of holding " unorthodox views as to the Trinity," and later was burned at the stake for them. Kett left Cambridge in 1580, the year of Marlowe's arrival. Whether these two men met or not is a matter of little importance. That an impressionable youth with an innate tendency to free thinking, should have remained uninterested and unaffected by influences that were notorious at his university when he entered it, is simply unthinkable, the more especially that we now know that Marlowe's actual " deflections from orthodoxy " appear to have been much those of Kett. The tale that Marlowe was an actor of riotous life in London "who brake his leg in one lewd scene " has now been definitely traced to the fabrication of that able scholar and antiquary gone wrong, John Payne Collier. As a matter of fact we know much less about Marlowe than we know about Shakespeare; and about Marlowe's life, his character and his authorship hover the same clouds of doubt which have given rise to guess-work and conjecture in lesser mass only because the world is naturally more interested in the greater man. Marlowe's authorship as a dramatist begins with *Tamburlaine,* a stupendous effort to treat in two whole dramas the subjugating career of Timur Kahn, the conqueror of Asia. Here, the young poet's choice of subject was as daring as his treatment was novel and untrammelled by previous examples. Moreover, he was entirely conscious of what it was that he was doing and as confident of success as his hero. *Tamburlaine* must have been on the stage by 1586 or 1587; it is a moot question whether it preceded or followed *The Spanish Tragedy.* Even if Marlowe wrote later, he could have owed little to the work of Kyd. On the other hand, there is none of the boisterous and dynamic romanticism that characterises *Tamburlaine* in the modified Senecanism of *The Spanish Tragedy.* Kyd's play is above all things a drama; indeed its merits lie along the line of action and in the forcible stage realism of an effective story; *Tamburlaine,* on the contrary, is essentially an epic in which the sheer force of poetry has triumphed over difficulties to produce, with all its faults, a really surprising result. It is impossible to make clear except by actual example how far the poetry of Marlowe, the quality of his words, the pomp and music of his lines, tower above the rhetorical niceties of Lyly, the effective eloquence of Kyd, or the graceful prettiness of Peele. Marlowe's *Tamburlaine* caught the age no less by its poetry than *The Spanish Tragedy* by its tragic quality and the problem of the character of Hieronimo; and Marlowe held his audience as long, beginning the series of conqueror plays — Greene's *Alphonsus of Aragon, Selimus,* Peele's *Battle of Alcazar,* and his lost *Turkish Mahomet* among them — as Kyd's *Tragedy* inaugurated the tardier tragedy of revenge.

The play of Marlowe next in chronological order is *Doctor Faustus,* on the stage by the year of the Armada. It has come down to us unhappily in a fragmentary and imperfect text. *Faustus* tells the world-story of the man who, seeking for all knowledge, pledged his soul to the devil, only to find the misery of a hopeless repentance in this world and damnation in the world to come. The motive, like much of the conduct of this tragedy, is that of the old moralities, witness the alternate promptings of the good and the bad angel and the dance of the seven deadly sins. More important is the typical character of Faustus who is any man and every man. But Faustus is, none the less, an individual in whose pathetic plight we are interested for himself, and the appeal of the work is primarily artistic. *Doctor Faustus* is a better play on the stage than the careless reader might suppose it; and it is worthy of note that what the old story has gained in other hands in variety of incident, by the infusion of the love story of Margaret for example, it has lost in the singleness of purpose with which Marlowe concentrates attention on his unhappy protagonist. Even the wide allegorical significance, the masterly obliteration of time and space of the second part of Goethe's *Faust* with the hero's redemption, scarcely compensate for this loss. The tragic and untimely death, too, of Marlowe, the daring character of his genius and the stories of his doubts of God have conspired to make this play one of the most interesting in our literature. Beside all this, it is unimportant what editions or translations of the *Faustbuch* Marlowe utilised in his work. His was the poetry that fired the genius of Goethe, who sophisticated with modern brilliant philosophical speculation a theme which was the product of an age of sterner and, dare we say, of sounder theology than that of his own.

Our interest in *The Jew of Malta,* 1589-90, is of a different kind and concerns Shakespeare's relations to it. In the Jew, as in the figures of Tamburlaine and Faustus, we have a creature of heroic and overweening passion; but, in the place of the passion for conquest or the passion for all-knowledge, we have substituted a gigantic malevolence that degenerates from its very excess into inhuman caricature. The Jew in Elizabethan, as in other ages, is a subject more interesting to those of the Hebrew race than to others. Shakespeare owed something in his Shylock to Marlowe's Barabas who is more nearly the conventional Jew of scandalous mediæval tradition. It is only fair to Marlowe, as to Shakespeare in this connection, to remember that both simply recorded for the stage the prejudices of an age not much more bound by such prejudices than the world of to-day, if somewhat more brutal in its avowal of them. Barabas is a monster, but the play in which he perpetrates his impossible crimes is, as a drama, decidedly an advance on its predecessors, even if, as must be acknowledged, less sustained by the buoyancy of Marlowe's poetry. The dramatic masterpiece of Marlowe, however, is his one chronicle play, *Edward II*. Recurrence has been made in these pages more than once to this species of drama, and early suggestions of it have been described in the figure of Bale's King Johan, in the subject-matter of *Gorboduc* and elsewhere. A chronicle play is a drama based as to source on the chronicle history of Great Britain, a history transformed into a play, and it is conceivable that it may exist in many varieties. *Edward II,* which appears to have been first acted in 1592, is by no means an early specimen of its class. In the probable collaboration with Peele, Greene and Lodge, we have met with such productions as *Jack Straw, The Troublesome Reign of King John, The Contentions of the Two Noble Houses of Lancaster and York* and *The Chronicle History of Richard Duke of Gloucester*. All are chronicle plays, and so, too, in a sense, are the plays on mythical British history, *Locrine, The Misfortunes of Arthur* and *King Leir*. The epic character, which imbues most of these plays, was not preserved by Marlowe in his *Edward II,* and it may be suspected that he wrote his play more for the tragic pathos which the story of the unkingly and discrowned sovereign exhales than for any other reason. It is worth noting, however, that in this tragedy Marlowe raised the whole species of the chronicle play to a higher artistic level and reached the crown of his own dramatic art. *The Tragedy of*

Queen Dido, published as his in collaboration with Nash, in 1594, is below his independent work; and *The Massacre at Paris,* acted 1592-93, save for the character of the Duke of Guise, is distinctly inferior. Historically, however, this work is of interest, as apparently the earliest effort to apply the method of the chronicle play to the history of a contemporary foreign country; and it led to important things after. Marlowe has been thought a collaborator with the others of this group in several plays, Shakespearean and other: *Henry VI, Titus* once more and even *Richard III* among them.[17] It seems, however, less consistent with his independent and insolent spirit thus to have submitted his genius to harness, and the degree of such servitude, if it were ever his, is likely to continue indeterminable.

There remains one matter as to Marlowe. His age, especially after his indubitably tragic death, acclaimed him, in the loose language of the time, "an atheist." Indeed Greene had touched him on this point in his *Groatsworth of Wit,* and, when Marlowe was killed, there was out against him a series of accusations, brought by a professional informer, named Baines, in which specific charges of this tenor were maliciously set forth. So far as we can make them out, the bases for Marlowe's disrepute in these matters are several. First, there was the association with Kett or at least with his ideas at Cambridge — many a man has been made or unmade by the reputation thrust upon him at college. Secondly, Marlowe was the personal friend of Sir Walter Raleigh and a choice circle of kindred spirits, poets and men of science who discussed many things with a greater freedom than the cautious orthodoxy of the age was likely to approve. The misfortunes and unpopularity of Raleigh in the next reign caused this little set of inquirers to be spoken of as a "school of atheists"; but it was the zeal of the Jesuit, Father Parsons, that so dubbed them. Again, Marlowe was evidently a man of free and unguarded speech, imprudent and incapable of concealment. He may even have enjoyed the intentional mystification of such an unimaginative fool as the informer Baines, whose " Note Containing the opinion of one Christopher Marley concerning his damnable judgment of religion," be it remembered, is wholly *ex parte*. More

[17] See C. F. Tucker Brooke, *The Authorship of the Second and Third Parts of King Henry VI,* New Haven, 1912.

serious than any of these things is an extant letter in which
Thomas Kyd under indictment of a similar charge, declares
that Marlowe was "irreligious," adding that he was also "intemperate and cruel of heart." But Kyd was in difficulty himself and it was the cue of a cowardly spirit to shift as much of
his misdemeanour as possible on the man who had shared his
room and his writing table. Fortunately we are not left in
this matter wholly to conjecture. A second document, turned
up in the scholarly researches of Mr. Boas not long since and
flamboyantly endorsed, "vile heretical conceits denying the deity
of Jesus Christ our Saviour," turns out on examination to be
"a methodical defence, based on scriptural texts of theistical
or Unitarian doctrines," denying neither God nor the authority
of the scriptures.[18] Lastly, let him who believes that Marlowe ever said in his heart with the fool, "there is no God,"
read the poignant scenes of _Doctor Faustus_. We do not really
know the circumstances of Marlowe's death. He was buried
June first, 1593, in the churchyard of St. Nicholas, Deptford,
near Greenwich, and in September of that year so little had
been the noise of his death that Gabriel Harvey, a notorious
ghoul, reported that he had died of the plague. The disgraceful particulars which tradition has attached to the poet's death,
— the quarrel, "the bawdy house," the serving man and the
rest — begin four years later when the Puritan author of _The
Theatre of God's Judgment_ employed the fate of this playmaker and "atheist" as one of his warning examples of the
vengeance of God. In 1598 the parallels of Meres' _Wits'
Treasury,_ a "comparative discourse" throughout of classical
and English authors, suggested that Marlowe was stabbed to
death by "a rival of his in his lewd love," for such was the
"parallel" death of the Greek poet, Lycophoron. And so the
matter grew until the poet became the aggressor and the
"atheist" was cut down in the very act of murder and
"blaspheming God." It seems worth while that we should
now recognise that the disgraceful particulars of the death
of Marlowe are wholly the invention of pious, ingenious

[18] On these documents, see Boas, _Works of Kyd_ as above and J. H.
Ingram, _Christopher Marlowe and his Associates,_ 1904. Mr. Ingram
attacks the validity of these documents. For a summary of the matter
more at large than is possible here, see the present author's _Elizabethan
Drama,_ i, 234 ff.

and untruthful good men who used this glaring example of the
fate that befalls the ungodly to point a moral and adorn a
tale.

The youngest of " the predecessors of Shakespeare " is Thomas
Nash, and he was truly " a university wit," although his touch
with the history of the drama is really exceedingly slight.
Nash was born in 1567 and entered St. John's College before
Marlowe left Cambridge, forming an association with that
poet, further proved by the joint authorship, at an uncertain
date, of *The Tragedy of Dido*. However, the talents of Nash
were of a different type, as the notable series of his satirical
prose pamphlets, his controversies, the Marprelate ones and
those with Harvey, go to show. While at college, Nash was
in difficulties for a satirical Latin comedy, and his *Isle of Gulls,*
in English and equally sharp of tongue we may believe, kept
him a prisoner in the Fleet for months and was so successfully
suppressed that we have not a shred of it. As a matter of
fact but one dramatic composition remains from the pen of
Nash — the masque-like comedy *Summer's Last Will and Testament,* 1597, acted before the queen and a late following of
Lyly's mythological and allegorical court drama of much elaboration and exceedingly little plot.

If we turn back to the group of writers just discussed re-
viewing them as a whole, it is clear that while they formed in
no sense a coterie, they must have been more or less intimately
acquainted in a small city such as Elizabeth's London. We
may assume that Lyly dwelt more continuously in the precincts
of the court; though Nash, Bohemian of the Bohemians, fought
by his side in the Marprelate controversy. Nash, as we have
seen, was associated with Marlowe and was Greene's champion
against the attacks of Harvey. Peele, Greene, and Lodge variously collaborated. Kyd, who was not a university man, appears to have stood apart from the group; and yet he was
room-mate of Marlowe. It is a mistake to suppose most of
these men actors. Only of Peele are we certain; and it is not
impossible that these university bred men may heartily have disdained " the quality," as the profession of acting was then
designated. Indeed " the actor-playwright " originated, as we
have seen, in personages such as illiterate Tarlton and Wilson
with his belated moralities; wherefore Greene's attitude of
resentment towards the " upstart crow beautified with our
feathers," for Shakespeare too, was an actor-playwright.

The third decade of the reign of Elizabeth (1579-1588) is the period of Lyly with whose popularity none could vie unless it may have been Dr. Gager with his Latin plays at Oxford or an occasional academic success such as the comedy *Pedantius,* the work of Anthony Wingfield or Edward Forcett, staged at Cambridge in 1581. As to the popular stage, the best that it could boast in the early eighties was Wilson's *Lords and Ladies of London, The Famous Victories* of Tarlton and Peele's parodies (may we believe them such?), *Locrine,* the Senecan craze outdone, and *The Old Wives' Tale,* lively take-off of the heroical romances. But in *The Spanish Tragedy, Tamburlaine* and *Arden of Feversham* English Tragedy sprang to maturity. Enough has been said of the other two, the outcome respectively and the protest against Senecanism; *Arden* is the most truly indigenous of our earlier English tragedies. Here is told with realistic and simple frankness the story of a faithless wife, her infatuation for a coward beneath her and the busy plotting of the wretched couple to rid themselves of Arden, the unfortunate husband who suspects their amour. The story, the unknown author found in Holinshed and it has been followed with a fidelity that might be called slavish were not the result so effective. And yet the material has been well ordered and the personages rationalised to a degree that no other English tragedy had reached before the year 1590. There is a power in the conception of the character of Alice Arden and a dignity about her repentance that places her among the great heroines of Elizabethan drama, and justifies a curious inquiry into the authorship of tragedy of such superlative merit. *Arden* has been thought the work of Kyd. But surely its unvarnished tragic actuality is widely in contrast with the romantic spirit and heightened Senecanism of *The Spanish Tragedy*. More strenuous has been the advocacy of Shakespeare's authorship, concerning which it is sufficient here to say that the art of the author of *Arden of Feversham* is mature in its " ease and restraint of style," in its weight and power to sustain character and in its grim mastery of humour and a peculiar irony of its own. None of these qualities were Shakespeare's at any time before the year 1592, the date of the publication of *Arden;* and moreover never is the quality of Shakespeare's art so divorced from the magic touch of poetry.

The period from 1586 to 1593 is *par excellence* the period of Marlowe. Therein are contained not only his own tragic successes but those of his imitators, and the chronicle play develops by rapid strides from the stuttering attempts of Tarlton and the panoramic trilogy on Henry VI to the realisation of historical character in the older *King John* and the grasp of inevitable tragedy in *Edward II*. No less important here is the natural comedy of rural life, compassed by Greene in *Friar Bacon* and *The Pinner of Wakefield* and his success in the more serious romantic comedy of *The Scottish History of King James IV*. Nor need we recur to other matters already sufficiently treated. Happy as Shakespeare was in his art and his genius, he was no less fortunate in these his " predecessors." It is somewhat remarkable how thoroughly they prepared the ground before him with experiment in what he was afterwards to triumph. Lyly offered to Shakespeare's imitation court manners and dialogue, wit and repartee; Greene the naturalness of every day comedy, its humour, on occasion, its pathos. Kyd is the most constructive tragedian, touching with rough but not unskilful hand the psychology of revenge; while Marlowe gave the supreme example up to his time of tragic force and the power of the magic of poetry. And now having acted each his part, like well tried players, each hurried from the scene; Greene, Marlowe and Kyd were gone respectively in 1592, 1593 and 1594; Peele by 1597. Only Lyly and Lodge were left to know the future of the drama the foundations of which they had helped to lay. But Lyly's was a repute of the past; Lodge was now interested in other matters.

CHAPTER IV

SHAKESPEARE AND HIS CONTEMPORARIES IN HISTORY AND ROMANTIC COMEDY

For the production of great works of art, we are told that the man and the moment must conspire. The moment in the history of our drama had now arrived. The time of preparation and experiment was past. Early rivals had done their part in warning and example, and now had gone their way. In Shakespeare were realised the ideals of Elizabethan life and thought about life as such ideals had never been realised before. In his dramatic poetry is to be found the breadth and heights of Elizabethan hope and aspiration as well as an interpretation of the things that inexorably *are* in the fulness of their reality. At this last we sometimes repine, wishing in him more circumspection, more reserve, after the manner of these our later days of propriety and innuendo. But the largeness of Shakespeare lies in his fidelity to the actualities of human life and conduct in all its phases; and sweeps such as his take us both aloft into regions that we can see, however they may remain unattainable, and into the depths, the petty nooks and crannies in which hide the littleness, the baseness, and even the bestiality of men. Shakespeare's scope is the widest among poets and the most completely justified; for he sees things in their true relations. There need be no limits to the freedom of an art such as this, for he is at will idealist, realist, sentimentalist and satirist unerringly where ideality, realism, sentiment or satire apply. To see the world habitually through any one of these lenses is to be biased, unsteady, and afraid. Shakespeare's is the courage of freedom, and we may commit ourselves unreservedly into his hands, sure that, wherever he may lead us, ours is ever the steadying hand of truth in a cosmos, sane, ordered and eminently rational.

As to the man, in a work such as this, there can assuredly be no need for the rehearsal of an often told tale. Shakespeare's extraction out of the sturdy yeoman stock of England, neither too high nor yet too low, was certainly no disadvantage to him. Nor could he have been happier than in the midland place of his birth, however it leaves the critics at a nonplus to explain his wit as an inheritance of the leavening salt of Gaul or his poetry by that magic wherein he is easily first, although he was assuredly no Celt. In his education and earlier experiences in life, too, Shakespeare was fortunate. In Stratford neither men nor ideas were crowded. There was time to think and time to dream; but who that knows those trifles of easy allusive memory, "Will Squele, a Cotswold man, and Perkes of the Hill," "Marian Hacket, the fat ale-wife of Wincot," or "the whisters in Dachet-mead," can suppose that in Stratford Shakespeare only thought and dreamed? A mayor's son might learn a little Latin and with it anatomize the character of a pedant in Holofernes or Hugh Evans. A mayor's son, too, as a mere lad, might welcome the return, at no infrequent intervals, of player-folk from London and receive in their rude performances the powerful bias of his life, to be turned to an immediate and unexpected account when the necessity of providing for wife and child struck home to the youth of twenty.

Of late the painful industry of generations of biographers of Shakespeare has been supplemented by a number of additional facts. We learn that Shakespeare's name appears in a couple of subsidy lists as a delinquent in the payment of his share of certain grants to the queen, a matter accounted for by the entry that "the said William Shakespeare had removed from Bishopsgate (the neighbourhood of the Theatre) to the Liberty of the Clink in Southwark," a locality not far from the Globe. Once more, in the case at law, Mountjoy vs. Bellott, the name of Shakespeare occurs as a witness again and again. In one of these occurrences he is described as "William Shakespeare of Stratford on Avon, gentleman," another is his deposition signed with his own hand. From these documents it further appears that Shakespeare lodged with Mountjoy, the plaintiff, who was a wig-maker and resided at the corner of Silver Street and Monkwell in the parish of St. Olave, not far from Cripplegate. We have thus no less than three localities of residence established for Shakespeare in London. Another case incidentally describes at length the details of the organisation and process of sharing which characterised the company of players to which Shakespeare was for years attached. By means of it we learn

that Shakespeare held originally a tenth share in the Globe
theatre which by the admission of other sharers was finally
reduced to a fourteenth, though the process could have involved
no decrease in the value of his share; that he also owned a
seventh interest in the private theatre in Blackfriars; and that
these shares seem originally to have been acquired merely by an
agreement to assume responsibility for the rental and main-
tenance of these playhouses. In time these shares became very
valuable; but the statement of the plaintiff in this case that an
interest such as Shakespeare's was worth £300 in the contemporary value of money, and therefore £2000 or more in our
money, is clearly an exaggeration intended to increase damages.
Shakespeare was well off for his station and for his time, and
it is a credit to the discernment and taste of his contemporaries
that his plays should have made Shakespeare's fortune. Still
another case, turned up as were these two last in the Records'
Office by the industry of Professor C. W. Wallace, is endorsed
with the remarkable caption, Shakespeare vs. Bacon.[1] Few
will deny, indeed, that Shakespeare has had of late years, owing
to the activity of certain eccentric and uninstructed persons in
cryptograms and in digging under English rivers, an unusually
good case against Bacon. But unhappily the defendant in this
Jacobean law suit was not Francis, but an obscure Matthew
Bacon who, according to the poet's bill of complaint, dated
April 26, 1615 (just about a year before his death), was
alleged wrongfully to have detained certain "letters patent,
deeds, evidences, charters, and writings," concerning the title
of Shakespeare and others plaintiffs to various houses "within
the precinct of Blackfriars in the city of London." The inference as to Shakespeare is not unimportant, as it discloses him
actively interested in his business and property ventures in the
city to the last, and not, as has hitherto been accepted, in his
latter years retired from them as from writing for the stage.

Other new discoveries concerning Shakespeare are less important, however interesting: That he was paid " 44s in
gold " for the design of an impressa or semi-heraldic pictorial
badge with its attendant motto for the Earl of Rutland; that

[1] See the various publications of C. W. Wallace in *The London
Standard*, Oct., 1905; *Englische Studien*, xxxvi, 1906; *The Times*, Oct.
2 and 4, 1909. *Harper's Magazine*, March, 1910; the *Century Magazine*, Sept., 1910, and elsewhere.

he was regarded by a splenetic contemporary critic of the
Heralds' Office as one of those who "outrage truth and decency" in his endeavour to secure a coat of arms; that his
father, described as "a merry cheeked old man," is reported to
have said that "Will was a good, honest fellow, but he darst
have cracked a jest with him at any time."

Conjecture is easy where the facts are so disconnected and
remote, and there are many more varieties of pen portraits of
Shakespeare than there are pictures of the day and of later
fabrication that purport to record the features of his face.
With the plays before us and their attendant poems, with the
circumstances of their writing so far as we know, their acting
and their publication, all so natural and so absolutely in accord with the practises of the time, it is wantonly gratuitous
to find any difficulty or invent any mystery about them. As to
Shakespeare personally, we have a hundred contemporary testi-
monies and traditions galore that he was "excellent in the
quality that he professed," that he was gentle, thoughtful and
kindly, that he was capable and alert in argument. What
more could we wish to know of his estimable nature, for example, than the fact that he "was adored on this side of idola-
try," by a man like Jonson who customarily adored, however
he may occasionally have approved them, few men and poets
save himself. As to the plays, judiciously considered and at
large, they tell us indubitably what manner of man Shakespeare
was, however they may fail in those petty matters biographical
that men, infinitely meaner in their natures, may conceal with
unimportant cunning in the pages of their works. We may
assume with confidence that Shakespeare was neither an
abandoned sensualist, a sinner the loss of whose immortal soul
was the price of his matchless experience in the world, nor yet
an impeccable Prospero, exercising his art of legerdemain with
a condescending pity for that human weakness and passion in
which he had never shared. There is no condescension in
Shakespeare, and the absolute success with which he has made
himself one with his personages, that actor's power that has
enabled him to wear many masks, each for the nonce sympa-
thetically, without once disclosing the actual face behind it,
alone is sufficient to account for the many portraits that ingenious malice and ignorant adoration have contrived in distortion.
To the superficial reader who takes his impressions from the
passage before him, and then, laying his Shakespeare aside,

generalises a cosmos from his chosen point of departure, this great poet and philosopher must remain an enigma if not a subject for ingenious speculation. To him who knows the age, his Shakespeare entire and the other writers that stood, a mighty forest, rich in undergrowth as well, about him, to him who remembers that the first condition of the drama consists in a " notable feigning " and in the sinking of the author's self in his personages, there is no higher example of order and consistency than the works of Shakespeare. With his hundreds of personages and thousand situations, expressing opinion and idea, we can usually tell none the less the author's position and learn his attitude towards the personages involved: and this attitude is commonly more charitable, more kindly, more logical, too, and just than our own. Wherefore Shakespeare's consistent fulfilment of the highest function of poetry, that of offering us a guide to a wider and truer outlook on life.

The details of Shakespeare's career as a dramatic writer are as irrecoverable as are similar details concerning his contemporaries who were similarly circumstanced in life. There is danger in assuming too early and phenomenal a success for the countrybred lad of Stratford. Shakespeare even must have needed time in which to learn and to observe. At any rate he must have been well past the period of mere apprenticeship by the year 1590, for two years later he had attracted the envy of Greene and inspired his slighting allusions in a *Groatsworth of Wit* together with Chettle's recognition and apology in *Kind-Heart's Dream* which immediately followed. In the succeeding years come the dedications of *Venus and Adonis* and of *Lucrece* to Shakespeare's patron, the Earl of Southampton and the beginnings of the long series of entries of published plays in the Stationers' Register. Shakespeare had found himself by the date of the death of Marlowe and the town had recognised him. As to the manner of his apprenticeship, there is no reason to believe it different from that of other playwrights. Shakespeare must first have been " a hired man " or assistant about the theatre, charged with bringing out and putting away the properties and aiding the actors and sharers. He was undoubtedly employed very early in small parts and, possessing less the genius of mimicry than that of creation, never rose to the repute of his friend, Richard Burbage, as an actor. Tradition relates that Adam in *As You Like It* and the ghost in *Hamlet* were rôles of Shakespeare. Clearly a sonorous voice and a fine bearing must have been imperative in the latter part. Perhaps, as Professor Matthews believes, Shakespeare preferred the rôles of thoughtful elderly men. The folio of Ben Jonson's *Works,* 1616, is witness that Shakespeare took a part in the Roman tragedy of *Sejanus* and in the comedy of *Every Man In His Humour;* but what parts it is impossible to say. The listing of actors came into vogue only late in Shakespeare's career, hence the paucity of our information on the subject. But Shakespeare's opportunity came otherwise. In the incessant revision to which acting dramas were subject under the exigencies of revival, performance at court, in the provinces, with a greater or a smaller number of players, a ready pen and inventive dramatic cleverness were in urgent demand. And here Shakespeare was able to show his mettle. The degree of Shakespeare's participancy in the plays assigned by common consent to the earliest period of his authorship must remain matter of perennial debate; for the evidence recoverable is and must continue insufficient, however assured we may feel of the general proposition. It is not enough for the critic to feel in his inner consciousness that Shakespeare could or could not possibly have written this, that or the other line or passage; his doubts must be based on external evidences, however graceful a superstructure of inference his ingenuity may be able subsequently to rear. For example, take the whole vexed question of the trilogy of plays on Henry VI, included by general consent and the sanction of the folios in all editions of Shakespeare. For the first of these plays, no version save that of the folio exists; the other two occur in a very different form as the first and second parts of *The Contention between the Two Noble Houses of York and Lancaster,* printed in 1594. A comparison of this version with that of the folio discloses a line for line revision of the two *Contentions,* a correction of obvious mistakes and an occasional reordering of material in the interest of a more effective dramatic presentation. As to the first part of *Henry VI,* there is no opportunity for such a comparison; but there is a striking allusion by Nash to the extraordinary success, in 1592, of a play in which Talbot figured as a hero in his warfare against the French. The scenes that concern Talbot in the first part of *Henry VI,* as we have it, are written with peculiar animation as compared with many other scenes of the same play. The all but certain inference is that the success of this revision of an earlier and now lost version of the play, now known as Shakespeare's first part of *Henry VI,* was due to Shakespeare's insertion or rewriting of the scenes that depict Talbot. Once more, there remains extant an old drama in two parts called *The Troublesome Reign* *of King John* which covers very nearly the ground traversed by Shakespeare's play on that king. Here comparison reveals a different process. What Shakespeare did was to retain the general course of events and the personages of the old play, and then refashion the material into one drama of a superior unity and workmanship. But it was not in the chronicle play alone that we find Shakespeare thus working over old material. Similarly it is problematic to what extent Shakespeare's hand remade *The Taming of a Shrew* into *The Taming of the Shrew;* certainly the scenes between Katharine and Petruchio are thoroughly remodelled; while even as to *Romeo and Juliet,* existent in two Shakespearean versions, who knows, had we the lost tragedy alluded to by Brooke as on the stage three years before the birth of Shakespeare, that the case might not exhibit a parallel in the matter of revision, to that of *King John?*

This period of work with the material of other men must have been well over for Shakespeare before the death of Marlowe; more definitely than this it is impossible to speak with confidence. And now there succeeded a time of experiment and imitation. When Shakespeare first came up to London the popular stage was ringing with the successes of Kyd and Marlowe, and tragedy and chronicle history held the vogue of the moment. If Shakespeare had any hand in *Titus Andronicus,* which the present writer would like to believe that he had not, this must have been the time when writing of matter at the furthest extremity from his own feelings and experience, he strained his art to outdo the grewsomeness and horror of popularised Seneca in this revolting tragedy. We are on safer ground when we turn to *Richard III,* the most Marlowesque of the Shakespearean dramas. Richard is conceived, by the help of tradition and previous stage representation, as a monster of moral depravity, a figure of heroic proportions and heroic wickedness and perfidy, stalking through life regardless of anything but his own ruthless ambition. This is Marlowe's conception of the tragic protagonist and comparable not only in conception but likewise in execution — in a certain largeness of phrase, force of passion and objectiveness of poetic spirit — with Tamburlaine, Faustus and Barabas, the heroes of Marlowe. Plainly the young Shakespeare recognised this commanding genius in tragedy and strove here to rival him in his own art. In comedy, too, Shakespeare was at first equally imitative, and here his supreme example was as naturally at hand. Comedy lagged after her sister tragedy on the popular stage, and there could be little choice of models between the jejune moralities of Wilson, heroical absurdities such as *Fair Em* or even light, trivial *Mucedorus* and the finished comedies of Lyly at court. *Love's Labour's Lost* is Shakespeare's endeavour to write an original comedy in the manner of Lyly. Shakespeare's play is as politically allusive and as personally satirical, as bright and packed with wit and repartee. And it has, too, the Lylyan quality of having been carefully prepared and of not always being resonant with the timbre of spontaneity. Shakespeare threw aside mythology and allegory in his play which Lyly had for the most part preserved. To mythology Shakespeare afterwards returned for atmosphere in *A Midsummer Night's Dream,* the latest of his plays to be affected by Lyly's art of the court. *Love's Labour's Lost* has the distinction of being the only play of Shakespeare's in which the plot has not been traced to an extraneous source in whole or in part. Clever and interesting though it is, its picture of the conversation and manners of gentlewomen and courtiers is amateurish, however excellent a copy of like converse in the comedies of Lyly. It is perhaps worthy of note that in both *Love's Labour's Lost* and *A Midsummer Night's Dream* a play is attempted within the play by ridiculous amateurs before great people, and in both the conduct of the great as to these well meant endeavours is not above reproach on the score of consideration and common civility. Could Shakespeare have known the merciless banter that takes advantage of intrenched position? Or did Shakespeare laugh, as most of us are wont to laugh, with the majority and feel, even as early as *Love's Labour's Lost,* the professional's contempt for that creature, most loathed of gods and men, the would-be player.

Shakespeare made no second attempt at the allusive court drama of Lyly; but he tried other experiments. The fun and mischance of disguise, already well represented in Gascoigne's *Supposes* and in the intrigue of Roman comedy, now attracted his attention and *The Comedy of Errors* was the result, a play in which the improbabilities of mistaken identity, as exhibited in his source the *Menæchmi* of Plautus, are frankly seized and doubled, and all attempt at characterisation is as frankly and rationally sacrificed to farcical situation. But although Shakespeare employed the mistake in identity again (in Viola and her brother Sebastian in *Twelfth Night* for example), *The Comedy of Errors* remains his only experiment, his one success, in Plautine comedy. With *The Two Gentlemen of Verona* Shakespeare found his bent in comedy. Free from the allusive satire of Lyly, the intrigue of Plautus and the impeding morality element of Wilson, here was a romantic love story, told dramatically for its own sake with opportunity for event, character and situation, all harmoniously to develop into artistic unity. *The Two Gentlemen of Verona* is not among the most successful comedies of Shakespeare; but it is the first comedy of a kind destined to become exceedingly popular and a production of extraordinary promise. Moreover it presages many of the personages that Shakespeare afterwards worked up into a completer realisation. Julia, the resourceful maiden, arrayed as a page, seeking her lover yet womanly withal, Lucetta, the pert waiting-woman, the contrasted "two gentlemen," the faithful and the recreant, Launce, the droll serving man, all are sketches subsequently developed and differentiated among the enduring comedy folk of Shakespeare.

To return to the chronicle play, if Shakespeare imitated the gait and manner of Marlowe in *Richard III,* he had that poet almost equally in mind in *Richard II. Edward II* must have been Marlowe's latest play. It was published very shortly after his death and we have no reason to doubt that it maintained to the full the repute of his earlier dramas. The theme of *Edward II* details the fate of an unkingly king, one whose unfitness to rule and wanton disregard for the obligations of his office and his manhood convert him into a pitiable object, dethroned, disgraced, and at last miserably murdered. The only other English monarch, whose career and end can be described in terms almost identical, was Richard II, the careless and dishonourable son of the Black Prince. It seems incredible that Shakespeare should have chosen such a theme and produced his *Richard II,* not long after the death of Marlowe, without a full recognition of his own daring. Moreover, whatever its similarity in subject, *Richard II* is written with an independence and spirit, new as compared with Shakespeare's previous efforts in the chronicle play. *Richard II* is Shakespeare rivalling Marlowe but free from his leading strings and example; for what could be further removed from the Marlowesque hero than the poetic egotist and poseur, Richard II, consoled in the hour of his discrowning and almost in the very moment of his taking off by his theatrical sense of picturesqueness. Richard II is Shakespeare's first great study in character; for John was a copy, and Richard Crookback the imitation of an established tradition. In the tragedy of *King Richard II* Shakespeare emerged absolutely from tutelage in serious drama to display unmistakably that fine scrutiny into the mainsprings of human passion and conduct, ever subordinated to artistic and dramatic limitations, that distinguishes him above other poets.

It is familiar to students and to most general readers that our popularly accepted chronology of the Shakespearean plays is the result of a consensus of scholarly opinion and that much of it is founded on inference and argument, neither lightly to be disturbed nor yet to be accepted otherwise than in a spirit of hopeful and provisional faith. The famous mention by Francis Meres, in 1598, of twelve plays by name has been described as " our one rock of certainty in a sea of surmise." Yet even this rock is not absolutely secure. Meres' book is entitled *Palladis Tamia, or Wit's Treasury,* " a comparative discourse of our English poets with the Greek, Latin and Italian poets," and his method requires a nice balancing of names, titles, and characteristics, in all of which he is somewhat priggish. Moreover, Meres may not have been infallible. His testimony in including *Titus Andronicus* among the tragedies of Shakespeare has fastened that dubious clog about the poet's neck; and the critics are still happily undecided as to what comedy Meres could have had in mind under his title *Love's Labour's Won.* Was it *All's Well That Ends Well* or *Much Ado About Nothing* where Beatrice and Benedick in a sense both win? Was it *The Taming of the Shrew* wherein the hapless Katharine is won with labour but assuredly not with love? Or may it have been some comedy, now lost save for this solitary record of its title? Moreover does the mention of just twelve plays by Meres preclude the possibility of Shakespeare's having written more, unknown to this pragmatic critic of 1598? As to the order of the plays of Shakespeare thus far mentioned, leaving the revisions of the plays on Henry VI aside, the poet seems to have been busy with the three experimental comedies, *Love's Labour's Lost, The Comedy of Errors,* and *The Two Gentlemen of Verona,* up to the close of 1591, when apparently

he turned seriously to chronicle history, writing *King John,*
Richard III and *Richard II,* perhaps in this order during 1592
and 1593, and then turning back to comedy in *The Merchant
of Venice* and *A Midsummer Night's Dream* in 1594 and 1595.
Romeo and Juliet, published in a form suggesting revision in
1597, comes in somewhere here and, in 1597 too, Shakespeare
continues his work in the chronicle play with the first part
of *Henry IV.* So much for the generally accepted order of
Shakespeare's dramas up to the date of the list of Meres.

And now Shakespeare bloomed forth in the full strength of
his dramatic maturity, freed once and for all from competition that he need never to have feared. In some respects
there is no completer example of Elizabethan dramatic art
than *The Merchant of Venice,* however our appreciation may be
staled by the base use of this exquisite comedy in childhood for
" educational purposes." Here is a just intermingling of
romance with the hard actualities of life, passion trembling on
the verge of tragedy and comedy charmingly triumphant after
all. To the Elizabethan, Shylock was the ogre in the fairy
tale, a mixture of the fearful and the comically grotesque; Antonio was the Christian gentleman who spat upon him as a
creature noisome and righteously detested; Bassanio, the gentleman adventurer, frankly a suitor for the golden Portia's wealth
as much as for herself, and unashamed. Modernity plays
frightful pranks with the artless truth of our old drama and
nowhere more so than in this play. We sigh as we think of
Portia, sacrificed to the fortune-hunting Bassanio and, recognising modern, perhaps Ibsenesque, examples of like occurrences,
wonder if the couple could possibly have been happy after. In
Antonio, we find that his heartlessness in not claiming the Jew
from the first as a brother is really the cause of his all-but undoing; and we feel dissatisfied that the drama should not have
ended as a tragedy. But our greatest transformation is that
of Shylock in whom some unwise critics have discovered the
prophetic answer to current anti-Semitism. Save for the unfilial daughters of King Lear and Iago perhaps, Shakespeare has
scarcely ever drawn a personage wholly and irrevocably bad;
and that is because he is so unaffectedly true to human nature.
The pathos of Shylock is totally of nineteenth century manu-
facture and as absurd as it is gratuitous. It is referable, like
our modern shudder at the robust punishment meted out to the
Jew, to our emasculated contemporary sentimentality that habit-

ually meddles with clumsy hand to interpose between human acts of folly and criminality and their logical consequences. Least of all writers does Shakespeare need our help in reading into his works high ideals, fine distinctions and the metaphysics of twentieth century conduct. Barring some cases in which the conventions of his time clung about him, as they must about all whose lot is mortal, Shakespeare's are the ethics of all time; ours, when we seek to expand his humanity or explain away the conditions of the world in which he lived, are ridiculous and misguided.

A Midsummer Night's Dream is Shakespeare's latest return to the manner of the old court drama. The intention of this play for a performance at court or as part of the entertainment on the occasion of a noble marriage has been thought sufficient to explain its nature in this particular. Whether the comedy is to be interpreted as containing no more than a passing allusion in complimentary terms to the Earl of Leicester's courtship, some twenty years before, of the imperial votress fancy free or much more, now hidden from us by the lapse of time, must depend largely on the success of ingenious scholarship. In these matters it is as easy to treat the subject carelessly with preconceived ideas as to probabilities drawn from our own contemporary experiences as it is to carry our own interpretations of this old drama into details that must remain forever beyond us. Indubitably the age was fond of enigmas, involved allusions, veiled compliments to monarchy and the nobility and the like, and Shakespeare was not above his time in these respects, witness the allusions to Elizabeth in this play and the more direct ones in Henry V to the friend of his patron Southampton the unfortunate Earl of Essex.[2] More interesting to us is Shakespeare's composite art in this fanciful comedy and his delightful uplift of the fairy-lore of his country into a dainty mythology that has set the standard in this particular for all literature that has followed. What for example, could be more unpromising than the current superstitions of the countryside as to that uncouth oaf, Lob-Lie-by-the-Fire, a lout and the conception of louts, and the malicious goblin Robin Goodfellow, fused and transformed into the lithesome and volatile Puck, winged servant of those delightful little creatures Oberon

---

[2] A Midsummer Night's Dream, ii, 1. 148-174; Henry V, the chorus preceding Act V.

and Titania, with their human foibles and bickerings, and their delicate retinue Cobweb, Mustardseed, Pease Blossom and the rest. And then the daring juxtaposition of these sylphs with the delicious humour of Bottom and his base mechanicals, the wandering lovers in the mazes of the wood and the semi-classical figures of Theseus and Hyppolita a background for all. Never has there been art more unorthodox, more incongruous, more warranted in its success, than this. We have only to compare Shakespeare's fairies with those of his contemporaries, Jonson or Drayton say, for example, to see how immeasurably he stands above them in this world of imaginative fancy as in that which has to do with the realities of human passion.[3]

It was about 1596 or 1597 that Shakespeare turned once more to the chronicle play to reach in the trilogy of *Henry IV* and *Henry V* the height of Elizabethan attainment in this species of drama. In these plays Shakespeare returns to the epic quality of this variety of drama and retains another early feature, their mingling with deeds of high historic import, an invented underplot of humorous relief. For his material the poet has recourse as usual to Holinshed's *Chronicles of England,* his customary quarry where the history of his native country was in question; but, as usual with Shakespeare in his earlier work, here, too, an old play intervened to suggest the subject. The play in question is the half-illiterate *Famous History of Henry V,* ascribed to Richard Tarlton. In no place has Shakespeare so transfigured the old material; although the suggestion of the relations between Prince Hal and his austere father, the scene of the purloining of the crown and even the hint of a humorous companion of the Prince, old, stout, unvenerable and named Oldcastle, all come from the older play. Apropos of Oldcastle, a couple of allusions in Shakespeare's text point to the circumstance that that was the name under which Falstaff first appeared in Shakespeare's first part of *Henry IV*. Nothing could have been more unsuitable than such a misrepresentation of the famous Lollard nobleman of old time and, whether because of objection by those interested or for other reasons, the name of Sir John Falstaff was soon substituted for the part.

[3] On the general subject, see the present writer's " Some Features of the Supernatural as represented in Plays of the Reigns of Elizabeth and James," *Modern Philology,* i, June, 1903.

Such an opportunity was not to be lost and in *Sir John Old-castle,* a rambling chronicle play by Michael Drayton and three collaborators, " the true story of Oldcastle " was set on a rival stage and the Shakespearean personage, Falstaff, was frankly imitated in the character of the " humorous " hedge priest Sir John of Wrotham. It was the success of Falstaff that encouraged not only his appearance in *2 Henry IV* but the composition of *The Merry Wives of Windsor* which was written, according to an old tradition, at the request of Elizabeth who was desirous of seeing Sir John in love.

Falstaff was by far the most popular comedy figure on the Elizabethan stage; he is more frequently mentioned in contemporary allusion than any other personage and was again and again imitated but never approached. The idea of a group of " irregular humourists," as they have been called, such as Falstaff and his rout of folly, may have been suggested by the immediate success of the moment, Jonson's comedy, *Every Man In His Humour.* Certainly Ancient Pistol, with his playhouse phrases and his Cambyses vein of rant and bombast, is a personage simply enough compact of " humours," and so is Nym and, to a less extent, bottle-nosed Bardolph. As to Falstaff, the complexity of his personality and the triumphant transcendency of his wit stand out immeasurably beyond anything that Jonson, with all his power and constructive ingenuity, ever compassed. It is a moot question as to whether the Falstaff of *The Merry Wives* is really the same personage as Prince Henry's resourceful, and incomparable companion in arms and mischief; and assuredly it is something of a shock to find the Hector of Dame Quickly and Doll Tearsheet, he who fought with fierce Percy of the North for a long hour by Shrewsbury clock — for have we not his word for it? — reduced to the adventure of the buck-basket and to pinching at the hands of mock fairies to reduce his lecherous blood. Yet it might not be difficult to show that an absolute artistic logic rules the character of Falstaff throughout the plays in which he appears. Indeed nowhere is Shakespeare's fidelity to human nature and to those invisible laws that rule human nature more consummately exercised than here. With a personal charm absolutely irresistible we recognise none the less in Falstaff to the full his worthlessness, his immorality, his chicanery and incurable grossness and we approve while we regret the rigour of the Prince's final repudiation of him, however we share

Dame Quickly's pious hope, expressed in her pathetic account of his death, that " he is in Arthur's bosom."

That Shakespeare was led on from *Richard II,* his earliest independent study of historical character, to the plays on Henry IV seems, considering their probable sequence in point of time, altogether likely. Politic Henry Bolingbroke offered a striking contrast to Richard, " the skipping king"; and no less distinctly is Henry represented once more in contrast with the son whom he so little understood as the Prince is set against his engaging rival, Hotspur. A fine heroic spirit pervades Shakespeare's scenes of the old chivalric warfare. Too humane to take joy in the barbarism of these internecine feuds, their pageantry, pomp of war and ceremony lent themselves admirably to Shakespeare's artist's sense of the picturesque while the deeper well-springs of thought and action which life involves offered him his true theme to raise his historical plays immeasurably above the contemporary craft of most of his competitors. It is difficult for the educated modern reader to do justice to the historical personages of Shakespeare because he is habituated to think so absolutely in their terms. The pathetic child figure of Prince Arthur, the monstrous Richard III, calculating Bolingbroke, smitten with the mouldering fire of remorse, thick-spoken, impetuous Hotspur, devout, heroic Henry V — these princes of England have received, like many a lesser personage, the stamp of Shakespeare's royal mint once and for all, and mere history may interpret and explain as it will, the impression of the master poet alone remains lasting. It is not usual to think of Shakespeare as a patriotic writer. Yet which of our poets has devoted a third of his activity to the celebration of the heroic deeds of English men and princes? And which has accepted love of country so unaffectedly, so as a thing to feel and not to prate about as this same gentle Elizabethan? To the noble list of his chronicle plays Shakespeare was to add but one more, *Henry VIII,* and that at a later time when the recent death of Elizabeth called the attention of the nation to the annals of the Tudor princes which were staged in play after play as we write up the career of a deceased monarch in our newspapers upon his demise. Thither we shall not follow now but turn back to some of Shakespeare's immediate contemporaries in romantic comedy and history more particularly during the last dozen years of the old queen's reign.

Shakespeare wrote many more chronicle plays than any one of his fellow playwrights, but several of them joined, as others had preceded him, in this endeavour to place history in a series of vivid epic and dramatic scenes on the popular boards. Were we looking so wide afield, it might not be difficult to make clear that this vogue of historical drama was only one manifestation of the national consciousness which the repulse of the Armada and other English successes in arms and diplomacy had fanned into blaze. In literature this begot, besides these patriotic plays, the ponderous prose chronicles of Halle, Holinshed and Stow, innumerable lesser " histories " and biographies, and poems lyric, epic and topographical such as those of Daniel, Drayton, Warner and more.[4] To return to the drama, the rise of the chronicle play in the hands of the predecessors of Shakespeare, Greene, Peele, Marlowe and the rest, and the place of earlier chronicle histories such as the older *King John,* the older plays on Richard III and the two *" Contentions "* which concern the Wars of the Roses and furnished Shakespeare with materials, are matters already sufficiently discussed. Besides these more kingly plays, there were, in the nineties, several biographical chronicles, as they may be called, that differed very little from the main species in their conduct and subject-matter. Such a play is the anonymous *Sir Thomas More* which so prudent a critic as Spedding once thought good enough in parts for Shakespeare's hand. Such, too, was *The History of Thomas Lord Cromwell,* the capable Machiavellian minister of Henry VIII and that of *Captain Stukeley* in which is set forth the career of a fascinating adventurer who endeavoured to carve out a kingdom for himself and found comfort and abetment among the enemies of England, to die at last an heroic death as the ally of Don Sebastian against the Moors at the battle of Alcazar.

An important name among the immediate competitors of Shakespeare in the chronicle play is that of Thomas Heywood, long to maintain, as we shall see, for other dramatic work, a high place in the favour of the lovers of popular drama. Heywood began experimentally, as did Shakespeare, and one of his earliest endeavours was chronicle history. The subject-matter of this early attempt, Heywood found in the annals of King

[4] For a list of these works and their relations to the historical drama, see the present writer's *The English Chronicle Play,* 1902.

Edward IV; but he combined with material merely historical the pathetic story of Jane Shore, the royal mistress, thus giving to his scenes a bias towards the domestic drama in which he was later to reach his most permanent recognition. *Edward IV* is a rambling production, containing however many scenes not only dramatically capable but reaching the heart with that unaffected pathos of which this old poet was one of the masters. I have not hesitated elsewhere to declare that touching little scene in which the two youthful princes, children of King Edward, are represented in the Tower, separated from their mother and their protectors with the shadow of murder stalking towards them, as capable of holding its own in its natural simplicity against the poetry that Shakespeare employs to describe the same situation; [5] and the whole episode of Jane Shore and her relations to her wronged husband is as wholesome ethically as it is effective from a dramatic point of view. But all this is little of the stuff of chronicles. The Heywood of later years and achievement will claim our attention in his place. *Edward IV* represents the chronicle history diverted into a drama of the domestic relations. Other interests entered in to dilute history: thus the anonymous *Look About You,* 1599, although the story includes King John among its personages, is mainly a diverting comedy of disguises; Munday and Chettle's two plays on Robert Earl of Huntingdon (otherwise Robin Hood), 1598, concern also the unlawful pursuit by the same John Lackland of " Matilda Lord Fitz-Walter's daughter," while many other plays make the historical setting of the scene in the reign of a given English sovereign simply the background of a play of totally different interest. None the less it is possible to gather together of dramas treating English kings and historical personages a goodly number. And this can be extended to more than a hundred titles if we include plays on subjects set in the scene of the mythological Britain of Geoffrey of Monmouth and his like. To this class belong *Gorboduc, Macbeth,* and *King Lear,* as well as many plays the titles only of which have been handed down. The easy faith of a credulous age made no attempt to distinguish between the historical authenticity of Brutus, founder of Britain, Merlin the magician or King Arthur, with his knights of an impossible chivalric age, and such personages as Edward I, the Black Prince or Henry Monmouth; and the playwrights scraped up

[5] *Ibid.,* p. 147.

every adventure, every war, intrigue and petty conspiracy, and
added matter of their own from British and Roman times to
the coming of the Saxons, Danes and Normans, to say nothing
more of later times. There is no English monarch from Edward the Confessor and William the Conqueror to Philip and
Mary who is unrepresented in some one of these plays and
some of them, as for example Richard III, enter into half a
dozen plays or more.[6] When James came to the throne he
might have seen the " facts " of the Gowry conspiracy, a personal adventure of his own, enacted on the stage. The age
was free spoken and, certain matters of state, religion and
foreign affairs excepted, any man might say what he liked.
Elizabeth meddled very little with freedom in such matters
and most of the cases of royal intervention, that have come
down to us in her reign and even in the next, are referable to
the complaints lodged by an ambassador or other foreigner of
importance. One matter regarding a play of Shakespeare deserves a word in this connection. It appears that in 1599,
when the conspiracy of Essex was in process, several of his followers induced the Chamberlain's men (Shakespeare's company) to act before them a play " of King Harry the IVth
and of the killing of Richard II " by promising the players
" forty shillings more than their ordinary for it." Elizabeth
was very much affected by this and afterwards told her Recorder
of the Tower, Lambarde, that by Richard she herself was intended and her dethronement aimed at therein.[7] It may be
remarked that the scene of Richard's deposition in *Richard II*
does not appear in any of the quarto editions of that play and
that it was restored to its place in the text for the first time
in the folio, years after Shakespeare's death.

The chief contemporary rivals of Shakespeare in the production of chronicle plays were the playwrights employed by Philip
Henslowe who was the backer and exploiter of two or three
theatrical companies, and who fortunately left behind him a
Diary, as it has been called, of which we shall hear much more
in the next chapter. Henslowe employed many poets and the
habit of collaboration was prevalent among them, sometimes as
many as four — as in the familiar case of *Oldcastle,* the work
of Drayton, Chettle, Munday and Wilson — engaging in a

[6] See the table and classification of these plays in the same.
[7] See Nichols, *Progresses of Queen Elizabeth,* iii, 552.

single play. It was thus that a ready supply was to be had for an immediate demand; and the only wonder is that work thus hastily and even perfunctorily done should often remain so vital and readable. As to the authors just named, Michael Drayton was the friend of Jonson and Shakespeare and became, in later years, the most popular successor of Spenser in general poetry. He appears to have been somewhat ashamed of his connection with the stage and covered up his tracks with a success discouraging to the modern investigator. Henry Chettle is memorable, aside from one extant play, as the editor of Greene's notorious *Groatsworth of Wit* and for his own apology to Shakespeare in his pamphlet *Kind Heart's Dream* soon after. Robert Wilson the younger is distinguishable from Robert Wilson the elder, author of *The Three Lords and Ladies of London,* and of him we know little more; while Munday was a well known balladist, translator and pamphleteer in addition to his contribution of much loose work to the drama. These men, together with Day, Wilkins, Haughton, Hathway and several others, continuously appear in *Henslowe's Diary,* although their work was by no means confined to the chronicle play but ranged through every variety of drama which the teeming imaginations of their fertile time could invent.

Besides his *Edward IV,* Heywood is the author of one of the less interesting of the group of plays which chronicle Tudor subjects, *If You Know Not Me You Know Nobody,* 1604. This rambling production concerns the life of the late Queen as did likewise Dekker's strange allegorical *Whore of Babylon* in which, suffice it to say, King Henry VIII appears as the fairy King Oberon. Of the same date and kindred in title to Heywood's *If You Know Not Me,* is Samuel Rowley's *When You See Me You Know Me,* the coarse and occasionally ribald scenes of which detail events in the life at court of the same monarch much as they might have been seen from below stairs and traditionally reported. The relation of this play to Shakespeare's *King Henry VIII* (at some time known to the stage as *All Is True*) appears in the prologue of the latter. Its probable later revision by Fletcher does not concern us here. Still another chronicle play of the Tudor group is the slightly earlier *Sir Thomas Wyatt,* 1602, in which the well known dramatists Dekker and Webster collaborated to tell of the unfortunate young conspirator who attempted to antedate the accession of Queen Elizabeth by a few months to his own

complete undoing. Among authors in the kindred group of
plays on mythological British history we find Thomas Lodge
accredited by some with the older version of the story of King
Lear, 1593, which he spelled " Leir " and concluded happily;
and Robert Armin, the comic actor, author of *The Valiant
Welshman,* 1595, a mediocre play on Caractacus diluted with
much invention. *The Birth of Merlin* and *The Shoemaker a
Gentleman,* both interesting works of William Rowley, later
the distinguished collaborator of Thomas Middleton, and Middleton's own *Mayor of Queenborough,* in which is told the
supposedly historical matters relating to the first landing of
the Saxons on British soil, are all deserving the attention of
the student of our English historical drama however their subjects stretch out into the domain of sheer fiction.

A romantic spirit informs much of this material and this
is true likewise of the kindred group that sets forth the adventures of Englishmen beyond the seas, of notorious pirates and
other matters as strange as circumstantial. Thus *The Travails
of Three English Brothers* by Day, Rowley and Wilkins is a
hastily dramatized version of the actual experiences of the
Shirley brothers in Italy, Russia and Persia, transferred direct
from a contemporary pamphlet; and *A Christian Turned Turk*
by Robert Daborne is even less, and might be called a dramatized penny-dreadful. On the other hand, in *Fortune by Land
and Sea,* Heywood and Rowley appreciated the possibilities of a
current story wherein a young man of broken fortune and in
disgrace, retrieves the past by a brave and happy capture of redoubtable pirates. Even more full and buoyantly smacking of
the salt of the sea is Heywood's fine play in two parts, *The
Fair Maid of The West* in which womanly faith and devotion
triumphs most unconventionally in a drama set in Plymouth,
at the court of the Sultan of Morocco and especially on the
high seas between. These plays come somewhat later, in the
early days of King James. It was in happy, off-hand dramas
such as these, taking up as they often did the current topic of
patriotic, curious or other interest, that Henslowe sought to
rival in his several play-houses the learning of Jonson and the
genius of Shakespeare. The not infrequent success of ephemeral drama and fiction lies in the very circumstance that it is
such. Which of us has not given the preference to a newspaper account of a contemporary scoundrel while poetry and
serious literature lay close at hand and postponed? We may

assume that many of these plays of our lesser drama reached their auditors as they can never reach the belated reader of to-day; for they were above all things timely, fresh and calculated for the consumption of the moment. And, the moment passed, they passed with it. It is a curious commentary on art that that which is most " up to date," as we express it, is invariably the least calculated to carry beyond the present. It is vastly to the credit of the Elizabethan age that it was able so unerringly to choose between the plays of the henchmen of Henslowe, which it suffered to lie to a large extent unpublished, and the permanent dramas of Shakespeare and his greater fellows which his contemporaries not only attended to applaud but purchased for after reading in a remarkable number of editions, if we take into consideration the population of the time and the illiteracy of the lower orders.

We found the romantic drama rising to art in the tragedies of Kyd and Marlowe while comedy flourished at court with Lyly to find in Greene all too chary a popular exponent. We have traced, too, Shakespeare's earlier career as a writer of comedies and turn now to other developments of the romantic spirit as well as to Shakespeare's fellows in that lighter art, before proceeding to consider Shakespeare's own later career. It will be recalled that one of the earliest manifestations in the drama of that craving of human nature for the novel and the strange that we denominate the romantic, we found in a variety of play which we called the heroical drama. Plays of this type developed directly out of the moralities and were closely akin to the prose and metrical romances that formed so staple an article of the literary diet of our mediæval forefathers. To their general kind Marlowe contributed the conqueror play represented by *Tamburlaine,* Greene his dramatization of *Orlando Furioso* and the writers of chronicle plays their dramas of Merlin, Arthur and other heroes of the Round Table. Even more strictly of the type are such productions as *Charlemagne,* an anonymous work of about 1590 which Mr. Bullen printed under the title of *The Distracted Emperor, The Thracian Wonder* (of dubious authorship and doubtless first acted about 1598), and *The Dumb Knight,* as late as 1607 or 1608, the work of two very young writers, Machin and Markham, who were following older example as the uninspired young are apt to do. All of these plays deal in knightly prowess, heroic combat, remarkable adventure, and they occasionally add the element of magic, although this last led to the differentiation of another group. They must have enjoyed an unusual vogue, with the citizens of London in particular, as the titles of many now no longer extant — *Dick Whittington, The Life of Sir Thomas Gresham with the Founding of the Royal Exchange* for example — would go to prove; and they reached the height of their absurdity in Heywood's *Four Prentices of London* which must have been acted not later than 1594. In this preposterous performance (wherein Heywood is clearly writing down to his auditors), we hear how the good old Earl of Bulloigne, suffering from poverty, apprenticed his four sons to four honourable trades in London, how they and their sister as well — the last clad as the inevitable page — went forth into the world to carve out each his own fortune; how each won a kingly crown and their sister a royal husband, and all were reunited at the siege of Jerusalem. Such material begot its own antidote in satire. Beaumont's famous *Knight of the Burning Pestle* is a take-off on the whole class of heroical romances and on Heywood's play in particular. It was the work of a clever young literary man of whom we shall hear considerably more in this volume and appears to have been somewhat belated in point of time, as it was not printed until 1613. *The Knight of the Burning Pestle* is an apprentice lad who is literally thrust upon the stage and into the midst of the play by his master and mistress to act a burlesque part in accompaniment to other parody of the heroical drama. We are not surprised to learn that the city that so acclaimed *The Four Prentices* should not have appreciated the joke. The drama has seldom been reformed by means of parody and it was reserved to more cultivated and courtly auditors of the next reign to appreciate to the full this remarkably clever production that resembled in spirit more than it borrowed in kind of Cervantes' immortal *Don Quixote*.

However, romantic comedy less outrageously absurd than *The Four Prentices* and its like was not wanting among the playwrights contemporary with the young manhood of Shakespeare. But with them for the most part it is found as a component element in plays made up of other material as well. Thus the charming episode of Margaret and Lacy in Greene's *Friar Bacon* is subsidiary to the element of magic for which the comedy exists, as the graver royal temptation of Lady Salisbury in *Edward III* and the courtship of Cordella by "the

Gallian Prince" in *King Leir,* each is but an episode in a chronicle play.   So, too, *The Weakest Goeth to the Wall* is a romantic comedy of Italian origin told history-wise and *A Knack to Know an Honest Man,* also of unknown authorship, with its duels, its banishments, and tests of loyalty in friendship and love, comes nearer to material of Shakespeare, naïve though its spirit, than many a more ambitious performance.

Among Shakespeare's contemporaries in whom the romantic note in comedy ruled however the stridency of other tones, the result of forced work and necessity, came to mar it, is Thomas Dekker.   There is an unaffected tenderness about certain of his work that is as engaging as it is rare.   Among early comedies of Dekker none is so pervaded with poetry as *Old Fortunatus,* 1599, in which is told the old tale of folk-lore of the beggar who offered by Fortune his choice of " wisdom, strength, health, beauty, long life and riches," chose the last and, despite the addition of the wishing cap to his wealth, dies unhappy.   All this, with the continuance of the story of the sons of Fortunatus, the whole set in an allegorical contention of Vice with Virtue, is admirably poetic.   No subsequent work of Dekker's is so completely romantic in spirit until we reach, late in his career, *The Sun's Darling,* "a moral masque," 1623, in the compositions, perhaps revision, of which Dekker appears to have been assisted by John Ford.   Dekker's intervening work in the chronicle play has already been indicated.   His domestic dramas and his touch with Jonson fall more logically within the next chapter.   Dekker's *Fortunatus* is only one of a considerable group of Elizabethan romantic dramas that employ for the stage the delightful material of folk and fairy lore.   To this group belong Greene's *Friar Bacon* and even Marlowe's *Faustus* which it emulated, as we have seen, and *A Midsummer Night's Dream,* however different its immediate sources.   A curious old play by Anthony Munday, half chronicle half fairy tale, but depending mainly on unexpected and almost farcical situations, is *John a Kent and John a Cumber,* 1595, in which two wizards strive in their art each to outdo the other much as Friar Bacon strove to overcome his German rival Vandermast. *The Merry Devil of Edmonton,* 1604, of unknown authorship, links on to the Faustus story in which the supernatural accomplishes little more than the straightening out of the crooked course of two interesting young lovers.   As to fairies in comedy, however they may have obtruded before his time in Lyly's

Maid's Metamorphosis for example, or in Greene's *Scottish History of James IV,* where we meet Oberon for the first time, subsequent to *A Midsummer Night's Dream* all fairies wear the livery of Shakespeare.

This is only one example of the extraordinary and immediate influence which Shakespeare exerted on the drama of his time; for, however his followers might fail to imitate the simple romanticism of his earlier comedy, the influence of his refinement of tone and sentiment and of his ideal treatment of character appears in many contemporary plays. John Day, whose vivacious comedies were printed in the reign of King James, is more Lylyan and Jonsonian than Shakespearean. His two memorable plays (if we except the delightful *Parliament of Bees* which is satire in dialogue and inconceivable acted) are *Law Tricks* and *Humour Out of Breath*. But even Jonson in a first effort, *The Case is Altered,* 1598, fell momentarily under Shakespeare's spell. This comedy Jonson never acknowledged as his; and, Plautine though the source of the intrigue, Jonson never approached nearer to romantic art than in the character of Rachel, the fair and virtuous beggar maiden of this play: indeed it might almost be said that Rachel is Jonson's only vital female figure.

With the completion of the trilogy of *Henry IV* and *Henry V,* Shakespeare returned to romantic comedy to which he adhered in some half dozen plays, from *Much Ado About Nothing* to *Measure for Measure,* which followed in quick succession within the last half dozen years of Elizabeth's reign. There are no more perfect comedies of light and joyous type than *Much Ado, As You Like It* and *Twelfth Night,* all of them referable in theme as in atmosphere to the well-born, social life of Italy which was recognised, and justly, by the Elizabethans, as marking the very *beau ideal* of modern cultivated living. The atmosphere of youth hovers in a golden haze about these charming scenes and nothing is so serious as to impair, save for momentary pathos, the joy of life that sparkles in their exquisitely conceived personages and in the delightful poetry that clothes them. Moreover, the romantic people, Duke Orsino, Viola, Benedick and Beatrice, Orlando and his Rosalind — only to name which is to remember fascinating friends of intimate acquaintance — exist always, in Shakespeare as in the world itself, in a *milieu* of the practical, the commonplace, the stupid and the absurd, all of which the

the Italian and other foreigner in his national traits. Indeed the first has so impressed certain of his foreign critics that they have credited him with journeys to Venice, to Elsinore and elsewhere, notebook in hand, wherein to transcribe the impressions of " local colour " that he subsequently transferred to his plays. Such is the method of pedantry, not that of genius. Though, after all, the local colour of Shakespeare has been much exaggerated and most of the touches so praised by his commentators are the result of that honest employment of his material, ultimately Italian or other, in which faithfulness and an equal fidelity to the portrayal of the familiar things around him Shakespeare leads all dramatists. As to Shakespeare's personages in comedy, it seems altogether probable that they are all contemporaneous English men and women, practising the graces, the mannerisms or the absurdities that were prevalent in the England of his own day. And it is unlikely, save in a few definite cases, such as Othello the Moor or Shylock the Jew, that Shakespeare thought very definitely of those race differences and diversities of nationality to which it is easy, after all, to attach an undue importance. The foreigner as a subject for comedy, if not for ridicule, Shakespeare used after the manner of the time. Already in *Love's Labour's Lost* we meet with Don Armado, the fantastical Spaniard, in the second part of *Henry IV*, with the Welsh, Scotch and Irish captains, the admirable Fluellen first among them, while the broken French of Henry V and the gibberish of Dr. Caius, in *The Merry Wives*, may have amused a class whose lineal descendants go numerously to the theatres of the present day to applaud similar "humour." The period from 1593 to 1603 from the death of Marlowe to the close of Elizabeth's reign, is *par excellence* that of Shakespeare. Therein were contained not only the comedies and histories of which we have heard in this chapter, but likewise the tragedies of *Romeo and Juliet, Julius Cæsar* and *Hamlet,* beyond which Shakespeare attained many varied and tragic notes, but few deeper. Chronicle history, save for the obituary plays of a year or two after, was dead with the death of Queen Elizabeth. Further to proceed in the story of romantic comedy, would bring us into touch with Chapman, Marston, Middleton and Fletcher, each distinctive for new departures in the drama, for the most part to come. This much, however, may be said: Chapman appears to have been not uninfluenced by Shakespearean comedy in *The Gentleman*

Usher and *Monsieur D'Olive,* ambitious and romantic efforts
at romantic comedy of a graver type and both in print by 1606.
Chapman's métier hitherto had been Terentian comedy of intrigue. These later comedies are of higher type and the former, at least, is by no means unworthy either of its author or
their example. Marston, too, with all his vaunted originality,
again and again essays the Shakespearean gait, as his serious
and able *Malcontent,* in which the hero is affected with a
melancholy not unlike Hamlet's, plays a rôle not dissimilar to
the disguised Duke of Vienna in *Measure for Measure.* The
romantic note in Middleton came later by way of his collaborator, William Rowley, not by way of Shakespeare; but
that of Fletcher, however resonant of Shakespeare in some of
the earlier plays, soon became a note as different as it was
insistent and prevailing among Fletcher's own compeers. These
matters we shall postpone for the nonce, as things of closer
sequence claim the next chapter.

CHAPTER VI

DEKKER, HEYWOOD AND THE DRAMA OF EVERY DAY LIFE

LINES of classification and division in a subject so complex as the drama can never be more than provisional, helpful in making clear what would otherwise remain in confusion. Obviously life may be seen through a pane of clear glass as well as in the dilation of romance or scrutinised with the belittling lenses of satire. In neither of the latter cases is the world, reproduced from such a point of view, in any wise accurately represented, though each method of art in its success again and again substitutes the higher truth for a mere category of realistic facts. The literature of fact is the oldest, imagination and amplification came after. So, too, in the modern drama, the earliest amplification of the facts of bible story added material within the observation of the playwright's every day experience whereby Cain became a boorish yokel, the wife of Noah a village scold and Joseph an awkward craftsman diffident before strangers and superiors. There is, in a word, no stronger strain in our drama than this strain of simple realism, however affectation or passing fashion may have overlaid it at times or genius have transformed it. It was this strain that made the success of John Heywood and our two earliest English comedies, however foreign suggestion may have intervened. Indeed it may be doubted whether, with all its poetry, its flights of imagination and its transmutations of things mundane into things rich and strange, there is a more characteristic trait of Elizabethan drama than its contemporaneousness, the quality by which all things are translated into immediate terms, comprehensible to the average man and therefore universal in appeal. Shakespeare possessed this quality; he possessed likewise, as we know, much more. But many a contemporary of Shakespeare succeeded in his time because of this quality alone. It is with the drama of every day life during the lifetime of Shakespeare that we are concerned in this chapter; less with this drama as a feature that enters into plays as one component

among many, than with that very definite group of Elizabethan
dramas in which the realism of every day life is the ruling
spirit.

And first a word as to what went before. *Gammer Gurton's
Needle* was only an amplification into a complete drama of the
interlude and the comedy scenes which the moralities, and even
the miracle plays, had long popularised. So *Gammer Gurton*
became the mother of a large progeny in which types, such as
the thick-witted, blundering husband, the clever shrewish wife
none too honest, the mischief-making Diccon of Bedlam, are
repeated again and again. For example in *Tom Tyler and his
Wife* that stupid victim of his wife's neglect and unreasonable
temper regains a momentary mastery by following the advice
of a friend and giving his spouse a sound beating; but pitying
her miserable condition, he confides the source of his sudden
mastery to his immediate loss of it and total undoing. In several plays, *Like Will to Like,* the underplot of Edward's *Damon
and Pithias* and *Grim the Collier of Croydon,* a personage of
this name figures who is as diverting and homely as he is
thoroughly English. Such plays were, some of them, on the
stage before the birth of Shakespeare and their material remained
the essential material of comedy and a part, according to immemorial usage, of many in other respects devoted to more lofty
subjects. In the group of Shakespeare's immediate predecessors,
Kyd and Marlowe were always more or less lofty and tragic;
the rest all employed comedy scenes of common life. But chief
among them was Greene who, had he but known it, might have
stood foremost in his age for the simple truth of his dramatic
talent in scenes such as those that concern the love affairs of
Margaret, the fair maid of Fressingfield, and her noble suitors
and the delightfully fresh rendering of a Robin Hood theme in
George à Green and the jolly shoemakers of Bradford. Shakespeare might well have had Greene for his example, had he
needed it, in these scenes drawn from the observation of English
daily life; and it was the same thing that Shakespeare was doing
(howsoever he transcended the lighter art of Greene) in *The
Merry Wives of Windsor* and in the comedy scenes interspersed
throughout the chronicle plays. Among early plays of the type
the authorship of which remains doubtful, is *Wily Beguiled,*
certainly on the stage as early as 1595. There occur early types
of several well known Elizabethan personages, Gripe the usurer,
Churms the confidential rascally lawyer, Fortunatus the bluff

soldier and a capital, loquacious nurse who seems more like a possible suggestion for the immortal Nurse of Juliet than an inferior borrower of her humour.

But if we would know the little that can be known of the contemporaries of Shakespeare who wrote for the lesser theatres this drama of every day life, we must make the acquaintance of Philip Henslowe, pawnbroker, moneyed man and exploiter of plays and players. What we know of Henslowe depends, in the main, on the fortunate survival of one book, popularly known as *Henslowe's Diary*.[1] This is really a manuscript book, employed by Henslowe from 1591 to 1609 in which to note all manner of accounts, memoranda, private and domestic, as well as those connected with his various ventures of the felling of trees, the lending of money and the fitting out and performance of plays. These last entries assume different forms. One series gives us the name of the play, the date of acting and Henslowe's share in the takings in of that day; another concerns advances and payments to playwrights and property men; a third records disbursements by Henslowe on behalf of the several companies in which he was interested. Incidentally a great many signatures of poets and others conversant with the stage are preserved, witnessing agreements, acknowledgments of payments or promises of plays. Finally, outside of the *Diary,* but preserved with it among the Alleyn papers at Dulwich College, are certain lists of properties once Henslowe's, letters and other documents, all of interest to the history of the stage, concerning half a dozen companies and almost as many playhouses beside the mention of scores of plays. Henslowe was a shrewd, illiterate man of business who grew rich by his foresight in building playhouses where they were wanted and in furnishing them, at the least expense to himself, with the kind and number of plays that met with the popular demand. An alliance by marriage with the famous actor Edward Alleyn, creator of the chief rôles of Marlowe's tragedies, gave Henslowe a standing in the theatrical world that enabled him to dictate terms to the poets. Henslowe does not appear to have been more avaricious than many of those who have exploited the drama since his time and there is nothing to show that his appreciation of the theatrical art was much below theirs. Without his book we should lose a valuable chapter in the history of the popular stage.

[1] See the excellent edition by W. W. Greg, 1904-08, 3 vols.

From the *Diary,* then, we learn that Henslowe managed two
or three theatres simultaneously and that he employed both
actors and playwrights at his own terms. Of the latter he had
at times no less than ten or a dozen on his books, and he appears
to have averaged something like a new play every two weeks.
Although Henslowe's relations with his men were close, it
cannot be shown that he was altogether unfriendly to the shift-
less bohemian small poets to whom he advanced money on
promises, often badly kept, or bailed out of that " consistory of
unthrifts," the debtors' prison. His books disclose that he occasionally bestowed small gratuities on the authors of unusually
successful plays or paid for a supper at the Mermaid on some
business occasion. But for the most part he so contrived to dole
out payment that he kept his people securely in his grasp. In
the palmy days of Henslowe's traffic with the stage " an acting "
play commanded from six to eight pounds sterling, and this was
often divided among three or four authors. In the reign of
James the price of plays rose with other things, and three years
before, 1613, Robert Daborne, a very second rate dramatist,
received twenty pounds and declared that he could have had as
much as twenty-five. How the playwrights of the day contrived
to live would remain a complete mystery, even with William
Rowley producing fifty-five plays in twenty years or Heywood
with his two hundred and twenty in twice that period, did we
not recall the contemporary system of patronage and the circumstance that some of the playwrights were also actors on regular
wages or sharers in the playhouses. For example, take the case
of Michael Drayton, next to Spenser the most popular general
poet of his day. For a period of a little more than three years,
Drayton gave his attention to the writing of plays, mostly in
collaboration with others in the employ of Henslowe. He was
concerned in twenty-four plays during that period and collaborated with eight other writers. In his best year he received forty
pounds for play-writing. But Drayton had noble patrons, had
been a tutor and must have received some income from the
many editions of his poems. It is not remarkable that only one
or two of the plays, in which he had a hand, are extant and capable of identification. Moreover, Drayton covered up the tracks
of his sojourn in captivity to Henslowe, ashamed of that to
which his hand had been subdued. Many others were not so
fortunate.

In no respect, however, is *Henslowe's Diary* more interesting than in the contrast which it offers to what we may justly infer to have been the conditions governing the company of Shakespeare. Indubitably, Shakespeare's fellows no less than Henslowe, were in the theatrical business for what they could make out of it; and both succeeded, Shakespeare and Burbage as well as Henslowe and Alleyn, dying rich, according to the standards of their time and station. But Henslowe's success was based on shrewd dealing with his poets and on a willingness to follow wavering popular taste. Shakespeare created and guided the taste of the public in the very act of reaching its favour as it had never been reached before. From a table of court performances between 1594 and 1603 [2] it has been estimated that the Lord Chamberlain's company of players (that is Shakespeare's) performed twice as many plays at court as its four competitors together. The success of the latter in the popular playhouses may have been less disproportionate, but the fact remains. In short, the romantic dramas of Dekker, Heywood, Rowley and others among Henslowe's writers wanted the finish and perfection that Shakespeare could give them. Their chronicle plays were rude and straggling in comparison to his, nor did any other dramatist so specialise in English history. In the simple comedy of every day life and in serious domestic drama alone, whether tragedy or less, did the authors of Henslowe's eclectic, haphazard, experimental school succeed in rivalling the writers of the Chamberlain's company and in giving to the London tradesman a drama based on a faithful rendering of the life of his own class.

If we look at this citizens' drama, as some have called it, we find it falling naturally into several classes as action prevails or passion. There is rural life and London life, the latter by far the more popular, dependent as it was on local colour and typical allusion, the success of which lay in its familiarity to the auditor; and within the limits of each there were farce, intrigue, comedy, satire and tragedy, all centring in domestic scene and realistic in presentation. The dramas of Greene, that is those of the domestic type, already mentioned, turn upon the simpler emotions, love, generosity, wifely devotion and the like, and their scene is, for the most part, rural or at least not urban. An exceedingly interesting comedy of the type is Henry Porter's *Two Angry Women of Abington,* on the stage by 1598 and

[2] See F. G. Fleay, *Chronicle History of the Stage,* p. 125.

exceedingly popular. The plot turns on a quarrel between two
" curst wives " and the consequent embroilment of their families.
The action depends as much on situation as on vivacious dialogue
and humorously drawn personages. Porter is a typical poet of
Henslowe's mart. We hear of him twenty-five times in the
Diary and in connection with five plays, all, save this one, lost;
and we know no more. But in this, his repute in the comic
drama is sufficiently established; for *The Two Angry Women*
is verily " full " in Charles Lamb's phrase, " of business, humour
and merry malice." Another comedy of rural English life, *The
Merry Devil of Edmonton,* 1600, has been doubtfully ascribed
to Drayton. Here we are introduced, at the outset somewhat
seriously, to the English Faustus, Peter Fabel; but the current
of interest changes to a very pretty love-tale and a group of
" humourists " whose wanderings and mistakes through Enfeld
Chase by night parallel a similar concluding scene of *The Two
Angry Women*. It is interesting here to note a third comedy
of English village or country life, which ends, as these, in a
night scene in a park and agrees with them in point of date.
It is usual to remember *The Merry Wives of Windsor,* as we
have above, for its connection with the chronicle plays through
Falstaff. But *The Merry Wives* is conspicuous among the
comedies of Shakespeare as the only one in which he lays his
scene frankly in England, an experiment never repeated. Perhaps the romantic spirit that achieved remoteness in time by the
former age and setting of the historical plays needed remoteness
of place in comedy to preserve it from that which was too familiar. Yet if we are seeking Shakespeare's contribution to the
drama of every day life, we may find it not alone in the vivacious
scenes and admirable personages of *The Merry Wives of Windsor,* but in the delightful comedy that follows Falstaff and holds
over into *Henry V,* who in his palmy days, as Prince Hal at
least, lived not afar off in the atmosphere of an heroic Agincourt, but in the streets and taverns of Elizabeth's own England. Shakespeare has brought us up to London from Windsor
and the country-side. Before we sojourn there with some of
his lesser fellows, we may mention an experiment of Ben Jonson's that agrees here in date and kind. *A Tale of a Tub,*
which may be assigned to the neighbourhood of 1600 rather than
later, is a rustic comedy of English village life, in which, with
characteristic accuracy, the poet endeavours to heighten the

effect by the use of dialect.   This comedy of Jonson is unworthy
his genius which lay elsewhere as we shall see.

If our subject were Elizabethan prose instead of Elizabethan
drama, we should recognise in Thomas Dekker and Thomas
Heywood the successors of Greene in that ready writing up of
things of contemporary interest, that journalistic instinct that
turns anything into copy, which is the distinguishing characteristic of the group of writers known as the pamphleteers.   It was
precisely these qualities that made Dekker and Heywood most
successful in domestic drama and enabled them to add a life-
likeness to the scenes of many a drama otherwise below the level
of some of their more ambitious contemporaries.   Thomas
Dekker was born somewhere between 1567 and 1570, in London.   The form of the name suggests a Dutch extraction, which
a knowledge of that language in some of the plays and a power
of minute relation as to common things which we associate with
Dutch art, go far to confirm.   Dekker is first mentioned by
Henslowe in 1598; some have thought that his career as a playwright began a few years earlier.   He continues traceable in-
termittently well into the thirties, and it is not certain when
he died.   Dekker was a born unthrift, constantly the victim of
poverty and often in the debtor's jail.   He appears to have
turned his hand to many varieties of writing, following closely
the example of Greene in pamphlets realistic, moral, satirical
or religious and mending, changing, adapting and rewriting
plays, his own and other men's, for Henslowe year after year.
Dekker is a notorious example of the Elizabethan practice of
collaboration in play-writing.   In one of the earliest plays with
which his name is associated, *Patient Grissil,* 1598, he had, as
coadjutors, Chettle and Haughton.   This comedy is a dramatic
version of the favourite mediæval story of the much enduring
wife, and is memorable for several very beautiful songs which
common assent has given to the authorship of Dekker.   Dekker's
lyrical gift, slender though its runnel of song, is as exquisite and
tuneful as that of any poet of his time.   Further expression of
it may be found in *Old Fortunatus,* already described in the
last chapter for its romantic and poetic spirit.   *The Shoemakers'
Holiday,* on the stage by 1599, is Dekker's typical contribution
to domestic comedy and here we have the daily life of the small
trades-folk of London done to perfection; their humours, their
pleasures, ambitions and hearty good fellowship.   The person-

ages of this delightful comedy are as distinctly drawn and differentiated as the story is naturally unfolded. Simon Eyre, the bluff and hearty master-shoemaker, with his crew of jolly apprentices about him, must have been an admirable character in the hands of a great comedian such as Kempe or Armin; and the circumstance that Dekker had his plot from a well known novel, as we should call it, of the day, *The Gentle Craft,* by Thomas Delony, enhanced its popularity. Much of the genial humour and kindly spirit, Dekker had from his original. But he lightened all, gave a touch of the romantic to the story of "Hans," who became a shoemaker because of love, a touch of pathos to the underplot of the faithful lovers, Ralph and Jane, and raised the whole production to a higher literary and artistic plane.

In *Patient Grissil* we have a favourable specimen of one of the most important groups of the domestic drama, the story of the faithful wife. The underplot of *The Shoemakers' Holiday* has just been noted as concerned with a not dissimilar theme. The ideals of Elizabethan days were, of course, not ours, and it was not only in Puritan circles that talk was at times of " the weaker vessel " or that the dominion of man was upheld by men and women alike and commended. It is a mistake to confuse the status of Elizabethan women with that which came to obtain in the degenerate days of gallantry when the Merry Monarch thrust English manners down with English morals to a level with those of the brothel and the tavern. There is a charm about the free and natural intercourse of the young people in the comedies of Shakespeare, Greene and Dekker, which we lose sensibly in the next generation when manners turned towards sophistication. There is a candour, a give and take in dialogue, a recognition of woman and a delight in her power and charm, which comported none the less with a recognition that after all she is not the stronger animal. Wherefore the many dramatic pictures of that favourite of the day, the faithful, the much enduring wife, often contrasted, not only with the obvious foil of her own sex, but with that incorrigible rascal, the favourite of fiction and of life, the prodigal son. To be sure, the scene of these dramas is by no means confined to England nor their portrayal to the conditions of any one age. Shakespeare's Hermione, devoted and forgiving beyond the range of our present ideals, and his Mariana at the moated grange are both of the type of patient Griselda, and so, too, is innocent and confiding Desdemona. But it is needless for us here to stray into the lofty regions of romantic tragedy or even where a satirical outlook has transformed our ideals from the simpler representations of the drama of every day life. Thus in *How a Man May Choose a Good Wife from a Bad, The Fair Maid of Bristow,* in *The London Prodigal* and in Marston's *Dutch Courtesan,* all of them between 1602 and 1605, we have practically the same group of personages: the faithful wife, the neglectful, spendthrift husband, the alluring, faithless and cruel courtesan, with the emphasis, as the case may be, on the one or the other. Marston's is by all odds the best play, indeed it rises above its species for its style, its variety and its substitution of an artistic for a moral contrast. Heart and soul of the domestic type, on the other hand, is the homely, circumstantial drama entitled *The Miseries of Enforced Marriage* in which George Wilkins staged, in 1605, the actual details of the unhappy married life of one Calverley. Wilkins, we now know, was personally acquainted with Shakespeare and was concerned in some way, not altogether clear, with *Pericles.* As to Calverley, his prodigal life soon after led to crime, and his murder of his wife and children was made into a play, *The Yorkshire Tragedy,* though not by Wilkins, soon after. Here, as so often, we have the old drama performing a function of the newspaper in disseminating knowledge of some recent event. The drama of our English-speaking lower playhouses has never lost this practice, though the moving picture lends itself more readily to this obvious mode of exploiting topics of current interest. Still another play of this same group is Heywood's *Wise Woman of Hogsdon,* not printed until 1638, but unmistakably of far earlier acting. Here the familiar story is varied, the spendthrift husband becomes a recreant lover and prodigal, seeking to recoup his fallen fortunes in a wealthier match. "The faithful wife" is here a resourceful country maiden who follows her betrothed up to London and succeeds, with some help from the "wise woman," not only in winning him back but in marrying her wealthy, and in this case virtuous, rival to a worthier suitor. Here verily is the stuff of ordinary every day life, for Heywood relies on no art save the simple and truthful presentation of his story.

Thomas Heywood was born about 1575 in Lincolnshire and became a student at Cambridge and later a fellow of Peterhouse. We meet with him as early as 1596, in *Henslowe's Diary,* in a

covenant " not to play anywhere in public about London [for two years] but in my house." He is traceable as an actor up to 1622 and continued an active pamphleteer and playwright until the closing of the theatres in 1642, dying some five years later. Indeed, Heywood is by all odds the most productive of our old dramatists, confessing in one place in print to having had " either an entire hand or at least a main finger " in two hundred and twenty plays. This would make an average of five plays a year for forty years; and Heywood was productive otherwise. Of his dramas only some thirty-five have been preserved, and he, doubtless, would have thought that number too many; for Heywood was modest and rated his work, hastily done as it was and for the moment, at its true value. Indeed the little that we can glean as to the personal character of Heywood makes him out an estimable, scholarly but unbookish man who found in the average lives of the people about him abundant material for the smiles and tears, the pathos and the tragic emotions that make up the life of prince and beggar alike. Among the many cheap generalisations of this generalising age of ours, it is not uncommon to find remarks on what is called " the feudalism " of Shakespeare's age, the emergence of man as an individual somewhere in the later history of our fiction and other like things. A slight acquaintance with Heywood and the domestic drama might correct much of this; though, un-happily, anything but a superficial acquaintance with the past is disdained by these forward generalising members of the race.

Heywood's most important play is *A Woman Killed with Kindness,* printed in 1607. In several respects this drama is a remarkable departure from the traditions of its time. The theme of the major plot is that of " an ingrate friend and a wife unchaste," a situation almost precisely paralleled in two other plays of Heywood, the Jane Shore story of *Edward IV* and *The English Traveller*. It is familiar that the code of the day demanded violence at such a juncture. Heywood dared to solve the problem in a manner novel to his time, separating the unhappy wife from the husband whom she had wronged and from their children, and suffering even the seducer to go the victim of his own remorse. Not only does the story thus rise to the dignity and pathos of tragedy, but all is accomplished without the usual extraneous aids of bloodshed and terror. *A Woman Killed with Kindness* is constructed with a care and the plot developed with a skill beyond Heywood's usual power.

Nor did he surpass this success in the interesting recurrence to a similar theme in *The English Traveller,* notwithstanding the creation therein of the character of young Geraldine, described by Lamb as " one of the truest gentlemen of Elizabethan drama." In this matter of character, as is his treatment of incident and dialogue, Heywood is so natural, so unobtrusive, so truly modest in his art that we cease to wonder at an effect so easily accomplished. It is impossible to better the words of Lamb as to this admirable man and dramatist. " Heywood's ambition seems to have been confined to the pleasure of hearing the players speak his lines while he lived. It does not appear that he contemplated the possibility of being read by after ages. What a slender pittance of fame was motive sufficient to the production of such plays! . . . Posterity is bound to take care that a writer loses nothing by such a noble modesty." [3]

To the category of domestic drama belong the two slightly earlier plays entitled *The Honest Whore,* the joint work of Dekker and Middleton, however their scene is transferred after the current practice of the time to an imaginary Italy. The first of these two plays was on the stage about 1603, and the second part must have followed, as is usual in such cases, soon after. Here is told the story of Bellafront, who has fallen but who is regenerated by a sincere love and is aided in her determination to lead an honest life by her own father, who has repudiated her in her evil days but now in disguise befriends her. There is no finer dramatic presentation of the eternal struggle of woman and man than this play of forbidding title, and it would be difficult to find a cleaner one or one more ethically sound. The old age was more outspoken than ours, but it was no less clear in its perceptions of right and wrong; and it may be questioned whether the gain in reticence is always a gain in true delicacy. The story of Bellafront in both her unreclaimed and in her reclaimed condition is admirably told and the character of her father, " the merry seeming Orlando Friscobaldo," with his pathos and suffering at heart, alone is enough to keep this fine drama unforgetable. A clever foil to the main story is that of Candido, the enduring husband and his mischievous, teasing wife, a palpable take-off on the popular theme of patient Griselda. Indeed, the age was far from unappreciative of the comic possibilities of subjects such as these.

[3] *Specimens of English Dramatic Poets,* i, 130.

Have we not seen the repugnant dispositions of man and woman, the theme for the struggles of Noah and his wife, about to enter the ark, and one of the common topics of interludes which precisians would have us label "made in France"? The shrew is at least as old as the patient wife; and it is not altogether certain which Cain found for a wife in the land of Nod. A comedy entitled *The Taming a Shrew* was on the stage as early as the coming of the Armada, and it was this old play, still extant and to read, that Shakespeare made over in combination, with an underplot from Gascoigne's *Supposes,* as *The Taming of the Shrew,* about 1597. In both forms the play was an ever popular success and in due time was followed by a sequel, *The Tamer Tamed,* the composition of John Fletcher, wherein is told how Katharina dying soon, as the reformed are apt to do, is succeeded by the redoubtable Maria who turns the tables completely on Petruchio and solves the question once and for all in a manner the cleverness of which may be commended to her younger militant sisters.

We have found gravity of subject and a clear moral purpose characteristics of several of the plays already treated in this chapter. A striking group of the domestic drama is the murder play, already exemplified above in its most successful example, *Arden of Feversham,* in print by 1592 and on the stage probably before the Armada. From titles found among the accounts of the Office of the Revels, *The Cruelty of a Stepmother* and *Murderous Michael,* 1578 and 1579, it has been surmised that the murder play was of even earlier origin, and that perhaps the latter play was another version of *Arden.*[4] We may leave these earlier plays to note, in the nineties, a revival of interest among the playwrights of Henslowe in tragedies of this type. From other sources we have reason to believe that plays of Henslowe's mention, such as *Black Bateman, Cox of Collumpton, The Stepmother's Tragedy* and *Page of Plymouth,* were of the type of the domestic murder play. Chettle, Day, Dekker, Haughton and even Jonson are named among the authors of them; but all, in dramatic form, have perished. There remain however several tragedies beside *Arden* to make clear the continuance of the type. *A Warning for Fair Women,* 1599, recently shown to be by Heywood, relates the murder of one Master George Sanders, "consented unto by his own wife,"

[4] See Wallace's "Table," *Evolution of the Drama,* p. 207.

with her trial, confession, " godly contrition " and execution.
Two Murders in One details the sordid murder of one Beech,
a chandler in Thames Street. Finding the material scant, the
author, one Yarrington, eked out the play with an alternation,
scene by scene, with the old tale of the *Babes in the Wood.*
A year or two later, saw *A Yorkshire Tragedy,* staging, as we
have seen, a recent murder, and published, in 1608, as " by
Wm. Sh.," one of the many efforts of the dishonest publishers
of Shakespeare's day to profit by his name. Although this
short play is exceedingly well written and imitative in places
of Shakespeare's manner, we may feel sure that his pen was not
concerned in it. *A Yorkshire Tragedy* was acted by Shakespeare's company and so was *A Warning for Fair Women,* a
matter of wonder when we recall that these were the years of
The Merry Wives, Much Ado and *As You Like It.* The age,
be it remembered, was as robust as it was catholic, and theatrical
success, then as now, depended not alone on the verdict of the
judicious (as Jonson called those who appreciated his own
plays), but on the acclaim of the groundling whose many pence
far outweighed the gentlemen's half crowns. It is a comfort to
know that nothing so execrably bad as Yarrington's *Two Murders* was ever acted at the Globe or at the Blackfriars. This
was one of Henslowe's plays, and doubtless we have lost little,
in *Cartwright,* the murder of a clergyman, in *The Bristol
Tragedy* or in *The Six Yeomen of the West,* wherein one
Cole comes to his death, like Barabas in Marlowe's *Jew of
Malta,* in a boiling cauldron.

In *The Yorkshire Tragedy* we have apparently the last of the
murder plays which had flourished by this time some twenty
years beside the tragedy of revenge and other serious drama
that partook more or less fully of the romantic spirit. There
were later revivals of the plays of the type, such as *The Witch
of Edmonton,* 1621, by Dekker, Ford and Rowley. Into this
interesting drama of every day life a new element enters, that
of the supernatural, for its subject, like that of *The Lancashire
Witches,* 1633, deals with witchcraft, that dangerous outcrop-
ping of the primitive superstitions that cost so many innocent
subjects of King James and his son their lives. A homelier
and more certain revival of the old-fashioned murder play is
The Vow Breaker or the Fair Maid of Clifton, by one William
Sampson, printed 1636, in which apparently we have a making
over of the old lost play of Henslowe, *The Black Bateman of*

the North. It was the homeliness of the murder play, like several of the comedies of domestic life, that preserved them from that heightening of effect by means of the imagination that we denominate the romantic, as it was their seriousness that kept out of them the levity of satire. Among the many plays that suffered neither of these deviations may be named *The Fair Maid of the Exchange,* 1602, with its interesting and novel figure, the brave cripple of Fenchurch, and *Fortune by Land and Sea,* 1607, the story of the victory of a disinherited youth over fortune and false friends. Heywood, with the help of Rowley, contrived the latter charming, natural play, and while *The Fair Maid* is not certainly his, it is after all much in his manner. *The Hog Hath Lost his Pearl, The Honest Lawyer,* and *A Cure for a Cuckold,* are all later examples of the recurrence of the homelier manner or more familiar scene of the earlier domestic drama; and all were acted within a year or two of Shakespeare's death. In the first a repulsive crime is frankly told, but allowed to lead to a reconciliation where the logic of the older drama would have demanded tragedy. In *A Cure* recurs the theme of a demand by a heartless lady that her lover kill his best friend (already employed in *The Dutch Courtesan* and *The Fair Maid of Bristow*) ; whilst in *The Honest Lawyer* by a certain "S.S." we return to country manners in the town of Bedford, despite a repetition of several well known comedy figures, the usurer, the jealous husband and the faithful wife, once more among them. The gross titles of the first and third of the plays just mentioned, each of them taken from the underplot, denote the deteriorating taste of the hour of which we shall have more to hear in later chapters.

Before we leave the domestic drama, with its homely English scene and its direct methods, we may look forward to the finest, later specimen of its type, *A Fair Quarrel* by Middleton and William Rowley, printed in 1617. The subject turns on an insult to the fair name of his mother, offered a young man, Captain Ager, at the hands of his own Colonel. A challenge, after the custom of the age, is the immediate and inevitable result. But Lady Ager, fearing for the life of her son, who has but recently returned to her, to frustrate the meeting, insinuates that perhaps the Colonel's words are not mere slander. The meeting takes place none the less; but now the young and honourable Captain, feeling that he no longer has cause for a quarrel, refuses, to the disgust of his seconds, to fight. At last the Colonel calls him a coward, and thanking God that he now has a true cause, the Captain fights and desperately wounds his antagonist. In the upshot the Colonel recovers, retracts his calumny and the virtuous Lady Ager is forgiven by her son for her desperate ruse to save him. *A Fair Quarrel* is one of the great Elizabethan plays and unequalled in the two great scenes, that of Lady Ager's struggle between her pride, her sense of honour and her terror lest she lose her beloved son, and the admirable scene of the duel. *A Fair Quarrel,* however, like *A Woman Killed with Kindness,* mixes in the underplot more or less extraneous elements. In Middleton and Rowley's play we have mere intrigue and the play, like the same two dramatist's master tragedy, *The Changeling,* becomes disappointing as a whole. It was in present questions such as these that the Elizabethan presented the problems of his time. Dare a man fight in a quarrel in which he knows that he fights to uphold a lie? Is there any conduct, save that of traditional violence, justifiable to an honourable man who has been wronged by wife and friend? And is our charity and forgiveness never to extend to fallen womanhood in that most terrible of struggles in this world, the effort to regain lost honour? These are some of the questions that the Elizabethan dramatic casuists put to their audiences, giving them again and again, with all their direct speaking and occasional grossness, answers as sound, as charitable and as satisfying as any that we, with all our refinements, have reached in our time.

Were we to continue our search for scenes of dramatic realism in the drama of the age we should have to confess that, when all is said for outlandish romance and borrowings classic and other, it is this that remains the essential fibre of the writings of the age, whether we consort with Dogberry and Verges in their very unItalian adventures of the watch, peer into the very unGreek theatrical affairs of the Athenians, Snug the Joiner and Bottom the Weaver, or hurry Danish Ophelia into a grave dug with English spade and mattock. Jonson, with all his learning of the ancients, found the warp of his drama in his contemporaries about him; and the happiest scenes and personages in the plays of Beaumont and Fletcher are those, often to be found in the inventive underplots which they had not from

Spain, France or elsewhere, but found at hand in the England that they knew so well. With this acknowledged and filed as a caveat, we need not fear to proceed.

There remains one topic properly to be considered in this connection, and that is the dramas that have to do with the contemporary beliefs in the supernatural, more especially in the manifestations of witchcraft and demonology. Fairy-lore obviously belongs elsewhere, as it was fancifully raised to a poetic potency by the genius of Shakespeare, and there is a quality of the truly imaginative about that abiding human faith that gives to those mortals who have gone before the power to return and revisit the glimpses of the moon. To grasp the effectiveness of the old and popular superstitions, we must conceive ourselves in a very different environment from our own. There was a universal belief in omens, in lucky days and in the powers of devils and witches. Comets were thought to foretell disaster and wise-men and wise-women were consulted concerning serious actions and weighty affairs. To bleed at the nose was ominous, a notion used effectively in Heywood's *Edward IV* and in *The Duchess of Malfi*. The elements foretold and sympathised with the doings of men. Not only did a lioness whelp in the streets of Rome and sheets of rain and the terrors of lightning foretell the fall of Caesar, but foul weather accompanied the witches in *Macbeth* and the familiar stage thunder preluded many a tragic event. An excellent story is told, somewhere, of a provincial performance of *Doctor Faustus* in which, when the players had come to the dance of the Seven Deadly Sins about that abandoned scholar, they looked and behold, in the whirl, there were eight. Now they knew the number of their company, all were on the boards, there could be no mistake, whereupon with one accord they fell on their knees and prayed for forgiveness and their auditors stampeded terrorstricken out of the room. These beliefs were not only the superstitions of the vulgar; the Earl of Leicester consulted the celebrated Dr. Dee as to an auspicious day for the crowning of Queen Elizabeth, and her wise councillor, Sir Francis Bacon, with all his philosophy, shared many of the popular notions of his day. Ben Jonson, too, who attacked alchemy, dared not raise his voice against witchcraft, and Reginald Scott, who wrote a lengthy treatise on the abuses of witchcraft, hesitated to deny the existence either of witches or to question their supernatural interference in the affairs of men. With superstitions such as

these universally prevalent, many a scene that we read now
merely with a curious interest must have carried a conviction
and a terror difficult for us to conceive.

We may pass by the black magic of Faustus and the white
magic of his English compeers, Peter Fable and Friar Bacon,
as already treated. A sufficient illustration, too, for our purposes, of the employment of the superstitions of devil-lore and
witchcraft in the drama may be derived from a brief consideration of several plays, involving these things and allied, as well,
to the domestic drama from their general context and realistic
treatment. The well known mediæval tale of Friar Rush, in
whom a devil is disguised and sent into the pious precincts of a
monastery to tempt the brethren, was dramatized apparently
as early as 1568. Far later, in 1610, Dekker brought out his
dramatic amplification of the story in the elaborate, though
hastily written, production, *If this be not a Good Play, the
Devil is in It*. Here no less than three devils are sent to earth
to tempt respectively the virtuous court of Naples, a supposedly
upright merchant and a monastery, as in the original tale, and
there is an attempt to apply the story to present times by the
introduction of such contemporary malefactors as Ravaillac, the
assassin of Henry IV, and Guy Fawkes. Machiavelli's
satirical *jeu d'esprit, The Marriage of Belphegor,* which has
sometimes been confused with the tale of *Friar Rush,* also
furnished material for Elizabethan playwrights. The earliest
is *Grim the Collier of Croydon,* the major plot of which details how a suicide, Spenser's Malbecco, pled before the infernal judges that he was driven in desperation to his death,
because of the outrageous wickedness of his wife; and how, the
devils doubting this, sent one of their number, Belphegor to
earth to investigate the matter, which he did with such effect
that he returned assured that there was no wickedness that any
devil could teach mankind. This extraordinary story received
a further dramatic amplification at the hands of no less a personage than Jonson, in 1616, the year of Shakespeare's death.
Such an opportunity for satire on the depravity of mankind was
not to be lost by the great dramatic satirist, but with all its
merit, *The Devil is an Ass* of Jonson is not to be reckoned
among the unquestioned successes of the author. Notwithstanding the royal acceptance of a belief in demons and the
possession of men and women by them, set forth conclusively in
King James's *Demonology* of 1597, it cannot be said that his

age believed in devils with so simple a faith as did that of his predecessor. The satirical attitude of both Dekker and Jonson, in these two devil plays, is very different from the atmosphere that pervades *Faustus*. As we turn to witchcraft, which was nearer the folk, we find another attitude. "Witches and sorcerers within these last few years," the pious Bishop Jewel solemnly adjures Elizabeth, "are marvellously increased within this your grace's realm. These eyes have seen most evident and manifest marks of their wickedness;" and he begs that "the laws, touching such malefactors, may be put in due execution." This was in Shakespeare's boyhood. Shakespeare's own attitude may be variously interpreted by his retaining the burning of Joan of Arc for a witch in his revision of the first part of *Henry VI* and his representation of the wizard, Bolingbroke, and Margery Jourdain, a witch, in the second part of the same trilogy, or by his agnostic rejection, with the good Duke Humphrey, of the impostures of Simpcox in the same play. Much use of popular demonology will be found in the maunderings of Edgar while pretending madness in *King Lear*. As to the witches in *Macbeth,* they tell us less of what Shakespeare thought about witches than of his imaginative art that could transform the obscene hags of the superstition of the countryside, with their malicious tricks and trivial wickednesses, into supernatural agencies tempting the man prone to evil to the violation of eternal law. Shakespeare did for the witches in *Macbeth* what he had already done for the fairies in *A Midsummer Night's Dream,* translated them from folk-lore into the realms of poetry and the imagination. The age followed him as to the fairies; witches were another matter, for who could know, after all, that it was safe to doubt these malevolent ministers of evil?

For a popular exposition of current beliefs as to witches, we must turn from Shakespeare to Jonson and lesser men. Jonson's witch of Papplewick, in *The Sad Shepherd,* admirably presents us this picture. She is as repulsive as she is malignant; she assumes the shape of various beasts and even of persons, and is hunted as a hare with a full cry of hounds. Unfortunately Jonson's play, which is a fragment, ends just as we are coming to a full acquaintance "with her spindle, threads and images." This minute realism Jonson gives us in his *Masque of Queen's,* the antimasque of which is sustained by a bevy of witches, equipped with all the gruesome horrors that the reading and research of their learned author could lavish upon them. For the Elizabethan witch, outside Scott's famous *Discovery of Witchcraft,* there is no such authority as Jonson. The association of Middleton's drama, *The Witch,* with the witches of *Macbeth* has already been adverted to in this book. Middleton's *Witch,* with true Renaissance confusion of ideas, is first linked on (as in our version of *Macbeth*), to the classical figure of Hecate with whom English and Scottish witches have nothing to do, and then employed to elucidate the intrigue of a romantic tale derived from Belleforest. Middleton's play is unimportant except for its association with the revision of *Macbeth.* We may conclude this matter with two late plays that involve witchcraft and hark back as well to the older domestic drama. In the first, *The Witch of Edmonton,* Dekker was assisted by William Rowley and John Ford, if indeed the latter be not a reviser, about 1620, of the other's earlier work. In the other, *The Late Lancashire Witches,* printed in 1633, Heywood was associated with Richard Brome. This latter play is a perfect mine of current witch-lore and tells the story of the transformation of a supposedly respectable housewife into a witch by night, her escapades, her injury by a stroke of her husband's sword while transformed into a cat, the discovery of her converse with evil, her trial and delivery over to justice. The story was based on actual and recent happenings, so recent indeed that it is not impossible that the play may in some wise have affected the verdict against the unfortunate Mistress Generous and her supposed confederates. In *The Witch of Edmonton* we have a drama as superior to Heywood's in its execution as it is humane in its conception of this monster misconception of the age. The story is that of a forced marriage and its consequent tragedy which, it is suggested rather than insisted, is due to supernatural agency. Mother Sawyer, the witch, is represented as a wretched poverty-stricken old woman who is driven by the heartless ill-treatment of her neighbours to her converse with evil. A demon comes to her in the shape of a black dog and surprises her in one of her fits of impotent cursing. After the usual pledges, he becomes her " familiar." It is Mother Sawyer's black dog that brushes against the legs of Young Thorney and fawns upon him at a moment when his innocent young wife has become a burden to him, thereby instilling murder into his heart. But above the homely fidelity and truth of this latest of the domestic murder plays, is to be placed its pathos and the touch of sympathy for the miserable old hag whom the persecution and uncharitableness of her neighbours has driven to extremity. This recognition of an ultimate responsibility outside of the victim of persecution is remarkable in view of the fact that the play contains no word of doubt as to Mother Sawyer's actual possession by the powers of evil. This, too, was an actual event dramatized. Could we recover them we might find, among the lost plays of Henslowe and later, many other examples of the kind.

Our pursuit of the domestic drama has carried us far afield and in point of time ahead of our object. But other influences came so thick and fast in the reign of King James to confuse the simpler elements of earlier Elizabethan drama, that it seems best to anticipate in this respect. The close alliance of many plays already treated among romantic comedies and chronicle plays especially, will not have escaped the observant reader. Such a comedy for example as Heywood's *Fair Maid of the West* was as strong in its scenes of the tavern life of the adventurers of Plymouth as in its scenes on the high seas or in romantic unknown Morocco. The essentially English fibre of our English drama can not be too strongly insisted on. With this remembered we may leave the subject.

CHAPTER VI

SHAKESPEARE, WEBSTER AND THE HEIGHT OF TRAGEDY

In any analysis which seeks the discrimination of things so complex as the products of dramatic literature, classifications will arise that seem to contradict one the other. Tragedy is after all a relative term; but aside from that, who will deny that *Richard III* is not equally a tragedy with *King Lear* or *Othello;* or *Julius Cæsar,* in the conduct of its later scenes, as much a chronicle play as *Henry V?* The tragedies of Shakespeare which are of English historical source have received their treatment in a previous chapter, and with them have been considered the dramas of like theme, the work of others, which may be grouped, it would seem not without reason, in a class referable to the common national consciousness that begot them. We proceed now to a consideration of the other tragedies of Shakespeare and his immediate contemporaries with a lively appreciation of the inadequacy of the brief treatment of these important productions which a sense of proportion none the less here demands. Leaving aside *Titus,* which we would frankly discard from the list of Shakespearean plays, *Romeo and Juliet* takes precedence in point of time, corresponding in its fervour and in the exuberance of its poetic expression with the earlier more joyous comedies. Between 1591 the supposed date of the earlier Shakespearean form of this tragedy and 1597 the alleged time of its final revision Shakespeare had widened his experience as a dramatist with at least three tragical historical plays, to say nothing of an improved technique in comedy. But the regular structure of *Romeo and Juliet,* its lyrical sweetness, its passionate sympathy with the young lovers mark it as the work of a young man. In comparison with the storm, the heat and the ingenious wickedness of Elizabethan tragedy at large there is a naturalness, a directness, an inevitableness about this world drama of youthful passion that places it forever alone. Its tone has been likened to a midsummer day in which the sun broods hot and golden in an atmosphere suffused with beauty and ominous of catastrophe and change. The beauty of Juliet, the passionate unreason of Romeo, the wit of Mercutio, even the grossness of the Nurse, seem dilated in that surcharged air. It is somewhat remarkable that Shakespeare's *Romeo and Juliet* should be the first English tragedy of note to celebrate the passion of man and woman in its purity. Previous heroines of such romance, Gismunda, for example, or Belimperia in *The Spanish Tragedy*, each has loved before and her untoward fate seems not wholly undeserved. Romeo and Juliet alone are the ill-starred lovers, mere shuttles in the loom of fate leaving a flash of colour in the sombre garment of time.

It was some three or four years after the revision of *Romeo and Juliet* that Shakespeare recurred to tragedy in his *Julius Cæsar,* and here, befitting an historical theme, he returned to a modified form of the chronicle history. In this choice of a classical subject for the popular stage it is not impossible that Shakespeare may have been aware of something like a departure; for, common as such subjects were at the universities and at court under humanist and Senecan example, the groundling of the Cross Keys or the Red Bull knew little enough of ancient history. Yet even before Shakespeare the experiment had been tried. The *Wounds of Civil War,* by Thomas Lodge, which has to do with Marius and Sulla, and the anonymous *Wars of Cyrus,* both were publicly staged and date as early as most of the chronicle plays on English history. Later, in the nineties, Heywood appears to have staged no less than five dramas dealing in a series of epic scenes that depicted ancient mythology, beginning with " the lives of Jupiter and Saturn " and concluding with " the destruction of Troy." Another of Heywood's plays tells the tragedy of Lucrece.[1] So that Shakespeare could scarcely have found an ignorant audience when he staged the latter events in the life of the greatest man of antiquity. Even the subject was not novel, there are five plays about Cæsar on record before the date of Shakespeare's, though unfortunately no one of them has survived. In *Julius Cæsar* Shakespeare had recourse to Plutarch's *Parallel Lives,* his usual authority for ancient history — some have thought it his only authority. But he has used his material with freedom as well as discretion, ex-

[1] These six plays are *The Golden Age, The Silver Age, The Brazen Age,* two plays on *The Iron Age* and *The Rape of Lucrece.*

panding here the barest hint, as in the well-known orations of
Brutus and Antony, and elsewhere inventively shaping his
story. The character of Brutus especially develops under the
dramatist's hand in dignity and power, while Cæsar, his foil and
victim, correspondingly suffers. The striking detail that makes
the conspirators pause, their dreadful deed accomplished, to
"bathe [their] hands in Cæsar's blood" is Shakespeare's and
referable to an old English custom in hunting the stag, and so
is the touching incident of the sleepy page Lucius and his lute.
The classical atmosphere of his source and his story appear to
have given to this play a certain regularity of structure and
conduct as compared with the freer specimens of contemporary
romantic art: Shakespeare, in a word, is scarcely so restrained
elsewhere. But *Julius Cæsar* presents none of the familiar
mechanical features of contemporary Senecan practice, remaining equally free from Senecan rant and moralising commonplace.

We may postpone to consideration in another place the
several like plays of closer Senecan affiliation that succeeded
Kyd's translation of Garnier's *Cornelia,* towards the end of the
reign. It may be well, however, to anticipate somewhat our
treatment of Jonson to consider here, for the sake of contrast,
his two notable tragedies of classical subject. It does not seem
altogether unlikely that Jonson's *Sejanus, his Fall,* first acted
in 1603, was written in protest against what so excellent a
classical scholar could not but have considered the careless, slip-
shod romantic manner of depicting ancient life upon the popular
stage. Jonson was one of the few men of his day likely to
have been seriously affected by the historical anachronisms in
which the plays of the time abounded. He knew and remembered, even if Shakespeare did not, that the conspirators in the
orchard of Brutus were exceedingly unlikely to be disturbed by
the striking of a clock, a device not invented until centuries
after, and that the only effect of a pistol in the hands of
Demetrius Poliorcetes, in one of the plays of Fletcher, would
be to create laughter in the knowing auditor. We have one
little scrap of Jonsonian criticism as to *Julius Cæsar.* In it he
objects not to the conduct of the play but to the wording of a
passage which does not correspond to the wording of that
passage as we have it.[2] The specific question need not detain
us here. Nor need we stop longer than to notice that the allu-

[2] As to both these matters see, *Jonson,* ed. Gifford-Cunningham,
1875, i, 272; iii, 398.

sion in the prefatory matter of *Sejanus* (as published) to "a
second pen," as present in the earlier unpublished version of
that tragedy, has been thought by some to refer to Shakespeare.
Sejanus was acted by the company to which Shakespeare belonged and soon after *Julius Cæsar,* in all probability. Moreover Shakespeare was an actor in *Sejanus,* as we know from
the published list of actors in the Jonson folios. It is not impossible that the rivalry between these two exponents of contrasted romantic and classical ideals may have worked amicably
together in an endeavour to reach a solution or a compromise,
and it was honourable in Jonson when he came to publish
his play to "have rather chosen," as he expressed it in the
preface, " to put weaker and no doubt less pleasing [numbers]
of mine own, than to defraud so happy a genius of his right by
my loathed usurpations."

Sejanus is a master study in dramatic form of the early days
of the empire, following, in the presentation of that enigmatic
personage, Tiberius, and his pampered favourite, Sejanus, the
story as presented in Tacitus and Suetonius. Jonson has succeeded here, as no less in *Catiline,* in transferring to his pages a
remarkably effective picture of ancient Rome in which not only
the historians but the ancient poets and satirists have aided in
many a stroke inappreciable except to the classically trained
reader.[3] When Jonson came to publish *Sejanus,* he cited line
and chapter in the footnotes, after the exasperating manner of
scholars, to avouch his learning. The work has not been a
success on the stage; Jonson's habitual attitude of arrogant contempt for the multitude had something to do with this. Now
his critics and rivals took up this display of scholarship, Marston
especially, in the preface to his *Sophonisba* declaring: "Know,
that I have not laboured in this poem to tie myself to relate
anything as an historian, but to enlarge everything as a poet.
To transcribe authors, quote authorities and translate Latin
prose orations into English blank-verse, hath, in this subject,
been the least aim of my studies." The taunt is unmistakable,
coming as it did, immediately after the performance of *Sejanus.*
As to Marston's contribution to this rivalry in the representation of ancient life in tragic form, indubitably he enlarged more
things as a poet than he followed as an historian. Taking his

[3] "An Anachronism ascribed to Jonson," W. B. McDaniel in *Modern Language Notes,* xxviii, 158, 159.

subject, not from the classical authorities but from that old and favourite quarry of the dramatists, Painter's *Palace of Pleasure,* the atmosphere is as romantic as the substance is pseudo-historical. None the less Marston's *Tragedy of Sophonisba* is a fine play of its type and worthy of more praise than it usually receives. It may be worth while to note that *Cæsar, Sejanus, Sophonisba* and Heywood's *Lucrece,* all were on the stage within a period of two years; while, in 1603, likewise had appeared in print Dr. Matthew Gwinne's *Nero Tragoedia Nova collecta a Tacito, Suetonio, Dione, Seneca,* a Latin college drama of no small merit. In fact it might be interesting to know more concerning Jonson's relations to the Latin college drama of his time, for Jonson was learned not only in the ancients but in their modern Latin imitators and commentators. Gwinne's tragedy is only one of several *Neros, Pompeys, Cæsars* and other academic plays of the period, Latin and English. As to the popular stage, it was between 1606 and 1610 that Shakespeare's attention was occupied with stories of ancient times; *Antony and Cleopatra, Coriolanus, Timon, Pericles* and *Cymbeline* all fall within those years. In 1611, Jonson's *Catiline, his Conspiracy* was acted, once more by the King's players. Here Jonson followed, as a main authority, the well known narrative of Sallust, by no means reaching the excellence of *Sejanus,* but presenting, especially in the comedy scenes of the fashionable wanton Fulvia and Semphronia, vain of her Greek and her dabbling in politics, admirable pictures of ancient Roman social life. It is interesting to note that in *Catiline* Jonson reverts to certain of the Senecan practices from which *Sejanus* was measurably free. The classical ideas of Jonson, his theory of drama and the like will claim a wider attention in the next chapter. It is of interest to know that Jonson wrote a tragedy on *The Fall of Mortimer,* if we may trust the fragment remaining and a synopsis of what was to follow, even more Senecan in character than *Catiline.* Tragedy was not the forte of Jonson, yet no one can read his two admirable dramas of Roman history without a renewed respect for his scholarship and his powers as a poet and a dramatist of admirable ability.

Leaving any mention here of the scattered tragedies on stories of ancient history which came later and either imitated Jonson or partook of the ruling romantic spirit of Fletcher, let us return to the succession of Shakespeare's tragedies that follow upon *Julius Cæsar. Hamlet,* by general consent the closest of these, must have been acted in the very last year of Elizabeth's reign; but the topic, as a theme for drama, was already well known at least some dozen years before and we have already heard of the association of a lost tragedy on the story with the name of Thomas Kyd. The position of Shakespeare's *Hamlet,* the greatest of world tragedies, in breadth of its artistic significance unapproached and alone, causes any discussion of its position among the minor productions of its age to seem an impertinence. Yet, historically considered, *Hamlet* is accountable like other plays and susceptible of classification with others of its kind in that orderly sequence which governs the productions of genius with no less certain laws than lesser things in other realms of human activity and thought. Thus considered, *Hamlet* is one of a series of dramas, the works of several authors, which extended from 1599 onward for a number of years and is known under the specific title, the tragedy of revenge. The earliest authentic examples of this class of plays are Kyd's lost *Hamlet* and his *Spanish Tragedy,* on the boards, as we have seen, a year or two before the Armada. Which preceded the other it is impossible to say; but the likeness of the two stories is striking. A secret crime, a perpetrator above the law, the burden on the avenger suggesting at least the unseating of his reason, the discovery (or avenging) of the crime brought about by a play within a play — all these things are not only common to both stories, but they remained, however modified and variously emphasised, recurrent notes in the entire series. The revival of the species seems referable to John Marston who placed on the stage, in 1599, a continuous drama in two parts entitled *Antonio and Mellida* and *Antonio's Revenge.* The first is a drama of Italian court intrigue, unconnected with the series except for the Hamlet-like melancholy with which the hero, Antonio, is endowed. His revenge, in the second play, is for his father's murder and consequent upon a visit of his father's ghost who discovers to Antonio " the deep damnation of his taking-off." Moreover, the revenge is finally compassed by the agency of a masque. Marston, who was born in 1576, was a young law student and partly Italian in his blood; moreover, he was something of a coxcomb in literature. In the previous year he had gained a sudden repute by a series of satires which were as strident and impudent as youth, cleverness and inexperience could make them. There is much noise, effort and talent in these

plays, with their blood, terror, yet genuine imaginative force
in places. Evidently Marston was striving hard after originality and in *Antonio's Revenge* he succeeded in outdoing the horrors of his original. It is not until 1602 that we have actual evidence of the revival of Kyd's old *Spanish Tragedy,* though certain parallels between that play as revised and *Antonio's Revenge*
point to an earlier date.[4] In 1601, at any rate, Ben Jonson was
paid for certain "additions" to Kyd's old tragedy and those
additions — some six in number — are easily traceable in the
printed editions of the play that have come down to us. Jonson's "additions" involve an increase in the meditative speculation and in the irony of the part of Hieronimo, the father who,
in *The Spanish Tragedy,* is the avenger; and they involve likewise a vivid dramatic presentation.

It was in 1603 that the earlier quarto of Shakespeare's *Hamlet*
was published. It had been registered in July 1602. The
text of this quarto is imperfect and only about half as long as
the text of the second quarto of 1604 and the slightly different
text of the folio. On this, as on all other subjects Shakespearean, the critics have fallen apart. But when we recall that
the second quarto declares in its title that the play has been
"enlarged to almost as much again as it was" and that it is
"newly imprinted . . . according to the true and perfect copy,"
it is not unreasonable to harbour serious doubts as to the
authenticity of the earlier version, if indeed it may not be a fair
surmise that it contains material which may once have formed a
part of Kyd's lost *Hamlet*.[5] Into the intricacies of this question it is impossible to enter in a work of our present limitations.
Suffice it to remark on the interesting correspondence in point of
time between Marston's *Antonio's Revenge,* acted by the Paul's
boys at their singing school late in 1599, Kyd's *Spanish Tragedy,*
revived by the Admiral's men at the Fortune with new additions by Jonson in 1600 and 1601, and Kyd's *Tragedy of
Hamlet,* revised and subsequently wholly rewritten by Shakespeare in 1602 and 1603, and acted by the Chamberlain's men
at the Globe. It was out of the heat of such contemporary
rivalry that the *Tragedy of Hamlet* as we have it was evolved

[4] See especially *Antonio and Mellida,* v. 1 and *The Spanish Tragedy,*
III. xiii. 72. Also cf. Boas, *Kyd,* p. 66.

[5] See on the general topic, C. M. Lewis, *The Genesis of Hamlet,*
1907.

and the struggle was between the veritable dramatic Titans of the age.

A larger number of " questions " have arisen out of the reading and pondering of *Hamlet* than out of any other play; and the mass of commentary goes on increasing. With a lively sense that these words must add, however inappreciably, to the heap, it seems none the less necessary to proceed whether we shall ever reach anything like a consensus of opinion as to the psychology or anything else concerning this most absorbingly interesting figure of fiction. And here is an essential first point. Hamlet is a creature of the poet's imagination, a figment of the dramatist's creation, not an historical personage. The language which Hamlet speaks is that of the art which created him; not that of the human material which forms the subject of the alienist's or the criminologist's researches. However true the dramatist's touch with nature, art is not nature nor is nature art. Another essential to keep in mind is the absolute irrelevancy of the extra-Shakespearean Hamlet, whether the monster of Saxo-Grammaticus as set forth in Belleforest's *Hystorie of Hamblet,* the distorted shadow of the German early version, *Der Bestrafte Brudermord,* or the Senecan avenger as we have some right to conclude Kyd's " Prince of Denmark " to have been.[6] Shakespeare's Hamlet, reduced to the simplest terms, is a man who has seen a ghost and Shakespeare's interest as a dramatist — and psychologist if you will — centres about the question: how would a man behave who had really seen a ghost? that is, how would a rational, honourable, capable man behave? and that in Shakespeare's time, not in ours. When, moreover, the supernatural message entailed upon him a responsibility that altered the whole aspect and tenor of his life. The story of Hamlet is not the story of a madman; Shakespeare was too good an artist for that. And I do not think that the play was written either to depict the man of thought infirm of action, or the man of action confronted with a question that required and received no thought, as some have actually argued of contrariety. *Hamlet* is the story of a man in a state of nerves, a man in whom an unexpected contact with the invisible after-world has created a tensity of emotion that

---

[6] Cf. the words of Lodge in *Wits Misery,* 1596: " The ghost which cried so miserably at the theatre like an oyster-wife, ' Hamlet revenge! ' "

sets up an incessant struggle between the calm and self-restraint that marks the normal man and the unfortunate who is " passion's slave." It is this that transforms the Prince momentarily from the courteous gentleman that he is by nature and goads him to words of rudeness and insult. He can not stand the tediousness of Polonius, so he mocks him. The untruthfulness of Ophelia drives him to anathema of the whole sex. The bombast of Laertes' grief maddens him. Another thing the sight of the ghost has done for Hamlet. With the excitation of the nerves comes a marvellously quickened perception. He sees through Rosenkrantz and Guildenstern at a glance, penetrates the deceptive devices of Polonius and the King and wrings his mother's heart unerringly to bring home to her her wickedness. He can act, too, cleverly and efficiently as in his outwitting of Rosenkrantz and Guildenstern. In a last analysis may we not discern that it was not Hamlet's hesitancy and inaction that denied to him the processes to his own revenge; but that the mockery of Fate (which rules all men) tossed him that bauble, his revenge, before it could have fallen logically and by his own act, within his reach?

But the story of the tragedy of revenge is not yet all told. Aside from several titles of plays now lost, there was Chettle's *Tragedy of Hoffman or a Revenge for a Father* which corresponds in point of time with Shakespeare's *Hamlet* as it strives to outdo its supernatural horrors; and there is Chapman's *Revenge of Bussy D'Ambois* (a far finer play and the continuation of an earlier drama on the same hero), in which, far more unmistakably than is Hamlet, the man of thought is thrust into a place of action. Chapman's *Revenge* was published later, in 1608, but before that date had appeared the two lurid and effective plays commonly attributed to Cyril Tourneur, *The Atheist's Revenge* and *The Revenger's Tragedy* in both of which we reach alike the height of the melodrama and the extremity of the exaggeration of the species. Of Tourneur little is known save that he was the relative of Captain Richard Turner, "water bailiff of Brill," and apparently held a like semi-military office in the Low Countries. *The Atheist's Tragedy* alone contains his name on the title page and a difference in diction, conduct of plot and ideal of life has raised a question as to Tourneur's authorship of *The Revenger's Tragedy*. Both plays, however, agree in the stridency of their melodramatic art, however the latter surpasses the former, as it transcends most of its species, in its mastery of ingenious horror. To compare these lurid pictures of the depth of human depravity and ravening passion with Shakespeare is as unjust as it is inevitable. We may neglect Chettle and remain consolable that time has left only *The Tragedy of Hoffman* of the fifty plays in which he had at least a finger. With Chapman and Tourneur we are in the presence of stronger men, for neither their art, their poetry, nor their power to realise their terrible scenes is for a moment to be denied. *The Revenger's Tragedy* of the latter with Webster's *White Devil,* of which more below, stand almost alone among Elizabethan romantic tragedies in the supremacy of their dramatic realisation of the wickedness and debauchery that characterised the Italy of the Renaissance.

Kindred in scene and general source to these tragedies of revenge is *Othello* which disputes with *Macbeth* a place immediately following *Hamlet,* about 1604. The transformation which Shakespeare has wrought in the sordid, dismal and protracted novel of Cinthio, from which the tale is ultimately derived, should alone be sufficient to refute the statement, sometimes made, that the great poet was not a creative genius of the first order. It might almost be said that the beautiful name, Desdemona, was the only poetical thing to be found in the old story; everything else — the light-headedness of Cassio, the dignity and noble suffering of Othello, the subtle malignity of Iago — all are the inventions of the dramatist, to say nothing of the conduct of a plot as cleverly knit as it is naturally unfolded. *Othello* is the arch-tragedy of jealous passion, the more terrible in that the Moor is not by nature suspicious nor prone to evil imaginings. Iago is the arch-villain of all literature, for his villainy is wanton and gratuitous and his victim the man who has loved and trusted him. It is impossible to regard Iago's foul suggestions in this respect otherwise than as the baseless fabrications of a malignant mind; just as any mitigation of the " sooty bosom " of the Moor in the interests of modern race-prejudice destroys the veritable cause out of which the tragedy of this amazing marriage was inevitably to spring. However pitiful the catastrophe, Shakespeare never sinks to the despairing pessimism of our modern conception of human tragedy that leaves man, innocent or guilty, the sport of an impersonal fate in which a hideous apathy has usurped the place of the comprehensible Greek envy of the gods. Desdemona, lovely and innocent, even in thought, of Iago's devilish insinuation, had been none the less an undutiful daughter, bringing her father's white head literally in sorrow to the grave, and Othello, for his credulousness as well as want of faith, might serve for argument in this regard to one less subtle than a casuist.   In a word, the catastrophe of Othello and Desdemona is not unjustifiable in an orderly world such as most men persist to believe in, nor could anything save disaster be predicted for so ill-sorted, so hasty and so ill-advised a union.   Indeed, whatever the niceties of our distinctions between æsthetic and ethical values in the realms of art, it is their coincidence after all that marks the supreme artistic creations of man.

There is a passage in *Macbeth* that has caused some to suppose that it followed hard upon *Hamlet*.[7]   Whatever the fact, in the matter of text no two works could be in greater contrast. Not only have we for *Macbeth* no quarto, only the folio, but the text seems mutilated and interpolated in parts with alien material, some of which, especially the speeches of Hecate and the attending dialogue, have been found in a play of Middleton already adverted to called *The Witch*.   Not unlikely the version that we have is one that suffered later revision.   This would account for the fact that *Macbeth* is one of the shortest of the tragedies, besides explaining certain inconsistencies in the conduct of the story.   In *Macbeth* Shakespeare returned, as is well known, to Holinshed's *Chronicles* for his materials, using them, however faithfully to the bare fact, with that imaginative freedom that transformed the vulgar, meddlesome witches of Scottish folk-lore into a supernatural embodiment of human temptation to evil with its attendant, supernatural terrors. Whatever the explanation, nothing could be in greater contrast than the leisurely development of situation in character in Hamlet and this swift, lucid and vigorous story of the degeneration of a loyal thane into a cruel and infatuated tyrant, tenfold more interesting for the intrepid, devoted and equally infatuated figure of Lady Macbeth, whose ambition was the fruit of her love for her husband, not, like Macbeth's, the spur of vulgar, personal aggrandisement.

Close to *Macbeth,* perhaps even before it, came *King Lear.* *Lear* like *Macbeth* follows the old chronicles, but with far greater freedom and with the almost certain intervention of an older drama known as *The History of King Leir*.   This was

7 See *Macbeth*, i. 7. 10-12.

acted, according to Henslowe, in 1594, registered in that year
and printed, so far as we know, for the first time in 1605.
This publication of an old play with the false statement, " as
it was lately acted," marks a clear attempt on the part of a
piratical publisher to palm off a spurious production as Shakespeare's, a misrepresentation which was responded to in un-
equivocal terms on the title page of the quarto of 1608. " *Mr.
William Shakespeare his True Chronicle History of the Life
and Death of King Lear.*" Shakespearean innovations on the
sources are the conversion of the drama into a tragedy, the
banishment and disguise of Kent, the creation of the fool and
the addition of the underplot of Gloucester and his two sons
derived from an episode in Sir Philip Sidney's *Arcadia*. But
little does this tell of the transformation of a pleasing and pathetic comedy of no very serious import into this stupendous and
torrential tragedy of the irrational, imperious Lear, the strident,
unfilial daughters and their sweet-voiced, womanly sister, Cordelia, the faithful Kent and the sad-eyed clown — all etched
into the picture on the background of an elemental war of nature with the mordant acid of tragic genius. In *Macbeth* and
King Lear, as in the lesser tragedies of *Coriolanus* and *Timon
of Athens,* there is a higher unity of passion that preserves each
drama in its own essential key. As *Macbeth* is the tragedy of
murderous royal ambition and *Lear* the cataclysm that follows
on human folly, however regal its masquerade and pathetic its
consequences, so *Timon* is the tragedy of misanthropy and
Coriolanus that of arrogant, self-willed pride. It is not the
least of the merits of Shakespeare that in no one of these cases
has the attribute obscured the individuality of the hero. The
minor position of these two latter plays is referable to other
reasons. *Timon* is of uncertain date and there is nothing to
show that it was ever acted during Shakespeare's lifetime.
Moreover, the text is unequal and it has been doubted if it is
wholly his. *Coriolanus,* on the other hand, is certainly Shakespeare's and the latest of the tragedies, in all likelihood, as to
composition; but it, too, was badly printed and external evidence as to its composition and acting is altogether wanting.
Yet *Coriolanus* in its major portraiture of the egotistic, self-
willed hero, the patrician Roman matron, Volumnia, his mother,
and admirable, garrulous old Menenius, is not unworthy of its
place beside the other Roman plays of Shakespeare. It may be
doubted if the spirit of old Rome is better preserved in either of

the greater plays, to say nothing of the many dramas by Shake-speare's contemporaries — always excepting Jonson — that lay their scenes in the august capitol of the imperial city of antiquity.

There remains *Antony and Cleopatra,* if we are to judge by the Stationers' Register, on the stage by 1608, although unpublished until its appearance in the folio. Here, as in *Julius Cæsar,* Shakespeare's immediate source was Plutarch whom he followed with even more than his customary fidelity, however he succeeded in his usual amazing transformation of his material into something possessed of a new artistic organism. Seldom has the æsthetic acumen of Coleridge so completely forsaken him as when he advises that *Antony and Cleopatra* "be perused in mental contrast with *Romeo and Juliet,*— as the love of passion and appetite opposed to the love of affection and instinct." And nothing could be more admirable than the late Dr. Furness's refutation of this idea.[8] In this great tragedy even more than in the case of some others are we prone to confuse the figures of the diverse kinds of fiction that we call history, drama and poetry. The impression which any cultivated man retains of an important personage in history is at best a composite of the reading that has happened to be his, superimposed on tradition and, we may add, modified by his own personal prejudices. This is why we often have such difficulties with Shakespeare's historical characters, reading into them extraneous matters and distorting the significance of his text. To Shakespeare the love of Antony and Cleopatra was no mere vulgar liaison between a sensualist conqueror and a royal trull, intriguing to postpone the inevitable collapse of a degenerate dynasty. Nor was the story, as Dryden heroically conceived it, a struggle between unlawful love and forfeited honour for the restoration of Antony's peace of soul. To Shakespeare the all important thing was the personality of his characters. What must have been the fascination of Cleopatra thus to have won to his destruction the greatest captain of his age? And what must have been this great love for what Antony conceived his honour, his life, the world well lost? Such a love Shakespeare knew could not be wholly ignoble, hence while he never for one moment condones this heroic infringement of accepted moral law, he compels us to see how heroic, after all, it is and how

[8] Cf. the New Variorum ed. of *Antony and Cleopatra,* 1907, p. xiv.

inconceivable it would be to form so lofty a structure on mere sensuality and moral degeneracy.

Shakespeare's chronological range in tragedy extends from the year 1590 at earliest, when *The Spanish Tragedy* and *Arden of Feversham* were new to the stage, to 1609, before the Fletcherian dramatic compromise, known as tragicomedy, had come into popularity. Shakespeare's competitors in tragedy during this period were many and discrimination as to their activities is not always easy. There were, first of all, Kyd and Marlowe, already sufficiently treated, whose plays maintained their hold upon the stage for a generation despite the deaths of both in the early nineties. In these years tragedies derived from English history — *Edward II, Richard III, Edward IV* — appear to have held the popular voice against romantic tragedy, to be followed by a temporary interest in topics derived from Roman history. This we have already found exemplified in several fine dramas by Shakespeare and others, especially Jonson who endeavoured to compromise between the extravagance and inconsistency of romantic art and a slavish following, on the other hand, of Senecan traditions. Another, perhaps more immediate, outgrowth of the chronicle play is the extension of its method to subjects derived from foreign modern history. So far as we know, Marlowe's *Massacre at Paris,* 1593, was the first important drama of this particular species, and it was Marlowe's example that turned the attention of George Chapman to the tragic possibilities of contemporary French history in the plays of the brothers D'Ambois, the Duke of Byron and Chabot. About Chapman and his comedies of manners we shall hear more below; we have met him already as a writer of serious romantic comedies not unaffected by the contemporary example of Shakespeare. We have found, too, *The Revenge of Bussy D'Ambois* in its place among the tragedies of revenge. The informing spirit of this play, as of *Bussy D'Ambois,* its predecessor in the series of Chapman's French tragedies, is romantic. Bussy is an upstart courtier and bravo raised by the whim of Monsieur, brother to the king, to a favour and acceptance at court that gives full vent to Bussy's intolerable egotism. In the end he falls traitorously, if morally justly enough, by the hand that raised him. But no mere recital such as this could make clear the mingled excellencies and defects of Chapman's remarkable work. Chapman, as became the translator of Homer in a romantic age, has the grand heroic manner.

In his diction the rhetorical tone, which he caught from the prevailing Senecan influence of his time, is often raised to a higher power by his sheer poetry. As we read *Bussy D'Ambois* we are struck again and again with Chapman's wisdom, his mastery of the phrase, his imaginative eloquence; as we lay down the play we wonder that a course so devious and apparently without design could have compassed a dramatic effect so complete and lasting. Nor would an estimate involving some such ideas be less applicable to Chapman's other historical tragedies. The two plays on Charles, Duke of Byron, appear to have been acted soon after *The Revenge of Bussy* about 1608. In all, the atmosphere of political intrigue in an elegant but corrupt court is preserved with excellent fidelity, and the personages of contemporary neighbouring France are represented so faithfully, at times so scandalously, that we hear of a remonstrance from the French ambassador at London and of the arrest of several of the actors concerned. Chapman later protested vigorously against the ruling of Sir George Buc who excised certain passages of *Byron* when license to print was requested. Indeed one of these plays remains to us in its mutilated condition, a proof of the effective censorship which King James exacted where political allusion was concerned. The fifth of Chapman's historical tragedies is *Chabot, Admiral of France*. In the version that remains to us this fine tragedy was revised by the skilful dramatic hand of Shirley, at some time in the early sixteen thirties. The theme is both novel and interesting; it concerns an honourable and upright servant of his king who dies broken-hearted because of his sovereign's suspicion and mistrust, the result of the machinations of his enemies. While less imaginative and uncontrolled than Chapman's earlier work in this kind, Shirley has made out of Chapman's material by far the best drama of the series. It seems unwise to include either *Revenge for Honour* or *Alphonsus of Germany* among the works of Chapman. The former is a tragedy of Turkish court life and the work of Henry Glapthorne; the latter a play not impossibly of the revenge series, but alike indeterminable as to date and authorship. It has attracted the attention of German scholars from its German story and the circumstance that in it is to be found considerable quotation in the language of the fatherland.

Other employment of French history came later, save, perhaps, for the rough and ready product of the playhouse, *The*

Noble Spanish Soldier by Dekker and Samuel Rowley, from its similar subject in parts and from the nature of its allusions to the court of King Henry IV probably of a date not far from that of Chapman's two plays on Byron. Wiser than their predecessor, the joint authors of *The Noble Spanish Soldier* evaded the pains and penalties of contemporary allusion by transforming the scene of their drama to Spain and making a tragedy out of events that had not reached, in their reality in Henry's court, so serious a termination. Not dissimilar was the device afterwards pursued by Fletcher and Massinger in *Thierry and Theodoret,* 1617, not improbably a revision of an early play of other authorship, known in 1597 under the title *" Branhowlte,"* Henslowe's approximation to *Brunhalt.* Here, once more, it has been thought that contemporary happenings in the neighbouring court of France were staged under the disguise of a story of Merovingian times. The play itself is powerful and forbidding, and a favourable specimen of the Fletcherian art of dramatic contrast. Scarcely less forcible is *The Bloody Brother or Rollo Duke or Normandy,* variously dated between 1606 and 1624 and the work of several hands, Fletcher, William Rowley and Jonson supposedly among them. But no such duke apparently disgraces the annals of historical Normandy.

But France was not the only modern country to lend historic material to Elizabethan dramatic treatment on the stage. The diversity of tragic scene, as of comic, was to a large degree accidental, the subject-matter of our old plays commonly grouping for other reasons than these. Thus the tragedy of revenge gives us Italian Antonio, French D'Ambois, German Hoffman and Danish Hamlet; and it began in a Spanish Hieronimo. Besides the famous play of Kyd, Greene's *Alphonsus of Aragon* and Peele's *Battle of Alcazar* touch on material more or less historically Spanish, to say nothing of *The Spanish Moor's Tragedy,* referred to the authorship of Dekker, Haughton and Day in 1600, and perhaps *Lust's Dominion,* printed as Marlowe's in 1657. This play is certainly not Marlowe's; it is a shameless following of *Titus Andronicus* especially in the figures of " the lascivious queen " (the alternate title) and of Eleazer the Moor who at once recall Tamora the Gothic queen of *Titus* and Aaron, her paramour. Towards the end of the reign of King James, Spanish subjects, for political and other reasons, came into great request. To these we shall return; for the present it is enough to note that in the year 1619, William Rowley's *All's Lost by Lust* was acted, a tragedy of remarkable frankness and effectiveness, in which is told the famous old story of Spanish ballad literature, that of *El Rey Rodrigo*, the last Christian King of Spain, and his fall before the treacherous King of Barbary. We have met with William Rowley as an alleged collaborator with Shakespeare in *The Birth of Merlin;* we shall meet him again, especially in his dramatic association with Middleton. William Rowley is distinguishable from his namesake, Samuel Rowley, whose name does not appear in *Henslowe's Diary*. William has been described as "beloved by those great men Shakespeare, Fletcher and Jonson." He was the junior of the youngest of these by several years. His collaborations were numerous and with many different playwrights.

Of tragedies the scene of which is German, Chettle's *Hoffman* and the anonymous *Alphonsus of Germany* have already been mentioned. The marriage of the king's daughter Elizabeth to Frederick, the Elector Palatine, in 1613, is responsible for a mediocre play, entitled *The Hector of Germany or the Palsgrave Prince Elector* by Wentworth Smith, a busy minor poet in Henslowe's employ. The extravagance of the wanderings of the Hector from history and over the face of Europe need not concern us. A point of interest is the circumstance that the tragedy was acted at the Red Bull Theatre, not by professional players but by a troupe of "young men of the city." When all has been said, however, it was Italy that figured to the Elizabethan imagination, in tragedy as elsewhere, as the golden land of romance. Personages of Italian history appear in the titles of many plays from *The Duke of Milan and the Duke of Mantua*, in 1579, to *Macchiavelli,* the *Medici, Pope Joan* and others of Henslowe's mention in the nineties. An exceedingly effective tragedy of Italian quasi-historical character is *The Devil's Charter* by Barnabe Barnes, the Italianate sonneteer and lyrist. Here is told the life and terrible death of the wicked Pope Alexander VI and the story is correlated to the Faustus cycle by assuming the papal success in worldliness and wickedness the result of a compact with the devil. In a finely conceived, if melodramatic climax, the dying Pope catches at a curtain which conceals from him the future and, tearing it apart, beholds enthroned in all the regalia of priestly pomp and seated in the chair of St. Peter, Satan himself. *The Devil's Charter* was acted by the King's company in 1606.

With our return to Italy we have returned to romantic tragedy. The years 1609 to 1612 gave to the stage four great dramas in which woman is represented in the deadly perversion that brings destruction to man. The first of these in point of time is Fletcher's powerful *The Maid's Tragedy* which from its relations to his tragicomedies is best treated below; the latest was *The Insatiate Countess,* printed as Marston's, in 1612, and perhaps not wholly his. The subject, " the difference betwixt the love of courtesan and a wife," Marston had already treated with effect in his comedy, *The Dutch Courtesan.* Both plays belong, in a sense, to the domestic drama, and the tragedy, in its terrible picture of the career of a veritable queen of wantons, however it horrify, for its subject cannot but be commended for its vigorous art. Middleton's *Women Beware Women,* acted about 1612, is neither less forbidding in subject nor inferior in dramatic power. This tragedy tells the story of a recent Italian scandal, that concerning Francesco de' Medici and his abandoned mistress, Bianca Capello. In his underplot Middleton touches the foul topic of incest, maintaining here, as in his comedies, his repute as the most veritable realist of his age. The fourth of these tragedies of misguided and perverted womanhood is Webster's *The White Devil,* the dramatization of a recent *cause celèbre,* the outcome of another scandal in Italian high life.

Of John Webster very little is known save that " he was born free of the Merchant Tailors' Company " and was a fellow-worker with Dekker, Middleton and Marston. His earliest work, now no longer extant, belongs to the very last years of Elizabeth's reign. Thereafter he was concerned in something less than a score of plays and pageants, comprising historical drama such as *Sir Thomas Wyatt,* comedies of manners and intrigue like *Westward Ho* and *Northward Ho,* and classical tragedy represented in *Appius and Virginia.* Of the several comedies doubtfully attributed to Webster at least in part, it is unnecessary to speak here. Webster is remembered in the history of English literature for one thing and that is for his extraordinary power in romantic tragedy, alike in the creation of character and in the skilful handling of material; and his two masterpieces are *The White Devil* and *The Duchess of Malfi,* both acted before 1612. In the first we have the story of the infatuation of the Duke of Brachiano for the beautiful Vittoria Corombona, his murder of her husband and his own wife at the instigation of Vittoria, their subsequent trial, flight and marriage with the vengeance of the brother of the late Duchess on the guilty pair. The radiant beauty of Vittoria pervades the play and, conscious though we are at all times of her abandonment to passion and her calculating cunning when brought to her defence, we too feel the fascination that perverted her judges and the spectators at her trial. Scarcely less effective are the figures of the profligate Brachiano, of Flamineo, the cynical pander to his own sister's shame, and the distracted mother of these extraordinary and brilliant creatures of vice. *The Duchess of Malfi,* which is usually regarded as the later play, preserves the same atmosphere of intrigue and counter intrigue in the ducal courts of Italy and portrays, in the " Arragonian brothers " and in their creature Bosola, three of the most consummate portraits within the range of our drama. Bosola the intelligencer, depraved, discontented, absolutely clear-sighted as to his wicked acts and their consequences, unvisited by compunction in his cruelty yet smitten with remorse in disappointment of his reward,— such a villain is worthy to stand beside Iago himself. Above all in her beauty and pathetic fate, stands the Duchess of Malfi, victim of unparalleled indignities, losing all, husband, children, life itself, yet victor over the machinations of her wicked brothers against her in her equally unparalleled fortitude. In depicting the ingenious horrors with which the half-crazed Ferdinand tortures his unhappy sister of Malfi in the vain endeavour to break her unconquerable spirit, Webster proclaims himself our master poet in the domain of the terrible. Sustained as is all by a competent diction, a power over language and illuminated by single lines of flashing genius, Webster takes his place for these two tragedies as second only to the master poet himself.

We have seen how popular romantic tragedy was affected from the first by the example of Seneca, the cult of whose tragedies, beginning at court with the reign of the queen, was extended to the playhouses of the city by such men as Peele and Kyd. But Kyd was author not only of *The Spanish Tragedy,* which was Seneca popularised for the vulgar, but also of a translation of Robert Garnier's *Cornélie* which, though unsuccessful on the stage, led to a series of academic dramas imitative of the Roman tragedian in a new solution, this time French. Recent investigation into the sources of Elizabethan literature tend to show that the age was affected by the literature of France far more and much more directly than has hitherto been accepted. The Elizabethan lyric turns out, for example, to be extensively imitative of that contemporary in France and many a story, formerly imagined to have come to England directly from Italy or Spain, has been shown to have arrived by way of the same intermediary.[9] French Seneca, as we may call this small group of tragedies, centres about the Countess of Pembroke and her immediate circle. As early as 1590 the Countess herself had translated Garnier's *Antonie,* preserving the lofty tone, the frigidity and stately air of her original; and Kyd's *Cornelia,* as well as his projected translation of another tragedy of Garnier, his *Porcie,* which was not completed, both are referable to this impetus. The rest of the group include several original tragedies by Daniel, Brandon and Sir Fulke Greville, all of them falling, in point of date of composition, within the last ten or twelve years of Elizabeth's reign. A little later, Sir William Alexander, afterwards Earl of Stirling, brings up the rear with his *Monarchic Tragedies,* 1603 to 1607, whether as an actual intimate of this noble literary circle or as an imitator of its achievements may be left in question.

By far the most important person in this group was Samuel Daniel, to be recorded recognition in any history of the literature of the time for many estimable qualities as a man and a poet. Daniel was the son of a musician and born in 1562. His education he had at Oxford, beginning his career as a poet as early as 1584 with his graceful Italiante sonnets to Delia, the first series to follow in the wake of Sidney's famous *Astrophel and Stella.* While chronicle plays were holding the stage, Daniel wrote his narrative poem, *The History of the Civil War,* which enjoyed like other productions of its class, Warner's *Albion's England,* and Drayton's *The Baron's War,* for example, a greater popularity in its day than its merits now appear to warrant. It was later, in the reign of King James, that Daniel gained further literary laurels for his masques and pastoral dramas. And it was then that Jonson's enmity overtook him. In the interim came his two contributions to " French Seneca," *Cleopatra,* 1594, and *Philotas,* 1600. There is eloquence, choice diction and much poetical spirit in both these

[9] See especially Sir Sidney Lee, *The French Renaissance in England,* 1910.

tragedies. More, there is a queenly grace and dignity about the figure of Cleopatra, here represented in the heroic resolve of her last hours, that the reader remembers with pleasure; but neither production is truly dramatic, nor, with all his talent, was the dramatist in Daniel. We read with interest that there was some fear on the part of the author lest his *Philotas,* the story of a young noble, full of pride, and outspoken in criticism of his sovereign, Alexander, might be held to touch " too nearly the like story of the Earl of Essex, in this very year disgraced and on trial for his foolish and disloyal outburst against his queen. A similar fear caused Greville to destroy the manuscript of a play of his on Antony and Cleopatra. Clearly more importance was attached to the words of courtiers and scholars than to the treatment of historical topics by the poets or common players. Innuendo and " dark writing " was one of the accepted arts of the time and what those within the precincts of the court might say, was a thing of moment. Samuel Brandon's *Virtuous Octavia,* 1599, is by no means devoid of merit though chiefly interesting here for its subject taken in conjunction with the efforts on the story of the same hero by Lady Pembroke, Daniel and Greville. Of Brandon personally nothing is known.

In turning to the extant tragedies of Fulke Greville we meet with work of a higher order. Greville was the boyhood friend of Sir Philip Sidney and born in the same year. Like Sidney he enjoyed the personal favour of his queen whose memory with that of his friend he embalmed, years after, in one of the sincerest and choicest of Elizabethan books, Greville's *Life of Sir Philip Sidney.* Greville became an important councillor of King James under his later title, Lord Brooke, and, as owner of Warwick Castle, dispensed noble hospitality in his day. He lived to an advanced age being finally murdered by a servant in 1628. The two plays of Greville are *Alaham,* written about 1600, and *Mustapha,* probably some five or six years later. We have here evidently works of maturity, very different from the efforts of young literary men like Daniel and Brandon in intent and based alike on a wider reading and a wider experience in life. Indeed it may be questioned if the particular dramatic form in which these dramas were cast was more than accident, the author taking the mode current in his own circle and concerning himself not at all about anything outside. In story these tragedies draw on material as remote as possible, one would think, from contemporary interest. The scene of

Alaham is laid in "the kingdom of Ormus," *Mustapha* is drawn from the history of the Ottomans, not impossibly from Knollys' *General History of the Turks,* a new book at the accession of King James. Both are stories of palace intrigue, of malevolent ambition, noble fortitude and suffering under cruel infliction. Moreover, both are exceedingly original in conduct, in conception of personage though almost parallel in plot. But for none of these things were these tragedies written. Greville declares for us his intention, in them as in his poetical *"Treatises"* on government, ambition and other like themes, to be " to trace out the highways of ambitious governours, and to show in the practice, that the more audacity, advantage and good success such sovereigns have, the more they hasten to their own desolation and ruin." These tragedies differ from all the dramas of their age in existing for a speculative, not an artistic or merely moral, purpose. Greville is not alone in abstract moralising, Daniel did that in this group of plays before him and Stirling especially after; nor is Greville alone in writing for a purpose ulterior to the artistic one, that was common enough. Greville is conspicuous in the purely intellectual processes of his art and in the extraordinary logic of his Stoicism, which causes him to regard all human activity, whether virtuous or depraved, as varieties of folly; the only true wisdom is patience. It was this, with some misapprehension as to the dramatic purpose of certain utterances that led to the notion that Greville was irreligious. His tragedies are the most truly philosophical of their time, for they exist for their speculative thought and thus presage such modern productions as Goethe's *Faust* and Browning's *Sordello*. The amazing thing about them is that the circumstance that their personages stand out with a vividness and an individuality little to be expected in work of such a design, and that passage after passage is sustained by sheer poetry. With Stirling's four *Monarchic Tragedies, Darius, Croesus, Cæsar* and *The Alexandrean Tragedy,* variously published between 1603 and 1607, and outlying productions such as *The Tragedy of Mariam* by Lady Elizabeth Carew and *Cynthia's Revenge* by one John Stephen, these two latter printed in 1613, the tale of French Seneca comes to an end. Stirling's dramas are not without a certain historical value; Stephen's, in its obscurity, allegory and bombast, may be pronounced the most intolerable of Elizabethan plays. We may add that it seems unlikely that any of these dramas were written for acting either privately or at court. All observe a more or less minute attention to the technical processes of the drama of Garnier, the brothers La Taille, and Grévin and rhyme, in couplets or alternately employed, abounds in the dialogue. It may be doubted if this series of exotic imitations had any effect whatever on the popular stage, unless it may have been to call attention to classical subjects; and of these on the popular stage enough has been said.

Our tale of Elizabethan tragedy at its height is told; but there are some things that we may gather up by way of summary. Of the fifty or more tragedies which have been mentioned in this chapter, it is somewhat surprising to find nearly half referable to ancient story, however a proportion of those on the popular stage were romantically conceived and presented. The place which Kyd and Marlowe take as theme-givers to English tragedy is notable. The former's *Spanish Tragedy* and *Hamlet* led to the line of the tragedies of revenge, and *Tamburlaine* started the war drama or conqueror play and, through Greene's *Selimus* and the like, the group of plays on eastern subjects. To the Elizabethan the annals of the Turk were of a very live interest, for it was only the Battle of Lepanto in 1571, that put a stop to Ottoman aggression in Europe. Hence popular dramas like Peele's lost *Turkish Mahomet,* scraps of which are quoted with *Tamburlaine* by Ancient Pistol; and hence rude melodramas such as *Mulleasses the Turk,* 1607, by one John Mason, and the lurid Turkish tragedies of Thomas Goffe. To return to the influences on tragedy, it can hardly have been merely an accident that Kyd's *Cornelia* in 1592 and Marlowe's *Dido,* in the next year, should have been followed on Henslowe's stage by a *Cæsar and Pompey* and a "second part of *Cæsar;*" while Marlowe's inspiration of the French histories of Chapman appears as certain as inference from historical material can ever be. Tragedy on classical subjects is as old as the drama. Such plays existed at the universities, as we have seen, and as Bower's *Appius and Virginia,* 1563, and Geddes' *Cæsar,* in 1582, with many other examples, attest. The new infusion of Senecanism from France we have sufficiently examined. Its courtier cultivators were oblivious of the popular drama; though it is not so certain that the playwrights of the London theatres may not have turned to topics derived from ancient history partly because of these literary efforts at court. Certainly when Shakespeare tried his hand at

Julius Cæsar, Henslowe's poets, in this case described as " Munday, Drayton, Webster and the rest," responded almost immediately with *Cæsar's Fall;* and Jonson, Heywood and Marston put forth, soon after, each his rival tragedy in this kind,
Chapman following a little later with his *Cæsar and Pompey,*
a production not worthy his great name.   The rivalry went on,
rising to its height in *Antony and Cleopatra,* and closing in
Coriolanus, 1608, and in Jonson's *Catiline,* 1611. Of the
tragedy of revenge no more need be said. Shakespeare's *Lear*
and *Macbeth* hark back to earlier times, for each is, in a sense,
a glorified chronicle play. *Romeo and Juliet* and *Othello* belong to the general class of romantic tragedy founded on Italian
story and differ from their kind mainly in the individualism of
their art, what genius has wrought above their species. Save
for Chapman's definite group of historical dramas touching
French history, only one remaining group stands notably forth
among the various themes of the tragedies of the days of James;
and this is the terrible series which details the life of the noble
harlot, beginning with *Titus* and *Lust's Dominion,* which has
been attributed to Marlowe, and including *The White Devil*
of Webster, Middleton's *Women Beware Women* and Marston's *Insatiate Countess.* An atmosphere more or less historical dominates some of the remaining dramas, *The Noble
Spanish Soldier* and *All's Lost by Lust* for example; others rise,
like *The Duchess of Malfi,* in their artistic isolation above the
circumstantiality of fact. To the writing of these tragedies
during a period of some twenty years was brought the genius
and the talents of a score of writers at court, in the universities
and especially on the public stage. And their theories of
tragedy were no less diverse than their stations in life, their
learning and their opportunities. Assuredly the disparity between the learned Dr. Gwinne of Oxford, ransacking Tacitus,
Suetonius and Dio Cassius accurately to write his Latin
Nero and Samuel Rowley, dramatizing a contemporary scandal
of the French court, disguised as a " Spanish story," is as great
as that between Webster, intent on a faithful and artistic
picturing of the deeper passions that animate and ruin mankind,
and Greville, oblivious to all save a vivid illustration of his
theory of speculative stoicism. And the variety of this drama
is equally great, ranging from the rhetorical frigidity of Daniel
to Jonson's vigorous historical portraiture, and from the significant poetry of Chapman and Shakespeare's masterful grasp

down to the melodramatic extravagances of Chettle, Mason and Goffe. The range of this wonderful musical instrument, Elizabethan drama, is always amazing, as often as we are beguiled to listen to the rich, full harmony of its music in master hands. There has been no age in which, proportionate to the population, so many wrote dramas, and there has been none in which so large a number of these rose above respectability to a memorable excellence. The new age was to care more for the horrors of tragedy than for its significance. Up to within a few years of Shakespeare's death there was still no form of the drama which carried such an artistic weight and message, none in which we meet with a deeper philosophy or with more imperishable poetry.

CHAPTER VII

JONSON AND THE CLASSICAL AND SATIRICAL
REACTION

WE know more about Ben Jonson than about any other literary
man of his age; and barring Shakespeare, Jonson is by far the
most significant literary figure of his time. A posthumous son,
born in Westminster, some nine years after Shakespeare, Jonson
survived to long outlive his friend and carry the authority of
his name and the sanction of his dramatic practices into the reign
of King Charles. Jonson died in 1637, long the victim of ill
health and a certain amount of neglect at court. We have
now to chronicle his palmier days. Jonson "was brought up
poorly," his mother having remarried and beneath her, a brick
layer; calumny even whispered that Jonson had at some time
exercised his step-father's trade. But the antiquary Camden,
then an usher at Westminster School, befriended Jonson and he
received his schooling there, though unable afterwards to proceed to either university. Degrees he had later from both
"by their favour not his study," and it is interesting to think
of the academic world of those times so honouring a purely
literary man. Jonson married quite as imprudently as Shakespeare and when almost as young. Thereafter he went abroad
and "trailed a pike" in Flanders, on one occasion, as he delighted to tell, singling out a champion from among the enemy,
calling him forth, and killing him in sight of both armies.
He returned from Flanders penniless, and had recourse, like
many another, to Henslowe's mart in the drama. This must
have been about 1595 or a year later. At any rate Henslowe's
entries show, as to Jonson, at first called familiarly "Benjamin," the usual course of apprenticeship, the revision and
refashioning of old plays when revived, collaboration with others
and general services about the playhouse. There are contra-
dictory traditions as to Jonson as an actor. We have no list
in which his name so figures, as we have in the case of Shakespeare. He was taxed by his enemies with having once played

the part of Hieronimo in *The Spanish Tragedy;* but it is unlikely that he ever made much of a success. He was a raw-
boned lad and later became corpulent, and he describes himself
in later life as possessed of " a mountain belly and a rocky
face." By 1598 Jonson had begun, however, to receive
recognition, for he is mentioned in that year by the pragmatic
Meres as one of " our best in tragedy." The earliest work of
Jonson has perished. Henslowe named however three tragedies,
Page of Plymouth, a murder play, *King Robert II of Scotland*
and *Richard Crookback,* these latter clearly contributions to
the current chronicle plays. Only a sketch of the last remains;
the others were written in collaboration; all of them fall later
than the mention of Meres. Jonson was sensitive about these
experiments of his nonage and appears to have succeeded in
covering up his earlier footsteps towards success. Only *The
Case is Altered,* a comedy of romantic type, not unaffected by
Shakespeare, remains of these early efforts, and of this Jonson
never acknowledged his authorship.

In the autumn of 1598 Jonson's pugnacity of disposition resulted in a duel in Hogsdon Fields in which he again killed his
man, a fellow player and by all accounts something of a bravo,
named Gabriel Spencer. The prevalence of duelling in Elizabethan England needs no comment for him who knows Elizabethan plays. But it was one thing for noblemen and gentlemen
so to defend their honour and settle their differences; it was an
impertinent assumption of gentility on the part of a common
player. Accordingly Jonson was tried at Old Bailey, convicted
and sent to prison, and such possessions as he had " were forfeited." Indeed, Jonson only escaped the gallows by pleading
the benefit of clergy and was branded on the thumb with a " T,"
for Tyburn, to commemorate that escape. While in prison
Jonson became a Roman Catholic, a form of religion that he
afterwards abjured to return to the faith of England. On his
release, which seems to have been speedy enough, Jonson offered
his services to the Chamberlain's men, in which company
Shakespeare was now a leading shareholder. And here falls
the pleasing story first related, it is believed, by Betterton:
that Jonson, departing with the manuscript of *Every Man in
his Humour,* refused by the reader, was recalled by Shakespeare
who himself read his play and reversed the decision of the company. Whatever the truth of this tradition, Jonson's comedy
was accepted and acted within the year, 1598, Shakespeare tak-

ing one of the parts. *Every Man in his Humour* made the reputation of Jonson. This first success is commonly reckoned an epoch-making play, for in it the poet set forth in practice certain very definite theories concerning English comedy which were his. Jonson was an observer of the life about him as well as a student of the past. He desired to compass a satirical picture of contemporary life presented vividly and amusingly, and to do this with a becoming regard for the practice of comedy as exemplified in the best classical models. The plot of *Every Man in his Humour* is exceedingly simple: an intercepted letter reveals to a father that his supposedly studious son is really somewhat of a gallant; the father follows the son to the city and their adventures with the personages they meet, together with those of their knavish servant, Brainworm, who follows both on his own account, form the fabric of the plot. The novelty of the comedy lies in the conception of the personages, each governed by some salient trait or characteristic. Brainworm with his passion for "gulling everybody," gulled in the end himself, Bobadil, eager to appear the supreme duellist though, unfortunately for his ambition, at heart a coward; Knowell, Downright, their very names, as often in Jonson, betray them. Now, to this kind of thing, Jonson gave — or at least gave popular currency to — the term a "humour," defining it as a ruling trait or bias of character such as determines the customary attitude and habitual conduct of the personage possessing it. He especially reprobated the abuse of the word to signify some trivial peculiarity or mannerism of costume or speech, a significance to which the term was subsequently sometimes degraded.

A satirical representation of life on the stage was of course no new thing. The elder drama was full of it, though never systemized as here. But this simplification of complex human nature to a leading typical trait was only a part of the poet's more general theory. Jonson was a classicist, that is, one who believes not only in the sanction and precedent of the ancients in literature and art, but one who believes in the restraint and respect for precedent which a study of former art should inspire. Jonson objected especially to the extravagance and unprofessional spirit of Renaissance poetry and drama. He believed that there was a professional and responsible way of doing all these things and that example for much of it can be found in the practices of ancient Greek and Roman authors. What

Jonson did not believe — however ignorant misrepresentation of his own time or later may affirm it — was that the salvation of English literature was to be found in slavishly following classical ways. " I see not," he says " but we should enjoy the same license, or free power to illustrate and heighten our inventions, as they [the ancients] did; and not be tied to those strict and regular forms which the niceness of a few, who are nothing but form, would thrust upon us."[1] His theories Jonson held to through a reasonable and triumphant practice of some forty years, standing manfully in a position counter to the extravagant romantic trend of his age. And in the end the age came around to him. In poetry at large Jonson exercised a more powerful influence on his time than did any other author, not even excepting Shakespeare and Spenser, and it was Jonson's ideals and practices that led on logically to Dryden and Pope. As to immediate effect on the drama of his own time, the Jonsonian " humour " became the rage. Jonson followed up his own success with a play of companion title, *Every Man Out of his Humour,* and later completed the cycle of his dramatic work with *The Magnetic Lady or Humours Reconciled.* There was Chapman's *Humorous Day's Mirth* in the same year with Jonson's second *Humour,* an inferior anonymous comedy, in 1600, called *Every Woman in her Humour,* and Day, a few years later, named one of his sprightly comedies *Humour Out of Breath.* More important than titles, Chapman and several lesser men came wholly over to Jonson's manner of writing comedy by way of humour and even Shakespeare disdained not to employ the method in personages such as Bardolph and Pistol, in Dr. Caius and his group in *The Merry Wives* and in the " humorous " Scotch, Welch and Irish captains of *Henry V.* In Falstaff and Malvolio we have Shakespeare's most serious efforts to model dramatic character along the line of Jonsonian humorous simplicity. We can conceive of Falstaff or even of Malvolio under situations different from those which surround them in the dramas of which they are a part; it is difficult to think of Captain Bobadil, outside of the entertaining scenes of *Every Man in his Humour.* Shakespeare's genius even in shackles transcended the ingenious art of Jonson.

With the success of his " comedy of humours," Jonson turned his attention determinedly in the direction of dramatic satire.

[1] See *Every Man in his Humour,* " Induction."

Jonson was always sure of himself; and, however generous to his intimates, he was arrogantly contemptuous of the great multitude amongst whom he included all whom he had not personally chosen to be of the number of his friends. As he looked about him, towards the end of the year 1598, flushed with success, three persons especially attracted his satirical attentions and for reasons not altogether accidental. There was John Marston, two years his junior, recently from Oxford, author of several plays, in his new book, *The Scourge of Villainy* proclaiming himself a satirist, and quite as opinionated and self-satisfied as Jonson himself. Secondly, there was Samuel Daniel, of whom we have also heard, the accepted entertainer of the court, Italianate, fashionable and effeminate — or at least so Jonson thought him — turning sonnets in the manner of Petrarch whom Jonson despised, and writing drama in the manner of Garnier whom Jonson did not understand, on easy terms, moreover, with great people, and these as yet Jonson did not know. Lastly, there was Anthony Munday, pageant master to the city, translator of romances, and collaborator with anybody in anything theatrical or other. These men in particular Jonson attacked in the three dramatic satires which form his contributions to what Dekker called the "*poetomachia*" and later critics have dubbed "the war of the theatres." It is interesting to note as to Jonson's personal ambitions respecting two of these men, that he became in later years chronologer of the city of London, a better post than that of pageant-poet, and that he also became poet laureate and the accepted entertainer of the court in a larger sense than Daniel had ever conceived the latter.

Jonson's three famous dramatic satires are *Every Man Out of his Humour,* acted by the Chamberlain's men in 1599, *Cynthia's Revels, or the Fountain of Self-Love,* and *The Poetaster, or his Arraignment,* following in the two successive years, and acted, not by the Chamberlain's men, but by the children of the royal chapel: the change of company is significant. However the opinions of individual investigators may diverge, all must agree that in these plays Jonson satirized several of his fellow poets in terms as unmistakable as they are vigorous, though the three dramas may be differentiated as devoted more or less ostensibly to an attack respectively upon the follies of citizen life, of the court and of the poets. The causes, origin and the details of the conduct of this "war" must remain obscure from the nature of things, although much has been done to elucidate the subject.[2] We may feel reasonably sure that Jonson and Marston were the principals and that Dekker was later called in as a mercenary, so to speak, contributing only *Satiromastix* to the fray. According to Jonson, the whole thing began outside the drama in certain satirical allusions of Marston's to Jonson in the former's *Scourge of Villainy;* and Marston's dramatic contributions to the quarrel have been found in *Histriomastix,* 1599, an allegorical drama of heterogeneous contents which he made over, in a romantic comedy of intrigue called *Jack Drum's Entertainment,* 1600, which Marston never acknowledged, and in parts of *Antonio and Mellida* which falls likewise within these years. On the other hand, there are epigrams of Jonson, variously charging one "playwright" (supposed to mean Marston) with cowardice, scurrility and plagiarism. Jonson told Drummond that "he had many quarrels with Marston [and that he] beat him and took his pistol from him." But, when all is said, we must not take these, valorous dramatic combatants too seriously. Two or three years later found Marston and Jonson in amicable collaboration with Chapman in an excellent comedy, *Eastward Ho,* and in 1604, Marston printed his *Malcontent* with a dedication "to Benjamin Jonson, that most grave and graceful poet, his very candid and beloved friend."

To return to the dramatic satires, Jonson's method is simple and direct. The story in these three plays counts for very little, although the successive episodes are made sufficiently interesting to hold the reader's attention and, we may surmise, far more certainly that of the auditor, when the matter was fresh. It is in his matchless power of satiric characterisation and in the brilliant, humorous, allusive dialogue with which all is clothed, that Jonson shines above all his competitors and justifies his title, the English Aristophanes. We can understand the contemporary success of these plays in the hands of the competent fellows of Shakespeare and in those of the clever lads that acted them; we can understand, too, how the town must have acclaimed the "war" and went about from playhouse to playhouse to hear how Marston would take off Jonson or "what

[2] The best account of the whole matter is that of J. H. Penniman in the Introduction to his edition of *Poetaster* and *Satiromastix, Belles Lettres Series,* Boston, 1913.

Jonson could say now?" We can likewise comprehend how,
towards the end, the town wearied of Jonson's arrogance and
self-righteousness — witness the almost incredible portrait of
himself which he draws in Asper-Macilente in *Every Man out
of his Humour* — how even the very wealth of his eloquence
was his undoing, and the palm of victory was awarded, by his
capricious hearers, to Dekker for his *Satiromastix,* a warmed-
over performance, inferior to the least of Jonson's.

Into the particulars of the "war" and especially into the
quagmire of personal identification there is happily no need for
us to trespass. In *The Poetaster,* Jonson lampooned the inferior poets of the day whose "petulant styles," he declares, had
"provoked" him for years "on the stage." The parable is
that of the virtuous Horace and his friend Virgil at Rome, with
their incomparable talents and impeccable perfections in the
high light of contrast with the envy, stupidity and spleen of the
poetasters, their natural enemies. In a climax more diverting
than elegant, Marston-Crispinus is represented as cured of his
"tumorous heats" of calumny against Horace by certain pills
"of the whitest kind of hellebore" which, acting after their
kind, relieve him with some struggling of his affected vocabulary and work an absolute cure. Dekker worked up the reply
of his *Satiromastix* by a parody of Jonson's subject, uniting its
Roman scene very inartificially with a species of chronicle play
of the time of William Rufus which he appears to have had by
him. The grossness of his workmanship in this case is best
discerned in his degradation of Jonson's braggart Tucca into a
scurrilous bravo. Many interesting surmises have been in-
dulged in as to Shakespeare's probable attitude among these
broils; and some have surmised that he is intended in Virgil,
the presiding judge of Jonson's court of the poets. Others
have given this place of honour to Jonson's known "friend and
lover," Chapman. There is a famous allusion to the "war"
in an academic play called *The Return from Parnassus,* acted
at Cambridge in 1602 in which occurs this much-quoted passage:
"Why here's our fellow Shakespeare puts them all down; aye,
and Ben Jonson too. O that Ben Jonson is a pestilent fellow!
he brought up Horace giving the poets a pill, but our fellow
Shakespeare hath given him a purge that made him bewray his
credit." And the question arises was Shakespeare's "purge" a
play? and if so, what play? Some have thought it enigmatic
Troilus and Cressida, the significance, we must fear, to be dis-

cerned only as in a glass darkly. Others have more wisely given up the matter. Shakespeare's comment on the "war," which, be it remembered, had come latterly to be a match between the adult players and the children's company of the queen's chapel, is contained in Hamlet's remarks to Rosenkranz. After hearing of the success of "the little eyasses," and the terrors of those whom they had lampooned, his thought is only for the little actor's welfare and he declares that "their writers do them wrong to make them exclaim against their own succession," that is, imperil their future as players by thus falling out with the adult fellow-members of the profession. Was it because of Shakespeare's disapproval of the excesses of this dramatic warfare that after *Every Man Out of his Humour* Jonson transferred his satires to the boy players? *Satiromastix* was acted by the Chamberlain's men and therefore with Shakespeare's approval. Perhaps, after all, it was Dekker's play that was the "purge" wherewith Shakespeare "put down" Jonson.

And now Jonson turned his attention elsewhere, as we have already seen, in his "additions" to *The Spanish Tragedy,* which fall within the year 1602, and to the composition of *Sejanus,* acted by Shakespeare's company in 1603. This fine tragedy, in its relations to the series of dramas on classical historical subjects, we have sufficiently discussed in the last chapter. It may be repeated here for emphasis that in his tragedies, no less than in his comedies, do the theories of Jonson fall into contrast with the prevalent romantic ideals of his day; and that these theories, however they were grounded in a recognition of the importance and weight to be attached to the example of the ancients, became reasonable, in Jonson's application of them to what he recognised as conditions far other than those governing ancient times. And now an even more important immediate interest absorbed Jonson. In the later, declining years of the old queen, the shadow of her successor in the north began to fall upon English affairs. It was this that armed the abortive Essex rebellion and cast suspicion on the literary tragedies of Daniel and Greville. After the acting of *Richard II,* by actors of the Shakespeare company, to inspirit the Essex conspirators, one Lawrence Fletcher visited King James in Scotland with a troupe of English actors and was cordially received. Fletcher was not a member of the Chamberlain's company on his first visit to Scotland in 1599; we are not quite so sure about his status on a second trip, in 1601. At any rate, in May 1603 letters patent were issued wherein it appears that the Lord Chamberlain's company had now become "the King's servants" and three names head the list of actors, Lawrence Fletcher, William Shakespeare and Richard Burbage.[3] By this thrifty piece of forethought Shakespeare and his fellows preserved their prestige in the new reign. Under such conditions it is not surprising that Jonson likewise should have bestirred himself. We do not know the means by which he received an introduction to King James, but we find Jonson in rivalry with Daniel in the entertainments of welcome tendered to the new sovereign on his royal progress from Scotland to assume his English crown; and he was also the author, with others, of entertainments celebrating the king's entry into London. This was a turning point in Jonson's career. His activities were henceforth divided between the court and the theatre; to the former with the author let us first turn.

The entertainments of royalty smacked of the dramatic from time immemorial. We have heard of the dialogue form given to speeches of royal welcome by Lydgate in the fifteenth century and of the development of the dramatic element in the hands of Heywood into the interlude, forerunner of domestic farce and comedy. It is out of an even earlier form of entertainment that the masque, properly so called, arose, and this was the disguising or mumming, a usual pastime very early at court and referable, if we are to seek deep enough in the past, to some of the most primitive of the customs of the folk. It might be easier, as well as more logical, to trace out the growth of such an entertainer of royalty as Cornish in Henry VIII's court, for example, from the occasional minstrel, whose songs, mimicry and inventive pageantry amused Henry's mediæval predecessors, than to find in his devices of masking, speech and costume any close relation to true drama. It was to supervise these things and the dialogues and interludes that grew with them that the office of the revels was raised from an occasional function in times of festival into a permanent organisation which provided not only for the entertainment of the sovereign in his court and on progress, but which came in time to superintend the drama at large. The records, moreover, go to show that

[3] The text of this interesting document has often been printed, see Hazlitt, *English Drama*, 38-40.

masquing, mumming and disguisings in all their varieties were as common among the people in mediæval times as at court.   Indeed, it is only the place and circumstance of their performance, their greater elaboration and their occasional rise into the categories of drama and poetry that account for our knowing so much about the entertainments at court.

In number, variety, elaboration and poetic beauty the masques of Jonson surpass those of all others, and but for him the species need hardly be chronicled at the hands of the historian of English drama.   By the time that Jonson came to write them, the nature of court entertainments had been fairly well determined, though few, except Gascoigne, Sidney, Campion and Daniel had done anything memorable in this lesser form of the drama. A masque, to be technical, is one of several species of quasi-dramatic productions of which an " entertainment," in its strict Elizabethan sense, and a " barriers" are two others.   The nucleus of an " entertainment " is a speech of welcome; the nucleus of a " barriers " is a mock tournament.   The " masque " exists only because of a dance, as a setting, or frame, so to speak, for what we should designate a ball.   These terms were used with precision by Jonson and most of his contemporaries. All involve more or less the dramatic elements of personification, costume, dialogue, music and scenic setting, although the masque alone of the three (save for one or two of Jonson's efforts) became dramatically effective.   But the masque needs a closer definition than this; for however it be made up of " a combination in variable proportions of speech, dance and song, its essential feature is a group of dancers, eight, twelve or sixteen, called the masquers.   These neither speak nor sing, but make an imposing show " by their fine presence, their gorgeous costumes and artistic posing, grouping and evolutions." [4]   These last, which always involve dancing, are premeditated and rehearsed, and they are known as the " entry," the " mean " and the " going out."   The unpremeditated dances, joined in by the auditors as well as the masquers, are known as the " revels " and include galliards, corantos and lavoltas, the popular dances of the day.   The masquers were always gentlemen, and often ladies of the court; both were usually of high rank.   There is no record that Queen Elizabeth, though proud of her dancing, ever took a part personally in any such entertainment.   And

[4] Evans, *The English Masque,* 1897, p. xxxiv.

indeed these technical niceties in the masque came to their maturity late in her reign. But her father, Henry, had been a confirmed masquer in the mummings of his time, and Elizabeth's successor, Queen Anne of Denmark, the wife of King James, delighted in masques, taking part herself with a bevy of her court ladies or witnessing the stately dancing and noble bearing of her sons, Prince Henry and Prince Charles, in the parts which they also took at times.

The pageantry and sumptuous costuming of the masque is as old as the middle ages. The dances, save for greater ingenuity and inventiveness, were not much changed. An obvious symbolism, too, was no new thing. The developments which mark the Jacobean masque are its superior scenic representation, a matter referable to the talents of the King's architect, Inigo Jones, who had been abroad and profited no little by his sojourn and study in Italy; and its enhanced poetic and dramatic qualities in which Jonson led all his fellows.

When Jonson turned his attention to the writing of masques, at the beginning of King James's reign, he found the general form well established in such productions as *The Masque of Proteus* by the lyrist Francis Davison and Campion, the musician, 1595. In Daniel's *Vision of the Twelve Goddesses,* 1604, the first masque of the new reign, we have the symbolism — so characteristic of those entertainments — for example, a temple of Peace, erected on the four firm pillars signifying the virtues that support the globe of earth; we have likewise the classical allusion and allegory in the familiar figures of goddesses and virtues —" Juno in a sky colour mantle . . . figured with peacock's feathers, Sibylla," decked as a nun " in black upon white," together with song and fitting verse. Jonson observed that what was wanted was the infusion of life and dramatic spirit into this sort of thing, and to this task he devoted his attention, devising for this purpose especially the antimasque by means of which he was able to maintain the element of humour and comic relief and to add the professional entertainer to the masquers, though keeping the two carefully apart. This raised the artistic standard of the masque without disturbing the formal parts and gave the poet endless opportunity to exercise his ingenious learning as well as his admirable poetic taste.

The masques of Jonson range from his *Masque of Blackness* at the opening of 1605 to *Chloridia* in February, 1631. All were presented at court, generally before the king, with careful and painstaking rehearsal and elaboration and often at great expense. Jonson wrote a few other masques even later, so that if we include his several entertainments of welcome to the king in 1603, his activity as a writer in this general kind extended over more than thirty years, summing up a total of no less than thirty-five pieces, twenty-three of them strictly masques. Indeed, the sum total of all other masques, those of Campion, Daniel, Marston, Chapman, Beaumont, Browne, Townsend and others, his contemporaries, scarcely equal, the half of his; and in Jonson's masques alone do we find, habitually united, drama, invention and poetry. In the earliest group of them, *The Masque of Queens,* 1609, stands out conspicuous for its happy solution of the many questions which must have arisen as to the antimasque. The contrast here is effected by a bevy of witches who, rushing forth out of " an ugly hell which flaming beneath smoked unto the top of the roof," go through a series of grotesque dances, songs and gyrations until driven away to their dark abode by the lady masquers, radiant in their glittering " house of fame," and personating, each appropriately habited, the famous queens of history from Penthesilea and Boadicea to " Bel-Anna," royal spouse of King James who alone needed neither mask nor disguise. Jonson's earlier *Masque of Blackness* began a new fashion, that of setting the end of the presence-chamber with a scene in perspective and changing it. In this case a wood was succeeded by a scene of the sea, in which billows rose and fell, and the masquers arrived in a concave shell. In *Hymenaei,* the masque which celebrated the ill-omened marriage of the young Earl of Essex with Lady Frances, daughter of the Earl of Sussex, the lady masquers descended on clouds, ushered by Iris and her rainbow, and the gentlemen represented an allegory of " humours and affections," issuing from a microcosm or golden globe, figuring man, so arranged as to hang apparently in mid-air among clouds and turn on an invisible axle. In this masque, Jonson's poetry is at its highest level, especially in the exquisite " Epithalamion " with which the whole concludes. In a rival masque of Campion, in the next year, a feature was the extent and choiceness of the music.[5] But at this time, Daniel was still Jonson's chief rival and his *Tethys' Festival,* 1610, was a sumptuous masque offering the novelties of three changes of scene (one involving

[5] *Masque at the Marriage of Lord Hayes,* celebrated at Whitehall, 1607.

ships moving on the sea), of gold and silver framings for the scene, artificial fountains and moving lights, the last so devised as to mask the changes of scene. Nor is Daniel's poetry unworthy of these gorgeous settings which, rising in expense to £1600, surpassed all that had gone before.

Into the inventive intricacies of Jonson's masques it is impossible to go at any length in a book of this size. In *Love Freed from Ignorance,* for example, Cupid, bound and beset by fools and follies, is rescued by the Muses. *Oberon the Fairy Prince* is preceded by a lively antimasque, conducted by several satyrs; and in *Love Restored,* the antimasque becomes a piece of realistic farce in which Robin Goodfellow satirically tells of the difficulties to be encountered by a plain man in his endeavours to gain access to a masque. It was the custom to publish the more important royal masques individually and soon after the event. With a zest in which his own taste coincided with that of his sovereign, Jonson was wont, in these publications not only to describe the action as well as print the text, but to discourse, most learnedly and with exact references, concerning his classical sources and authorities. Indeed never has there been so complete a union of poetry and curious learning in one man as in Jonson, though it is always to be recalled that it was Jonson's pedantry and his coarser humour — for Jonson is a very Rabelais at times in this respect — rather than his poetry that received the sanction and admiration of his gross and learned royal master.

It was in 1613, on the occasion of the marriage of the Princess Elizabeth to the Palsgrave, that the Jacobean masque reached its height. Jonson, for some reason unknown, did not write a masque to celebrate this event; but Campion, Chapman and Beaumont vied, each with the other, in three of the most elaborate productions of this kind of which we have any record. Campion's was called *The Lord's Masque.* For it Jones devised four changes of scene, and it contained two antimasques, together with novel musical effects worthy of the excellent quality of its poetry. Chapman's is a portentous effort. It was presented by the gentlemen of the Middle Temple and Lincoln's Inn and, according to Chapman's own indignant confession, was not a success, although preceded by a procession in which hundreds of people took part. The Inner Temple and Gray's Inn followed, the next day, with Beaumont's masque which was borne from Winchester House by water in a gallant flotilla, as their rivals in the study of the law had come by land. This masque had to be postponed by reason of the fagged condition of the court after several days of revelry; but it was finally given with success. Beaumont wrote his masque as a member of the Inner Temple, not as a hired poet; and it was "financed," as we might put it, by Sir Francis Bacon, then solicitor general, for the honour of Gray's Inn where he had his legal education. Bacon's interest in court entertainments was of long standing and is declared, besides this, in the devising of dumb shows for a Senecan tragedy as far back as 1587, in the writing of " speeches " for the *Gesta Grayorum* of 1595, and in the furnishing out of *The Masque of Flowers,* in 1614, at a cost of £2000. The dramatic activity of Bacon lies wholly within the precincts of Gray's Inn. His essay *Of Masques and Triumphs* should be carefully read by those who would know at first hand the great man's opinions of " these toyes," and his wise and worldly observations on their practical utility in that great game for worldly advancement that he played all his life, only to lose his stakes in the end.

With the new year, 1615, Jonson was once more established, the chief writer of masques for the court, and from *Mercury Vindicated from the Alchemists* to *The Fortunate Isles,* written to celebrate the betrothal of Prince Charles to Henrietta Maria, Twelfth Night, 1624, and the last of Jonson's masques in the reign of King James, no important celebration occurred at court without the poet's helping hand. In two or three of these productions, Jonson made so much of the antimasque that the masque itself practically disappears. *The Masque of Christmas,* for example, is pure drollery; in it figure such personages as Carol, Wassel, Minced-pie and Venus, described as " a deaf tire-woman "; while *The Masque of Gipsies,* which hugely delighted the king and was twice repeated at his request, is mere whimsicality and horseplay, however clever, when it is not worse. In this period, too, Jonson fell out with his old friend and coadjutor, Inigo Jones, declaring to Drummond that " when he wanted to express the greatest villain in the world, he would call him an Inigo." We do not know the reasons for this quarrel or its patching up and subsequent outbreaks. It was certainly regrettable; and towards the end, Jones appears to have used his influence at court against Jonson when the old poet was sorely in need of subsistence. One masque, not Jonson's, deserves mention in this place for its poetic beauty and a certain cogency of subject-matter, too rare in these occasional poems.   This is *Ulysses and Circe,* the work of William Browne of Tavistock, the Spenserian pastoralist and lyrist. This, too, was a masque of the Inner Temple, of which Browne was a member, and it was acted by the templars in 1615.

In leaving the Jacobean masque, we must keep in mind its occasional character and the temporary conditions to which it was fitted.   With the light and colour of performance, august court setting and cogent contemporary allusions, all gone and lost to us, we can only wonder that so much of literary interest should survive.   We find throughout, a persistence of allegory which admonishes us of the continuity of English dramatic taste from the morality of mediæval days.   The allegory of the masque, however, is always artistic, even in Jonson it is rarely tinged with the didactic; and, outside of Chapman's one effort and some minor exceptions, it was simple and comprehensible without effort or study.   Another characteristic of the Jacobean masque is its profuse employment and continued adhesion to classical allusions and personages, for the most part obvious to the cultivated man, however a sealed book to the unlettered. We might readily, in this, overestimate the culture prevalent in the court of King James, did we not remember that all education came, in those days, by way of the classics and recall that the use of such imagery and example was a settled mannerism of the time.   Lastly, it is not to be denied that the elaborate setting and *mise en scene* of the masque much affected the contemporary drama.   The plays from 1608 or 1610 on are full of "masques": the "antic dance of twelve satyrs" in *The Winter's Tale,* the betrothal masque with its classical goddesses in *The Tempest,* besides the antimasque in the same play of "strange shapes," to mention no others.   *The Two Noble Kinsmen* appears to have borrowed the idea of Beaumont's antimasque in his *Masque* of 1613, including the taborer, the bavian and five wenches with their morris dance. Far more important was the effect of the masque on the staging of popular plays, although of this we have less evidence than we should like and the most notable effects come later.

Leaving the masque of King Charles's time to the future and going back to the regular drama, in the year 1605, Jonson returned to the writing of comedy with his new court prestige about him.   To this he was not improbably drawn by the current success of Thomas Middleton in his vivacious and satirical comedies of London life. We have already met with the localized comedy of the city as represented in Dekker's *Shoemakers' Holiday,* that buoyant picturing of the tradesman's daily life dashed with romance, and with the lively personages of comedies such as the *Two Angry Women of Abington.* Middleton's art is of a somewhat different type. He is as realistic as any of his predecessors; if question on this score arise, he may be declared the most realistic of Elizabethan writers of comedy; but his attitude, while invariably falling short of that of the moralist, is inevitably that of the satirist. In this last he is at one with Jonson; but Jonson was nothing if not a moralist. Perhaps we may best put it thus: Dekker is a realist seeking often with kindliness of spirit or his dash of romance to lighten the inevitable sadness that follows the knowing of things human as they actually are. Middleton is a man of the world, cynical about realities, without being in the least concerned to improve them. Jonson's is the moralist's point of view, outraged by the prevalence of folly and evil, attacking them valorously, bitterly disclosing the incongruities of human professions, tempered in his zeal only by his passionate admiration for intellect and intellectual cleverness. Out of these aspects of life came three kinds of comedy — though the lines that distinguish them are not to be drawn too sharply: the comedy of every day life, life seen and delineated simply; the comedy of that same life, viewed more or less satirically, best known as the comedy of manners, and Jonson's variety of this last, the comedy of humours in which more than in the others is the method that of caricature and the impetus the moralist's *scaeva indignatio.*

Thomas Middleton was a slightly older man than Jonson. Educated at Cambridge and at Gray's Inn, Middleton was rather better bred than Dekker and Heywood and to all appearances, less a victim of bohemianism and poverty. The range of his work includes pamphlets and city-pageants as well as dramas and even masques. He began his theatrical career toward the end of Elizabeth's reign and with Henslowe in association with Munday, Webster and Dekker; and he joined the last, in 1604, in an entertainment to the newly arrived king. Not impossibly it was his conjunction with the same dramatist, in *The Honest Whore,* that brought Middleton into

repute, though several of his plays have been dated earlier.[6]
The most striking event in the dramatist's life was the performance of his notorious political satire, *The Game at Chess,*
in 1624, some three years before his death. Prince Charles
had just returned with Buckingham from a fruitless errand
to Spain in search of a wife, and Spanish pride, delay and
subterfuge had at last forced even King James to recede from
his darling project, an alliance with Spain. At this moment,
Middleton placed his satire on the stage in which, under the
disguise of a game between the white English chessmen and the
black Spaniards, not only were ambassadors and dignitaries of
the church figured forth, but the royalty of both countries.
Such " an indiscretion " was not to go unnoticed. On complaint
of the Spanish ambassador the play was " stayed " the actors
summoned before the privy council and severally reprimanded.
Middleton himself only escaped arrest by contriving " not to
be found." It has been doubted if the English court was really
as displeased as appears by the records. But we return to the
earlier and more distinctive work of Middleton. His comedies
of manners range from *Michaelmas Term* in 1604 to *No Wit
no Help like a Woman's,* 1613, and exactly correspond with
Jonson's period of renewed activity in comedy. The features
of the Middletonian comedy of London manners — besides the
two just mentioned, *A Trick to Catch the Old One, A Mad
World My Masters, Your Five Gallants, A Chaste Maid
in Cheapside* for example — are remarkably constant. Certain
figures recur with a regularity as certain as their variety is unexpected. The dissolute heir, going the pace, excellent at heart
but guilty of much that needs forgiveness, the hard, niggardly
usurer, tricky, vicious and generally overreached, the raw college lad who knows little of books and far less of the world, the
clever, intriguing Abigail, none too virtuous herself and serving
a merry open-hearted heroine none too virtuous either — these
with the despicable husband dupe and a variety of serving men
make up the dramatis personæ of Middletonian comedy. When
we add that all is done with ease and a certain competent grace,
without the least assumption of superiority over the auditor
and with a complete absorption of the personality of the author

[6] *Blurt Master Constable,* for example, 1601 or 1602; and *The Old
Law* in a supposed earlier version even 1599.

in his work, we can comprehend Middleton's easy success in his time.

Obviously Jonson's comedies are made of sterner stuff. He returned to the popular stage, save for *Sejanus*, in *Eastward Ho* in which he accepted the collaboration of Marston and Chapman. The title of this comedy is referable to that of a predecessor, *Westward Ho,* the work of Dekker and Webster, 1603; and it was followed by *Northward Ho,* by the same authors, a year or two after the play in which Jonson was concerned. The first two comedies were named from the familiar cries of the wherrymen on the Thames as they plied eastward to London bridge or westward to the politer precincts of Westminster. The two plays of Dekker and Webster are of the most pronounced Middletonian type, quite outdoing Middleton, it is fair to state, at his worst and making perilous the glib assertions of the historians of the drama concerning the deterioration of Carolan morals from those of the elder age. *Eastward Ho* is a very different production, and curiously enough, although the work of the three most strenuous playwrights of the age, really easier in manner and more perspicuous in plot than the unaided work of any one of them. *Eastward Ho* tells the universal story of the contrasted careers of the industrious and the idle apprentice with the amusing group of people about them that assist more particularly in the downward progress of Quicksilver, the idler. The personages of this delectable old comedy stand out with admirable distinctness: the honest goldsmith, Touchstone, his silly wife and sillier daughter, the latter with her head full of romances, the contrasted 'prentice lads, the good boy tiresomely estimable in his bourgeois virtues, Sir Petronel Flash with his imaginary castle, Seagull with his tales of far away Virginia, all is easily and well done, with just enough of the moralist's consciousness to give the play a universal application. A somewhat pointed allusion to the ubiquity of the Scotch, who had followed their king, a needy horde clamorous for place, caused the arrest and imprisonment for a time of both Jonson and Chapman. Marston, really the offender, escaped. This allusion, though later expunged, assured the popularity of the comedy on the stage and caused likewise the publication of three issues of *Eastward Ho* in the year 1605.

Jonson's next comedy in point of date was *Volpone or the*

Fox, acted in 1606. *Volpone* offers a fitting transition from the
personal satire of *The Poetaster* to the more genial humour of
The Silent Woman and *The Alchemist*. Not that there is
anything genial in *Volpone,* but that there the satire is general-
ised into a consummate study in villainy. In point of fact this
story of the wicked Venetian grandee, undone by his own
subtlety and chicanery, is pervaded by a spirit of absolute mistrust of mankind and there is scarcely a virtuous personage
in it. Jonson's philosophy of life, it would seem, was of an
extreme simplicity, and presentable in the form of a dilemma.
There are two kinds of men in the world for Jonson, the
knaves and the fools, those that prey and those that are preyed
upon. The fools are commonly laughable but contemptible;
the knaves deserve the righteous man's castigation, though often
truly admirable in their wit and forgivable for their cleverness.
Who would be a fool especially in a world of knaves? As to
Volpone, it is truly a question (as in Shakespeare's *Troilus and
Cressida,* if for a somewhat different reason) whether we have
here a comedy or not. The punishment which is justly enough
meted out to Volpone and his scoundrelly creature Mosca,
seems less dependent on their crimes among rascals nearly as
bad as themselves than upon the accident of their division and
want of a dominating cleverness. None the less, for its well-
knit and original plot, its vigorous characterisation, animated conduct and brilliant dialogue, *Volpone* must be esteemed one of the best of Jonson's plays. In the titanic
farce *Epicoene or The Silent Woman,* 1609, and in *The
Alchemist,* acted in the next year, Jonson reached the height of
his originality and ingeniousness of plot and broadened into a
geniality and capacity for mere fun that is nearer his earliest
dramatic success. It would be impossible to conceive of comedy
interest more happily sustained than in the successive surprises
of these admirable comedies, and we learn without surprise
that they captured the stage and held it, with *Volpone* and
Every Man in his Humour, for four generations. It is characteristic of Jonsonian comedy that, with all its merits and
ingenuity, it is usually so constructed that the entire group of
personages is set in motion by one dynamic character. It is
Brainworm's knowledge of the plans of his masters, father and
son, and his knavery that runs *Every Man in his Humour;* it
is Delphine, playing upon his uncle's hatred of noise in *The
Silent Woman,* that evokes that extraordinary personage, Epi-

coene, with all the fun and folly of this laughable farce.   So, too, in *The Alchemist,* all depends on the resourceful, capable and absolutely immoral Face who fascinates the reader, as he fascinates his master in the play, into forgiving a campaign of successful roguery that deserved only condign punishment.   The vitality, liveliness, rapidity and humour of the best scenes of these incomparable plays of Jonson remained unequalled in English comedy and served as examples to generations to come. With *The Silent Woman* and *The Alchemist* Jonson became a convert to the superiority of English scene and English personage for the comedy of manners.   Both are so set; and upon the republication of *Every Man in his Humour,* in his folio of 1616, he carefully revised that comedy so as to transfer the scene from Venice to London, a change materially for the better. To this English practice the poet adhered to his last great comedy the Gargantuan *Bartholomew Fair* which gives us a conception of the Elizabethan forerunner of a London bank-holiday, a picture large, gross, humorous, coarse and boisterous, but not unworthy the pen of this intimate knower and satirist of the life about him.   Jonson wrote other plays; but they belong neither to the time nor to the full-flowing genius that begot these master comedies.

Among dramatists, his contemporaries, none so resembled Jonson in his tastes and theories as his friend, George Chapman, the famous translator of Homer.   Chapman was a much older man than Jonson, born as far back as 1559.   And he appears to have taken up the drama, at first at least, as no very serious addition to his more important literary work as a translator and general poet.   He must have been quite thirty-five years of age when he produced his first comedies, although it is a moot question as to whether he may not, after all, have preceded Jonson in the employment of the word "humour" in the Jonsonian sense, if not in the actual writing of comedies, more or less of the type.[7]   The comedies of Chapman range from several dubious entries and allusions of Henslowe, as early as 1595, to the romantic comedies *The Gentleman Usher* and *Monsieur D'Olive,* both printed in 1606.   All the others are comedies of manners almost strictly at times of "humours";

[7] Cf. Henslowe's mention of a "comedy of humours," in May, 1597, ed. Greg, p. 52 and elsewhere and see a discussion of the subject in *Elizabethan Drama,* i, 460.

and they extend from the trivial *Blind Beggar of Alexandria,* 1596, with its preposterous disguises and confusion between trickery and felony, to *All Fools,* 1599, esteemed by no less an authority than Swinburne one of the best comedies in the language. Chapman's source here is patently the *Heautontimorumenos* of Terence, and he has worked up an intrigue and counter-intrigue in which his ingenuity is only equalled by his wit and originality. Considering that *All Fools* is free from the slightest suspicion of any Jonsonian intention to preach, we may affirm that it is the best example of an English comedy conceived and carried out on the lines of Roman comedy. While less successful, *A Humorous Day's Mirth,* and more especially, *The Widow's Tears,* are equally diverting. In the latter is dramatized with much gusto the scandalous story of the *Ephesian Matron,* who was won, in an incredibly short time and literally on her husband's tomb, from the abandonment of bereaved widowhood to a delighted acceptance of the blandishments of a new wooer. This is only an extreme example of Chapman's habitual attitude of contempt towards woman which has been thought referable to personal experience, but which more probably he caught, like Jonson in lesser degree, from the prevalent atmosphere of Latin literature.

From what has just been written it is clear that Chapman's idea of comedy, even more strictly than Jonson's, was that of Plautus and Terence. Each of Chapman's comedies is impelled by the impetus of one dynamic personage — Tharsalio, the irresistible wooer in *The Widow's Tears,* Rinaldo, the roguish mischief-maker in *All Fools* — and it is his business, as it has been wittily said, " to set all the rest by the ears." The intricacy of Chapman's intrigue is often bewildering, although the action is not always well sustained. The personages, too, while lively and entertaining enough in the dialogue, are little distinguished and scarcely one of them is individually memorable. Obviously Chapman wrote his comedies for a livelihood, and he seems to have fared none too well with them. To his tragedies we have seen that he brought a more strenuous effort. His ambition was to become famous as " *Georgius Chapmanus Homeri Metaphrastes."* That fame he achieved and deserved, but he is not to be forgotten in the distinguished list of playwrights who added excellent comedies to their more serious dramatic work.

From an historical point of view, Chapman's scholar's use of

Roman comedy popularised on the contemporary stage, may
be regarded as the climax of a long preparation in which we
begin with the humanists and schoolmasters, imitators of the
Roman poets, and meet with Gascoigne's *Supposes,* derived
through an Italian intermediary, and Shakespeare's *Comedy of
Errors* by the way.   At the universities Plautine comedy continued in high repute, sometimes direct in its derivation, sometimes imitated from Italian imitators.   None of these many
plays are important to a history of the popular drama, however interesting many of them are in themselves.   Typical examples are *Pedantius* (variously ascribed to Anthony Wingfield or to Edward Forcett) 1581, and the clever trilogy of
"Parnassus plays," 1601-02, from which we have already
quoted.   Both were of Cambridge.   Another still later Cambridge comedy was *Ignoramus,* by George Ruggle, acted in
1615 and immensely to the delight of King James who revelled
in its witty speech and coarseness.   This production is imitated
from an Italian play of Batista della Porta entitled *La Trap-
polaria* which in turn owes no little to the *Pseudolus* of Plautus.
This was a familiar derivation and sets one to wondering if,
after all, some of the intricate intrigue and the narrow range
of the personages of Chapman's comedies may not be found,
like so much else, in the enormous unread minor dramatic
literature of the Italian Renaissance period.   As to Jonson, we
find an interesting parallel in the hints derived from Giordano
Bruno's *Il Candelaio* which he worked up into the fabric of
The Alchemist.   His later use of Machiavelli's story of *Bel-
fagor* is less in accordance with his usual method.   Jonson
prided himself on his originality.   Ordinarily it was his wide
reading in the classics that supplied him with the suggestions
out of which he developed his original plots, although his position on the subject is clear from his own words where he declares that he regards the power " to convert the substance and
riches of another poet to his own use " as an endowment only
second to " natural wit." [8]

Chapman, Jonson and Middleton were the chief contributors,
in the order mentioned, to the new comedy of manners, the
range of which was from the lower toned domestic comedy to
the heightened caricature of the comedy of humours.   But

---

[8] See his *Timber or Discoveries,* 1642, on this subject and his theories
of composition.

they were by no means alone. Chapman's closest imitator was William Percy who left behind him half a dozen amateurish comedies, dating about 1601. Only two of them have seen print, and only one apparently was ever acted. A better comedy of much the same date is the anonymous *Sir Giles Goosecap* in which a story suggestive of that of *Troilus and Cressida* is enlivened with a group of irregular humourists, more in the manner of Jonson than in that of Chapman. The borrowings of title which Jonson's use of the word "humour" begot, we have already noted. Jonson's most successful immediate disciple, until we come to the days of Brome, was Nathaniel Field who had been among the several lads kidnapped by Gyles, and pressed into the profession of acting by an abuse of the queen's license "to take up singing boys" for the royal chapel of which Gyles was then master. Jonson taught the young actor Latin and how to make plays, and Field became notable as a player, especially, at first, in women's parts, and later as a dramatist as well. The best work of Field is contained in *Woman is a Weathercock* and *Amends for Ladies,* both on the stage by the date of the death of Shakespeare. The following of Middleton was even more general. Resembling his method in comedy though preceding him in point of time, is Haughton's lively *Englishmen for my Money,* 1598, in which the foreigner is satirized in a manner much to the taste of the groundlings. *The Fair Maid of the Exchange,* 1602, an excellent play, is more like Heywood in its touch of pathos and serious intent. With Edward Sharpham's *Fleir* and *Cupid's Whirligig,* 1606 and 1607, we are in the irresponsible atmosphere of the satirical comedy of manners once more, impertinent and shameless rather than clever; while in Lodowick Barrey's *Ram Alley or Merry Tricks,* published two years later, we have a vigorous and well-written comedy of low London, however broad of speech, that equals Middleton almost at his best and preserves, take it all in all, a wholesomer tone than is usually his. This play enjoyed great popularity, and so did Joshua Cooke's *Tu Quoque* known as *Greene's Tu Quoque* from the clever hit that the comedian, Thomas Greene, made in the rôle of Bubble, a humorous serving man. Another well-known actor in comedy, Robert Armin, is the author of *Two Maids of Moreclack (Morlake)*, printed, in 1609, a similarly merry production, full of disguise, bustle and merry intrigue.

We have deferred John Marston's comedies of manners to

this late place in this chapter, dealing with the classical and satirical reaction, because, despite his position as a nondramatic satirist and his part in the satirical sword's play of the war of the theatres, his attitude of egotist and doctrinaire, there is always more of the romantic spirit in him than in either Jonson, Chapman or even Middleton, except where William Rowley was Middleton's collaborator. Besides his part in *Eastward Ho,* Marston is the author of five comedies in all of which save one, the scene is Italy. As the country of his mother, whose language he evidently knew well, Italy may be imagined less remote to Marston than to many of his fellow playwrights, and his recognition of the " romance " of some of his subjects may have been less than ours. Marston's most characteristic comedy is *The Malcontent,* acted about 1600. This is a well-knit, original and perspicuous drama of intrigue, involving the disguise of a Hamlet-like prince in the court of the usurper of his dukedom and the consequent test of the character and loyalty of certain of his subjects. The general theme and the sombre tone of this able play suggest *Measure for Measure.* Like this play of Shakespeare, his *Troilus and Cressida* and Jonson's *Volpone* we have here rather tragicomedy than comedy although none of these dramas end in violence. Lighter in touch are *What You Will,* 1601, and *The Parisitaster or Fawn,* 1606. In the latter the device of *The Malcontent,* a prince in disguise, is employed to a less serious purpose; the former dramatizes an entertaining story of Boccaccio, afterwards employed by Shirley in his *Witty Fair One,* in which a clever young woman wins for herself a husband by making her own father the go-between while pretending dutifully to confess to him her lover's aggressive, but purely imaginary, courtship. Marston's work is exceedingly unequal. At his best, in poetry, originality of situation, inventiveness and power to portray character, he deserves his place beside the greatest dramatists of his day, at his worst, he sinks below Middleton to the buffoonery and indecency of Dekker or Webster in the lowest of their comic vein or to a bombast and noisiness in tragic heroics which is absolutely his own. Perhaps Marston's two dramas of this lighter type might be best called comedies of manners in romantic disguise. The type became no uncommon one.

In the preceding paragraphs we have endeavoured to segregate, for the sake of clearness, some of the more striking elements in popular Elizabethan comedy that stood in contrast with the romantic trend of the age and created a reaction against it. To this we have added an account of the Jacobean masque, Jonson's other distinctive contribution to the drama in the reign of King James. To the comedies of Jonson, Chapman and Middleton were added those of Marston, notwithstanding a certain incurable romanticism that is his, because his satire, his pose and his self-consciousness, all are reactionary. The collaborators in *Eastward Ho* were men of a more scholarly type than any of the popular dramatists who had preceded them, and they applied their scholarship in a manner unparalleled to their writing. All of them had theories about poetry and the stage; all, too, were inclined to take a more or less satirical view of life and to affect a greater or less independence of present conditions and popular demands. This is why even the success of Jonson was uncertain, now carrying court and city away, together with his adored " judicious few," by sheer force of genius, at other times provoking retaliation from rivals not his equals, which brought, not to him, but to them the palm, or gaining only that cool " success of esteem " which is more chilling to the ardency of genius than opposition. Were we looking for a generic phrase by which to designate these three writers collectively it might be difficult to find one more appropriate than the school of conscious effort. For not only had all three decided theories as to how to write a play, a satire or a masque, but they seem to have tried hard, each in his way, to carry them out, to be original in story, thought, personage and phrase; and they agreed likewise in a certain disdain of efforts elsewhere which they esteemed not so strenuous, so consistent or so in accord with precedent and experience as their own. Jonson's penchant for the unities, which he was, for the most part, too sensible to abuse (although there are two trials of the same culprits for the same offence in one day in *Volpone*), Chapman's limitation of comedy to a logical development of Plautine character and situation, these are illustrations in point; and so in lesser degree is Marston's transfer to his plays of whole episodes of classical origin, such as the wooing of the Ephesian widow from Petronius Arbiter. Neither Marston nor Chapman take any rank of importance in the masque, each producing but one, neither of them remarkable. This was Jonson's undisputed field which he owed, as much as his success on the popular stage, to his industry, his ingenuity and his adaptation to his purposes of his wide classical reading.   Marston's dramatic career was short; no play of his dates later than 1613.   We do not know when Marston took holy orders.   He was presented with the living of Christ Church in Hampshire in 1616, which he resigned in 1631, dying three years later in London.   Chapman long survived his dramatic career which closed, so far as we know, about the time of the death of Shakespeare.   Chapman is dimly traceable, however, in an alleged collaboration with Shirley in the early thirties.   He died also in 1634.   Jonson survived his fellows, leaving behind him the double achievement of a repute unparalleled as a writer of masques for the entertainment of royalty and a name in the popular drama, second alone to that of Shakespeare.

CHAPTER VIII

BEAUMONT AND FLETCHER, AND THE ROMANTIC
CONTINUANCE

IN the year 1647, when England was in the throes of civil war and Charles had already surrendered to the victorious Parliament, a handsome folio came from the press entitled "*Comedies and Tragedies* written by Francis Beaumont and John Fletcher, gentlemen." This edition was appropriately edited by James Shirley, till recently, when the theatres were closed, the successor to their popularity; and it contained thirty-four plays, as the title added, "never before printed." A second folio edition of 1679 reprinted the first with the addition of all the plays which had been previously printed in separate quarto form under the name of either author. This raised the number to fifty; and since that time some half-dozen dramas have been added to the list. The assembling of plays in collective editions was, up to the time of the death of Shakespeare, a thing practically unknown. The posthumous collection of an author's works, such as the Caxton *Chaucer* for example or more recently the folio of *Spenser,* 1608, even, was rare; although men like Daniel, and Drayton, especially, were always tinkering with their poetry in new collections and revisions which their popularity in their time seems to have demanded. It was in the very year of Shakespeare's death, 1616, that Ben Jonson collected and published his own works, the plays and all which he had written up to that time; a second volume followed only several years after his death, in 1640-42. A strong piece of evidence as to Shakespeare's contemporary popularity is to be found in the speedy collection of his plays in the folio of 1623, only seven years after his death, together with the demand for a second edition of this large and expensive book within nine years of the first. A second complete edition of Jonson with all his repute, was not issued until just fifty years after the first. As to the other Elizabethans, save for the publication by a belated enthusiast of *Six Court Come-*

dies of John Lyly in 1632, there is no other example of the collection of a dramatist's work either within his lifetime or soon after, until we come to the days of the Commonwealth when, there being no other use for plays, an occasional collection appeared, like that of Shirley's *Six New Plays* or *Five New Plays* by Brome. Marlowe, Chapman, Middleton, Webster, Massinger and all the rest remained uncollected — to say nothing of editing — until modern critical times. Shakespeare, Jonson and " Beaumont and Fletcher " stand in this respect alone, appreciated and acclaimed each on the stage of his time, to be read as well as acted in the next generation and in many to come.

Personal details as to this famous literary partnership, " Beaumont and Fletcher," are sadly wanting as usual in dealing with our old dramatists. This much, however, we know. Fletcher was the older, born in 1579, probably at Rye in Sussex where his father was then a minister. Richard Fletcher the father, afterwards rose through several preferments to become Bishop of London; but fell into disgrace with Queen Elizabeth because of a second marriage,— an act which the queen abhorred — and died poor. John Fletcher received his education at Bene't college, Cambridge, but there is no trace of him there nor of his earlier literary associations in London. It seems likely that he soon came to know Jonson and it has been thought by some that through Jonson, Fletcher became acquainted with Beaumont, a supposition altogether likely. Fletcher appears to have written dramas for a livelihood; his many collaborations and his industry go to show it. Besides his enduring friendship with Beaumont, we know that he was closely associated later with Massinger. Jonson esteemed Fletcher and praised him; later poets, such as Sir Aston Cockayne attempted a vindication of his authorship. From all that we can gather, Fletcher must have been a man of a singularly modest, cheerful and unaggressive nature. He died of the plague in 1625 while still at the height of his dramatic activity. Francis Beaumont was some five years Fletcher's junior, born in 1584 or 1585, a younger son of Sir Francis Beaumont of Grace-dieu, Leicestershire, a justice of the common pleas. Beaumont was educated at Broadgates Hall, Oxford, and became a member of the Inner Temple in 1600. He became intimate with Jonson, writing commendatory verses on *Volpone* in 1603 and on other plays, and imitating the Jonsonian comedy of humours unmistakably

in *The Woman Hater,* acted in 1606. Beaumont was certainly
less dependent on the theatre than Fletcher. His personality
and position in life gained for him the respect and esteem of
his contemporaries, even Jonson deferring to his judgment in
a manner remarkable considering Jonson's intractable temper
and the disparity of Beaumont's age. Beaumont evidently
shared Jonson's independent attitude and contempt for the opinion of the vulgar, as he appears to have shared somewhat his
theories as to drama. Another association of Beaumont's, that
with Sir Francis Bacon, has already been considered. Beaumont married a lady of some fortune, but survived only three
years, dying in March 1616, a month before Shakespeare.
Beaumont appears to have been little solicitous of the fame of
authorship. He apparently sanctioned the use of his name on
the title of his masque only. But there is abundant proof in
his own writings and in those of his contemporaries that he
was an intimate associate of the dramatists and men of letters
of his time, appreciating to the full " the things we have seen
done at the Mermaid," although he lived not to the days of
" the Sun and the Triple Tun " nor to subscribe to Jonson's
later *leges convivales.*

With ten years of authorship at best and with a majority
of the plays, included in the Beaumont and Fletcher folio, acted
for the first time certainly after his death, it is obvious that
Beaumont could have had no very large share in the volume.
Even contemporaries to its publication protested against the
assignment to him of so important a place, Sir Aston Cockayne
especially informing us that these dramas were substantially the
" sole issues of sweet Fletcher's brain " and incidentally that
Massinger had been a collaborator in some of them. Modern
scholarship has been busy with this interesting question and substantial results have been reached, however minor points and
individual plays may still remain matters of debate. It is not
necessary in a work of this scope to set forth the methods of
this inquiry into the problem of divided authorship. Suffice
it to say that after a due consideration of external evidence,
date of performance, derivation of plot, contemporary allusion and the like, the question resolves itself into a discrimination of the qualities of style, characteristics of versification, conception of personage and general attitude discernible
in contrasted work of the two authors. Starting from a play
avowedly that of Fletcher and of Beaumont respectively un-

aided — the former's *Faithful Shepherdess,* for example, the latter's *Woman Hater* — these are the main points of distinction that have been formulated. Beaumont's is clearly the more conservative nature, and the more ready to act in conformity with literary and dramatic usages then in vogue. This it is that causes him to adhere to the stronger, more strictly decasyllabic versification of his master Jonson while phrasing with freedom and using run-on lines after the manner of his immediate time. To Beaumont has been assigned a more serious attitude towards life than is customarily Fletcher's, together with the higher moral sense which arms his satire with the sanction, if not quite of the moralist, at least with that of the thoughtful man. For Beaumont has been claimed, too, the more delicate sentiment, a higher order of humour, truer pathos and the greater power in tragedy. Fletcher, on the other hand, is more inventive in his art and more eclectic in his practice. He placed before him the ideal of a drama that should be at once novel and entertaining, and he was intent on this not on theories of the pedant or the moralist. He found in contrast of character and picturesqueness of situation effective steps towards the realisation of this ideal, and in his loosely knit verse an admirably rapid, colloquial, plastic and musical substitute alike for prose and for the older more formal blank verse. The lithe, supple blank-verse of Fletcher is his most distinctive "note." In it he readily admits additional syllables, especially at the end of the line, giving it what is technically called a hendecasyllabic character; but to preserve the sense of rhythm, the pause is commonly marked at the conclusion of each line, far more so than in the current practice of the moment, the later verse of Shakespeare for example. Indubitably Fletcher's nature, like his verse and sometimes rambling and repetitious style, is lighter than that of Beaumont. Fletcher has been designated ready, clever, offhand, hurried and careless. He was all these things sometimes. But he was likewise inventive, ingenious, poetical and possessed of no small insight into human character and emotion.

The results of modern inquiry into the relative parts, contributed by Beaumont and Fletcher, respectively and jointly, to the mass of some fifty-two plays that bear their names, may be summed up as follows: Beaumont wrote one of these plays alone, Fletcher almost as certainly some fifteen independently. Their collaboration seems certain in eight or nine, while something over a score, formerly thought their joint work, are now regarded as Fletcher's in co-operation with some other author, and in five or six more, apparently neither Fletcher nor Beaumont had any appreciable share. To these is to be added *Henry VIII* in which the hand of Fletcher as well as Shakespeare's is now universally acknowledged, *A Very Woman,* formerly considered Massinger's but in which Fletcher once more had his share, and the fine tragedy of *Barnevelt,* printed only in our late times, by the same two authors. In collaboration with Massinger, Fletcher thus appears in sixteen plays, about twice as many as those in which Beaumont worked with him. Elsewhere Fletcher co-operated with Jonson, Field, Tourneur, William Rowley and even with Daborne, if Henslowe is to be trusted.[1]

Without further distinctions we may now turn to the Fletcherian drama to examine wherein it marks a development out of what had gone before. Beaumont began, as we have seen, under the ægis of Jonson as the "humours" of *The Woman Hater* and the satire of *The Knight of the Burning Pestle,* which is largely if not wholly his, sufficiently go to show. This last, a delightful dramatic satire, it will be remembered, contains a burlesque of the popular dramatic romance of impossible adventure in which the hero is always a citizen of London and the civic virtues are extolled. It is not surprising that Beaumont's picture was too true to be pleasing to auditors who loved "the tossing of the pikes" in *The Four Prentices* and *The Adventures of Dick Wittington* actually dramatized in a play now lost. It used to be thought that Beaumont's *Knight* belonged wholly to the order de la Mancha. But the resemblances between his play and *Don Quixote* are superficial and have been pursued too far. If Beaumont began thus in "humours" and burlesque, it is equally clear that Fletcher's first example was the Middletonian comedy of manners. The difficulties in the chronology of the Beaumont-Fletcher plays are far greater than those which concern Shakespeare's; and the subject is complicated by the incessant revision to which popular plays, like the majority of theirs, were subject, so that first performance becomes at times a matter quite irrecoverable. None the less we recog-

---

[1] For this appraisement I am indebted to the excellent chapter on Beaumont and Fletcher by G. C. Macaulay, in the *Cambridge History of English Literature,* vi, 115, 116.

nise at once in comedies such as *Wit at Several Weapons, The Scornful Lady, Monsieur Thomas* and *Wit Without Money,* which date between 1608 and 1614, admirable specimens of the London comedy of manners, beginning altogether in the manner of Middleton, but surpassing him in vivacity, clever plotting and in personages, admirably conceived and discriminated. Monsieur Thomas, a young scapegrace returned from Paris, in a dilemma between a father who would have him wild and a betrothed who declares that she will none of him unless he mend his ways; Valentine who regards an approved ability to live by his wits, the first essential of a free man, both are excellent departures within the range of that darling of the comedy of manners, the engaging spendthrift. Whilst in the capable, witty and high spirited Mary, more than a match for her travelled Thomas, and in Lady Heartwell, as outspoken and as scornful of conventions as Valentine himself, Fletcher created a new and exceedingly pleasing type, the spirited, resourceful heroine, with which he rings many a merry chime in subsequent comedies. Even the usurers, the servants and the ninnies, Fletcher coins over again in a new mint, giving individuality to personages with an easy naturalness that conceals his art and disarms the judicial frown of criticism.

But these comedies, strictly of London life, represent only a part of the generous contribution of Fletcher and his compeers to the comedy of manners. A larger, and, for the most part, a later group are those that, laying the scene in foreign places, in Italy, France or Spain, exhibit elements more or less romantic. Indeed, it might not be difficult for the reader of Beaumont and Fletcher to arrange their comedies in an order that would display a gradation from these scenes of London life to dramas in which the interest is almost wholly romantic; and the scale might be continued through the tragicomedies to the tragedies. I say " almost wholly romantic," because there are few plays of these authors which do not contain either scenes of comedy or at least some comic and realistic personages. This is a matter often forgotten when we speak of the romantic poets, Shakespeare and Fletcher. Romantic they are, for they see things in the mists of beauty and remoteness or in the glory that lights up common objects and makes them matters of shadow and light, not of rule and plummet. But the romantic dramatist is not among the great, if his power of vision does not likewise extend to the discerning of things as they are when there is need of this first essential of literary, as of all other, art. The realism of Fletcher is no small part of his dramatic effectiveness and his comic personages deserve more recognition than they have commonly received. Returning to the comedies of manners of foreign scene, first among them may be named *The Woman's Prize or the Tamer Tamed* which some critics are inclined to place very early (in 1604) because of its relation to *The Taming of the Shrew*. Here we meet once more the merry, resourceful heroine, in this case Maria, successor to the miserably tamed Katharine, and the vindicator of her sex. This comedy is as inventive and original as it is amusing and, as we have it, is not the work of a beginner in play writing. To return to our scale of comedy, in the unpleasing but able play, *The Captain,* 1613, as in the three admirable later comedies, *The Little French Lawyer, The Wild Goose Chase,* and *Rule a Wife and Have a Wife,* which range about 1620, we meet with lively, diverting and eminently successful specimens of the lighter comedy of manners in Fletcher's best vein. In *The Honest Man's Fortune,* 1613, *The Elder Brother,* and *The Noble Gentleman,* the two latter revised after Fletcher's death, the tone is graver and the animating motive more romantic. Nothing, for example, could be in better comic spirit than " the little French lawyer," transformed into a fire-eater by the accident of success in a duel into which he had been literally "pressed," but cured at last by being mischievously left with his opponent on a raw morning not only without weapons but without doublets. A clever and inventive variation, too, on the old motive of the shrew, is the main story of *Rule a Wife and Have a Wife* in which a wealthy lady, seeking a complaisant husband, meets her master; and — according to an obsolete doctrine which few dare now even covertly to hold — with man's mastery comes contentment, happiness and love.

But the distinctive dramatic achievement for which Beaumont and Fletcher stand memorable in the annals of literature is romantic tragicomedy. Obviously a drama which, in one and the same plot, is both comedy and tragedy is an impossibility because a contradiction in terms. Even the yoking together of both in two separate plots is apt to be incongruous and inartistic unless the comedy is employed in a place of subsidiary importance and merely for relief. A tragicomedy is a drama which deals with serious emotions — such as might well lead to tragedy — but in such a manner as to conclude happily and to the satisfaction of the auditor. Fletcher was by no means the inventor of tragicomedy which had existed long before his time. Shakespeare's *Merchant of Venice* is an excellent familiar example of the general meaning of the term. In the trial scene tragedy and comedy hang in the balance. An heroic resolution on the part of Shylock to risk his life for his revenge, and the scene had turned tragic. To the Jew, however, the man of trade and barter, this species of heroism was impossible; and he forfeited not only his revenge, but his faith and half his fortune, to become the butt and the laughing-stock of his enemies: and so the play ends, a comedy. But when we speak of the tragicomedy of Beaumont and Fletcher, we speak of something definite and distinctive. If we look back to the varieties of romantic drama already described, the heroical plays that trace back to mediæval romance, the conqueror series their near kin, the historical and biographical dramas and the tragedies of intrigue and revenge, we find them animated, each in its kind, by certain very definite characteristics. They were, for example, for the most part unoriginal in subject, adhering, as a rule, to the course of human experience and to a more or less accepted code of conduct. They adopted Italy as the accepted locality of romance while, none the less, affecting a certain verisimilitude to their own contemporary manners; and, while as fond of rank and as deferential to it as Englishmen both before and after, the characters were not arranged dramatically to conform to the rules of precedence. Once more, we find the comedies and tragedies of strictly Elizabethan times commonly constructed about some central idea, the infatuation of Antony for Cleopatra, the consequences of the senile folly of Lear, the revenge of Hieronimo, the subjection of Benedick and Beatrice to love. Variety of personage and situation is characteristic of this drama, and it tends very little to repetition and to the perpetuation of types. The later romantic drama, especially in the tragicomedy set by Beaumont and Fletcher as an example, stands greatly in contrast with all this. Originality of plot in it often runs to ingenuity, even to improbability. The place of action is tied to no scene nor age, but is often laid in some no man's land, governed by heroic princes, possessed of exceptional virtues or deformed by extraordinary vices, troubled with unhistorical usurpations, intrigues and rebellions and ruled by conventional and courtly manners unlike the actual conditions of any time. For unity of plot and construction according to some ruling idea, is substituted multiplicity of interest, contrast and surprise; and the personages fall into well determined and conventionalized types which, repeated in a never-ending variety of sameness, draw further and further from nature in the hands of playwrights less clever than those who first broached them.

The actual collaboration of Beaumont and Fletcher belongs to the year 1608 and some three or four years thereafter at the most. Whatever the two poets' earlier separate affiliations (with the boys' companies it has been thought), we find them united in the composition of *Philaster* which was "acted at the Globe by his majesty's servants" at some time not long prior to 1610. In *Philaster or Love Lies a-Bleeding* we meet once more with an epoch-making drama; for in this justly famous tragicomedy combine all the qualities of the species to set a standard from which this type of play was little to vary until it declined into its logical successor, the Restoration heroic drama. The story of *Philaster* is built on contrast. Philaster, the young prince of Messina, has been set aside by a usurping king who seeks to perpetuate his rule by the marriage of his daughter, the peerless princess, Arethusa, to Pharamond, Prince of Spain. The princess has thus two suitors, Philaster whom she loves, noble, melancholy and interesting, and Pharamond, whom she detests, who turns out cowardly, immoral and ignoble. The lovers employ, for messages between them, a devoted page, Bellario, who is really the maiden, Euphrasia, hopelessly in love with Philaster and so disguised to be near him, he unknowing. The requited love of Arethusa thus falls into contrast with the hopeless and unrequited love of Euphrasia; and these two varieties of virtuous affection again are contrasted with sensual love in the intrigue of Pharamond with a malicious court wanton, Megra. Philaster, although a noble lover, is high strung, quick to suspect even those he loves and ready to avenge his honour; so when Megra insinuates evil things of Bellario's service to his mistress Arethusa, Philaster for a time believes her, repudiates Arethusa and in a frenzy wounds his innocent page. In the upshot, Philaster, Arethusa and Bellario are freed from prison, into which the king had thrown them, by a timely popular uprising, and from doubt and scandal by the disclosure of Bellario's actual sex. It will be observed that we have here a comedy of sentimental interest thrust into the midst of elements, heroic and potentially tragic. The contrast of personages, the complexity of the action and its rapidity,

all make against any development of character. The drawing
is in black and white, but the strokes are sure and the personages that emerge are unmistakable. However, little can mere
recital of the story or comment on it make clear the variety,
the swiftness, the poetry and effective dramatic quality of this
charming drama which may be taken, in a first reading, as the
touchstone of a taste for romantic art.

The sources of *Philaster* have been sought by the critics in
vain; and, however a general similarity has been observed between its character and conduct and the contemporary Spanish
drama *de capa y espada,* a contact between English drama and
that of the Peninsula at so early a date as 1610 has not been
established. But interest as to *Philaster* lies not only in the
play itself, but in the circumstance that it became at once the
norm not only for its authors — of whom we may well believe
Beaumont the more important — but for a long following by
other successors. The other plays of the *Philaster* type include especially *King and No King* and *The Maid's Tragedy*
which rings tragic changes on a similar group of personages.
In the latter, which must have followed *Philaster* closely, the
usurping king becomes the lustful tyrant, Philaster sinks into
the noble but wretched and bewildered husband Amintor, married to Evadne, the king's mistress, to preserve appearances,
and the love-lorn maiden recurs in the unhappy Aspasia, also
disguised as a page and a tragic variant of Bellario-Euphrasia.
The Maid's Tragedy is a drama of genuine power, carefully
plotted and thoroughly well written. It held the stage, like
Philaster, until long after the Restoration and the rôle of the
wronged and regenerated Evadne who, awakened to her wickedness kills her royal lover, first acted by Field and Kynaston, was
afterwards played by some of the most famous actresses of that
later time. This tragedy added two figures to the several types
of Beaumont and Fletcher, the lustful tyrant, repeated in subsequent drama *ad nauseam* and in Melantius, the bluff and
loyal soldier, long a deserved favourite. In *King and No King,*
licensed in 1611, the authors returned to tragicomedy, ringing
a new change on a similar dramatis personæ. Here the king,
Arbaces, is once more the heroic prince. But his headstrong
passionateness and unreason is carried to the borders of the
ridiculous to emphasise his really ignoble birth. So in Bessus,
who belongs to the type of Pharamond, folly and bluster rather
than cowardice and immorality are brought out as the ruling

traits. And for the love-lorn maiden, we have substituted
Spaconia, a young woman of capacity and address, sister of the
resourceful maidens of Fletcherian comedy. In dwelling on
the undoubted types into which the personages of these able
dramatists do fall, it is important to mark, too, the extraordinary cleverness with which they avoid mere repetitions. To
judge them by their unsuccessful imitators would be eminently
unfair. On the other hand, it is not to be denied that, however accurate the observation of Dryden that Fletcher more
truly represented the manners of gentlemen on the stage than
Shakespeare, there is a certain unknitting of the moral fibre
even in these earliest of the tragicomedies. The readiness of
Philaster to believe the reported unfaithfulness of his peerless
princess and his cowardly " pinking " of poor little Bellario with
his sword, the " loyalty " of Evadne's husband, Amintor, that
unnerved his hand to avenge the greatest wrong that man can
do to man, because the wrongdoer was his sovereign, the struggle of Arbaces and Penthea, in *King and No King,* against a
mutual passion which both believe to be incestuous though their
belief turns out an error — all these things are illustrations in
point and explainable to a large degree by the struggle for
novelty, surprise and effect which Beaumont and Fletcher inaugurated in the drama of the time of King James.

We have already learned how the lord Chamberlain's company of players by a judicious alliance with one Laurence
Fletcher, who had affiliations with the then Scottish king, contrived to pass into the immediate patronage of King James even
before he reached London. Thenceforward this company was
known as the King's company and the other theatrical troupes
soon followed this lead to the royal patronage, the Earl of
Pembroke's, later Worcester's, becoming the Queen's, the Admiral's Prince Henry's, while the Children of the Royal Chapel
were now known as the Queen's Revels. Paul's boy continued to be so designated until 1607, when we lose sight of
them and a new company appears known as the King's Revels.
The boy companies, so long successful, seem to have been finally
suppressed about 1607, and they were succeeded by two companies of men, the Duke of York's players and the Lady Elizabeth's. A year after Prince Henry died, in 1614, his company
became that of the Palsgrave, who was already betrothed to the
Princess Elizabeth, and the company, formerly called the Duke
of York's, became that of Prince Charles. These five com-

panies united under the royal patronage long held practically a
monopoly of the London stage.   As to their theatres, the King's
men continued acting at the Globe, except for the interruption
of the fire in 1613, until the closing of the theatres by Parliament in 1642.   The Queen's men were at the Rose, later at
the new Red Bull in St. John Street, Clerkenwell; Prince
Henry's occupied the Fortune.   In 1609 the King's players
began to act likewise at Blackfriars which had been leased by
Burbage to the children of the Chapel from 1596 to 1608.
The Globe excepted, the playhouses of the Bankside seem not
to have thrived far into the reign of King James although apparently Henslowe attempted a revival there by erecting, in
1613, on the site of the old bear garden, a theatre which he
called the Hope.   This was opened in that year with Jonson's
Bartholomew Fair and *No Wit No Help like a Woman's* by
Middleton and Rowley, but we hear no more of it after
Henslowe's death in 1616, and the primacy remained thereafter
indisputably with the King's company ocupying its two playhouses the Globe and Blackfriars.

The last group of Shakespeare's plays are commonly denominated " the romances."   They include *Pericles,* the rambling
stage version of a romantic tale, ultimately referable to the
Greek romance of the sixth century called *Apollonius of Tyre;*
Cymbeline, the interweaving of an Italian story from the *De-
cameron* with a bit of ancient British history derived from
Holinshed; *The Winter's Tale,* the dramatizing of a popular
" novel " of Greene, *Pandosto;* and *The Tempest,* the glorification by a poet's fancy of hints contained in a couple of prosaic
pamphlets concerning far off and " vexed Bermoothes," otherwise the Bermuda Islands.   It is only necessary to note the extraordinary variety of the derivation of these four plays to
appreciate their diversity of origin.   Their diversity of treatment is in some respects almost as great.   They range, in point
of probable date of acting, between 1608 and 1612 at latest,
and they differ materially in tone and manner from Shakespeare's own comedies and tragedies that preceded them.   With
Pericles in all likelihood Shakespeare had only a little to do;
and yet some of the scenes, notably that in which Marina finds
her father, are in his most beautiful and effective manner.   The
other three plays are not only wholly Shakespeare's, but in some
respects they offer us qualities of a rarity and an exquisite poetic
fancy not matchable elsewhere even in his works.   In Imogen,

for example, we have the quintessence of that deep discernment and appreciation of true womanhood in which Shakespeare has no second. In the imaginative conception of Ariel we have the mischievous and fanciful Puck, of the earth delightfully earthy, translated literally to the skies to breathe to us invisible in soft and musical zephyrs. In the story of Hermione and her noble reconcilement to her husband, Leontes, contrite, it is true, for his terrible crime of doubt, but according to our human standards unforgivable, we have a larger charity and bounty in forgiveness than most of us can rise to comprehend. And in all we meet with that familiar, competent technique, ranging from these greater things — if even they be greater — to the turning of a perfect lyric or the conception of that inimitable vagabond, Antolycus. I confess that I lose patience with the scholarship whose scrutiny and second sight can discover a falling-off in Shakespeare's art in these beautiful dramas of his later maturity. Must we have always the blare of the trumpets of war and terrors followed by the solemn pomp of tragedy? And is there no time of the year for comedy except the merry springtime with its frolics and its follies? It is true that each of these plays of Shakespeare ends in reconciliation and that three out of the four deal with passions and emotions as serious as those which are wont to animate tragedy. These plays are tragicomedies in that sense, and by strict definition. It is also true that one or perhaps even two of them may have followed *Philaster* on the stage and that Shakespeare, alive as he was to all that was about him, must have appreciated the talent, the originality and success of this excellent performance. But to group Shakespeare's " romances " in any sense or in any wise with the tragicomedies of Beaumont and Fletcher — Shakespeare's " romances " with their sense of nature and out of doors, and their personages as freely conceived and naturally differentiated as men and women are in the world, with Fletcher's court ladies and gentlemen, laced and starched, governed by the conventions of the romantic novelists, sentimental, heroic, to the lover of reality, be it confessed, with all their poetry, often frankly absurd — is to befog the understanding and to lead those whom such scholarship affects to guide hopelessly awry.

After the period of Fletcher's collaboration with Beaumont some have recognised a short period of similar co-operation on

Rowley's powerful tragedy *All's Lost by Lust,* 1619, which is founded on an old Spanish historical ballad. Among the best of tragicomedies is *The Spanish Gipsy,* 1623, the work of Middleton and Rowley, which tells the romantic tale of the gipsy maid, Pretiosa, and in the combination of this with another story of Cervantes achieved a lasting dramatic success. The early twenties witnessed a momentary interest in the stage gipsy. Besides this tragicomedy, a band of gipsies figure in Middleton's excellent comedy, *More Dissemblers besides Women,* 1622. Possibly Jonson's masque, *The Gipsies Metamorphosed,* 1621, a great success at court, which delighted the king, is responsible for this feature of both plays.

As to the plays of Spanish origin by Fletcher named above, *The Chances,* 1615, and *The Pilgrim,* 1621, are charming specimens of the romantic species to which they belong. The former deals with the "chances" or accidents that befell "two young students, unexpectedly become the protectors of a lady and her child "; *The Pilgrim* details the adventures of a lover, returned, as a beggar, to his native place to claim the lady of his love. In *The Chances* the "humours" of Mistress Gillian, the landlady, English additions to the comedy element, had much to do with preserving the play in popular esteem on the stage. Another exceedingly popular play of Fletcher's, which also held the stage like these long after the Restoration, was *The Spanish Curate,* acted first about 1622. Here the poet treated his source with great freedom, the lighter scenes being wholly his own. But Fletcher was by no means tied to any one source for material for his ready, inventive genius to work upon. In *Beggars' Bush,* 1622, the scene is Flanders and the humours of a group of professional vagrants — not unlike the gipsies of the moment's popularity — work into a romantic theme of disguises, fugitives, merchant adventurers and the like. This play has been thought in theme suggestive of *The Merchant of Venice,* as *The Sea Voyage,* also 1622, has been considered not unreminiscent of *The Tempest.* But such "similarities" with the many more that scrutinising scholarship has gathered give modern critics far more concern than the easygoing subjects of King James ever took even so much as to recognise them. In one or two tragicomedies that date somewhat earlier than these we have Fletcher's confirmed manner. *The Knight of Malta* represents Fletcher's ideal, for example, of knighthood in a somewhat intricate plot based on a more

than usually complete realisation of the method of contrast.[4]
The gradual degeneracy of Mountferrat, by means of passion,
from a brave and honourable knight to recreancy, shame and
degradation from his order is finely conceived and powerfully
written.   The contrasted triumph of his foil, the worthy knight
Miranda, in his struggle between an earthly and impure love
and fidelity to the ideals of his order is more open to criticism.
In this interesting tragicomedy we have one of the earliest
appearances in English drama of the heroic theme, soon to be
contorted into a hundred new and ingenious changes, the struggle between love and honour. *The Loyal Subject* is of much
the same date (about 1618).   Here Fletcher takes up another
theme soon to rise to an interest more than histrionic, the test of
loyalty under extraordinary and wanton royal infliction.   This
is a favourite Fletcherian situation, recurring in its more natural
tragic form in Amintor's plight in *The Maid's Tragedy* and
in the relations of Aëcius to his emperor Valentinian in the
tragedy of that title.   In *The Loyal Subject,* the loyalty of an
honourable old soldier is put to tests as absurd and extreme in
their kind as those to which patient Griselda was subjected
by her " curious " husband.   Both plays exhibit typical examples
of another favourite situation of the age, the eternal test of
woman's chastity.   In *The Knight of Malta,* Miranda, the
ideal knight vowed to a holy life, tempts by way of trial the
virtuous wife of his friend in a scene which no pure-minded
man could have conceived much less have enacted.   In *The
Loyal Subject,* a daughter of that impossible hero, sent on the
royal mandate, an innocent to the court, proves more than a
match for the dissolute duke whom she captures for a husband with unmaidenly effrontery before he has time to propose
himself her lover.   It is refreshing to turn from Fletcher's
treatment of this latter subject to Heywood's *The Royal King
and Loyal Subject* which deals with precisely the same story,
derived by both from a " novel " of Bandello, told in Painter's
Palace of Pleasure.   Heywood transfers the scene to an indeterminate period of English history.   Bandello's scene was
Persia; Fletcher had made it Muscovy, which might be anywhere.   No better example in contrast between the methods of
earlier drama and those which Fletcher brought in could be
conceived than that exhibited in these two plays, and this de-

[4] The powerful first and second acts of this play have been thought
not to be Fletcher's.

spite the fact that Heywood is trying to write in the prevailing mode. Heywood makes the contest one in courtesies in which the king wins only because of his imperious assertion of his royal power. Fletcher adds cruelty to the qualities of his king and unmanliness and heroic madness to the submission of his subject, and he transforms the sweet womanly daughters of Heywood's subject into the unmaidenly hoidens already mentioned. Fletcher's method of contrast demanded these high lights and deep shadows. The drama became of coarser fibre in his hands, less delicate in touch and feeling, gaudier in colour, shriller in tone, less true to nature, however successful theatrically. With *The Laws of Candy* we meet still another heroic theme. The contest here being one for military honours between a father and a son. This drama was probably rewritten almost wholly by Massinger. It is an effective play of its species, deserving more recognition than it has received. Lastly of this tale of Fletcherian tragicomedy, *The Lover's Progress* is a dramatized version of a contemporary French romance and a favourable specimen of the old-world courtesy, heroic disinterestedness and other fine virtues in which this excellent old literature had its life and justification. This pleasing drama is interesting in establishing Fletcher's direct contact with that heroic literature which several of his plays of Spanish source disclose, elements for the vogue of which in the next two generations Fletcher is more responsible than any other Englishman.

We must now turn back briefly to survey another species of drama which Fletcher essayed and affiliated to his new tragicomedy. This is the pastoral. Pastoral drama is only one form of pastoral literature, which may be in verse or prose, lyric or epic, artistic and without further design than to amuse or fraught with weighty satirical or political meaning. The mode is wholly of Italian origin and was popular in general poetry before it was attempted in dramatic form. Of the nature and origins of pastoral poetry this is not the place to speak; it enters the dramatic entertainments at court with Gascoigne and in such masque-like productions as Sidney's *Lady of May;* and it developed in the hands of Peele, with his *Arraignment of Paris,* and of Lyly into full dramatic form. The scene of Lyly's *Love's Metamorphosis,* for example, is Arcadia, and other illustrations of what may be called the mythological-pastoral school are not wanting among his other plays and among those of his follower, John Day. No true student of literature, on the other hand, can confuse the English love of free rural life, embodied in the national myth of Robin Hood, with anything so stilted, artificial and exotic as the pastoral; and therefore the classification of such plays as *A Midsummer Night's Dream* and *As You Like It* with pastorals, save for some delightful and delicate raillery in the latter, is peculiarly wide of the mark. It is in Samuel Daniel's *Queen's Arcadia,* 1605, that we meet with the first authentic specimen of the pastoral drama in England, according to the practice and example of the great Italian pastoralists, Tasso, Sannazaro and Guarini. And it was this very pretty, correct and poetical endeavour to imitate the best Italian manner in this kind no doubt that suggested to Fletcher his attempt to popularise the pastoral on the public stage. It is fair to Daniel to state that his play is both original and inventive; it is even furnished with satirical comedy scenes for relief in which the famous descant on tobacco and its attendant evils was nicely fitted to meet the approval of the royal author of *A Counterblast to Tobacco.*

Fletcher's one pastoral drama is *The Faithful Shepherdess,* acted in 1608 and printed in the next year with a confession of its failure on the stage. In this confession Fletcher gives us his theory as to the pastoral in which he adopts, almost as rigidly as Daniel, the rules of Italian sanction, attributing the popular failure of his play to a vulgar misapprehension of its meaning. *The Faithful Shepherdess,* as we now read it, is full of poetry, beauty of sentiment and charm of person and situation and we are not surprised to hear that it gained no inconsiderable popularity, especially at court in later performances. The story is strictly of the approved pastoral type and the author has carried out in it even more completely than usual his favourite method of contrast, running a whole gamut, so to speak, on the scale of the passion of love from ideal constancy to a dead lover down to mere wantonness. Indeed, ingenious scholarship has discovered a complete allegory of love in this play of which the author was doubtless quite unaware. Milton discovered more than this in *The Faithful Shepherdess.* He found there beautiful poetry and a dainty sense for nature which he disdained not to make the model for some of his own most beautiful poetry. The poet and the critic hunts, each after his kind. No further attempt appears to have been made by the greater men to popularise the pastoral drama, although Shakespeare, in 1611, utilised the pastoral in some of the most charming scenes of *The Winter's Tale,* glorifying his material in the process and ignoring, if he were ever cognisant, of the Italians and all their regulations. A neglected, but very pretty, pastoral of popular type is Robert Daborne's *The Poor Man's Comfort,* staged by one of Henslowe's companies in 1613. Daborne was one of the latest of Henslowe's hack-poets and some of his letters remaining exhibit a hand-to-mouth existence that reminds us of the career of Dekker. Like Marston, Daborne sought refuge from the stage in the church. He was the author of several other plays. A novel departure of his meritorious pastoral lies in the circumstance that his folk are really shepherds and do not turn out in the end to be princes in disguise. Daniel tried his hand once more at pastoral drama in a less elaborate and more masque-like effort. This was his *Hymen's Triumph* acted at court in 1614; and this was only one of several similar adaptations of the pastoral to royal entertainment, such as *Scyros* by Samuel Brooke, acted before Prince Charles at Cambridge in the previous year and *Sicelides* by Phineas Fletcher, first cousin of the dramatist, acted before the king at the same university in 1615. *Sicelides* is described as a " piscatory," that is a pastoral in which fisher folk take the place of shepherds. The type is classically authentic. Phineas Fletcher's play is never dramatic; but it is well written and possessed of a genuine love of nature that cannot but hold the attention of a reader who loves poetry.

When Jonson died a fragment was found among his papers and published in the folio of 1642 as *The Sad Shepherd.* It is a charming, fresh and effective piece of writing and represents the poet in full vigour. Moreover, the play is a bold attempt to combine pastoral figures and pastoral traditions with the English story of Robin Hood and with English witch-lore. It is regrettable that Jonson never finished *The Sad Shepherd.* Various opinions have been held as to the probable date of this fragment and the occasion of its writing. Some have thought it " a last spring blossom from a withered tree." Others would place the poem here, a year or so before Shakespeare's death, and make it synchronize with this early period of the vogue of the pastoral drama at court. Jonson's avowed rivalry with Daniel who had just produced *Hymen's Triumph,* which was a success, the character of Jonson's fragment, so different from his later dramatic " fallings-off," and the opportunity to confound a foe in theory and practice as well — all these things point to the earlier as the more probable date for the composition of *The Sad Shepherd.* Why the play was never finished nor staged, we do not know. The still higher popularity of pastoral drama in the reign of King Charles, we must defer to its proper place.

There remain of Fletcher the tragedies, and of these the most celebrated, *The Maid's Tragedy,* has already been discussed because of its close affiliation to the tragicomedies of the Philaster group. The tragedies, some eight in number, range from *Cupid's Revenge,* about 1608, to *The False One,* in the form in which we have it, 1620. In subject, they exhibit a greater range even than the tragicomedies which are at least four fold their number; though the Fletcherian romantic atmosphere envelops them all. In two, the scene is France. *Thierry and Theodoret,* a forceable, if forbidding play, is founded ostensibly on Merovingian chronicles, but seems written more particularly to stage under this cloak certain contemporary scandals in the court of France. *The Bloody Brother or Rollo Duke of Normandy,* in which Fletcher is only one of several authors, has not been traced, in its powerful subject of internecine fratricidal struggle, to a source either French or other. But for the inexorable rigour of chronology, however, from the resemblance of the stories, a certain kind of scholarship would surely long since have discovered a German influence on Fletcher exerted through Schiller's *Die Braut von Messina.* Four of Fletcher's tragedies have a more or less remote touch with the classics. These are *Cupid's Revenge,* the scene of which is Lycia, though the source is partly Sidney's *Arcadia; Bonduca* which combines the story of the British queen, Boadicea, with that of the Welsh hero, Caractacus; *Valentinian,* the expansion of an anecdote told by Procopius of that emperor; and *The False One,* which deals with the intrigue of Cleopatra and Julius Cæsar. This last shows Fletcher and his coadjutor Massinger, excellent classical scholars and capable of dealing with their historical material in a manner that would have been no discredit to Jonson himself. *Valentinian* is a typical example of the transformation of unimportant material by a rehabilitation of familiar personages into a something dramatically successful. The emperor is the lustful tyrant, Lucina the steadfast wife, Aëcius the bluff and loyal soldier, whilst Maximus repeats though it may have preceded) the theme of the degeneracy of a noble nature which we have noted in Mount-

ferrat, the knight of Malta. And yet with sure, swift touch
all is transformed into a something new and admirably effective. In many respects we have in *Bonduca* one of the most
interesting of these plays. In its employment of British stories
it is allied through a long descent with the chronicle play and
is more or less closely affiliated to dramas such as Middleton's
Mayor of Queensborough or Rowley's *Birth of Merlin*. On
the other hand, despite an intelligent use of Roman historians
of Britain, the play is altogether romantic. It is the pathetic
figure of the little Prince Hengo, the infatuation of the young
Roman centurion for one of the daughters of the queen, whose
impetuous and shrill-voiced patriotism falls into contrast with
the calm, magnanimous heroism of Caratach, that really interests the dramatist and with him his auditor or reader.

When all has been said however of Fletcher's tragedies, it
must be confessed that his and Massinger's *Sir John Van Olden
Barnevelt* stands alone as the finest English historical tragedy
of the age, dealing with material outside of classical or British
sources. Here, for once, the immediacy of the material caused
the authors to doff their romantic plumes and deal with their
material in a spirit which achieved the reproduction of a genuine historical atmosphere. The noble pride of Barnevelt in
his honourable career, the reluctance of Maurice of Nassau to
press him to his undoing, the skilful use of minor personages, the
friends and family of the great Advocate, even the crowd of
burghers, women and children, all combine with consummate
dramatic art to produce a tragedy that must have created a
sensation, staged, as it seems to have been, at a time almost
current with the events which it portrays. Historically viewed,
The Tragedy of Barnevelt is one of an interesting group of
dramas which touch on contemporary political occurrences; in
its freedom from ulterior satirical or political purposes, it stands
practically alone. In this connection it is enough to remind
the reader that Middleton's *Game at Chess,* two years later,
was suppressed on the stage for its representation, satirical and
undignified, of Spanish dignitaries and princes as pieces of the
game; that Chapman's *Charles Duke of Byron* had been mutilated by the censor for too vivid a glimpse into the domestic
scandals of the French court; and that Massinger to avoid the
same fate was compelled to translate a play of his on a Spanish
pretender, as we shall see, into the terms of a classical story
having to do with Antiochus the Great. The patriot, Barne-

velt, was executed in May 1619. Three months later there is mention of Fletcher's play, which was prohibited by the Bishop of London, though later acted. *Barnevelt* was not printed in quarto or in either of the folios of Beaumont and Fletcher. It remained in manuscript until its discovery and printing by Mr. Bullen in the year 1883.

The close personal friendship of Fletcher and Massinger and the latter's succession to Beaumont's place as the chief of those who co-operated with the popular dramatist is avouched by contemporary testimony and confirmed by the discriminations of modern scholarship. Philip Massinger was of about Beaumont's age; he was born at Salisbury, late in 1584, and the son of a gentleman in the service of Henry the second Earl of Pembroke. It has been supposed that the younger Massinger served as a page in the household of the Pembroke family, whose patronage at a later time he certainly enjoyed. Young Massinger was entered at St. Alban Hall, Oxford, in 1602; but left the university without a degree. The details of his beginnings as a playwright are as little known as those of his associates. We have evidence, however, that his was the hard school of Henslowe and that Field and Daborne were his immediate fellows in adversity. It was with the former that he wrote *The Fatal Dowery,* a tragedy of great power and excellence, and the inspiration (unacknowledged by Nicholas Rowe, the author, long after) of *The Fair Penitent,* a drama of extraordinary vogue in its day. The appearance of Massinger's name with Dekker's in *The Virgin Martyr,* licensed in 1620 and reckoned among the earliest of his plays, and with Middleton's and Rowley's in *The Old Law* doubtless marks his revision of the older original work of these playwrights. Massinger's association with Fletcher begins about 1613, and he indubitably revised some of the latter's work after Fletcher's death. To that work we need not here recur. Massinger survived until 1640 and was buried, according to the epitaph by Cockayne, in the same grave with Fletcher. Some of the earlier work of Massinger was written for the Queen's company; after Fletcher's death, he wrote wholly for the King's men.

It can not be affirmed that Massinger, in his unaided efforts, added any new form or unusual variety of treatment to the repertory of the Jacobean stage. And yet there are distinctive qualities that differentiate Massinger and give him his place in the august brotherhood of England's great dramatic age. Massinger's work is of two kinds, the comedy of manners, represented in three or more plays, an able combination of the easy method of Middleton and Fletcher with the stricter moral attitude of Jonson, and secondly, his tragicomedies and tragedies, all of them in the approved Fletcherian mode, wherein, however, Massinger at times almost equals his master. Let us consider first the comedies in which although he shared less than in the tragicomedies with his more famous coadjutor, he has left behind him none the less two admirable specimens of the drama of English contemporary manners. These are *The City Madam,* acted perhaps as early as 1619, and *A New Way to Pay Old Debts* which must have been written close to the end of the reign of King James. *The City Madam* echoes some of the motives of *Eastward Ho* in the idle and vicious apprentices and the citizen's wife and her foolish daughters with their ridiculous pride and affectation. But Massinger gives his comedy a more serious turn in the figure of Luke Frugal, a sometime prodigal, reduced to affected penitence and the acceptance of his brother's charity; but, when opportunity arises, on his supposed inheritance of his brother's wealth, revealed a monster of selfishness and avarice, assenting to a proposition to transport his brother's wife and daughters to Virginia and a life of slavery to be rid of their importunate claims upon him. *A New Way to Pay Old Debts* is Massinger's best known play; and here again we recognise how close a student the poet was of the drama that had gone before him: the situation of Wellborn and the behaviour of his creditors is much that of Witgood, in similar case, in Middleton's *Trick to Catch the Old One,* to pursue resemblances no further. But here, too, Massinger has given to his drama an original bias in the powerful figure of avaricious and unprincipled Sir Giles Overreach who, in the exorbitance of his villainy and its fitting retribution in madness, touches the borders of tragedy. Both of these comedies of Massinger long held the stage, however altered in form. *A New Way to Pay Old Debts* is even now occasionally acted, and always with success despite the somewhat artificial and obvious nature of some of the minor personages. Well written and capably plotted as are both of these excellent plays, it must be confessed that Massinger is less successful in lighter comedy than where some serious motive animates his muse to a rhetorical fervour. In *A New Way to Pay Old Debts,* we leave the city with its bourgeois manners and personages for rather better

society, though the elevation of the comedy of English manners
from tradesfolk to gentlefolk belongs specifically not to Massinger but to Shirley. Massinger was less successful in comedy
the scene of which is laid in foreign parts. *The Parliament of
Love,* 1624, is a disappointing performance in which a corrupt
text and the opportunities of a promising subject thrown away
conspire to produce an effect quite disheartening. Massinger
could make nothing of the imaginative conception of the trouba-
dours, a court for the sage determination of causes in love, except a series of conventional intrigues and a seasoning of conventional humour. *The Guardian,* 1633, is Spanish in character, if not in scene or in known source; it is a comedy as
coarse as it is able. Such work offers the greatest contrast
with the air of refinement which pervades Massinger's more
romantic dramas to which we now turn, and seems more a
concession to the taste of the age than the expression of the
poet's own personality.

In *The Bondman, The Maid of Honour* and *The Renegado,*
all on the stage before the death of Fletcher, Massinger worked
independently and effectively in the received conventions of
contemporary tragicomedy. *The Bondman* is based on the
classical story of Timoleon's deliverance of ancient Syracuse
from the Carthagenian invasion; but the story is translated, in
true Fletcherian manner, into a romantic tale of vengeance
diverted by love. *The Renegado,* as we have seen, is an independent English version of one of the comedies of Cervantes;
The Maid of Honour was long and deservedly one of the
most popular of Massinger's tragicomedies, and in it, whatever
its undiscovered source, we have Massinger's distinctive way of
looking at life. Bertholdo, a noble knight of Malta, owes his
deliverance from captivity to the Lady Camiola, but is refused
by her as a suitor because of his vows. She accepts, however,
his troth-plight, after the manner of the time, as a test of his
gratitude. But Bertholdo falls a victim to his love for the
Duchess of Sienna and wooes her for his wife, thus proving
false alike to Camiola and his knightly order. Denounced by
Camiola, the recreant is also repudiated by the duchess, and bid-
ding Bertholdo return to his order, Camiola herself takes the
veil. This ending, the nature of the story of *The Renegado,*
in which a beneficent Jesuit priest is the motive power, together
with the semi-religious character of *The Virgin Martyr,* have
led to surmise that Massinger had become a Roman Catholic.

This, his intimacy with several gentlemen of that faith, makes a matter not unlikely. But moral earnestness was a distinctive trait of the dramatist which other plays besides these go to show. In several dramas of this type Massinger continued the Fletcherian tragicomedy. *The Great Duke of Florence* is an admirable drama refashioned from an older anonymous play entitled *A Knack to Know a Knave*. There is nothing historical about it, nor about the less important *The Picture* which transports us to an equally imaginary Hungaria. *A Very Woman,* 1634, is one of Massinger's best romantic plays. It follows closely, but not slavishly, its original, *El Amanto Liberal* of Cervantes. And scarcely less effective is *The Bashful Lover,* of the next year, for the source of which diligent search has been made in vain.

Only a small proportion of Massinger's dramas end in tragedy; but some of these are among his best. *The Unnatural Combat* is a forceable play which shows acquaintance with the terrible story of the Cenci, although the stress is laid upon the feud between the father and son, not upon the more awful relations of Cenci with Beatrice, his daughter, and the scene is conveyed to Marseilles and the characters renamed. An effective and original catastrophe is the protagonist's death by a stroke of lightning in the moment of his impotent cursing the hour of his birth. *The Duke of Milan* retells a familiar story, that of Herod and Mariamne, already several times used in the old drama, again transferring the scene and renaming the personages and evolving a powerful situation that owes not a little to the suggestion of the similar situation of Othello. Finally of Massinger there are the dramas that deal, however romantically, with ancient times, the early *Virgin Martyr,* revised in 1620, *The Roman Actor,* 1626, and *Believe As You List,* 1630, all tragedies, and *The Emperor of the East,* of the last date also, a tragicomedy. Of these *The Virgin Martyr* tells the story of Saint Dorothea together with the conversion of Theophilus, the persecutor, and the martyrdom of both. This play, with its spirits of good and evil, alternately prompting each after his kind, suggests not only the earlier origin in a play of Dekker's, contemporary with the later popularity of *Faustus* — a matter borne out by external evidence — but also the still earlier influences of the morality. *The Roman Actor* Massinger himself " ever esteemed the best birth of his Minerva," an estimation nearer the mark *than is usual when poets appraise their own creations. The theme is of original interest and must have been written *con amore*. It tells how the infatuation of the Empress Domitia placed Paris, one of the despised profession of players, on a level, for the moment, with the master of the world and how the man in him rose to the heroic occasion. The conduct and writing of this tragedy deserve all the praises that they have received. *The Emperor of the East* is less important.

Believe as You List claims a separate paragraph. This able, and in places truly pathetic, tragedy relates the story of Antiochus, King of Upper Asia, supposedly left for dead on his field of defeat by the Romans, but really come to life and seeking for a recognition of his royal claim. But Rome outfaces him everywhere and terrifies even those who believe in his identity into silence or repudiation; so that in the end the unhappy king is sent a slave to the Roman galleys. This is really the story of one of the pretenders to the long vacant throne of Don Sebastian and the play was so set at first. But Herbert, Master of the Revels, objecting to the story because "it did contain dangerous matter, as the deposing of Sebastian, King of Portugal, by Philip, there being a peace sworn betwixt the king of England and Spain," Massinger rewrote his play, ironically apologising in the prologue — which Herbert probably did not see — for his want of "a knowledge of cosmographie," if he should seem to come "too near a late sad example." As to this play, a further analogy has been pointed out by Gardiner, the historian, between the Roman treatment of Antiochus and the attitude of King Charles, at this time, towards his unfortunate brother-in-law, the Elector Palatine and titular King of Bohemia. Indeed Gardiner goes much further to find in a succession of Massinger's plays from *The Bondman* to *The Great Duke of Florence* and *The Maid of Honour,* a representation of current political events coloured in the interests of his patrons, the Earls of Pembroke and Montgomery, under a thin dramatic disguise.[5]

We have thus in Massinger, when all has been said, a successor to Jonson and Middleton in comedy and a continuer of the art and practice of Fletcher in able and important tragedies and tragicomedies. Massinger confirmed the taste of the time

[5] *Political Elements in Massinger, New Shakespeare Society's Transactions,* 1876.

in this last species of drama and, while he not infrequently equalled Fletcher in originality of theme and in consummate dramatic craftsmanship, Massinger commonly falls below Fletcher in his conception of character and in his substitution of a rhetorical style for the poetry which Fletcher had ever ready on occasion. Effectively eloquent as Massinger often is, we feel in much of his work the same hurry and carelessness that we feel at times in Fletcher's, and we do not feel the same sustaining cleverness, skill under difficulty and ease. When Massinger flags, he does not so readily recover himself. Finally, Massinger's verse shows a further disintegration. Massinger writes evenly enough; he is less free in the license of the redundant syllable than Fletcher, or even than Shakespeare in the latter's latest manner; but he often expands his words in violence to common hurried utterance and he abuses the licenses of run-on-lines, the weak ending and the pause within the line. In a word, the end of such blank-verse as Massinger's, at his worst, is prose.

But Massinger was only the most important of the followers of Fletcher. Even in his lifetime there were minor imitators of his types, his Spanish sources, his method of contrast, even of his darting hendecasyllabic verse, though never has its lithe activity, when at its best, been equalled. Among tragedies in the manner of Fletcher, there is the forceable anonymous *Second Maiden's Tragedy* endorsed with this title by Sir George Buc, Master of the Revels, who licensed it in 1611. This drama smacks not a little, in its pursuit of a devoted maiden by a "tyrant" and its gratuitous horrors, of the old tragedy of revenge; and much the same is true of the not dissimilar story detailed by Robert Davenport in his tragedy of *King John and Matilda,* 1624, however its harrowing scenes refer back to the old chronicle play, *The Death of Robert Earl of Huntington.* Both belong to the specific group of *The Maid's Tragedy,* the situation of woman a prey to the passions of man, the situation of *Measure for Measure,* of Massinger's *Duke of Milan* and of Shirley's *Traitor. The Bloody Banquet,* "by T. D.," 1620, marks a similar reversion to the theme of the wanton queen, the topic of Fletcher's *Thierry and Theodoret* as of the earlier *Titus Andronicus* and Marston's *Insatiate Countess,* to name no others. Turning to tragicomedy, we find it commonly mixing its high themes — as already in Fletcher — with lighter comedy. This mixture of elements is characteristic, for

example, of the several "women's plays," as they have been
called that cluster about 1620. These include, besides
Fletcher's own *Sea Voyage* (wherein a commonwealth of women
sufficient to themselves constitutes a feature), and *Women
Pleased,* the able anonymous play on the same Spanish story
as the latter, *Swetnam the Woman Hater Arraigned by Women,*
a cumbrous title referable to a passing misogynist pamphlet
attacked in the underplot. Of a like character, though more
serious, is Dekker's fine play, *Match Me in London* and his
Wonder of a Kingdom, while *The Spanish Gipsy,* already
noticed, by Rowley and Middleton, and the slightly earlier
Cure for a Cuckold by Rowley and Webster disclose in various
degrees a more or less happy combination of the drama which
approaches the tragic with pure comedy. These tragicomedies
belong in the early twenties and to them may be added *The
Heir* by Thomas May which, however repetitious of old
material, is well written and not without genuine merit.

As to lesser comedy within the reign of King James, it, too,
had learned much of Fletcher, and that despite the continued
force of the earlier example of Jonson. Of the older and
greater men in comedy, we have heard in a previous chapter.
Suffice it here to recall that not only were some of them still
active but that continued revivals of the plays of the former
reign served to leaven the rapidly increasing output of new
plays. Heywood's important contributions to the domestic
drama, *The Captives* and *The English Traveller,* fall, the one
just before the conclusion of the reign, the other not far after.
And William Rowley's pleasing and vivacious comedy, *The
New Wonder or a Woman Never Vexed,* however a reversion
to the method of earlier London comedy, likewise falls late.
Lastly, there is Robert Davenport of whom we only know that
he "flourished," as the phrase goes, in the year 1624. To this
year or earlier have been referred his two comedies, *The City
Nightcap* and *A New Trick to Cheat the Devil,* the latter
especially a clever if somewhat extravagant play of the same
general type. Brome, most important of the immediate disciples
of Jonson, Mayne, Marmion, Cockayne and the rest come later.
For the nonce be it repeated in conclusion that the period from
1612 to 1625 was as pre-eminently the period of Fletcher as that
which preceded it had been Jonson's; for in it, above the many
other things which we have found, the dominant note was the

new Fletcherian romanticism which, as we have seen, supplanted with its contrast, its surprise, its gaudier colours and more insistent music, the more natural, the healthier and more humane romanticism of the Shakespearean supremacy.

CHAPTER IX

SHIRLEY AND THE LAST OF THE OLD DRAMA

WHEN King James died, in 1625, few of the great men who had made his reign memorable in the drama survived him. Beaumont and Shakespeare had retired long since, dying, as did the old manager and exploiter of plays, Philip Henslowe, in 1616, and neither Chapman nor Marston wrote certainly thereafter. Alleyn, the famous actor, had retired in 1604, and Burbage, active to the last, died in 1619, to be succeeded in the more important Shakespearean rôles by John Lowin and Joseph Taylor. Fletcher's work came to its end with the reign and Middleton's two years after. Of the older greater men, only Jonson, Heywood and Dekker survived, the last somewhat uncertainly in work with other men and in the making over and printing of earlier plays. Heywood's late dramatic work, too, is much of it uncertain and in large part lost. He was too old to learn the new tricks, however he essayed them in such tragicomedies as *The Royal King and Loyal Servant* or in his other drama of heroic contest, the interesting *Challenge for Beauty,* an Elizabethan effort to appreciate Cavalier ideals. As to Jonson, by this time the best of his work was behind him, although the old tree put forth annually its blossoms of inventive poetry for the pleasure of the court. Latterly Jonson was less appreciated as younger pens and keener courtiers competed for his place. To the honour of King Charles, be it remembered that he was kind to his father's old poet. In the very year of the king's accession Jonson had returned to the stage after having written no drama since *Bartholomew Fair,* six years before. But these later efforts, *The Staple of News, The New Inn, The Magnetic Lady* and *The Tale of a Tub,* acted between 1625 and 1634, while full of strong, satirical and " humorous " writing, mark a hardening in the poet's touch, a reversion to allegory and caricature, disclosing at times a bitterness, referable to the poet's struggle with poverty, failing physical vigour and the approach of old age. Jonson went down contemning and despising the opinion of the vulgar to the end; but he was beloved by many, even among the younger generation, for the talents that had made him great and for his honest worth, and acknowledged, at his death, to have been the one, sole leader and arbiter of the poetry and the drama of his time.

At the beginning of the reign Massinger was still the most conspicuous figure in the drama. Intrenched in his recent partnership with Fletcher and strong in the acceptance which his independent work had received, he confirmed the popularity of tragicomedy, contributing likewise, as we have seen in the last chapter, both comedy and tragedy to the stage for a decade or more. But in these years begins, likewise, the work of Shirley and Ford, strong rivals for the popular favour, and Brome and Davenant follow soon after.

As to the general conditions of the stage, King Charles, on his succession, continued to extend the royal patronage to the theatrical companies that his father had created. Not only did the new king take over his father's players, but he added his own, the Prince's men, to them, thus confirming the leadership of the King's players. The Lady Elizabeth's men became now the Queen's; and, in 1632, the players, known in the former reign as the Palsgrave's, found a patron in the infant Prince Charles. One other company received royal recognition as the King's Revels; but the Queen's Revels disappears in this reign, although a fifth company, without a name or a patron, continued to act at the Bull and the Fortune. Besides these two lesser older theatres, the new Cockpit, sometimes known as the Phœnix, housed Queen Henrietta's players and there was another new playhouse in Salisbury Court which was variously occupied. The King's men still acted habitually at their old houses, the Blackfriars and the Globe, and an attempt, in 1637, to revive a boys' company of players enjoyed only a short lived success. A feature of this time is the widening breach between the court and the Puritan city in respect to the regulation of the stage; a struggle that was to end at last in the closing of all the London theatres by the act of Parliament and in the discontinuance, for the time, of all acting of plays.

James Shirley was born in London in 1596 and educated at both universities. Of his family and extraction little is known; but an air of refinement and reserve seems to have been his, and he enjoyed a wide and general esteem among his contemporaries. Shirley took orders about the year 1620, receiving a charge at St. Albans; but on becoming a convert to the Church of Rome, he gave up his pulpit and, in 1623, took the mastership of St. Albans Grammar School, giving this up in turn and coming to London and play making two years later. The period of Shirley's dramatic authorship thus corresponds almost precisely with the actual reign of King Charles; for it was only the closing of the theatres that silenced the poet. Shirley succeeded easily in his new craft and, "without affecting the ways of flattery," soon acquired many friends and patrons, among them most conspicuous the king himself and his amiable queen, Henrietta Maria. To the latter Shirley was deeply attached. Through another of his patrons, the Earl of Kildare, Shirley was induced to go to Dublin, whither he carried the repertory and traditions of the London stage. Thither he returned more than once in the thirties, never losing, however, his touch with the King's players for whom he was the chief poet in these later years. In 1640 Shirley returned permanently to London, but his career as a dramatist was cut short, two years later, by the peremptory order of Parliament closing the theatres. With the outbreak of the Commonwealth wars, Shirley followed his patron, the Earl of Newcastle, taking what part we do not know. He was soon back in London, however, striving for a livelihood with his pen. To the year 1646, belongs Shirley's publication of his volume of miscellaneous verse; to the next, his preface "To the Reader," prefixed to the first folio of the plays of Beaumont and Fletcher. Soon after, Shirley was forced back into his old profession of schoolmaster and to that unhappy recourse of his kind, the writing of schoolbooks. Teaching, the printing of plays, hitherto unpublished, and hack work in translation from the classics for men like Ogilby, who never acknowledged Shirley's help, make up the drudgery of the poet's later years which were prolonged to the time of the great fire, in 1666, when, according to Wood, our only authority for the life of Shirley, he was driven with his wife from their home in Whitefriars by the flames and "being in a manner overcome with affrightments, disconsolations and other miseries occasioned by that fire and their losses," died soon after, both "within the compass of a natural day." Shirley was buried in the churchyard of St. Giles-in-the-Fields.

During the period of his activity as a playwright, Shirley wrote nearly forty plays and, owing to his personal care of his work, a larger proportion of them remain extant than of almost any other of our old dramatists. Shirley's first work was for the Queen's men who played habitually at the Phœnix; by 1635, however, he had succeeded to the place, as also to the popularity, of Fletcher. But Shirley really succeeded to more even than this, for, owing to his acceptance at court, he combined with the popularity of Fletcher on the boards of the public theatres much of Jonson's received position as chief among the entertainers and writers of masques at court, until he was outstripped in this by Davenant. Shirley was remarkably independent in his authorship, collaborating with no one unless we accept the somewhat doubtful case of Chapman and certain alleged revisions of plays originally Fletcher's.

The earliest of Shirley's plays is *Love Tricks,* afterwards published as *The School of Compliment.* This comedy is far from a satisfactory performance. In 1626 Shirley wrote his excellent comedy, *The Wedding.* Here the lighter elements are happily sustained in the humours of one Rawbone, a hungry variant of Middleton's eternal usurer, addicted to a legal jargon that reminds the reader of the academic comedy, *Ignoramus.* Shirley was plainly feeling his way, inventively employing as yet the material of existing drama as became the bookish man that he was. So, too, in *The Brothers* of equal date, he experimented, not unsuccessfully, with that favourite source of his immediate predecessors, Spanish story. If we would know Shirley at his best constructively, we must refer to *The Witty Fair One,* acted in 1628. This inventive comedy turns on the old device of a struggle between a clever girl and a determined father as to which shall decide the choice of a husband. Marston had used this motive in *The Fawn,* especially the device by which the lady encourages a faint-hearted suitor by false reports to her father of his audacity before his face. But Shirley, profiting by all this, converted his comedy into as veritable a series of dramatic surprises as Jonson compassed in *The Alchemist* or in *The Silent Woman.*

It has already been noted that Shirley raised the comedy of English life from the tradesfolk of Middleton and Jonson to the higher social grade which came in time to constitute what is now known as society. Three comedies in particular illustrate this, *Hyde Park, The Ball* and *The Gamester;* for here Shirley left his books to draw from the life that he saw about him. The interest of the first of these centres in the races (of men as well as of horses), at that time held in the rural regions of Hyde Park. The heroine, Carol, is an excellent example of the witty, free spoken but virtuous lady of fashion; and the conduct of Fairfield's courtship of her, a match of wits in which the end is a drawn game, reminds one of many like situations to come in the dramas of the next age when Shirley was forgotten. *The Ball,* in turn, called attention, by way of defence, to the new fashionable assemblies for public dancing. It seems that these meetings had been criticised on the score of morals and surmised, by scandal-mongers, to be a cloak for vice. In this play, however, Herbert, the Master of the Revels, tells us that " there were divers personated so naturally, both of lords and others of the court, that I took it ill and would have forbidden the play but that Beeston, [the manager], promised many things, which I found fault withal, should be left out." Clearly Shirley had indeed left his books; but he learned his lesson like a sensible man and did not, in this wise, offend again. *Hyde Park* and *The Ball* were both on the stage by 1632. When the latter comedy was printed, seven years later, the title conveyed the words, " written by George Chapman and James Shirley." Now Chapman was at this time seventy-three years of age, in poverty and long a stranger to the stage, while Shirley was at the height of his success at court and in the city. There is not a word in *The Ball* to suggest Chapman, as the comedy is dependent on the passing fashion of the moment in a kind of society that must have been totally unknown to the old translator of Homer. The only other alleged example of this strange collaboration is the tragedy, *Chabot Admiral of France,* printed in the same year. Either these ascriptions are sheer error or possibly — as seems less unlikely in the latter case — Shirley was willing generously to befriend his older, unsuccessful contemporary in an allowance to him of a larger share in work revised than the facts of his borrowing perhaps actually warranted.

Most conspicuous by way of scandal is Shirley's next comedy, *The Gamester,* acted in 1633 and a notable success not only on its first performance but in repeated revivals. *The Gamester* is the grossest of Shirley's plays; in fact no other play of his approaches it in this respect; and it is no excuse that what seems to the auditor during the action a highly " objectionable complication " turns out in the end to be no more than " a harmless stratagem." Moreover, the plot of this play was suggested and its conduct and writing praised by the virtuous King

Charles. In consequence, Kingsley gibbeted *The Gamester,*
in his *Plays and Puritans,* and Gardiner, the historian, has taken
this drama as a typical example of the immorality of the Carolan
stage. Without endeavouring to condone the lapses of Shirley,
the vigour of the characterisation and the capable management
of the plot is not for a moment to be questioned. The matter
at large is not to be argued here, but in justice it may be urged
that it is eminently unfair to judge an age, or even an author,
by a single work. There are as bad plays, ethically considered,
as *The Gamester,* both before it and after, and Shirley is full
elsewhere of poetry and elevated thought. It is not the range of
vibration that determines the tone, however violence may, for
the moment, destroy all beauty of sound. There is a difference
between the improprieties of Shakespeare and the improprieties
of Shirley, and yet both are dramatic and not necessarily referable to any defect in the author; and it is almost as unfair to
judge Shirley — and King Charles for that matter — in this
wise as it would be to anathematise Shakespeare — as some indeed have done — for the discourse of Mistress Overdone with
her tapster, Pompey.

Intermittent with his other work Shirley continued to furnish
the stage with vivacious and eminently successful comedies of
manners throughout the thirties. *The Example* and *The Lady
of Pleasure* offer particularly happy illustrations of the poet's
nice observation of contemporary manners, his inventive facility,
ease of execution and adaptability to whatever might be the
task in hand. In *The Example* recurs, in effective form, Shirley's favourite dramatic situation, the conversion of a libertine
to virtue in the pursuit of pleasure by the steadfastness or cleverness of his intended victim; and *The Lady of Pleasure* repeats
with sufficient variation the same theme. Indubitably Shirley
used the material of his observation among the people of fashion
and rank to association with whom his acceptance at court gave
him admittance. And he writes always more in the spirit of
a sympathetic participant in their life than as an observer
armed with the weapons of satire. And yet while Shirley's
comedy figures are measurably true to the life about him, they
fall, altogether naturally, into the grooves of type, already so
well defined by Middleton and Fletcher. The foolish youth,
the " humorous " suitors, the sundry kinds of gulls, Sir William
Scentlove, Alexander Kickshaw, Lord Rainbow — their very
names betray them — all are the descendants of Middleton;

whilst Fletcherian are Shirley's many delightful, vivacious and resourceful maidens, be Violetta, Carol or Celestina her name. With all his changes, turns and ingenuities wrought upon these older types, new dressed to move in high cross lights, Shirley's most successful and serious variation is that of the profligate reclaimed to whom he gives in Lord Fitzavarice of *The Example* and in the " Lord " unnamed of *The Lady of Pleasure,* a real worth, dignity and contrition. Above all the women of Shirley's comedy stand for the companion figures, Mistress Peregrine and Celestina, for example, in their combination of a competent knowledge of the world with a womanly sweetness and a steadfastness in virtue not to be moved even where the heart has been touched.

But Shirley's facile pen was by no means confined to comedy. If we turn to his romantic dramas, we find them embracing a wide range of subjects in which light comedy such as *The Humorous Courtier* and pure extravaganza, like *The Bird in the Cage,* hold one extreme and pseudo-history, like *The Politician,* or tragedies, like *The Traitor,* hold the other. The romantic plays scatter over the poet's career, ushered in with *The Maid's Revenge,* in 1626, and closing with *The Sisters,* licensed in April 1642. *The Court Secret* was apparently written too late to escape the order which closed the theatres, though it was acted after the Restoration. In observing the later products of our English romantic drama, while plays indubitably tragic or wholly comic on the other hand continue to be written, there is a tendency towards the breaking down of these formal distinctions. This tendency, the averted catastrophe of tragicomedy fostered, with its incessant demand for the happy ending, so that even in dramas ostensibly tragic, the conclusion becomes often less an expiation and triumph of fate than a meting out of rewards to the innocent and punishments to the guilty. In Shirley's *Politician,* described, for example, as a tragedy, all the conspirators and wicked figures of the cast suffer death and all the virtuous, save one, are preserved for future happiness. Such a play may be described as only half a tragedy; because the tilting of intrigue and counter-intrigue has been substituted for a moral struggle. Moreover, it is just this tilting of intrigue and counter-intrigue that is the soul of comedy and tragicomedy. So that while we recognise in dramas such as *The Cardinal* or *The Maid's Revenge* that Shirley is accepting the meaning of tragedy in its normal sense, and while of some comedies there can likewise arise no possible question, in the majority of these romantic plays the distinction really breaks down completely.

It was in the early thirties, when at the height of his fame that Shirley dramatized in his *Arcadia* a subject from Sir Philip Sidney already employed by Day in his *Isle of Gulls;* and to the same period belongs the extravagant *Bird in a Cage,* supposed, from its ironical dedication to the unfortunate Prynne to be charged satirically with allusions to the circumstances of the moment. *The Opportunity* has been reported a happy dramatization in English of a comedy by Tirso de Molina and exhibits with several other plays, *The Young Admiral* and *The Humorous Courtier* among them, Shirley's recourse to Spanish sources. *The Opportunity* is a model comedy of intrigue in which a mistake in identity, accepted in a spirit of adventure, leads to a perfect network of involvement, and the accident of a faltering resolution at the critical moment brings its own defeat. To classify any of the dramas of Shirley as historical is to misuse a much abused term. But *The Coronation,* a very interesting tragicomedy, details a story of disputed succession in ancient "Epire," *The Doubtful Heir* is placed in a setting supposedly of Spanish history, and *St. Patrick for Ireland,* nicely calculated for the meridian of Dublin, reverts, in its curious intermingling of the elements of a romantic tragicomedy with the miracles of the saint, to an earlier and cruder form of dramatic entertainment. Not content with this diversity of scene, the ambitious drama, entitled *The Politician,* takes the auditor to Norway and works out a plot of great intricacy with figures which it is difficult to think were not suggested at least by the tragedy of *Hamlet.* As further examples of Shirley's exhaustless ingenuity in working new things out of old, *The Grateful Servant* details the adventures of a princess disguised as a page in the court of her lover, and *The Duke's Mistress* manipulates new changes with the old puppets, an infatuated prince, an imperious beauty, a faithless intriguer, a neglected wife and a bluff and honest captain.

Among the four or five tragedies of Shirley as yet unmentioned, two deserve special note. These are *The Traitor,* on the stage by 1631, and *The Cardinal,* 1641, one of the latest of the poet's plays. *The Traitor* is still another example of the legerdemain of a clever playwright in converting old and trite material into new effects. The malevolent cunning and effrontery of the arch-schemer, Lorenzo, of this play, in his wresting of the virtues as well as the vices of those about him to work his ends, amounts to genius. It is little to the purpose to show that the real Lorenzino de' Medici was a man very different from the figure represented by Shirley. The logic of the drama is not the logic of life, and Shirley treated the material of history, precisely as he treated the material of fiction, with the inventive freedom of absolute ownership. *Barnevelt* is almost the last play of the old age that seems actuated by anything like an historical conscience such as chained Shakespeare to the details of Holinshed or sent Jonson to a scholar's study of Tacitus and other Roman historians. Returning to Shirley's tragedies, *The Cardinal* is generally recognised as the poet's best play of the type, although the relations of the chief characters remind the reader, who has an eye for resemblances, of *The Duchess of Malfi*. The plot turns on a struggle between the Duchess Rosaura, young, beautiful and wealthy, and the politic Cardinal (not otherwise named) who has gained the consent of the King that the lady shall marry the Cardinal's nephew, Columbo, the royal favourite. But the duchess contrives to obtain a release of his claim to her hand from Columbo and gains the King's consent to her marriage with Alvarez, the man of her choice, the Cardinal apparently accepting the decision and consenting to be present at the wedding as a sign of reconciliation. In a scene, incomparably well written and prepared by a prelude of comedy, the newly married bridegroom, in the height of the nuptial revels, is laid dead, assassinated, at the feet of his bride; and the remainder of the play is concerned with a leisurely but masterful unravelling of this extraordinary situation. A serious blot on this tragedy is the scene wherein the Cardinal, unable to satiate his revenge on the hapless duchess, now distraught and delivered into his hands as a ward, attempts her dishonour. This situation is the more amazing from the pen of a Romanist; but it is strictly in accord with the taste of the age for a strong diet and, in this instance, leads to an ingenious catastrophe involving the deaths not only of the protagonists but of the valiant Hernando who has slain Columbo as the champion of the duchess and now interposes to save her honour but not her life. *The Cardinal* is the last tragedy that was attempted along the trodden path of romantic drama. In tragedy, at least, Shirley remained to the end singularly free of the influence of Fletcher. He marks, in a sense, a return to the more direct, the less heroic and less inflated character of earlier tragedy. For, however intricate the intrigue, Shirley's plot is commonly single and the episodes of comic relief are not allowed to usurp an immoderate share of the interest. His personages, too, are clearly defined and distinguished, and neither in conduct, thought nor diction is there ambiguity, difficulty or dramatic delay. More poetical on occasion than Massinger, Shirley never falls into the latter's rhetoric and preoccupation with a moral problem. In a word, Shirley wrote frankly for his age and his product was acceptable for its ease, finish, inventiveness and sufficiency. He was less in the trend of his time than several of his inferiors. That is why he so little affected his contemporaries and why the next age speedily forgot him to take up with modified Fletcherian romance and brutalised Jonson.

There remains one thing more of Shirley, and that is his part in the elaborate entertainments at court which continued into the reign of King Charles. It was in 1634, the very year of Jonson's last efforts and the acting of *Comus,* that Shirley's magnificent *Triumph of Peace* was presented at court with un-exampled cost and sumptuousness by the united endeavours of the four Inns of Court. This occasion was heightened by the recent trial and condemnation of Prynne, sometime a student of Lincoln's Inn, for his ill-timed and outrageous attack upon the stage entitled *Histriomastix;* and his fellow lawyers took this means of disavowing his Puritanic principles. William Prynne was an Oxford man, as well as he was portentously learned; he had already written several pamphlets expressing his abhorrence of certain practices, religious and social, of which he happened to disapprove, among which the picturesqueness of its title has given *The Unloveliness of Lovelocks,* a conspicuous repute. In *Histriomastix,* Prynne not only attacked, in the most intemperate language, the stage (with which he was much less minutely acquainted than with the Christian Fathers), but he scored especially the disguise of either sex in the habit of the other and anathematised the appearance of women on the stage in terms brutally coarse and abusive. In this last he was voicing a common prejudice of his time; for as yet women as actors were unknown to the English public stage, and the actresses of a French troupe, in 1629, had been hooted from the London boards. Unhappily for Prynne, however, the queen had recently displayed an unusual interest in theatricals; and had actually taken a part, at a private performance at court, in *The Shepherd's Pastoral* by Walter Montague — for the benefit of her English it was said — just about the time of the appearance of Prynne's book. It is doubtful if Prynne really intended this personal application; but an enemy was found of course to make it at once. The penalties inflicted on the unfortunate pamphleteer on his condemnation — a heavy fine, the loss of his university degrees and the clipping of his ears in the pillory — were as brutal as they were excessive. Shirley's ironical dedication of *The Bird in a Cage* has already been mentioned. *The Triumph of Peace* is a monster masque alike for size and incongruity. There are eight antimasques in rapid succession, of abstractions, birds, thieves, huntsmen, projectors and beggars, and the scenes varied from a knight tilting at a windmill to a sinking moon in an open landscape. The persons engaged could have numbered no less than a hundred; the scene was furnished by the indefatigable Inigo Jones, the music by the celebrated composer, William Lawes, and the cost was enormous. In less than a week the court matched this performance with *Cœlum Britannicum,* contrived by the poet, Thomas Carew, with the same able assistance and exhibiting eight changes of scene with as many antimasques. Carew's masque is poetic in the lyrical parts, but it lacks the dramatic touch which Shirley seems able to have infused even into the inchoate material of *The Triumph of Peace.*

But a greater than either of these availed himself of the popular masque form in this very year, in the entertainment, presented at Ludlow Castle before the Earl of Bridgewater, Lord President of Wales, and known now as *Comus.* Milton had already essayed the masque, if so slight a performance as *Arcades* can be so denominated, and he was to return to the drama in its most serious form in the tragedy of *Samson Agonistes.* It was the friendship of Lawes that procured for Milton this opportunity for the display of his lyrical talent. *Comus,* however it express a coherent situation in a well sustained allegory, is not really a drama, though it cannot be said that it falls below contemporary masques even in this particular. How much it rises in its elevation of thought, exquisite expression and lyrical music above all contemporaries all know who know and love our English poetry. Milton's *Comus* historically groups with a number of private masques in which several of the minor poets of the time of Charles, such as Nabbes, Cockayne and others, were variously concerned. None of them are memorable. In the next year Davenant succeeded to the post of writer of masques for the court, shortly after to become poet laureate on the death of Jonson. Among Shirley's works are to be found several short dialogues, more or less masque-like and dramatic in form, and some of them, as for example *Cupid and Death,* of a real poetic beauty. Although one other, *The Contention of Ajax and Ulysses,* is described as "nobly represented by young gentlemen of quality at a private entertainment of some persons of honour," we do not know anything definite concerning the performance of either or the time of their writing. *The Triumph of Beauty,* which is a fully developed masque and was printed in 1646, contains a similarly vague statement as to its presentation.

Among the dramatists, Shirley's rivals, in the reign of King Charles, none has left a more permanent, if at times a more questioned, repute than "melancholy John Ford." Ford was the younger son of a Devonshire gentleman, and he was born at Ilsington, in that county, in 1586. Educated first at Exeter College, Oxford, and later at the Middle Temple, it has been thought that Ford was a lawyer by profession and the legal agent in London of the gentry of his county. He does not appear to have written his plays, in the first instance, professionally, although there is abundant proof of their popularity. Indeed, the attitude of several of his introductions displays almost too great a sensitiveness regarding his "amateur standing," and he assures us that his works are "the issue of his less serious hours," and that his "courtship of greatness never aimed at any thrift." Ford's earliest literary work was an elegy on the lately deceased Earl of Devonshire, addressed to his Countess, formerly Lady Rich, sometime Sidney's Stella. A more inauspicious beginning for an aspirant to literary fame could hardly be imagined; for Devonshire had died in disgrace for this very marriage and Ford had nothing to gain. It was characteristic of Ford, however, as we shall see by his dramas, thus to glorify this ill-starred couple who for love had literally cast away the world. Commendatory verses to his own works and elsewhere show that Ford was not devoid of patronage and friendship among the literary important of his time, although their works are singularly reticent as to the man personally.

Seventeen titles of plays have been assigned to the authorship of Ford, alone or assisted; of those seven are no longer extant: *The Witch of Edmonton,* 1622, and *The Sun's Darling* of the next year, disclose in their titles the name of Dekker with that of Ford, the former adding William Rowley's as well. *The Witch of Edmonton* is an effective and pathetic domestic tragedy and as such has already received our notice; *The Sun's Darling* is a beautiful masque-like comedy which, first acted at court in 1623, enjoyed a continued popularity. It seems not unlikely that Ford, in these cases, was the reviser of Dekker's earlier work. In *Perkin Warbeck,* which relates the story of that pretender to the English crown and his overthrow, Ford attempted to revive the chronicle play, a type of drama long since extinct; and in *The Queen or the Excellency of her Sex,* a tragicomedy of considerable worth which recent scholarship has assigned to the authorship of Ford, we have another excursus, this time into Spanish "historical" drama.[1] As to *Perkin Warbeck,* which is an exceedingly interesting tragedy, it may be fancied, however, that Ford wrote far more for the problem in identity involved than for any historical import. As to the plays of Ford in general, it has been well said that they fall naturally into two groups: "those in which he took hold of his subject, and those in which his subject took hold of him."[2] In the first group fall the two historical plays just mentioned and the two comedies, *Fancies Chaste and Noble,* acted about 1635, and *The Lady's Trial,* 1638; to the second belong the romantic dramas in which Ford may be said to have contributed as effectively and originally to the variety of English drama as he certainly contributed to its decadence. Ford is as far as author can be from that quick grasp and realisation of the trifling occurrences and incongruities of every day life that go so far to make up the equipment of the successful writer of comedy; wherefore when he descends to trifles, he is veritably trivial and when he forces his wit, he is coarse to the verge of indecency and beyond. The subject of *Fancies Chaste and Noble* is contemptible, and it is no excuse for the author that when we have been misled into "fancies" by the suggestions of his plot by no means to be characterised by either of the adjectives of his title, we are laughed at for our anxieties in a dénouement which is meas-

---

[1] See the edition of this play by W. Bang, *Materialien zur Kunde,* xiii, 1906.

[2] See the excellent paper by S. P. Sherman on Ford's "Contribution to the Decadence of the Drama," *ibid.,* Vol. xxiii, 1908, to which this paragraph is indebted.

urably harmless. *The Lady's Trial* is a better and a cleaner
play; though, with all its intrigue, it too suffers from what has
been justly called " a certain futility of plot."

The four dramas which were " thoroughly congenial with
Ford's spirit " are *The Lovers' Melancholy, Love's Sacrifice,
The Broken Heart* and *'Tis Pity She's a Whore.* In all the
atmosphere is wholly romantic, even effeminately so; for the interest is absorbingly that of the psychology of sex. *The Lovers'
Melancholy,* unlike the other three, raises no problem and ends,
after the manner of tragicomedy, happily; in the others we meet
with a momentous change in the dramatist's point of view, a
change both from the acceptance of the code of things as they
are and from the idealist's contentment with the beautiful and
unreal creations of his own imagination, to a recognition of the
essential conflict that must always exist between the ideals of
men and their realisation in a world of fact. Thus, *The Broken
Heart* gives us the problem of a wife, married against her will,
yet loving another; *Love's Sacrifice,* that of a passion which
springs up after marriage, with the struggle against it;
'Tis Pity is the awful story of a brother's and sister's incestuous
infatuation. And Ford represents these things, not as temptations to evil about the resistance to which there can be no possible
moral question among good men, but in the light of a struggle
towards a larger freedom and a higher morality. Ford is less
a sensualist and a voluptuary than a moral casuist; the intel-
lectuality of his conceptions is at least as vivid as his revel in
the beauty of sound, the loveliness of woman and the surging
of passionate impulse. In the conflict between the conventional
actual and his romantic ideals, his drama became more a drama
of revolution than merely of decadence, although he represents
to us, in the end, a world in which the accepted laws of men are
gone to naught or,— what is worse — converted into the bonds
of an intolerable tyranny. The pathos of the situation of
Penthea in *The Broken Heart* moves the romantic reader:
hapless Penthea who regards her married life a life of shame,
although her virtue is proof even against the passionate pleadings of her lover. So, too, the romantic reader is carried away
on the rising tide of that surprising scene in the same tragedy in
which the Princess Calantha, tall, passionless and fair, apprised
in successive climaxes of the starvation of poor Penthea, the
atrocious murder of her betrothed and the death of her father that
makes her queen of Sparta, steels her heart against all, sustains

the royal courtesy to her attending guests, arranges her father's obsequies, the punishment of her lover's murderer and the succession to the crown, and then falls dead, literally of a broken heart. On the other hand, to the wholly reasonable man — be he the redoubtable Prynne or the critic Hazlitt — all this is mawkish and, where not impious, perilously savouring of nonsense. Such questions as these of Ford were unknown to the comprehensive morality of Shakespeare, undreamed by the surefooted and judicious Jonson. Now, the problem story and the drama that questions all things human and divine is only too familiar to us with our Tolstoi, Ibsen, Hauptmann, Maeterlinck and Shaw. Underlying both *Love's Sacrifice* and *'Tis Pity* is that dangerous principle of the romantic revolt, a faith in the divine guidance of passion, in the supreme and irresistible authority of human impulse, a principle which, put into practice in a work-a-day world, is subversive of all established order and destructive, in the end, of the very ideals it adores. It is not enough to note in Ford originality of plot, a power to conceive his people in the manifestation of their passions, a charm and beauty of diction, and that true spirit of poetry that fashions words in the glow of an actual emotion. It is not even enough to admit in him that strange casuistry which, weaning the mind persuasively from a contemplation of the rule to the admission of the exception, forces home the inconsistencies of our human codes of morals and conduct. In Ford the modern way of looking at the world begins and his originality in this attitude is difficult for us to appreciate for the reason that we are so accustomed to his point of view. Ford applied to the drama and to the particular problems that interested him the same questioning spirit that inspired the Parliament of Charles to his overthrow. Ford is not only the poet that marks one of the most striking of the symptoms that characterised the old drama in its decadence, he is even more notably the harbinger of new things to come in a changing age.

Shirley bulks large in the history of English drama for the considerable amount of his achievement and its uniform attainment of the standard of excellence which the poet himself set for his work. Ford stands out above his fellows for the sincerity and intensity of his art and for his departures from the precedents and current methods of his time. Leaving these, the persistent dramatic influences throughout the reign of King Charles remained Jonson and Fletcher, and the name of their followers is legion.   With an occasional exception such as Richard Brome, it is notable that writing for the theatres was transferred, in this reign, from hack writers of Henslowe, professional playwrights, more or less addicted to the Bohemianism that has haunted poetry in all ages, to gentlemen, courtiers, even to peers of the realm, ambitious to be known, like the Duke of Newcastle and his lady, not only as patrons of letters but as contributors to literature as well.   As we look over the list — William Cartwright, Jasper Mayne, Thomas May, Shakerley Marmion, Robert Davenport, Thomas Goffe and Henry Glapthorne — all were gentlemen who wrote, not professional playwrights.   Many are writers of only a single play or known better in other walks of literature: William Habington, author of a sweet and belated Elizabethan collection of love poetry to his Castara; Sir John Suckling and Richard Lovelace, the well known and exquisite lyrists respectively of fickleness in love and of constancy; Cowley, most famous and popular poet of the day; and Sir John Denham, remembered in a later age for a single fine descriptive poem, *Cooper's Hill.*   These men, though most of them were writers of ability and capable dramatically in their various degrees, treated their work in an amateurish spirit; they are abundantly inventive and rhetorical, but they will commonly be found artificial and, when not overstrained, too often merely commonplace.   We have, in their romantic and serious endeavours, at times the fantasticality that distinguishes the other poetry of their time; and when we have not this, we have premonitions of the frigid restraint and the cold rhetoric that became prevalent among the minor writers of drama, their successors after the Restoration.   These gentlemen writers of the days of King Charles are in fact far less the successors of the popular drama than of the drama of the court and of the universities.   Their plays bear the same relation to the romantic dramas of Marlowe, Shakespeare and Fletcher that the romances of Mlle. de Scudéry, and such an imitation of them as Barclay's *Argenis* or Boyle's *Parthenissa,* bear to Sidney's *Arcadia.*   They are superficially of the same class; radically in the greatest possible contrast.

However, from among them we may find certain definite clues to lead us onward in our story of pre-Restoration drama.   The comedy of manners, for example, continued vigorous and unmistakably vulgar, not only in the hands of Brome, but in those of Marmion, Cartwright, Nabbes, Cockayne, Glapthorne and

Mayne. Marmion was the spendthrift son of a country gentleman and the friend of riotous Sir John Suckling; Cartwright
had university affiliation and became a preacher of repute for his
eloquence; both died prematurely. Mayne rose later to high
dignity in the church, and Cockayne was a gentleman of wealth,
a spendthrift, much travelled abroad. Glapthorne and Nabbes
were men of lesser position and of their lives less is known. But
all wrote comedies in the recognised Jonsonian manner and most
of them had known the great man in his literary presence-
chamber, the Apollo room of the Devil Tavern and were proud
to be numbered among the "sons of Ben." For example, the
Jonsonian butt, a "projector," our modern sharper, figures
prominently in Marmion's *Holland's Leaguer* and in Cartwright's only comedy of manners, *The Ordinary*. Mayne's
City Match repeats the familiar device of a merchant's pretended journey abroad to test the character and conduct of his
family and reverts to a motive of *The Silent Woman* for the
conclusion. While Glapthorne's *Hollander, Wit in a Constable*
and Davenport's *A New Trick to Cheat the Devil* take us back
to the low life of the city with Middleton rather than Jonson
for a guide; and Cockayne, more ambitious than some of his
fellows, in *The Obstinate Lady,* repeats situations of Massinger
and Shirley. Of the minor writers of comedy in this time
Thomas Nabbes furnishes by far the most original and favourable example. Nabbes was a Worcester man, apparently in the
services of a nobleman of that neighbourhood. His comedies of
London manners, all acted in the thirties, are *Covent Garden,
Tottenham Court,* and *The Bride.* The last is one of the best
comedies of its time and, turning upon the familiar subject, an
elopement, is alike a fresh, cleanly and natural story well told.
Nabbes deserves the praise that he has received for " his modest
well-conducted girls " and his virtuous and refined young men."
His freedom from obscurity and grossness, which are the darling
sins of this group of plays, is alike remarkable and refreshing.

But the dramatic influence of Jonson was not confined to the
scholars and gentlemen. Richard Brome was " a son of Ben "
in a somewhat different sense from that applying to Cartwright
or Randolph. Brome had been for years Jonson's body-servant
and remained such to Jonson's death. The old dramatist, whose
memory Brome ever after revered, had nothing to leave his
faithful servant, so he imparted to him some of the crumbs of
his learning and, as he had done before in the case of the boy

actor, Nat Field, taught Brome " to make plays." Brome is the author of upwards of a score of dramas, comedies of manners, and romantic tragicomedies after the custom of the age. The first are well constructed and illustrate contemporary manners, chiefly in low life, not without spirit and success; but they repeat with wearisome reiteration Middleton's category of gulls, usurers and spendthrifts, city wives and city husbands and in repetition the lines have become coarser, like the situations, and the humour at times falls into horse play and worse. Brome enjoyed much popularity in his day not only for his comedies of which *A Mad Couple Well Matched, The Antipodes* and *A Jovial Crew* are among the best, but likewise for his romantic dramas such as *The Lovesick Court* and *Queen and Concubine* wherein he is proclaimed " a limb of Fletcher." Brome's work is characterised by inventiveness and a practical knowledge of the workings of the stage, there is a certain rough honesty about him, and his anxiety not to intrude and eagerness " to keep " no more than " the weakest branch o' the stage alive " is at times ludicrous. It is astonishing that a man consciously possessed of so little poetry could have succeeded as well. In his comedy *The Northern Lass,* Brome achieved his best effort. Therein a country girl becomes honestly infatuated with a gentleman who has offered himself to her as a fit husband half in jest. She follows him to London to find him on the eve of marriage with a widow, and, in the midst of a series of intrigues, exceedingly well managed, stands forth a natural and pathetic figure, absolutely clear-sighted and absolutely honest.

The influence of Jonson and Fletcher has been much insisted on in these pages, but not beyond the warrant of the actual facts; for however the greater men triumphed in their individuality, the lesser not only began but continued, with a few exceptions, under their spell. Both of these great men had employed classic story in the drama, it will be remembered, Jonson rigorously and with a sense of the differences of ancient manners from those of his own day, Fletcher always more or less romantically. It was drama of the type of *Valentinian* or Massinger's *Roman Actor* that presented to the subjects of King Charles their picture of ancient Rome; and such pictures shade off into the no man's land of happy romance so that we cease to remember that Shirley's *Coronation* lays the scene in " Epire " or *The Broken Heart* in Sparta. Thomas May is chiefly remembered as the historian of the Long Parliament and as a translator of Virgil and Lucan.

He was a man of distinction in his day and, on his death, in 1650, was buried with honours in Westminster Abbey. In the history of the drama, May is interesting for his effort to follow in the wake of Jonson in writing dramas on classical subjects with a due consideration of the ancient authorities and of the ideals of ancient tragedy. Four plays are the result, written and some of them acted, none too successfully, between 1626 and 1631; they are by title *Cleopatra, Julia Agrippina, Antigone* and *Julius Cæsar*. The last remains in manuscript. Passing *Cleopatra,* which is a stronger play than Daniel's on the same topic, but which dare not of course try conclusions with Shakespeare or Dryden, we find in *Agrippina* a genuinely effective tragedy, swift, clear and eloquent in parts. *Antigone* is scarcely inferior, however the prevailing romanticism succeeded, with echoes of Macbeth and the witches and the death of Juliet in her tomb, in seducing this devotee of the classics from the stricter paths of his kind. May's tragedies are well planned and well written, and in an age less given over to the drama of intrigue and surcharged situation, might have enjoyed a success more commensurate with their worth.

The few other plays of the period that drew on classical subjects either take us back to the universities, where Seneca in the dilution of three generations still flourished, or over absolutely to the delocalised tragicomedy that was leading on to the heroic play. Among dramas of the general kind and worthy a mention is the meritorious *Hannibal and Scipio* of Nabbes, which transforms the victor of Lake Trasimene, however, into the infatuated lover of an unknown captive at Cannæ, Heming's *The Jew's Tragedy,* on the overthrow of Jerusalem by Titus, and *Messalina* by Nathaniel Richards, an able and interesting tragedy, as effective as drama can be without the lift of poetry. William Heming deserves a passing mention as the son of John Heming, Shakespeare's fellow actor and sharer in the Globe and Blackfriars theatres. We know little of him save that he was the author of another tragedy, *The Fatal Contract* and that, after he had proved his father's will in 1630, he proceeded to rid himself of his inheritance in short order. Richards was a more decorous person, a Devon man of good family, educated at Cambridge and latterly of the church. *Messalina* is his only play.

With William Cartwright, already mentioned for comedy, we go wholly over to the university and to tragicomedy. Cartwright was identified all his life with Oxford and noted for his

scholarship. His three tragicomedies fall wholly within the
thirties and include *The Lady Errant,* treating of a woman's
conspiracy in ancient Cyprus suggested by Aristophanes, *Love's
Convert,* a story of Pausanias transferred to a siege of Byzan-
tium, and *The Royal Slave,* a dramatic amplification of the Per-
sian tale of the Ephesian captive who was king for three days.
Notwithstanding the classical flavour of all these subjects Cartwright is altogether romantic. He " writes like a man," as
Jonson said of him and is a capable dramatist. The major situation of *Love's Convert* is much that of Maeterlinck's *Mona
Vana,* though the censor of Cartwright's time found no difficulty
in approving it and it is quite as clean a play. *The Royal Slave,*
acted before the king and queen on the occasion of their visit to
Oxford in 1636 and repeated later at the royal request at Hamp-
ton Court, was remarkable in its day for no less than eight
changes of scene.

In Elizabethan times the drama of the universities and that
of the popular stage were wide apart. Ruggle's *Club Law* personally lampooned the citizens of Cambridge in a manner not
much above the horse play of the old interludes while Shakespeare was penning the immortal scenes of Falstaff; and *Lingua,*
an academic allegory of extraordinary and tedious elaboration
and completeness, corresponds, in point of its alleged date of
earliest acting, with the first popularity of *Hamlet.* In 1607 an
epidemic of theatromania, so to speak, raged at Oxford in which
students and dons were alike infected. As we read, in a contemporary document, an account of the whole affair, of the
argument as to whether English were " a language fit for a
university," and of their scholar's joy in their petty histrionic
triumphs, we wonder if these youths could have been aware of
contemporary *Antony and Cleopatra* or if their taste reached
to the satirical comedy of *Every Man In his Humour.*[3] The
attitude of academic circles to the great romantic drama that
was to make the age renowned above the scholarship of all the
colleges, is to be caught in the offhand, patronising, critical dicta
of *The Return from Parnassus* in which it is deplored — and
this in the very year of *Hamlet,* after *Julius Cæsar* and the
chronicle plays — that the author of *Venus and Adonis* should

[3] See the account of these theatricals at Oxford by Griffin Higges,
Miscellanea Antiqua Anglicana, 1816, Vol. i; and the present author's " Thalia in Oxford," *The Queen's Progress,* 1904, p. 201.

not " content " himself with " a graver subject." And yet we know, by the title of one of the quartos, that this same *Hamlet* had been acted at both universities, and *Volpone* as well — though this was later. Whether such performances wrought in part the change or not, by the time that Charles came to his throne, we find no such divergence between the drama of the London theatres and that of Oxford and Cambridge. The popular stage had suffered a modification that made it alike the heir of Marlowe and Shakespeare and of Lyly and Daniel, and the scholars now strove with the courtiers and with lesser men in supplying the boards of the London playhouses as well as the halls of their colleges at home.

When all has been said, however, it must be confessed that the universities only produced one dramatic poet of note. This was Thomas Randolph, a Westminster lad who was first of Trinity College Cambridge and became later a master of arts of Oxford as well. Randolph was described in his time as a brilliant scholar, possessed of a bodily and mental vigour that literally exhausted itself in excessive effort. He died in 1635 at the early age of thirty, leaving behind him, besides a Latin comedy (though of his authorship of *Cornelianum Dolum* doubt has been expressed), three English plays and a version of the *Plutus* of Aristophanes as clever as it is ungovernably free. To these works may be added a couple of witty monologues, *Aristippus* and *The Conceited Pedlar.* It was for the royal visit to Cambridge in 1632 that Randolph prepared *The Jealous Lovers,* a comedy which enjoyed great success although written strictly on the accepted academic lines of Plautine intrigue. In *The Muses' Looking Glass,* which appears to have been acted in London, Randolph conceived an original theme peculiarly adapted to his light satirical genius. The scene is a playhouse into which two Puritans, Bird, a featherman, and Mistress Flowerdew, a pin-woman, have intruded to sell their wares. They are detained by Roscius the actor, to witness several scenes in which human vices or humours are cleverly represented in pairs, each the extreme of the other, according to the Aristotelian doctrine; and, in the end, the drama concludes with the glorification of " golden Mediocrity, the mother of virtues." Thus coldly described Randolph's play seems little more than a reversion to the method of the old moralities, conducted after the manner of the Jonsonian humour. *The Muses' Looking Glass* is in reality much more, however, in its originality, its wit and really clever characterisation within the accepted limits of abstraction. Among college plays by Randolph's immediate contemporaries may be mentioned *The Rival Friends* by Peter Hausted, "cried down" at Cambridge in 1631, " by boys, faction and confident ignorance," if the author is to be trusted. There is also Abraham Cowley's amusing Latin comedy *Naufragium Joculare,* founded on a boisterous episode of Plautus, already employed by Heywood in the underplot of his *English Traveller.* Cowley's satirical English comedy, *The Guardian,* 1641, was too impartial to the unworthy Cavalier, as to the hypocritical Puritan, for success at a moment when men were taking sides for the impending struggle of the Civil War, although it met with a better reception when reacted after the Restoration as *Cutter of Coleman Street.* *The Floating Island* by William Strode, orator of the university of Oxford and later canon of Christ Church, was one of the many answers to Prynne. Strode's play is a weighty allegory of the passions in which is mirrored the complacency of the Cavalier and his contempt for the " malignant " whose right even to be heard is denied and whose courage in arms was yet to be tested.

To return to Randolph, by far his most finished play is *Amyntas or the Impossible Dowry,* one of the most poetic and successful of English ventures into that exotic form, the pastoral drama. In thus recurring to the pastoral in the year 1635, Randolph was in the height of contemporary dramatic fashion, as a considerable succession of dramas by minor authors go to attest. Thomas Goffe, Ralph Knevet, John Tatham, Joseph Rutter, Walter Montague, are the names of some of these pastoral writers; and the diversity of their extraction goes somewhat to show the range of this kind of play. Goffe, author of *The Careless Shepherdess,* began with lurid tragedies on the Ottoman Turk when a boy at Oxford. Knevet was tutor or chaplain in the Paston family in Norfolk and his *Rhodon and Iris* is an allegory of " the relations and properties of various plants and flowers," by no means badly planned and written even although the allegory is beyond us. Tatham followed Middleton and Heywood as " laureate of the lord mayors' shows " and wrote other plays after the Restoration. His *Love Crowns the End,* 1632, is fittingly described as an " early blossom of a subsequent harvest which was not contemptible." Rutter was a member of Jonson's latest circle of wits and poets, and his *Shepherds' Holiday* was not only acted successfully before the king and at the Cockpit but was praised by the old laureate.

Finally Montague was a favourite attendant on Queen Henrietta Maria and the author of the tedious *Shepherds' Paradise* in which the queen acted and which, as we have heard, Prynne was alleged to have animadverted upon so outrageously in his *Histriomastix*. Better works than any of these are Cowley's *Love's Riddle,* which that extraordinarily precocious poet wrote when less than eighteen years of age and still a scholar at Westminster School, and Henry Glapthorne's *Argalus and Parthenia,* derived from the *Arcadia* and conspicuous among pastoral dramas for a tragic conclusion. Pastoral drama, when all has been said, remained an exotic in England despite the grace of Daniel, the dramatic art of Fletcher and the ingenuity and literary capability of Randolph, for his *Amyntas* can hardly be overpraised for its poetical qualities, its clever conduct of plot and its wit, grace and pathos. The age of Charles appears to have derived a real pleasure in following the vicissitudes of the delicate amorous throes and anxieties of Daphnis and Amoretta, a matter wrapped up in a more general tendency of the age, its delight in the new heroical romance. For Daniel and even Fletcher, the home of the *lares* and *penates* of the pastoral was Italy and its prophets were Tasso, Sannazaro and Guarini. By the time that Randolph and his confreres had come to write, these *lares* and *penates* had migrated to France and Mlle. de Scudéry and Mons. D'Urfé had succeeded to the office of high priest and priestess. But to this we must soon return in another connection.

Ben Jonson died in 1637; in the next year William Davenant succeeded to the laureateship. Davenant, who became Sir William, was the son of an Oxford inn-keeper who rose to be mayor of his town. Young Davenant was born in 1606 and Shakespeare stood sponsor for him at baptism. Early in life he entered the service of Lord Brooke, better known in literary annals as Fulke Greville, the friend of Sir Philip Sidney and author, as we have already seen, of two remarkable Senecan tragedies. It is questionable if Davenant was in any wise more drawn to literature by association with his lordship than by a recollection of the example of Shakespeare. It is not to be questioned that Davenant's first model was the Fletcher of *Thierry and Theodoret* and *The Bloody Brother,* for to precisely the same category of the semi-historical tragedy of blood belong his *Albovine, King of Lombards,* 1626, and *The Cruel Brother,* of the next year. In this latter play we have a signal premonition as to the side which the dramatic poets would be likely to take in the coming difficulties of the crown as well as a specimen of the nice punctilios of honour which were constantly arising to perplex the gentlemen of Davenant's day. "Honour" compelled "the cruel brother" to kill his sister because she had fallen a victim to the royal lust; "loyalty" preserved her royal betrayer. Fletcher had solved the problem very differently some twenty years before in *The Maid's Tragedy* which the polite Mr. Waller rewrote as to the last act in a still later age, converting the dénouement into a reconciliation not to offend the susceptibilities of the royal lover of Nell Gwyn.

We may pass the able military drama, *The Colonel,* afterwards rewritten as *The Siege,* and *The Just Italian,* Davenant's first venture in comedy. A severe illness now overtook the poet, but he returned to the stage in 1634 with two comedies of manners, *The Wits,* merrily vindicating "the claims of town gallantry to a monopoly of the art," and *News from Plymouth,* a somewhat novel situation of three young officers of the royal navy, wind-stayed in port with their adventures, chiefly amorous, ashore. In certain personages of these comedies Davenant declares his adhesion to the Jonsonian mode. But this was not his most important work. To these years belong his several contributions in pre-Restoration times to the forebears of the heroic play and likewise his masques. "For heroic plays," says Dryden, "the first light we had of them, on the English theatre, was from the late Sir William Davenant," and the first unmistakable beam of that light was his *Love and Honour,* first known as *The Courage of Love.* A noble lady is a prisoner and in danger of her life in reprisal for the supposed death of a prince. She is attended by three young gentlemen who are all devotedly and chivalrously attached to her. One is filled with remorse that his misplaced valour should have taken her a prisoner, a second, her fellow in captivity with his sister, is equally disconsolate that he was unable to defend her, the third, son of the Duke, who has decreed her death, plans incessantly for her delivery. Moreover, each is generously "delighted" that the "others in their love concur with mine." And the lady and her attendant, sister of the second cavalier, both are equally generous and disinterested. The drama that is evolved out of this situation is both ingenious and interesting, and examination of the texts goes to show that, though rewritten after the Restoration, the original version contained all the elements of the heroic which the situation suggests. To the same year belongs Davenant's most successful masque, *The Temple of Love*. Here the poet seems to have endeavoured to bring back the masque to its former reasonable status and redeem it from the extravagance and excess which it had reached earlier in the year in Shirley's monster *Triumph of Peace*. The subject of Davenant's masque touches on the affectation of the moment, Platonic love, and tells how Divine Poesie has obscured from the unworthy the temple of chaste love to re-establish it, in all its pristine glory, by means of the influence of Indamora's (the queen's) beauty. This was a very appropriate compliment, for Henrietta Maria, whose delicate romantic temper had been nurtured in the *salon* of the Marquise de Rambouillet, was the true leader in her husband's court of the new French preciosity, one of the refinements of which was the cult of Platonic love.

The vogue of the new preciosity in England was extraordinary and its influence on society, manners and literature exceedingly great. The *salons* of literary ladies such as those of the Duchess of Newcastle and the Countess of Carlisle were conducted in accordance with its laws; the letters of Sir John Suckling to the lady whom he addressed as Aglaura were charged with it as were the lyrics of Waller to his Saccharissa. In the drama, although French preciosity continued into the next age as one of the characteristics of the heroic play, the feature of it, know as Platonic love, received but a short shrift. As early as 1629, Jonson had described a true " Platonique " in that "most Socratic lady," Lady Frampul (in *The New Inn*), whose " humour " it is to regard " nothing a felicity, but to have a multitude of servants (*i.e.,* Platonic lovers) and be called mistress by them." And James Howell expresses the English attitude towards the whole matter, in a letter which coincides with the date of Davenant's masque, in the words, " this love sets the wits of the town on work." An example of this is the curious anonymous dramatic satire, *Lady Alimony,* which has much to tell of " Platonic confidents " and " cashiered consorts "; another is Davenant's own *Platonic Lovers* which followed hard upon his masque. In this contrast of a pair of lovers, who love Platonically and discourse soulfully " against fruition of love in marriage," with a wholesome couple who frankly court that they may marry, Davenant, though arguing the case ingeniously enough, leaves us in no doubt as to his own attitude on the subject. It was upon these general achievements in the drama that Davenant received the laureateship; and justly, when everything has been considered. The rest of his work prior to the Restoration is less important save for the thoroughly heroic drama, *The Fair Favourite,* 1638, which likewise contains much dignified and elevated discourse on the casuistry of heroic love. The other pre-Restoration dramas of Davenant include *The Unfortunate Lovers,* a tragedy purely of the old type of Fletcher and *The Distresses* (later called *The Spanish Lovers*), which is little more than the translation of a typical Spanish drama of cloak and sword. Davenant's three or four other masques, *Prince D'Amour, Britannia Triumphans* and *Salmacida Spolia* (with perhaps *Lumenalia*) by no means equal *The Temple of Love,* but are meritorious efforts to follow in the wake of the previous great laureate without a tithe of his lyrical gift or his inexhaustible inventiveness. Davenant is less easily disposed of than he who has read only about him might suppose. Truly poetical he is not, although he comes near to the simulation of poetry at times; eloquent and no mean master of the devices of rhetoric, he is often. His dramatic aptitude is not to be questioned and his practical conversancy with the stage makes every one of his plays thoroughly practicable. Davenant was English to the core and remained such despite his Frenchified name and certain experiences later in France. But there was a streak of the impracticable and romantic in him of which his rhyming epic, *Gondibert,* a poem of genuine worth, however fanciful, is a patent example, and it was this that made him the chief conduit by which the heroic play was carried over, as we shall see, into a new age.

But Davenant was by no means the only conduit. In the now forgotten tragicomedies of Lodowick Carlell and those of Thomas Killigrew we have equally certain forerunners of the heroic play of Orrery and Dryden. Both men belonged to the intimate circle of the court and both reached success in their work because it fell in with the contemporary taste, in fashionable circles, for the intricate adventures, elevated sentiment and conventionally heroic virtues and passions that made for the vogue, each in its degree, of the Spanish romantic drama and the French heroic romances. Carlell, who came of the border stock of the Carlyles of Bryde Kirk, rose through various preferments to be one of the royal keepers of the great forest at Richmond; he died in 1675. The six or seven tragicomedies of Carlell begin with *The Deserving Favourite* the plot of which is lifted from a contemporary Spanish novel, in 1629, and conclude with *The Fool would be Favourite,* 1638, the intricacy and artificiality of which alone should be sufficient to establish its originality. Carlell revels in the heroic dilemma, the struggle between love and duty, "love without the possibility of satisfaction" (delight of the "Platoniques"), the duel of devoted friends on a punctilio of honour and the like. In *Arviragus and Philicia* he lays his scene in ancient Britain and runs through the gamut of Fletcherian figures — the tyrant king, heroic prince, faithful friend, sage counsellor, imperious princess, and the steadfast maiden, masquerading as a page, all are there. But his situations are turned to the heroic pitch and his ingenuities of plot carry us off into a world equally well described in *The Passionate Lovers* as "Burgony." Carlell marks more than a degeneracy in design, personage and situation. His medium of expression is a loose mixture of blank-verse and prose, which flows easily enough, but is too fibreless for good verse and too rhythmic for successful prose. Nor is Killigrew substantially different in kind. Killigrew was reared as a page in the court of King Charles I and continued a favourite companion of Prince Charles. He wrote his earlier plays while abroad, between 1635 and 1640, and lived to be a theatrical figure of note in the next age. His tragicomedies are full of action, adventure and melodrama. In *Claracilla* the princess of that name is rescued from a usurper by her lover and his friends; in *The Prisoner,* an heroic pirate holds princes for ransom and kidnaps their women folk, and much of the story takes place at sea. In *The Princess,* one of the personages is known as "Virgilius, son to Julius Cæsar," and the plot of another play, *Cicilia and Clorinda,* is confessedly derived from *Le Grand Cyrus,* itself enough to explain all this heroical inspiration. Killigrew wrote with fluency, not to say volubility, but his work in this kind, like that of Carlell, is without distinction. His one pre-Restoration comedy, *The Parson's Wedding,* acted in 1640, marks the lowest degradation of the old stage in the unblushing effrontery of its situations and in its unparalleled ribaldry. Two brothers of Thomas Killigrew, Henry and Sir William, contributed several plays to the degenerate tragicomedy of adventure in which the family seem to have been especially practised, but neither *Palantius and Eudora, Silindra, Pandora, Ormasdes,* nor *The Siege of Urbin* are in any wise memorable or likely to delay any one except the most valiant and curious reader.

More attention has been given here to Carlell and the Killigrews than the intrinsic value of their work deserves. They were by no means conspicuous save for their fertility in those last years of the old drama. John Gough, Sir William Berkeley and Sir William Lowes shared, each in a single play, in their fluency, romantic novelty and absurdity. Lowes, strangely enough, was a translator of Corneille and other contemporary French dramatists, but he learned nothing from them. His *Phœnix in her Flames* runs rampant over Arabia, Egypt and Persia, and the peerless princess, his heroine, dies like the fabulous bird of the title, smothered in the fumes of sweet incense. This effort deserves mention as the very extremity of extravagant romance, preposterously dramatized; and Berkeley's *Lost Lady,* with its ridiculous dénouement, the discovery of the identity of the heroine, though blackened to simulate a Moor, by the laving of her face in water, is assuredly a good second. No wonder that this kind of thing, written by persons of quality, should have led to a recrudescence of the old heroical plays of the class of *The Four Prentices of London,* and that we meet with the " dolent history " of *Guy of Warwick, "* by B. J." (not Ben Jonson), in 1639, a personage who figures triumphant among Paynims, giants and fairies, and with *The Seven Champions of Christendom,* by one John Kirke, and acted at the Cockpit, in which " the heir to great Coventry " slays Mahometans in Trebizond and dragons in Tartary, a place where, to the accompaniment of thunder and lightning, " devils run laughing over the stage." Nor did comedy suffer a less complete degradation, if we remember Killigrew's outrageous venture which enjoyed a huge success, and such coarse if vigorous sketches of low life as *The Gossips' Brawl, The Walks of Islington* and *The Ghost, or Woman Wears the Breeches.* Occasionally, in these late years, we meet with something better. *London Chanticleers* is a fresh and odd little play of unknown authorship on the city's street vendors; *The Swaggering Damsel* by Robert Chamberlain, a favourable specimen of the minor domestic drama; and *The Country Girl* " by T. B." and *The Cunning Lovers* by Alexander Brome are good comedies of manners, of London and foreign scene respectively. Moreover, scholarly men and men of attainments in other walks of literature still busied themselves with the drama. Francis Quarles, for example, the serious if fantastic religious poet, left behind him " a comedy " of no great merit entitled *The Virgin Widow;* and William Habington, author of *Castara,* a tragedy, *The Queen of Aragon,* staged at court and at Blackfriars, we are told, at great expense. Of the unfortunate Richard Lovelace, exquisite lyrist of constancy, the titles only and a few scraps of two lost plays remain. The conscientious student will find several titles of plays of these closing years to add to his list, if he will search the later volumes of Dodsley's collection. Among them and elsewhere he will find a late recurrence to Seneca in the virile tragedy, *Imperiale,* by Ralph Freeman, and a repetition of the story of Plangus from the Arcadia, already used by Fletcher, in *Andromana, the Merchant's Wife.* *The Rebellion* of Thomas Rawlins is replete with bandits, disguises, rescues and visions, and Nabbes' *Unfortunate Mother,* " refused by the actors," has also been placarded by a modern editor as a play " that hardly allows itself to be read."

In these very last years, one writer of plays stands out above his fellows, howsoever he wrote in the prevailing modes; and, strange to say, that writer was Sir John Suckling, the lyrical poet, spendthrift and trifler. But Suckling, who was fortune's darling as to wealth, personal endowment and station in life, had enjoyed excellent training at Oxford and, above all the rest of his contemporaries, knew, admired and honoured the poetry of Shakespeare. Suckling left three plays. *Aglaura* was staged by the author in 1637 with the same prodigality that he bestowed two years later on the equipment of a company of horse for his king. *Aglaura* is a somewhat gloomy drama possessed of the pseudo-historical atmosphere of its kind and full of the " Platonics " of the passing moment. With a flippancy altogether characteristic, Suckling wrote an alternative final act so that the play might be acted a tragedy or a comedy. *The Goblins* is a sprightly comedy of intrigue involving a couple of very hackneyed situations, two noble houses at feud and a prince's relinquishment of a maid whom he loves to a more fitting suitor of her own choice. *Brennoralt* is Suckling's best and most ambitious effort and interesting for its Byronic hero who is doubtless a projection of the poet himself when he was not in his habitually flippant and cynical pose. Suckling, however, is not a dramatist, with all his wit, his mastery of style, his poetry (in which he towers over the playwrights in this last decade), and his occasional weight of thought. The best thing in *Brennoralt* is a certain fine heroic note that tells us that even in this sybarite and trifler there was a spirit within that might have risen to better things than atonement for a misspent life in suicide.

The Puritan had been at variance with the drama from the very earliest times, and by no means without reason; for the abuses of the stage have been many and only too glaring in all ages. The hostility of the city was now grown into a more serious matter, the hostility of Parliament, and the intent to regulate the performance of plays and the building of playhouses became manifest early in the reign. In the very year of the king's accession, the acting of plays on Sunday was again forbidden and a petition for the building of an amphitheatre in Lincoln's Inn Fields failed, in the next year, when it was discovered that it was intended to house players. The notorious Nathaniel Gyles, who, as Master of the royal chapel, had trafficked for a generation in boy actors, was forbidden any longer to take up boys, on plea of the royal service, to make players of them; and, in 1631, the Bishop of London was petitioned by the inhabitants of Blackfriars for the removal of the theatre from among them because it interfered with traffic, trade and the worship of God. The friends of the drama at court had their hands full in this phase of Puritan aggression and the bitterness of the prosecution of Prynne marks the height of the Cavalier counter action. In 1636 and 1637, the plague kept the playhouses closed for a month; and Collier is the questionable authority for an order issued to suppress the players as early as 1640. Finally, in September 1642, came the ordinance of lords and commons putting a stop to the performance of all plays because of the outbreak of the war. The Puritan suppression of the drama was an actual one, and most of the players sought service in the camp of the king. In 1647, in consequence of certain attempts on the part of the actors to resume acting, the war being now over, all players were declared common rogues within the meaning of the old statutes, their playhouses were dismantled and even attendance at a play became a statutory offence.

CHAPTER X

DRYDEN AND THE DRAMA OF THE RESTORATION

THE ordinance of 1642 had closed the theatres and brought to an untimely end the brilliant drama that had flourished with such luxuriance during three generations. In the civil war, the players followed the king almost to a man, though there are indications that some of them sought a livelihood in the continuance of the practice of their profession abroad. With the conclusion of the war, some of the players attempted entertainments of various kinds, only to be met with more drastic regulations by their triumphant Puritan enemies. Thus Fletcher's *King and No King* (a somewhat suggestive title in 1647), was announced at Salisbury Court, only to be stopped by the sheriffs; in the next year, the provisions of earlier acts having expired, the players promptly opened to large audiences at the Fortune, the Red Bull and the Cockpit, again to be dispersed, in the last instance, by a party of soldiers. Angered by these efforts on the part of the actors, Parliament passed the ordinance of February 1648, authorising the destruction of all playhouses and the compulsion of all actors, on pain of flogging and imprisonment, to enter into a recognisance "never to act or play any plays or interludes any more." Even with this, there seems to have been some connivance at performances during the Commonwealth; those in lesser authority could, on occasion, be reached so as to wink at plays not too openly acted. And private performances could, of course, not be controlled. In later Commonwealth times the laws were less stringently enforced. Cromwell himself was no such enemy of the drama as the Parliament which had preceded him in power, though he, too, continued to invoke the law on occasion.

During the ban upon the drama, various devices were employed to evade the letter of the law. Among them, by far the most successful was the "droll" or "droll humour," which was commonly a single scene or situation, humorous or other, derived from some well known popular play and acted, or recited at least, in character. In the " address to the reader " prefixed to a collection of drolls entitled *The Wits, or Sport upon Sport,* 1673, the publisher informs us that performance was " only allowed us . . . by stealth . . . under pretence of rope-dancing"; but notwithstanding, drolls were " acted in public and private, in London at Bartholomew fairs . . . in halls and taverns . . . at Charing Cross, Lincoln's Inn Fields and other places," and that they were " as great get-pennies to the actors as any of our late famed plays." This collection contains no less than thirty-six such scenes, serious and comic, pastoral, none of them tragic, and they are derived from more than a score of well-known plays, mostly Fletcher's; but *Hamlet* (for the grave-diggers' scene), *Henry IV* (for Falstaff's monstrous account of the robbery on Gadshill) and *A Midsummer Night's Dream* (for " the merry conceits of Bottom the Weaver ") are among them. Some of the drolls are mere foolery, especially those written by the chief actor in them, Robert Cox; others take over some of the coarsest scenes of the older drama. It seems not unlikely that this particular kind of evasion of the Puritan ordinances against the stage enjoyed, during the Commonwealth, a somewhat greater vogue than it has usually been accredited.

When at the height of his reputation in the reign of King Charles I, Davenant had become governor of the King's and Queen's players and had obtained a royal patent, empowering him to erect a playhouse. Nothing came of this, however, in those troublous times; and two years later, in 1641, the poet was driven to seek safety in France for his part in a royalist conspiracy. But he soon returned to England and, following the king, was knighted for distinguished service at the siege of Gloucester in 1643. He served the queen thereafter as a confidential agent on more than one mission; and, as such, was arrested, off the coast of France, in 1649, and sent to Cowes Castle. It was during this imprisonment that Davenant wrote his epic *Gondibert,* published in 1651 and already mentioned. On the lifting of the rigorous restrictions heretofore placed on dramatic performances, Davenant obtained permission to produce an " entertainment," as he called it, of declamation and music, " after the manner of the ancients," and actually staged it at Rutland House in May 1656. Davenant's " entertainment " was made up of two pairs of speeches, the first on the pertinent topic, " against and for public entertainment by moral presentation," the second in a lighter vein, the whole interspersed with good music by musicians of repute. It was really a " feeler " to test how far he might venture, and was sufficiently well received to encourage him to the preparation of the famous *Siege of Rhodes,* " made by the art of prospective in scenes and the story sung in recitative music." In his address " To the reader," Davenant carefully explains that " the story as represented . . . is heroical, and, . . . I hope, intelligibly conveyed to advance the characters of virtue in the shapes of valour and conjugal love." This was a sop to the Puritan Cerberus who had still power to bite. Much was made, too, of the scenic, musical and operatic features to obscure as far as possible the circumstance that *The Siege* was in any wise a play. And indeed the production, save for its change of scene, variety of costume and general characterisation, can claim very little dramatic merit. Acted in August 1656, *The Siege of Rhodes* was an immediate success; and, the wedge now entered, Davenant opened the Cockpit in 1658, producing there two similar " operas," as he called them, on the historical topics, *The Cruelty of the Spaniards in Peru* and *The History of Sir Francis Drake.* The " historical " matter and " improving " purpose of these performances were nicely calculated to disarm Puritan suspicion and an intended inquiry into their nature was frustrated by the rapid movement of events. *The Siege of Rhodes,* it may be remarked, is neither the first English opera, the earliest English play to employ actresses on the stage, nor the earliest play in England to make a change of scene. All these things have been erroneously stated about it. Only the author's own misuse of the term could have caused it to be designated an opera; the women who appeared in it were chosen for their voices, not for their acting, and at least one of them, the well known Mrs. Coleman, had already appeared in Davenant's previous " entertainment." As to scenery, we have already heard of eight changes of scene in Cartwright's *Royal Slave* acted at Oxford in the year 1636.

This is not the place in which to detail the events that led to the Restoration of King Charles II. Soon after the arrival of General Monck in London, February 1660, John Rhodes, formerly a wardrobe keeper in the King's company, received permission to open a playhouse in Charing Cross, and other companies soon followed at the Red Bull and Salisbury Court. In August Thomas Killigrew and Sir William Davenant secured

a royal patent empowering them to " erect " two companies of
players. And now Sir Henry Herbert, the long quiescent
Master of the Revels, intervened to assert the authority which
he had held over from the previous reign. Out of the disputes,
divisions, combinations and compromises that followed there
emerged two recognised companies, the King's, presided over by
Killigrew, and the Duke of York's company, headed by Davenant. From 1661 on, the latter company acted at the playhouse in
Lincoln's Inn Fields, Portugal Row, until transferred, in 1671,
three years after Davenant's death, to their new and handsome
theatre in Salisbury Court, Fleet Street, on a site known as
Dorset Garden. The King's players occupied the Theatre
Royal in Drury Lane (although the house was not yet so called)
from 1663. Thus fostered by the royal patronage, staged by
those practically acquainted with the demands of the theatre and
acted by distinguished actors, Thomas Betterton foremost among
them, the stage entered, histrionically at least, on one of its most
brilliant periods. To this the innovation, which rapidly became
the rule, that women's parts should be acted by women, contributed not a little. For whatever the consequences from the
point of view of society and morals, the superiority of the new
actresses — many of them like Mrs. Barry and Mrs. Bracegirdle superior artists as well as beautiful women — over the
squeaking boys of the previous age was patent.

After the Restoration, Davenant, immersed in management,
took no such position as an original dramatist as had been his
in the previous reign. A second part of *The Siege of Rhodes,*
acted and printed with the first part in 1662, is inferior like
most sequels. *The Siege* and *The Distresses* (doubtless the
same with *The Spanish Lovers*) are capable romantic comedies
which the author carried over from earlier times. In *The
Playhouse to be Let,* Davenant utilised the material of his two
historical entertainments of the time of Cromwell, already mentioned, to concoct a diversified performance, devoid of the slightest pretensions to unity. Some topical satire on the untoward
theatrical conditions during the recent suppression of the drama,
may have carried it off. And in *The Man's the Master* we
have a couple of the comedies of Scarron, rather cleverly combined. The rest of Davenant's work after the Restoration is
made up of adaptations, chiefly of Shakespeare, in which he set
a vicious example, the continuance of which has gone on to our
present day. Thus, Davenant's *History, Murders, Life and*

Death of Macbeth was acted in 1666, " drest in all its finery, as new clothes, new scenes, machines, as flyings for the witches, with all the singing and dancing in it . . . being in the nature of an opera." [1]   And Davenant's and Dryden's adaptation of *The Tempest* which duplicates the rôles of Ferdinand and Miranda on contrasted islands and gives Caliban a sister, was staged with unexampled effects in the next year.   Both enjoyed an extraordinary success.   Killigrew, who had become groom of the king's bedchamber and later chamberlain to the queen, contented himself, so far as his own works were concerned, with the revival of his *Parson's Wedding* against which, when it was scandalously acted only by women, even the easy-going Pepys exclaims.

The repertory of the earlier years of the Restoration was made up largely of revivals of the older drama, Fletcher leading in popularity, with Shakespeare a close second.   After Davenant's example, it became the custom to alter the older plays on these revivals, a thing which indeed had long before been done, but never so brazenly avowed.   There was scarcely a playwright, from Dryden and Betterton to Vanbrugh and Farquhar who did not take part in this merry game of pillaging and " improving " the works of their predecessors.   Earliest in point of time, were several pieces of dramatic journalism, satirizing the Puritans and their discomfiture, such as *The Rump or the Mirror of the Late Times* by Tatham, Sir Robert Howard's *Committee*, Crowne's *City Politics* and Lacy's *Old Troupe;* and here belongs Cowley's revival of an older comedy under the title of *Cutter of Coleman Street*.   The comedies of several " gentlemen of quality," too, were staged in the sixties, one of Sir Robert Stapylton, one of Roger Boyle, Earl of Orrery, and a very few of the many penned by the Duke of Newcastle and the innumerable more by his literary Duchess. [2]   None of these productions are memorable.   Indeed, until Dryden came, in the drama, to his own, but one playwright stands out with any distinctness.   This was John Wilson, born at Plymouth and a lawyer by profession, who became later secretary to the Duke of

---

[1] Downes, *Roscius Anglicanus*, p. 33.

[2] *The Stepmother* by Stapylton, 1664; *Mr. Anthony,* probably Orrery's; *The Humorous Lovers* and *The Triumphant Widow* of Newcastle were both acted before 1673.   The work of the Duchess is earlier as an edition of twenty-one of her plays was printed in 1662.

York in Ireland and recorder of Londonderry. Wilson's four plays belong to the earliest years of the new reign; and the first of them, *The Cheats,* enjoyed an unusual as well as a deserved popularity. This comedy deals with the quack astrologer, the sharking bravo, the Puritan hypocrite, all of them stock personages and frankly conceived in the manner of Jonson. The very name of Wilson's second comedy, *The Projectors,* proclaims it of the same type; and Wilson's names for his personages, Bilboe the swaggerer, Scruple the Puritan minister, Suckdry the usurer and Sir Gudgeon Credulous his dupe, declare how true " a son of Ben " the author was. But Wilson in these vigorous and able comedies has succeeded in imitating the best of his master and stands high in his class. In another of Wilson's plays, *Belphegor or the Marriage of the Devil,* the author treated a story of Machiavelli, already employed by Jonson in *The Devil is an Ass.* But Wilson's work is his own and no mere adaptation after the custom of his time. Lastly in *Andronicus Comnenius* we have an exceedingly well constructed tragedy, conceived with power and written in a strong-fibred blank verse that recalls an earlier age. Here, too, although the historical material closely parallels the story of Richard III, Wilson displays a literary conscience, strange in his or any other day in the drama, and refutes any possible charge of borrowing by his inventiveness and originality. Wilson came too late. In an earlier age he might have taken an even higher place with his manly talents as a dramatist.

John Dryden was born of a good family which, on both sides, had lent its aid and countenance to the Puritan cause. The poet was educated at Westminster and at Trinity College, Cambridge, where, however, he proceeded only to his bachelor's degree. His father dying in 1654, Dryden came into a small estate, which was increased somewhat by his marriage with Lady Elizabeth Howard with whose brother, Sir Robert Howard, the poet was intimate from his youth and with whom he collaborated in his first heroic play, *The Indian Queen.* Dryden began his career as a poet in 1658 with a panegyric in heroic stanzas on the death of Cromwell. This was followed in publication by *Astrea Redux,* a similar poem on the happy restoration of King Charles. Dryden was a young man with his way to make. He swam with the tide at a moment when everybody, save an occasional Marvell or Milton, was doing likewise. The new theatrical ventures of Killigrew and Davenant soon offered Dryden an opportunity of another kind; and, after one or two false starts, he reached a qualified success in *The Rival Ladies,* 1664.

Into the details of the interesting literary career of Dryden at large, his successes as a panegyrist, satirist, translator, critic and general poet, it is impossible to enter here. His controversy with Sir Robert Howard as to the use of rhyme in the drama belongs to the years immediately following his first dramatic recognition; and here he was interrupted by the intervention of the plague and the consequent closing of the theatres for a time. In 1667 Dryden renewed his dramatic efforts with *Secret Love,* the highly successful play in which the acting of Nell Gwyn reached the heart of her susceptible royal lover; and the association of Dryden with Davenant and the Duke's theatre followed and, later, a more permanent agreement with the King's players on Dryden's part to supply that company with three plays a year. For this Dryden was to receive a share in the profits of the company; and this he did receive, notwithstanding that he never contributed more than one play within a single year. Later, difficulties arising, Dryden transferred his services back to the rival house. In 1670, he succeeded Davenant as poet laureate. This put Dryden, on its face, in a solid financial position; but so irregularly paid were all the offices of the crown, in the impecunious court of Charles, that Dryden, no less than preceding dramatists, was compelled to write for his bread. It was this necessity that palliates, if it cannot excuse, the poet's complacency in writing so loosely in comedy that even that loose age at times decried him; and it was this doubtless, too, that caused him to attempt to catch the popular taste in a gross misrepresentation of the Dutch in their alleged cruelties to English merchants, in *Amboyna,* and to perpetrate the bitter attack upon the Roman clergy, in the time of the excitement of the Popish plot, that the character of the Spanish friar, in the play of that title, conveys.

Between 1668 and 1681 no less than fourteen plays of various kinds came from the productive pen of Dryden, who, be it remembered, was writing much besides. Comedy, tragicomedy, the new heroic play, the new hybrid, opera, tragedy in the older manner, tragedy in the new manner of Corneille, all these things were attempted and — everything considered — surprisingly well accomplished by this extraordinary, industrious, adaptable and brilliant genius. Dryden, with all his triumphs, was not altogether a dramatist by nature. He recognised his own comparative failure in comedy, and in those fine, frank, lucid intervals that recur in his critical writings, acknowledged his own limitations. He wrote incessantly, both in season and out. Hence there is, in his dramatic writings, an extraordinary inequality that ranges from the eloquent hyperbole of the heroic plays and from tragedies in which he followed with honest freedom and individuality the footsteps of Shakespeare and Corneille, down to the garbling spoliation of *Troilus and Cressida,* the " tagging" of *Paradise Lost* into a rhymed opera, and the perpetration of the disgusting dramatic satire called *Limberham.*

The most recent authority on Dryden has given us so excellent a classification of the plays of the poet that we can not do better than follow it.[3] First, the comedies, some six in number, range from *The Wild Gallant,* a failure in 1663, to *Amphitryon,* a deserved success, in 1690. Of the others, *The Assignation* and *Marriage à la Mode* are altogether negligible, and *Limberham,* already adverted to, while better planned and written than almost any of the group, is of an intolerable grossness. *Sir Martin Mar-all,* which dates 1667, enjoyed a long continued popularity in the author's life-time and, we may agree, is " the most uniformly amusing of Dryden's comic plays," notwithstanding that he is alleged in it merely to have " corrected " previous work by the Duke of Newcastle on the basis of a combination of two comedies respectively of Molière and Quinault. *Amphitryon* is an exceedingly diverting comedy on the old story of Jupiter's visit to Alcmena which Plautus himself doubtless borrowed from an earlier Greek comic poet and Molière tried his hand at as well. The comic situation of the two Sosias, it will be recalled, is that of the two Dromios, prolonged and amplified. It can not be denied that Dryden has bettered his Greek and French models, for his work is far more than an adaptation of either. Dryden's comedy, like everything else that he attempted, is admirably written; his touch on occasion is light, his wit abundant. What he lacks is the moisture of humour. While he is clever enough in construction and uniformly happy in his dialogue, his ability to portray and differentiate character falls short of that of many lesser playwrights. Few better illustrations of this could be found than Domenic, the

[3] Sir Augustus Ward in *The Cambridge History of English Literature,* viii, pp. 15-33.

famous and popular personage who gives title to *The Spanish Friar,* which is more a comedy than a serious drama from his prominence in it. A momentary comparison of Dryden's friar with Falstaff discloses the difference. Both are gross, fat, essentially dishonest and knavish; yet, from their humorous appeal, intended to be attractive rather than repellent. We condone the lies and transgressions of Falstaff, open and palpable though they are, because of his inimitable wit and charm. In contrast, we may well believe that the success of Domenic depended largely on the actor and that even Anthony Leigh, who, Cibber tells us, was so famed for the part, must have struggled against the unsympathetic depravity of this would-be genial liar and disgrace to his order.

A second group of Dryden's dramas are the tragicomedies in the old sense. The earliest is *The Rival Ladies,* of Spanish origin or example at least. In this, his second dramatic venture, two scenes are written in rhyme by way of experiment. The inartificiality in the device of two ladies, each in the disguise of a page for love of the same man, leads to some pretty complications, but is proof of the dramatist's immaturity; the inroads of robbers, nicely timed to the action, suggest an acquaintance with some of Killigrew's tragicomedies or their sources. This surmise becomes a certainty in the case of *Secret Love or the Maiden Queen,* already mentioned, which is founded, as to the serious parts, on the famous romance of the day, *Le Grand Cyrus.* The light comedy part of Florimel seems written for the pert talents of Mistress Gwyn; and, indeed, Dryden is never better in comedy than in the vivacious fencing of gallantry, which, however much he may have learned of the past, set a model for many a scene to come.[4] Of *The Spanish Friar* enough has been said. The remaining tragicomedy is *Love Triumphant,* the poet's latest work for the stage, acted in 1694 and a failure. The best that can be said for it is that Dryden seems in this instance, as in some others, to have been working against the grain, for not only is the action " forced and unnatural," but even his habitual command of verse fails him at times.

---

[4] Cf. especially the mock articles of agreement between Florizel and Celadon with the similar scene of Congreve's *Way of the World* between Millamont and Mirabell.

In the heroic play, using that term in its strictest acceptation, we have the most characteristic group of the dramas of Dryden. There are two ways in which to view the heroic play. One, which it is not to be denied certain of the utterances of the poet himself go far to warrant, makes the term equivalent practically to a drama written in rhyming couplets.[5] If we look somewhat more closely into the matter, we see at once that there is something more in the heroic play than this. It was no less a person than Davenant who first employed the term, " heroique play," to designate not only his *Siege of Rhodes* (which he calls elsewhere an opera) but likewise his blank-verse tragicomedy, *Love and Honour,* as we have already seen. That play, if we look back to its paternity, marks only a step from such dramas of Fletcher as *The Knight of Malta* or *The Loyal Subject,* in which heightened situation and personages conceived in the dilation of heroic passion hold contest in generosity, magnanimity, faithfulness to plighted word and other of the larger virtues. The heroic, indeed, is an element of incessant recurrence in the drama as in other art. It crops out in Alphonsus of Aragon who levies tribute on three continents, in Tamburlaine who conquers the world, in Bussy D'Ambois whose proud heart will yield to no man. This is the hero superhuman, the hero of the old exorbitant romantic drama of action and may be classified as an excess of the hero passionate which is exemplified in Lear, Othello or Macbeth. Now the heroic spirit in the newer drama, beginning with Fletcher, is of a totally different type; it expresses itself primarily neither in action nor in passion, but in heightened sentiment. Substituted for event and character, we have analysis of conduct; in place of the hyperbole of poetry, we have, too often, merely the flights of rhetoric. Exaggeration here leads, as I have written elsewhere, not to the dilation of the supernatural, but to the humanly extraordinary and amazing. " The hero superhuman and the hero passionate have been displaced by the hero supersensitive, by 'the paragon of virtue and the pattern of noble conduct.' The themes of the heroic drama are 'honour won by valour,' and 'valour inspired by love.' 'Its rivalries are rivalries in nobility of soul;' its combats, less those of the sword

[5] See L. N. Chase, *The English Heroic Play,* 1903, pp. 3 and the list of rhyming plays in which even comedies are included.

than those of fortitude, loyalty, and the sacrifice to honour and plighted word." [6]

The personages of the heroic play are of exalted rank, its scene lies in some outlandish country — Mexico, China, Tartary, Persia — or one indeterminate geographically at least. Its background is one of war, conspiracy and court intrigue. Now all this is Fletcher; and equally Fletcherian is the accepted method of the heroic play, that of a heightened contrast. Some have found a greater simplicity of plot characteristic of the heroic play, a quality in which its greatest exemplar, *The Conquest of Granada,* is far from conspicuous. But simplicity of plot was one of Shirley's contributions to the tragicomedy of his time; a characteristic which was by no means followed by the degenerate imitators of the heroic in Fletcher, to wit, Carlell, Killigrew and their like. As to the sources of the heroic play in Spanish fiction and drama and, more immediately, in the French romances, Fletcher had already broached the first, Massinger the second, and Fletcher, still again, with Killigrew and Carlell after him the last. So that, when everything has been said, all that the authors of the new heroic play accomplished by way of actual novelty was to exaggerate what had already been exaggerated, to heighten still more and make more florid an already exalted diction, and to substitute for the supple blank-verse of Fletcher or the hybrid prose-verse of Carlell, the regular tread of the rhymed couplet.

A nice question here arises: who first wrote rhyming plays? In the old age, the group of dramatic writers that imitated French tragedy in the manner of Seneca employed rhyme and many a poetic play of the same earlier time had done likewise. So a rhyming play was really no new thing. It was the rhyming heroic play that was the innovation,— the form clearly suggested by the practice of French tragedy — and the question who first wrote in this particular manner in England lies between Davenant, Sir Robert Howard, Roger Boyle Earl of Orrery, and Dryden. We may rule out Davenant, as his *Siege of Rhodes* is heroic but not strictly a play; the claim of Howard is wrapped up with that of Dryden. The order of the earliest group of rhyming heroic plays is *The Indian Queen* by Howard and Dryden, acted in January 1664; *Henry V* by Orrery, in

[6] *Elizabethan Drama,* 1908, ii, 349, where the topic is discussed more at large.

August of the same year, and his *Mustapha,* April 1665. Of
Dryden's *Indian Emperor,* a sequel to *The Indian Queen,* we
only know that it was staged early in 1665. It may have
preceded *Mustapha;* the question is not important. As to Sir
Robert Howard, it may be remarked that both he and two
brothers were emulous of success on the stage and wrote several
plays among them. Sir Robert's comedy, *The Committee,* an
attack on the defeated Puritans, and his *Duke of Lerma* deserved their contemporary success. The Earl of Orrery was
alike a more important man and a better poet. He is a pleasing
example of that large and interesting class of noblemen and
statesmen in active life whose leisure is given to the assiduous
cultivation of letters; and no less than eight dramas attest that
interest in his case. Four of these were acted in the sixties
while the heroic craze was at its height. When it is recalled
that Orrery had written in his youth a prose romance in the
approved manner of Calprenède and the Scudérys, entitled
Parthenissa, we are not surprised to find his *Mustapha,* his
Tryphon (dealing we are told, with Syriac history) and his
Herod the Great, all of the heroic type. Even in his *History
of Henry V,* that prince and Owen Tudor heroically strive
with a passion, which the Princess of France has inspired
equally in both, and in devotion and sacrifice of self to their
noble friendship. To return to the question of priority, Dryden's interest in rhyming plays is traceable earlier than his first
venture in writing one; for not only have we the experimental
scenes in rhyme of *The Rival Ladies,* but, in the dedication of
that play to the Earl of Orrery, the matter is discussed — first
word of a long critical interest of Dryden in the subject — and
his lordship is paid a neat compliment: " But, my lord, . . .
I must remember to whom I speak, who have much better commended this way by your writing in it, than I can do by writing
for it." The whole matter turns on Dryden's part and influence in *The Indian Queen,* which must have been considerable. The alleged priority of the Earl of Orrery in the application of heroic verse to the heroic play depends on a compliment by a poet who knew admirably how to pay compliments
and never spared small matters of fact in the process. Dryden
is the innovator, the leader in form, as in spirit, of the new
heroic play.

The list of rhymed plays already alluded to includes nearly
fifty titles and ranges, in point of date (omitting *The Siege of*

Rhodes and *The Rival Ladies*) from 1664 to 1680, with a few
sporadic examples later. If we throw out of count the comedies and other non-heroic pieces, the actual number of plays
which fulfil the strict conditions of the rhyming heroic play is
reduced to something not much more than half this number.
On the other hand, if we classify by spirit, not by form alone,
we can readily double the first list within the period in the now
forgotten works of Lee, Crowne, Settle, Banks, Durfey and
lesser men. Even Otway began in rhyming plays of the heroic
type. But when all is said, Dryden not only set the fashion of
the heroic play; he was alone truly eminent in it; for he alone
of all these writers had the force, the eloquence and the sustaining poetry to carry this enormous weight of magnificence, noise,
bustle, sentiment and exaggeration. To take an example, in the
two parts of *The Conquest of Granada,* acted in 1670, Dryden
is equally independent of the trammels of fact and of the dull
sequence of historical events. His hero, Almanzor, supposed a
Mahometan prince, is in reality the son of the Christian Duke
of Arcos, and he carries out to the full the new heroic ideal.
He is, to use Dryden's own words, " of an excessive and over-
boiling courage . . . a character of eccentric virtue . . . I design in him a roughness of character almost approaching to arrogance, but those errors are incident only to great spirits; [for
his, too,] is a frank openness of nature, an easiness to forgive
his conquered enemies and to protect them in distress; and, above
all, an inviolable faith in his affections." Almanzor's actions
are in keeping with these traits. He takes the weaker side,
always and without question. He changes sides whenever he
thinks himself personally ill-treated, and he brings unfailing
victory to the party whose cause he espouses. He liberates his
prisoners habitually without a ransom and obeys with absolute
literalness whatever he believes to be the wishes of his beloved.
Almahide, his incomparable lady, is no less noble in her unas-
sailable fidelity and unexceptionable propriety of conduct. It is
not until we are far advanced into the second part, that the hero
is permitted so much as to kiss her hand. To give even in outline the ins and outs of the action of *The Conquest of Granada*
would take four or five pages of print in this size. Factions,
dissensions, sallies, skirmishes, discoveries, and executions de-
layed, mutinies, ordeals of battle, the visitations of ghosts and,
ever and anon, " sighs and flames " from the three or four pairs
of lovers whose protestations of fidelity or struggles of gen-

erosity play an incessant obligato to the trumpets of war — these
are some of the contents of this play. The drama is obviously
written for its great scenes; and the love-making, renunciations,
and pleadings, the lofty decisions as to conduct and the eloquent
bombast, all go to make a bewildering succession of brilliant and
rapid scenes, under the spell of which, even in our own age —
beguiled as we are by the banalities of grand opera — we might
well fall the victim. It is much easier to laugh at the absurdities of the heroic play, read in cold print, than to appreciate
what must have been the charm of its novelty and the lofty
nature of the ideals which it upheld in an age that needed moral
ideals to sustain it beyond any English time that we know. As
we read these heroic dramas of Dryden, we fall insensibly into
the swing of his swift, agile succession of thought, sustained on
a current of enthusiasm for these outlandish creatures of his
imagination and though we find them again and again grotesque,
judged by any standards that are ours, we can not wholly decry
an art that was after all sincere in its way and eminently successful in the thing that it set out to do.

With the success of *The Conquest of Granada,* imitation set
in. In the next year, 1671, Elkana Settle, a clever and pre-
sumptuous young man of three and twenty, produced his *Empress of Morocco* with rival magnificence and, by means of the
influence of Rochester, the enemy of Dryden, the play was twice
presented at court and was repeated by Betterton with signal
approval on the popular stage. A few years later, Settle followed this up with his *Ibrahim the Illustrious Bassa* (direct
from Calprenède), which enjoyed almost as enthusiastic a reception. But thrust in this manner into Dryden's glittering
heroic car, Settle's fall was speedy. His petty politics and
changes of party, with the absence of anything like poetic spirit
or the uplift even of rhetoric in his work, soon reduced him to
a more fitting sphere, that of poet of the city's pageantry. None
the less his activity in writing for the stage continued in the
production of nearly a score of plays; although the name of
Settle is now remembered solely for Dryden's contemptuous
portrait of him as Doeg in the second part of *Absalom and
Achitophel.* An abler rival of Dryden, also brought forward
by Rochester, was John Crowne, who began literary work in
1665, with a prose romance, and some five or six years thereafter
resorted to the stage. In his eight serious plays, written between
1671 and 1692, Crowne is eclectic enough in his practice but

imitative throughout of the passing fashions of his time. Thus, his *Charles VIII of France,* acted in 1672, is, like Orrery's *Henry V,* history transformed into heroic rhyming drama, concocted with a love story which is wholly fictitious; and his *Destruction of Jerusalem,* 1677, is sheer imitation of *The Conquest of Granada,* even to being written in two parts. This second play of Crowne's enjoyed a success on the stage incredible to us as we read its commonplace and unilluminated lines; and we realise how much these dramatic spectacles depended, then as now, on their gorgeousness of costume, novelty of scenery, ingeniousness of effect and the excitement of things seen in crowds in the bewilderment of dazzling light. Crowne gave up rhyme when Dryden did so, writing his most vigorous and original tragedy, *The Ambitious Statesman,* 1679, in blank-verse on the lines of Marlowe and *The Spanish Tragedy* but emulating the extravagance rather than the merits of those ancient plays. Again following Dryden, he reverted to classical subjects in *Thyestes,* a tragedy of revolting horror, in *Darius, Regulus* and *Caligula,* reducing all the heroes of antiquity, after the accepted manner of his time, to conventional gentlemen wholly preoccupied with the passion of love. Crowne's five comedies were acted between 1675 and 1694. They enjoyed a greater reputation than we feel it possible to allow them now. The best of them, *Sir Courtly Nice* long held the stage. But Crowne's most interesting production is his " court masque," *Calisto* which Rochester's influence engaged him to prepare in 1675, less to advance Crowne than to humiliate the laureate Dryden. *Calisto* is a well-written effort to revive a lost form, but it is scarcely poetical. Crowne was an estimable man and he enjoyed the good will of King Charles. Fortunate he was not and he drops out of sight in the nineties.

One other writer of heroic plays, from a certain spirit and fire that was in him as well as from his collaboration with Dryden, deserves more than a passing mention. This is Nathaniel Lee. Lee was the son of a minister who had contrived to deserve well as a Presybterian in Cromwell's day and better, as a divine of the Church of England, later on. After leaving Cambridge, the younger Lee led a dissolute life, while enjoying the unstable patronage of Buckingham and Rochester; and, after failure as an actor, despite extraordinary powers of elocution, became one of the most popular dramatists of his day. Lee rejoiced in ambitious subjects and in splendour of the settings

of great historical personages; he was possessed of an extraordinary extravagance of imagination and an ear that delighted in
sound and the volume of a large heroic utterance. It is not to
be denied, that, in his huge and panoramic dramas, he glutted
these tastes. With a frank acceptance of the substance, method
and versification that Dryden had sanctioned, Lee threw himself
passionately into the composition of his *Nero, Sophonisba or
Hannibal's Overthrow,* his *Gloriana or the Court of Augustus
Cæsar, The Rival Queens or Alexander the Great,* all of them
poured forth and acted, between 1675 and 1677, in all their
glory, exorbitance, erotic passion, poetry — for there is poetry
in them — and bombast. They were followed by similar
dramas on Mithridates, Cæsar Borgia, Brutus, Constantine, ending with *The Massacre of Paris* in 1690. In these latter, Lee
followed his mentor into blank-verse. It would seem that this
exuberant spirit would leave no historical hero unsubjugated to
this preposterous new land of heroic romance wherein a lovesick
Hannibal loses Rome because of his infatuation for " a Capuan
lady," and Alexander the Great becomes the shuttlecock between the battledores of the two imperious queens. This drama,
The Rival Queens, enjoyed an unexampled popularity and continued to hold the stage to the days of Edmund Kean and Mrs.
Siddons. Something of the secret of this success is explained in
the words of Colley Cibber who tells us: " When these flowing
numbers came from the mouth of a Betterton, the multitude no
more desired sense to them, than our musical connoisseurs think
it essential in the celebrate airs of an Italian opera." [7] Lee
represents, whether in rhyme or in his plays in blank-verse — it
matters not which — the *ne plus ultra* of the species. To change
in any wise, the heroic drama must become sane, and to become
sane was to cease from heroics. As to the poet himself, who was
a man of unquestionable talent, his dissipations brought him in
1687 to the madhouse and, on his release, a return to them cost
him his life.

In 1671, while *The Conquest of Granada* was still a new
wonder, appeared the clever dramatic burlesque and satire entitled *The Rehearsal* which ridiculed the whole species in admirable fooling and parody. Here Dryden was represented in the
person of Bayes, in all his peculiarities of speech and habit, as
in the act of superintending and commenting on a preliminary
performance of one of his own plays. *The Rehearsal* is the

[7] *Apology,* ed. R. W. Lowe, i, 105, quoted by Ward, iii, 409.

work of the dissolute and witty Duke of Buckingham, assisted
by several others, Clifford, Sprat and Butler (author of *Hudi-
bras*), it is said, among them. The play discloses neither unity
of authorship nor unity of plan, and it was in process of making, it is reported, as far back as 1663, when Davenant was to
have been the hero. Then Sir Robert Howard was to have
taken Davenant's place; but performance, for which the play
was ready in 1665, failing because of the plague, the drama was
again rewritten and the new poet laureate made the butt of
attack. *The Rehearsal* is after all no very venomous matter;
the authors were content merely to laugh at the absurdities of
the heroic spirit at large, the want of serious plotting or motive
in plays of the type and the bombast and high-flown language
in which much of them was written. The effort was an immediate success, both on the stage and in the many printed editions that were called for; and Dryden recognised, with his
usual good sense, that the case was hopelessly against him and
made no reply. Indeed the nickname Bayes clung to him ever
after, and it is not impossible that *The Rehearsal* may have
hastened Dryden's repudiation of rhyme for dramatic writing
and his return to blank-verse, although this came later. To say,
however, that *The Rehearsal* killed the heroic play, is to say far
too much; for the species continued in high repute for at least
a decade after, animating, even later, the works of lesser or old
fashioned men. A more certain influence of Buckingham's burlesque is its example for a line of like dramas among which
Sheridan's *Critic* alone rivalled it in success. As to Dryden,
two other dramas of his belong to the category of the rhyming
heroic play, *Tyrannic Love,* which immediately preceded *The
Conquest of Granada,* and *Aureng-Zebe,* with which his heroic
series concludes, not staged until 1676. Both plays are absolutely within the type, although *Tyrannic Love* treats a subject
somewhat more actually historic than usual among productions
of its class, the subject of Maximin's persecution of the Chris-
tians and the martyrdom of Saint Catherine. The tragedy of
Aureng-Zebe only falls short of *The Conquest of Granada* because it less extravagantly exhibits the characteristics of its class.
The personage who gives his name to the play is described as the
last descendant of Timur Kahn, and he was actually alive at the
time of Dryden's play; but, as Ward well observes, " his name
can scarcely have come home more closely to Englishmen at
large than that of Mithridates," and the play is wholly con-

ventional in its setting and given over to the "factions," bustle, warfare and love-making of its kind.   In *Aureng-Zebe,* the plot is clearer, the action less confused, the poetry, which is abundant, more restrained, for in it, as both the preface and the prologue attest, Dryden was wearying of restrictions of rhyme and recognising more and more how inferior was all his art of strenuous endeavour to the simple touch of Shakespeare and his healthier age.[8]

Or Dryden's degradation of his dramatic art to pander to political prejudice and of his makings over of the work of greater men, enough has been said.   His *Duke of Guise,* written in collaboration with Lee, is an example of both these things. The tragedy of *Œdipus,* written with the same collaborator, is a nobler play.   *Albion and Albanius,* 1685, and *King Arthur,* 1691, are what Dryden called "operas," though the first is rather an elaborate political allegory in the manner of a masque and the second was suspected of concealing a similar second meaning.   These productions are sustained throughout by Dryden's poetry, which was equal apparently to any task put upon it, and they are better understood if we remember the Dryden of *Absalom and Achitophel.*   Of the fame and the enemies which this great satire brought, all know who read.   In the early eighties, Dryden held much of the literary dictatorship which had once been Jonson's, and he was greatly in request for his admirable prologues and epilogues in which especially he excelled.   On the death of King Charles, James, his successor, continued the royal bounty to Dryden; but that bounty was, as it had always been, precarious.   At this time the poet avowed himself a Roman Catholic, for which change of faith, he was roundly abused by his enemies.   It will be remembered that two famous argumentative poems of Dryden's disclose first why he was of the faith of England and then how he found a deeper religious contentment in the faith of Rome.[9]   It is not necessary to explain Dryden's conduct in this respect as a discredit to his convictions, although his flattery of "great ones" and his dependency on the royal favour make the suggestion that his change of faith was unworthy, not a thing wholly incredible.

[8] See especially the epilogue to *The Conquest of Granada,* beginning with the words: "Spite of all his pride, a secret shame invades his breast at Shakespeare's sacred name."

[9] *Religio Laici,* 1682; *The Hind and the Panther,* 1687.

With the Revolution of 1688, Dryden lost all his offices and had the mortification of seeing his rival and inferior, Thomas Shadwell, succeed him in the laureateship. Misfortune and ill health assailed him, but his mental powers remained unfailing and he continued his literary labours, translating and publishing to the end, howsoever his last play, *Love Triumphant,* had failed on the stage in 1694. Dryden died in May 1700.

There remain three tragedies, *All for Love,* 1678, *Don Sebastian,* 1690, and *Cleomenes,* 1692. Dryden was never better than when following with independence a great example. This was what he did in the first of these plays, and his example, on his own confession, was Shakespeare's *Antony and Cleopatra.* By this time, Dryden's taste and sound understanding had revolted against the rhyming heroics which he had essayed with such success; and acknowledging, as we have seen, the superiority of " an age less polished, more unskilled " than his own, he returned to blank-verse and a simpler and nobler dramatic art. Judged by abstract standards, *All for Love* is Dryden's finest play; for while he uses therein the subject of Shakespeare's greater tragedy, the conduct of the story, the conceptions of the great personages involved and the poetic vehicle by which all is conveyed are wholly Dryden's own. It is not to be denied that *All for Love,* estimated merely as a play, is of a superior construction, condensity and rapidity as contrasted with *Antony and Cleopatra.* And however we may prefer the larger and grander conception of the characters of these old-world lovers by the elder poet, Dryden assuredly carried out, in his more limited but intense realisation of their story, the thought conveyed in the title of his play, *All for Love, or the World Well Lost.* By some *Don Sebastian* has been given an even higher place, no less an authority than Sir Walter Scott declaring that, " Shakespeare laid aside, it will perhaps be difficult to point out a play containing more animatory incident, impassioned language, and beautiful description." And, indeed, the much famed scene of reconciliation between Don Sebastian and Dorax can not be matched in our English drama for its exquisite portrayal of the highest realisation of the chivalric and generous heroic ideal. Lastly, in *Cleomenes the Spartan Hero,* in which he had some help from Southerne, Dryden once more achieved splendid work on the lines of a definite model, in this case contemporary French classical tragedy. A resemblance in situation and pathos has been discovered between Cleomenes and his son, in their extremity perishing of hunger, and the catastrophe of Caratach and the little Prince Hengo in Fletcher's *Bonduca;* and once more, as always, even when at his greatest, Dryden pales before the stronger, truer, less affected and less conscious drama of the Elizabethan age.

Dryden's domination of his age in serious drama was absolute. No one thought of questioning his methods, his medium of expression or his ideals. But his age, despite his own exemplary labours in the translations of Virgil and the Roman satirists, possessed less sympathy with the ancients than almost any time that had gone before. So while his crew of imitators followed Dryden's choice of classical story in the drama, not one of these productions can lay the slightest claim to any attempt either honestly to represent the life of the ancients or to reproduce in any degree the lofty spirit of Greek tragedy. It is only after contemplating the confusion, stridency, extravagance and barbarity of the heroic dramas and tragedies of the Restoration that we can appreciate to the full how truly the poetic soul of Milton " dwelt apart." *Comus,* with its exquisite poetical allegory, had raised the masque, in the days of its degeneracy and abuse, to a permanent place in the categories of great and significant poetry. *Samson Agonistes,* licensed in 1670, the very year of Dryden's inflated *Conquest of Granada,* reproduced, in its restrained conduct of plot, its chaste and beautiful diction and its lofty theme, more nearly the conditions governing Attic tragedy, when at its best, than has any other play, before or since in our English language. Little need can there be in such a book as this to repeat what every schoolboy knows concerning the subject of *Samson Agonistes* in the biblical narrative of the *Book of Judges,* its conduct of plot in wonderfully close reproduction of the technical niceties of Greek tragedy, and the obvious analogy between the heroic Samson, blind and fallen on evil days, and both the poet's affliction and sorrow and the lost cause of Puritanism so dear to his heart. It matters, indeed, very little that Milton's tragedy was neither written for the stage nor is dramatic in the sense in which an actable play is dramatic. As the sincere utterance of a great soul in time of anguish, a lament for a fallen cause and for hopes cruelly bruised, if not shattered, *Samson Agonistes* has a significance and a power infinitely above the ephemeral triumphs of Dryden and the rest of Milton's time-serving, man-fearing, ingenious and forgettable contemporaries.

On the tragic stage but one contemporary of Dryden surpassed him, and this was Thomas Otway. Born in 1652, the son of a clergyman in poor estate, the poet was educated at Winchester and at Oxford which he left without a degree. To failure at the university he soon added failure as an actor; and an unhappy and unrequited passion for the celebrated actress, Mrs. Barry, almost completed his undoing. Otway was one of the many poets who languished in the fitful patronage of Rochester; although to that nobleman the poet owed his earliest encouragement and his opportunity. The first plays of Otway, *Alcibiades* and *Don Carlos,* were offered to the stage in 1675 and 1676, when the heroic play was still at its height, and both are written in the accepted heroic couplets. *Don Carlos* is a tragedy of much promise and, with Betterton in the title rôle, was an extraordinary success. Two adaptations followed, *Titus and Berenice,* from Racine, and *The Cheats of Scapin,* from Molière, the latter holding the stage for generations. The comedy, *Friendship in Fashion,* acted in 1678, was heartily applauded in its time; but it adds nothing in its flippant indecency to the author's reputation, nor can anything be said for Otway's flagrant plagiarism of the greater half of his *Caius Marius* from *Romeo and Juliet.*

Putting aside two military comedies, in which the author drew upon his own experiences in Holland, there remain *The Orphan* and *Venice Preserved,* the tragedies which raise the name of Otway to a place notable among the few of his age. The former, first acted in 1680, details the tragical consequences that followed the impersonation of a bridegroom by another on the wedding night, a subject in which the strong taste of Otway's age found a pathos of which our horror at the situation almost totally deprives us. However this harrowing theme had already been employed and whatever the dramatist's debt to the novel entitled *English Adventures,* the intensity and poignancy of the emotions which Otway raised in this play were quite new to the stage of his period. It is reported that Mrs. Barry, who created the rôle of Monimia, the injured heroine "invariably burst into genuine tears in the course of the performance," and the tragedy long continued, like *Venice Preserved,* which followed it in 1684, one of the great stock pieces, certain of appreciation and applause. The latter tragedy is a free dramatic version of an obscure episode in the late history of Venice, and Otway had it from an English translation of the French of the Abbé Saint-Réal, a writer already employed by him for the source of *Don Carlos*. It is not unlikely that Otway was willing to have his drama recognised, in its picture of Venice, weak and demoralised by the social and political corruption of its own senators, as symbolic, at least, of England in a similar condition during the recent great conspiracy known as the Popish Plot. In this it was, like many a play of its time, " a Tory document against the Whigs." But with all this, including the vilification of that much abused statesman, the Earl of Shaftesbury, in the vile Antonio, we need not concern ourselves. *Venice Preserved* has lived for something very different. For in it Otway has created two novel and truly tragical figures, the nobility and pathos of which it would be difficult elsewhere to equal: Jaffeir whom poverty and outrageous treatment have driven from despair into conspiracy, distracted between fidelity to his friend and fellow-conspirator and his devotion to an incomparable wife; and Belvidera, the wife, who, though repudiated by her father for her marriage and devotedly attached to her husband, none the less sacrifices husband and self to save the state. Nothing could be finer than the tenderness and pathos of the scenes between this devoted pair in this tragedy, nor anything more complete than the catastrophe in which the innately noble, though weak and unstable, Jaffeir, perfidiously defrauded of a promised amnesty for himself and his friend, kills both to cheat a felon's death on the scaffold. Constructive excellence, a clear and easy flowing diction and a poet's command of imagery, as well as the technicalities of an admirably smooth yet varied blank-verse, these things are Otway's. But above them all is his power to portray in his personages the tenderness of those who love and the throes and anguish which the virtuous and innocent suffer among the tragic vicissitudes and tossings of life. Otway's instrument contains not too many notes; but its few are of a surpassing and poignant sadness and sweetness. To those who can see in the fog and contagion of life somewhat more than the distortion and ruin of things, it may be possible to think of Otway as the one true lover of his faithless time, pouring out his own suffering heart in works of art to make immortal the woman whom he adored. To those, on the other hand, who are content that fog shall be fog and contagion contagion, the unhappy poet seems no more than one of the many men of talent whom association with the corrupt Rochester and a misplaced infatuation for a clever, but heartless and mercenary wanton, ruined body and soul.

Save for a few minor plays of the political reaction, Wilson's honourable following of Jonson, and Dryden's contributions to the lighter muse, trifling in comparison with his serious plays, the comedy of the Restoration remains for our consideration. Among older plays revived after the return of the king, the comedies of Fletcher and of Jonson, with a smaller number of Shakespeare's, still held the stage, and Davenant and Killigrew naturally staged work of their own and of their friends, the Howards, Stapylton, Orrery and others. But foreign influences made themselves manifest almost at once, in comedy as in tragedy; indeed it is better to recognise, in these influences, the continuance of what had gone before than to explain the new age, as was formerly done, as a more or less complete repudiation of England's own past. The important rôle which Fletcher played in opening the coffers of Spanish literature to the English drama has already been set forth, and it is sufficient for our purposes here to remember that his subjects of the kind were drawn, so far as we now know, wholly from Spanish fiction, and that it is not necessary to infer on his part — or on that of Massinger or Rowley, for that matter — either an acquaintance with the Spanish language or any knowledge of the Spanish stage. Even with Shirley, plays of whom have been confidently ascribed to sources in the dramas of Lope de Vega and Tirso de Molina, we are not on sure ground as to the precise nature and extent of these borrowings. In the last two volumes of Dodsley's *Old Plays,* several dramas, Spanish in scene, are to be found; most of them date before the Restoration.[10] It is likely that Sir Richard Fanshawe's translation of a couple of the plays of Antonio de Mendoza never reached the stage; but in Sir Samuel Tuke's *Adventures of Five Hours,* 1662, and the Earl of Bristol's *Elvira,* printed five years later, we have certain examples of the adaptation of Spanish dramas to the English stage. The Spanish *comedia de capa y espada* has been alluded to in these pages more than once. The recipe for its making is simple: two ladies, a gallant and his friend,

[10] These are *The Rebellion,* by Thomas Rawlins; *The Marriage Night,* by Henry Viscount Falkland, and *The Parson's Wedding,* by Thomas Killigrew.

their lovers; a jealous brother or a difficult father, with the attendant servants of all parties; mistakes, accidents, intrigue and involvement, honour touched and honour righted. Variation on the theme is infinite. Of English adaptations of this type, Tuke's well-written *Adventures of Five Hours* is by far the best. While the love that is intrigue and the touchiness, that go to make up much of what is accepted as Castilian honour, are the constant themes of the comedy of cloak and sword, it is a mistake to confuse such dramas with the heroic play, however the two may have reacted each upon the other. Without here entering into details, it is sufficient to notice that Orrery, Crowne, Mrs. Behn, and Wycherley, not to mention lesser names, all drew on Spanish comedies for some of their own and that Dryden himself was not unaffected by Spanish example, though perhaps less so than has sometimes been claimed.

But these influences from Spain are not of great moment, and they were frequently derivative, usually by way of France. It is to the latter country that the drama of the Restoration contracted its heaviest debt, and what could be more natural when we consider that, aside from the extraordinary draughts upon the heroic prose romance, there were, for serious drama, the refined examples of Corneille and Racine (in the England of this time, misunderstood) and for comedy, the commanding genius of Molière. As to the first, *The Cid* had been translated by Joseph Rutter as far back as 1637 and just before the Restoration, Sir William Lowes and, just after it, Mrs. Katherine Philips ("the Matchless Orinda"), Carlell and others were busy with *Polyeuctes, Horace, Pompée, Heraclius* and *Necomede,* the last three successfully produced variously in Dublin and London. Racine was adapted somewhat later; Crowne's inadequate version of the *Andromaque* in 1675 and Otway's *Titus and Berenice* are almost the only traces of that poet in English drama prior to 1700. On the other hand, the debt of Restoration comedy to Molière is extraordinary. His borrowers and beneficiaries include almost every name of importance from Davenant and Dryden to Shadwell and Wycherley; and some of the lesser people had their whole dramatic equipment of him.

Possibly Restoration opera is as well mentioned here as anywhere else, as the immediate foreign influence upon this biform hybrid of the drama was French and the librettos, as we should call them, are no serious matter at best. The introduction of

Italian opera into France as far back as 1645 and the subsequent transference of French opera to England are interesting subjects in themselves into which we can not here digress. It has been pertinently said, in view of all these alleged foreign influences, that "the manner in which instrumental interludes and dances and songs and passages of recitative were introduced into masques suggested the methods upon which composers might attempt incidental music to plays and operas." [11] And indeed, Matthew Locke, whose music to Shadwell's *Psyche* is sometimes spoken of as the first attempt at English opera, had written music for Shirley's masque-like, *Cupid and Death,* as far back as 1653, and portions of the vocal poets for *The Siege of Rhodes,* as well as for the far later revival of *The Tempest* with the Davenant-Dryden "amendments." With precedents such as these, it became the custom to make much of the incidental music on revivals of old plays with new splendours, and the names of Locke and Purcell, especially, attach to many a revival and to almost as many new performances. Purcell's *Dido and Æneas,* presented in 1680, has the distinction of being the first example in England of a story told in continuous dramatic music. As such it perhaps deserves to the full the title of the earliest English opera, although it would be difficult to determine what degree of recitative or spoken dialogue in a production of this kind should bestow or deny to it the coveted designation. The music of Purcell's *Dido and Æneas* has been highly praised: the libretto was by Nahum Tate, later to become poet laureate. The performance was a private one and interesting only historically. When Dryden turned to the writing of "opera," in *Albion and Albanius,* he employed Grabu, a foreign composer, to prepare the music; but, on his second venture, *King Arthur,* he returned to Purcell who had already written music for *Aureng-Zebe* and other plays. *King Arthur,* like its predecessor, is less an opera than "a play copiously supplied with incidental music." Indeed, when we examine the matter of opera in England before the coming of Handel, we find it, save for a few imported French performances, a vanishing quantity. Pepys uses the expression, "to the opera," habitually to denote a visit to the Duke's theatre in Lincoln's Inn Fields where he saw, under this designation, *Hamlet, Twelfth*

[11] See Sir C. H. H. Perry, "Music of the Seventeenth Century," *Oxford History of Music,* iii, 288.

Night, Davenant's *Love and Honour,* and Glapthorne's comedy, *Wit in a Constable,* with a score of other plays. The word was doubtless employed by more careful speakers than Pepys to signify any play in which considerable attention was paid to the music and setting.

Turning back to comedy, the earliest notable figure is that of Sir George Etherege who was born of good family in 1634. It is doubtful if Etherege was of either university, but he may have been at one of the Inns of Court. Possessed in all likelihood of some fortune, Etherege lived much abroad until the Restoration, and his easy knowledge of the French language and of French manners make it likely that he had spent much time in Paris. His work as a dramatist began with *The Comical Revenge, or Love in a Tub,* acted in 1664, the serious scenes of which are written in rhyme. This comedy was an immediate success and *She Would If She Could* and *The Man of Mode* (both written in prose), followed at long intervals after, the last in 1676. Both maintained and enhanced the author's repute for an easy ability to stage, with absolute freedom and abandon, the profligate manners of the fashionable society of his day. For, with his success, Etherege had joined the rout of Rochester, on more equal terms, however, than his lordship's creature poets, as a disgraceful broil at Epson and the dramatist's " protection " of Mrs. Barry after Rochester's death, both go to show. After marrying a fortune, Etherege went abroad and served as English resident, finally for several years at Ratisbon in Germany, where he appears to have lived riotously, neglecting his duties and finally losing his life, at Paris, in 1691 (it is supposed), in an accident that could hardly have befallen a sober man. It is a sordid story; yet this may be said for the comedy of Etherege, that it owed nothing to books or precedents. Fashionable, indolent, witty, charming and utterly profligate, Etherege knew at first hand the brilliant, shameless, deadly life in which he was alike a participant and a victim; and his conscienceless art enjoyed the popularity that an actual rescript of the time always deserves and usually obtains. Historically Etherege assumes importance when we consider that he determined a whole species of comedy which persistently held the stage, through Wycherley, Congreve and Vanbrugh down to very late times, increasingly more divergent from actual life. Etherege copied the life he knew, his successors copied Etherege.

Nearest to Etherege in point of time and literary manner is

Sir Charles Sedley, second in notoriety for his wit and his prof-
ligacy only to Rochester whom he resembles, too, in an admirable sense for the graces of prose style and for no inconsiderable lyrical gift. Attention has lately been called, with much
justice, to the fact that these gentlemen roisterers of the court
of King Charles were " too flagrantly industrious in the pursuit
of pleasure," too determined, in opposition to the gloom of
detested Puritanism, to be happy at all events, to make us altogether certain that they were not frequently bored in the midst
of their revelry and with all their dangerous hazards.[12] Sedley
lived, like some others, to become a grave, if none too stable,
politician. His plays reflect the influences of the moment; *The
Mulberry Garden* (borrowed in idea partly from Molière), is
precisely of the type of Etherege's *Comical Revenge,* even to
the writing of the serious scenes in rhyme; his *Antony and
Cleopatra,* a feeble tragedy, is wholly in rhyme, because Dryden
was so writing and on a classical subject for no better reason.
Bellamira, 1687, is Sedley's best play, for in it, however he
drew on the *Eunuchus* of Terence for his plot, he presents a
lively and realistic picture of the reckless life that he knew
so well. In writing of Restoration comedy, it is impossible
to avoid harping on the extraordinary license of speech and
conduct which the stage accepted as a matter of course. With
the taste and example of the king, the wits and the laureate
before them, the minor writers of comedy supplied what was
wanting in cleverness with the extravagance of license, while
appropriating from the past with consciences absolutely at ease.
John Lacy, who died as early as 1681, presumed upon his
popularity as an actor to turn playwright in some half dozen
efforts in which he laid violent hands on Molière, Shakespeare
and lesser men, making coarser whatever he touched. Edward
Ravenscroft was busy warming over the dramatic victuals of
other men for twenty years. His plays are described, by
Dibden, as " a series of thefts from beginning to end." His
most popular comedy, *London Cuckolds,* first acted in 1682,
was repeated on the lord mayor's day for nearly a hundred years
for its vulgar, humorous and scurrilous satire on the city.
Ravenscroft's one gift seems to have been that of boisterous
farce, a gift, by the way, that has carried off many a mediocre

[12] See Mr. C. Whibley, in *The Cambridge History of English Literature,* viii, 198 ff.

play and worse with the help of clever actors. Abler, but of
the same predatory class, was Mrs. Behn, interesting as the earliest example of a woman in England who made her way as a
professional author. Alphara Johnson was born at Wye about
1640, and reared in the West Indies, where she had unusual
experiences of which she made a literary use in her famous
story, *Oronooko*. In 1651, she married a Dutch merchant
named Behn who maintained her in good circumstances in London. Losing her husband about the time of the Restoration, she
lived abroad for a time at Antwerp, probably in the government
employ as a spy. But being neglected and unpaid, she returned
to England and began the writing of plays and fiction about
1671. Mrs. Behn's earliest efforts were romantic, tragedy even
in one instance, lifted from Marlowe; but she soon went over
to comedy in deference to the demands of her market. With
Killigrew for a model, she made over two of his unacted
comedies in *The Rover*, 1677, which proved to be her most
popular play. For other work she borrowed from Brome,
Massinger, Middleton, Wilkins and even Tatham, in *The
Dutch Lover, The City Heiress* and *The Widow Ranter* doing
her most characteristic work. She is fond of a swash-buckling
hero, sound at heart (according to Restoration standards), but
libertine in speech and conduct, and the certain victim of every
pair of bright eyes. Her writing is inventive, lively and made
up of incessant action; but she is boisterous, frivolous and a
match for any of her male competitors in foulness of speech and
frank immorality of dialogue and situation. Mrs. Behn knew
her age only too well, and she catered acceptably to its demands.
She was a clever and gifted woman who was forced to write
for her bread; and she loved the coarse fare that went by the
name of pleasure in her day. It is not fair to judge her by
harsher standards than those that we apply to her male contemporaries in the drama whose example she followed.

As we look at the complacent and satisfied countenance of
Thomas Shadwell, crowned with laurel, that faces the four
volumes of his plays, dedicated to King William (who could
not read them), and as we note how, for a period of nearly
twenty years, beginning with 1668, there was scarcely a year in
which a comedy of Shadwell's was not staged, often with applause, we can not but wonder that all this industry and assur-
ance of fame should be recompensed by so complete an oblivion.
Shadwell, owing to his bitter political feud with Dryden, has

suffered perhaps more than he deserves. Of an age with Mrs. Behn and Wycherley, King William's laureate received his education at Cambridge which, however, he soon quitted for the Middle Temple. In his first endeavours he enjoyed the encouragement of Dryden who wrote a prologue to *The True Widow* as late as 1679. In his day, indeed, Shadwell was a respectable figure, neither tampering with Shakespearean amendments nor with borrowings from France to a greater degree than his theatrical brethren, but holding at least one constant model before him for imitation and adoration. It is in the preface to his very first play, *The Sullen Lovers,* that Shadwell declares: "I have endeavoured to represent variety of humours . . . which was the practice of Ben Jonson, whom I think all dramatic poets ought to imitate, though none are like to come near, he being the only person that appears to me to have made perfect representations of human life." Shadwell endeavoured with honest industry, if not with any great illumination, to follow faithfully in those illustrious footsteps. In plays such as *The Humorists, Epson Wells, The Virtuoso,* and in the later *Bury Fair, The Scourers* and *The Squire of Alsatia* (esteemed his ablest comedy), Shadwell followed his model at a distance, often not greater than that of Cartwright or Brome, adapting his work to the "humours" of his own London, with the parade of an occasional moral and a more frequent descent to a coarseness and ribaldry below the level of *Bartholomew Fair.* Shadwell was a strong Protestant and a valiant Whig, both of which are abundantly proved in his outrageous attack upon "the Papists" in the scandalous character of Tegue O'Dively, the Irish priest of *The Lancashire Witches.* The play came just at the time of the excitement consequent upon the lying revelations of Titus Oates, and undeniably had more to do with Shadwell's supplanting of Dryden in the laureateship than had his poetry. Shadwell is not to be denied a certain power in dramatic invention, a broad rough humour in realising "the fops and knaves" which he thought were "the fittest characters for comedy," and an honest sense of right which was blind, however, to generosity and delicacy alike. It is probable that his vigorous pictures of the low humours of the London of his day are at least as true to the life which they depict as the tediously reiterated gallantries of the school of Etherege and Sedley.

The long continuance of the activity of Shadwell, who died in

1692, eight years before Dryden, has carried us forward. With William Wycherley, who was born the same year with Shadwell, we return once more to the earlier days of King Charles. Wycherley was educated first in France, at Queen's College, Oxford, and later at the Inner Temple. His position in life gave him access to that "best society" in which the king and Rochester were pattern and example. The comedies of Wycherley followed close on the earliest efforts of Etherege and Sedley, to whose school he unquestionably belongs, and they were written within the short period of five years from the success of *Love in a Wood,* in 1671 (which attracted to the author the somewhat questionable attentions of the Duchess of Cleveland), to *The Plain Dealer,* staged in 1674. Between these came the other two, *The Gentleman Dancing Master* and *The Country Wife.* In comparison with Etherege, Wycherley's comedies are of stronger fibre and better constructed; they are not nearly so well written. There is a vigour, however, a strength amounting at times almost to brutality about Wycherley that differentiates his "young gentlemen of the town," his coxcombs and match makers — to call his women no worse — from the superficial qualities of his predecessors. Wycherley was as frank a plagiary as any of his contemporaries, taking his *Dancing Master* from Calderon who in turn had found it in the bulging dramatic granaries of Lope de Vega; while his *Country Wife,* one of the coarsest comedies in the English language, derives its plot from two popular comedies of Molière. *The Plain Dealer* is Wycherley's most celebrated play, and, however it may have been suggested by certain scenes and personages of *Le Misanthrope,* was certainly made over by the English dramatist into something new and distinctive. Manly, a sea captain, is one whose natural honesty and frankness revolts at the hypocrisy and the faithlessness of the world. Instead of driving him from contact with his fellowmen, this creates in him such an infatuation for plain speaking and direct conduct, that these virtues become vices and the means of blinding him to the actual nature of the men and women about him. His mistress proves untrue, his bosom friend, false and an ingrate, and he is only saved from complete misanthropy by the faithfulness of the woman who, unknown to him, dearly loves him and serves him as a servant. In the gravity of Manly's disillusion and in the extraordinary and brutal demands upon Fidelia's devotion into which her master's eagerness for revenge betrays him, this comedy rises almost into tragedy. A diverting underplot is wholly of Wycherley's invention. *The Plain Dealer* is admirably planned and managed, the characters are roughly but clearly sketched and the dialogue, as usual with Wycherley, is written in prose, unadorned, forceable and natural. The thing which raises Wycherley above his class, strange as it may appear, is a certain moral earnestness which, despite the fact that there is scarcely a single truly virtuous person in all his drama, causes the careful reader to discern in all this brutality and plain speaking not a little of the gravity of true satire. After *The Plain Dealer,* Wycherley ceased to write, although he lived through various vicissitudes, an elderly man about town, now somewhat out of the mode, to receive a pension at the hands of King James and to form, in the reign of Queen Anne, a literary friendship with the precocious young poet, Pope.

The vogue and popularity of the stage during the period of Dryden's literary activity rivalled the busiest days of Elizabethan or earlier Jacobean days. Never before had plays been so in request, so elaborately staged or acted by so many talented and capable players. As we read the theatrical annals of the time: how Mrs. Hughes ensnared Prince Rupert and Nell Gwyn the king; how the Earl of Oxford betrayed the virtuous Mrs. Davenport by a mock marriage; of Mountfort dishonestly slain and of Goodman only too justly tried for a murder, we wonder that the drama could exist as an art in the midst of surroundings so foul and abandoned. But there is another side. Betterton made his début in *Hamlet* in 1661, Mrs. Sanderson, soon to become Mrs. Betterton, playing the part of Ophelia. Fifty years later, this great actor took leave of the stage, its acknowledged leader, for a lifetime, despite all temporary rivalries, and his wife was still by his side. Betterton was a man of sober, honest and industrious life, untouched by the vices of his age and equally the friend of Dryden the greatest poet, and Tillotson the greatest preacher of the day. His range of characters was enormous and his industry was only exceeded by his many gifts, and his success by his integrity and kindliness. It was sheer enthusiasm for the art of acting that took Rochester from the court and his dissolute pleasures to drill the tardy mind and unskilled gait of Mrs. Barry into the most consummate of actresses; and, however that lady may have repaid his lordship's condescensions, Mrs. Bracegirdle, her successor on the stage, lived in excellent private repute and was noted for her charities. As to the Restoration dramatists, Doran says that they exceeded in number the players and lists more than a hundred names. Indeed, nearly everybody wrote for the theatre. Besides the names already mentioned in this chapter — to add only two or three — there was John Banks, beginning in heroics rivalling Lee's, yet showing a certain melodramatic force in several plays of English historical subjects, treating of Essex, Lady Jane Grey and Anne Boleyn, that attracted public applause. There was Nahum Tate, almost the least of the poets laureate, a universal collaborator, giving us, among many other like things, a *King Lear* which is arranged to end happily with the marriage of Cordelia and Edgar, a version which Dr. Johnson defended and which held the stage into Victoria's reign. William Mountfort, the celebrated actor, followed Banks with English histories and wrote other plays, among them a *Faustus* enlarged especially as to its *diablerie* and "operatic effects"; and Charles Hopkins, beloved for his sweet temper by Dryden and Southerne wrote "promising" tragedies on Pyrrhus and Boadicea. Thomas Southerne, although his work for the theatre began in the eighties in association with Dryden, wrote on far into the reign of King George I. His *Fatal Marriage,* long a favourite and revised by Garrick, was acted in 1694, and his almost equally popular dramatic version of Mrs. Behn's novel, *Oronooko,* followed two years later. Southerne was an amiable man and conspicuous, among his fellow playwrights, for his long, prosperous and happy life. His four comedies (which are cleanly but of no great merit), and his six or eight other plays (several of them dramatized novels) deserve the contemporary appreciation which they inspired. Southerne's distinctive quality is a certain ability to move in the representation of pathetic situations in which he has been compared, not altogether unjustly, with Otway himself. Tom D'Urfey, the song writer, light hearted, convivial and imperturbably good humoured, began like Banks with heroic drama in the seventies, but carried his trivialities, dramatic and other, well over into the next age. It is something of a shock to recall that this Yorick of the court of the Stuarts was a nephew of Honoré D'Urfé the dignified author of *L'Astrée.* In the last decade of the century, too, Mrs. Behn was by no means alone in writing for the stage. There was the amiable and learned Mrs. Cockburn (Catherine Trotter) who combined poetry and philosophy and rejoiced in the friendship of Locke and Congreve alike; there was Mrs. Pix (Mary Griffith), her friend who, innocent of theory or practice in verse, none the less penned tragedies, succeeding measureably in the lighter mode. And there was the disreputable Mrs. Manley, society novelist and scandal-monger, whose adventurous biography with its political controlling wires is more interesting to read than her half-dozen forgotten plays. Mrs. Centlivre, the ablest of them all, began her work as a playwright later. The age was not unconscious of the innovation of women in authorship as a coarse but amusing comedy entitled *The Female Wits at Rehearsal,* acted in 1697, goes to show. Lastly, the scholars and critics were equally addicted to the universal habit. Lord Lansdowne, the patron of Pope, put forth the last flicker of the heroic play in his *Heroic Love,* 1698, which is written in blank verse and deals with the love affairs of Achilles. He also imitated Congreve at a long interval in comedy. While the notorious critic, John Dennis, fellow of Rymer and Gildon both of whom " wrote plays," not only rewrote Shakespeare as he ought to have been written but laid futile mines to success on the stage by way of Euripides and Tasso, to find a modicum of recognition when he mixed the concoction with party politics and abuse.

In William Congreve the artificial comedy of manners reaches its height. Born near Leeds, in 1670, the son of an officer whose professional duties carried him to Ireland, Congreve attended the Kilkenny school where he had Swift for a schoolmate. On coming to London, his indolence unfitting him for the law, Congreve ventured into literature with a novel entitled *Incognita,* of no great merit or promise. His earliest play is *The Old Bachelor;* it was acted with success in January 1693 and declared by Dryden the best first play that he had ever seen. The intricacy of the plot of *The Double Dealer* caused it to be not so well received; but the performance of it, in November of the same year, drew from Dryden an enthusiastic acclamation of the young dramatist as his poetic heir and successor with an exaggerated comparison of his talents to those of Shakespeare. In 1695, upon the secession of the older actors, headed by Betterton, from the patentee managers of Drury Lane, the opening of his new theatre in Lincoln's Inn Fields was signalized by the performance of Congreve's *Love for Love* which achieved an instantaneous and brilliant success. In consequence, the author received a share in the house on promise to write for it one new play each year. This success brought

Congreve, also, at the hands of Montagu, later Lord Halifax, an office as " commissioner of hackney coaches," the first of a happy series of like sinecures with which Congreve's political friends contrived to make easy his way of life, whether Tory ruled or Whig. In 1697, the poet's one venture into tragedy, *The Mourning Bride,* now remembered only for Dr. Johnson's eulogy, ran for thirteen days, an unusual time for the period, and saved the company from ruin ; and with *The Way of the World,* which was coolly received in 1700, the author gave up writing for the stage although he lived nearly thirty years thereafter.

Congreve has been variously estimated both as a man and an author. The man has been well described as " a gentleman of quality by nature " ; for his was ever the grand manner, the accepted course of conduct, the fitting word in that light, witty, risqué skirmish of repartee that went by the name of polite conversation. Congreve had too much wit to be a fop and too much good sense to throw away his life in dissolute living. He was much petted in good society and his plays were enthusiastically lauded and extolled. He took all naturally and gracefully, and was not too much spoiled. Indeed he professed (perhaps not without affectation) little more than a languid interest in the writing of plays, explaining that his first comedy was written " to amuse himself in a slow recovery from a fit of sickness," and declaring that success on the stage for his famous *The Way of the World* was almost beyond his expectation. When Voltaire called on him he insisted on receiving the visit as the civility of one gentleman to another, not as the meeting of two men of letters. None the less, Dryden, Swift, Addison, Steele, Gay and Pope, with many higher in station and less in prominence, valued his friendship and enjoyed it ; while the fascinating Mrs. Bracegirdle, who created the leading female parts in all his plays, and Henrietta, Duchess of Marlborough, daughter of the great duke, were alike devoted to him and beneficiaries, according to station, under his will.

The comedies of Congreve are of a literary excellence that overtops not only the comedies of their own age but that quality in all his imitators. There is no parallel in English to the directness, incisiveness, brilliancy and ease of his stage dialogue. And his personages, however they belong to the accepted categories of fops, gallants and ladies of fashion and intrigue, are conceived and executed with an air and distinction that raises them as much above their fellows of Etherege, Wycherley or Vanbrugh as Congreve himself excelled in the company he so loved. The plots of Congreve have been criticised as alike insufficient and difficult to follow. But Congreve was little concerned with story, however he prided himself on the construction of *The Double Dealer,* if what he had provided was thread enough on which to string the glittering beads of his epigram and repartee. It has been intimated above that the artificial comedy became less and less a transcript of life as successive playwrights accepted its conventions instead of observing afresh the life about them. Congreve's first comedy was written before he knew anything of actual fashionable life; and his last repeated as cynically, if more elaborately, precisely the same sorts of personages, the same intrigues and situations. These comedies exhibited a total absence of any standard of rectitude or honour in any sense whatever of that misused word. Mr. Archer has well called Congreve's art " a picture of society observed from a standard of complete moral indifference," and as such, it can in no sense be considered true satire. Whatever of social amelioration may have taken place between the early days of King Charles and the decade in which Congreve wrote, we may not unjustly conceive of that dramatist as a perverse or rather inverted idealist in the kind of life that he chose to depict, who magnifies alike the " gallantry," the wit, the heartlessness and the abandon of speech and conduct in this foul and glittering Utopia of his. There never were people quite so fascinatingly and brilliantly witty as Mirabel and gorgeous, petulant Mistress Millamont, these princes of the realms of the artificial comedy, nor beings quite so unutterably frivolous in their coxcombry as Brisk, Tattle or Witwood. And only the actual annals of the reign of King Charles can convince us that there were ever men and women as heartlessly wicked and depraved as Maskwell, Fainall, Mrs. Frail and Lady Touchwood. Judged by any standards applicable to actual life this entire Restoration comedy is hopelessly immoral and corrupt. Whether we are able to achieve the detachment that may enable us to accept it for its artistic and literary qualities (so far as it really possesses them) or anathematise it unconditionally with honest Jeremy Collier must depend less on our morals than on our attitude of mind.

It was in 1698 that the famous attack of Collier, *A Short View of the Immorality and Profaneness of the English Stage,* was printed.   Collier was a non-juror, which distinguished him as widely as possible from Puritan pamphleteers, like Prynne, from whom such attacks usually emanated, and therefore gave to his words a sanction which others could not have.   In his attitude of reprobation, Collier had had many respectable predecessors, among them John Evelyn, the diarist, Sir Richard Blackmore and others.   Moreover Collier's *Short View* is only one of more than two score like treatises of the author attacking " abuses," political, social and moral.   Collier's pamphlet has been commonly estimated as " a noble protest against evil," bringing immediate reformatory results; and neither his sincerity nor the need for his words is, for a moment, to be questioned.   But even a cursory glance at his pages, with their minute but evasive particulars, in which he hopelessly confuses the representation of vice with the approval of it, and makes no allowance for appropriateness of character or situation, must convince the most careless reader that Collier's *Short View* is a much overrated work which sought the destruction, not the reformation of the stage, and that its success was " one of scandal and no more." [13]   In the controversy that followed, Congreve, Vanbrugh, Farquhar and others took a hand and even Dryden, acknowledging his own short-comings, warily encouraged the fray from afar.   But the wits had no case; and despite a nugatory inquiry ordered by the crown and replies, rejoinders and surrejoinders lasting through many years, comedy continued her impudent way, actually little bettered if in any wise affected by Collier and his controversy.   It is neither true that the corruption of the stage set in with the Restoration nor that the attack of Collier brought about its reform.   That reform, if it can be said to have come at all, came in other ways.

[13] See Mr. Whibley's "showing-up" of Collier in *The Cambridge History of Literature,* viii, 163-169.

CHAPTER XI

STEELE, ROWE AND THE CLOSE OF THE LITERARY DRAMA

THAT two such minor names as these should head a chapter in the history of our English drama, following the illustrious succession that went before, may well give the thoughtful reader pause. Yet the great Augustan age, so famous for its wit and its satire, so satisfied that in it poetry and polite learning had reached a perfection beyond which it was impossible to conceive of a further advance, has no weightier names in comedy and tragedy to offer; and in the following reigns of the Georges, Goldsmith and Sheridan, the two that surpass them, stand historically more or less isolated and, in their talents, absolutely alone. It is true that the plays of older time still held the stage, those of Congreve, Wycherley, Vanbrugh, Otway and Dryden; while the pre-Restoration drama was now represented almost wholly by Shakespeare, largely in bastard versions in the making of which noblemen and wits complacently vied with the playwrights. Poetry died out of the drama with Otway and Dryden, save for a spluttering in Lee and a flicker in Southerne; the last glint is gone with Rowe. Literature and power over the phrase drops from Congreve to Steele, to be lost in excellent Cibber and his like, save for the satirical snap of Fielding, the light of Goldsmith and the flash of Sheridan.

Dryden died in 1700, and Congreve ceased to write for the stage; yet neither of these events nor the controversy that Collier had just raised in any wise materially altered the trend of the drama. An examination of the lists of first performances and revivals, kept by Genest, that careful enthusiast for our old drama, discloses *The Rival Queens* of Lee alone among the heroic plays in the frequency with which it was revived in the new century; although Dryden's *Indian Emperor* and *Aureng-Zebe* were occasionally acted, and *The Rehearsal* was repeated again and again, always with applause and appreciation. Clearly the heroic play was dead. Of Dryden's other dramatic works, few of the comedies were revived, unless we except *Amphitryon* and *The Spanish Friar,* which latter had caught the popular fancy, we may well believe, as much for its libel on the hated " Papist " clergy as for the humours of the incorrigible personage who gives the play its name. Otherwise, it was to *All for Love* and *Don Sebastian* that the public awarded the palm among Dryden's plays, however *Œdipus, Troilus* and *Cleomenes* were less frequently acted. As to Congreve, not only did he maintain his original popularity, he increased his hold; *The Double Dealer* and *The Way of the World,* both of them qualified successes at first, were now fully accepted and *The Mourning Bride* was often reacted as well. Among the comedies of other writers, Wycherley's *Plain Dealer,* Shadwell's *Squire of Alsatia* or Etherege's *She Would if She Could* appear to have led all others in popularity. Whilst among serious plays, outside of Shakespeare, *The Orphan* of Otway and his *Venice Preserved* had no rivals. As we look back, save for *The Mourning Bride* which was carried by Congreve's contemporary popularity in comedy, this list is by no means a discredit to the taste of the time, although it shows in the comedies no revulsion against the careless immorality of speech and conduct which had become an accepted convention of the stage. Omitting any enumeration of less frequent revivals such as Otway's *Cheats of Scapin,* Southerne's *Fatal Marriage,* or Crowne's *Sir Courtly Nice,* it is of interest to note how well the older dramatists held their own, though for the most part altered more or less to accord with prevalent taste. Of Mountfort's addition of " the humours of Harlequin and Scaramouch " to Marlowe's *Doctor Faustus* we have already heard; it was a deserved failure. More commonly these amended dramas of the older age were successful. As early as 1668, Davenant altered *The Two Noble Kinsmen* into *The Rivals,* Buckingham, if the critics are to be believed, took in hand *The Chances* to better it on the score of delicacy, while Settle " did " *Philaster,* Powell, *Bonduca* (bestowing four days on it), and Vanbrugh, *The Pilgrim.* Other plays of Fletcher appear to have been acted substantially as at first presented. One of the most popular of these was the lively comedy, *Rule a Wife and Have a Wife,* not amended before Garrick, and *The Maid's Tragedy,* despite the fifth act of Waller that transforms the story into a comedy, was acted, according to Southerne, in all its rigour and before King Charles. The most successful making over of a play of

Fletcher's is Farquhar's *Inconstant,* lifted bodily, however improved for acting, from *The Wild Goose Chase.* Among other "old plays," the popularity of which is attested, were Massinger's *New Way to Pay Old Debts,* Brome's *Jovial Crew,* Webster's *Appius and Virginia,* which Betterton worked over and called *The Roman Father,* and Chapman's *Bussy D'Ambois,* considerably damaged by D'Urfey. Further into these revivals we need not here inquire.

It was Shakespeare who was always the first quarry, and of some of these depredations upon him we have already heard. The subject, however, is of such interest, both in itself and for the light that it throws on the taste of the age, that a brief consideration of the nature and extent of some of these "changes" cannot here be out of place. During the fifty years following the Restoration no less than twenty-six rewritings, alterations and makings over of dramas of Shakespeare were made and the large majority of them acted. This list discloses some twenty different plays, the work of sixteen authors including three laureates, the actors Betterton, Lacy and Cibber, scholarly authors and critics such as Theobald, Dennis and Gildon, and hack writers like D'Urfey, Ravenscroft and Duffet.[1] Several reasons have been assigned for this pillage of Shakespeare and undoubtedly pressure for new material was the most important. It was this that must have actuated Davenant in his *Law Against Lovers,* 1662, the result of a union of the stories and much of the texts of *Measure for Measure* and *Much Ado About Nothing,* in which the Claudio-Hero plot drops out and the character of Mariana as well, and the play ends with Angelo's espousal of Isabella at the command of the duke. Pressure of time and utter carelessness as to the result alone could explain Otway's grotesque thrust of Caius Marius into the rôle of Romeo with Sulla in that of County Paris. Eagerness for novelty and pruriency, to the charge of which the whole age is open, account for the offensive additions made to the delightful and poetic conception of *The Tempest,* by which Ariel and Caliban each is provided with a sister and a youth who has never seen a woman is added to match Miranda and her sister "Dorinda." So pleasing was this subject that

[1] See on the whole topic, G. R. Lounsbury, *Shakespeare as a Dramatic Artist,* 1901, p. 302. To the twenty-six here mentioned may be added nearly double that number up to the end of the eighteenth century.

Shadwell transformed the reviser's work into an "opera" with new scenes and machines "admirably managed" besides songs and dances; and Duffet degraded it into a farce of the humour of the gutter in *The Mock Tempest*. It is the "new scenes and machines" with the spectacle involved that account not only for Shadwell's "opera" but for *Macbeth*, as revised in 1672, "with alterations, amendments, additions and new songs"; and so much were these features admired and accepted that Pepys declared it "a most excellent play in all respects especially in divertisement though it be a deep tragedy; which is a strange perfection in a tragedy, it being most proper here and suitable." [2] We need not wait until the Restoration to notice another feature of the popular taste that favoured alterations of our older plays. Tragicomedy had been called into being from the shrinking of later audiences from the inevitability of tragedy and the happy ending came more and more to be demanded. As early as 1663, James Howard had rewritten *Romeo and Juliet* to end in the wedding of the now truly "ill starred lovers." This effort has fortunately been lost; but Tate's *King Lear,* into which are injected several pretty love scenes between Cordelia and Edgar (who in Shakespeare's tragedy do not even meet), long held the stage and even Garrick did not dare to return to the original tragic version. Here, too, is involved still another reason for these Shakespearean alterations. Shakespeare recognises the love of man and woman as one of the many passions that animate mankind, and there are no love scenes the equal of his; but he recognised likewise the existence of other motives that are no less efficient for tragic than for comic use. We have already noticed that in the drama of the Restoration, comedy is almost solely preoccupied with the gallantry of amorous adventure and serious drama as undividedly with amorous passion or its reflexes, jealous enmity and revenge. For this various reasons have been assigned, among which the presence of women on the stage and their enormously larger proportion among the auditors, as contrasted with earlier times, are not to be overlooked. With Field or Kynaston, however complete their "makeup," affecting the graces of Viola or "boying" the greatness of Cleopatra on the stage, the illusion was at least sufficiently far from complete not to disturb the interest of the auditor in the play as a play.

[2] *Pepys Diary*, ed. Wheatley, 1904, vi, 125.

On the other hand, the auditors of *The Old Bachelor* of Congreve received with enthusiasm the stale and impossible dénouement of the marriage of the wrong woman in a mask, applauding to the echo, Davies tells us, as each of the four beautiful women who acted in the play unmasked and disclosed her identity. It was not only *The Rival Queens* that drew crowded houses; but Mrs. Barry and Mrs. Boutel, known rivals in their art as in their beauty for the favour of the town, and "'the accident," whereby, on one occasion, the dagger of Roxana reached the bosom of Statira with more effect than the author had demanded, effaced, as it surpassed in fidelity to nature, all the eloquent bombast of Lee's inflated rhetoric. In such an atmosphere it was essential that the poets should strive to enliven the older plays by an infusion into them of this popular element. Hence it is that Crowne worked into his alterations of *Henry VI* "a good deal of love making in which Warwick the king maker, Edward Plantagenet, his future queen Lady Gray and a new character Lady Eleanor Butler all have a share." Hence Shadwell gave to Timon of Athens a daughter, divided between the attentions of Alcibiades and those of a wealthier suitor, whilst Orrery, in an heroic play on Henry V, which has the merit at least of not having been stolen from Shakespeare, raised the love affairs of Catharine of France, Owen Tudor and the victor of Agincourt to an interest above that of the mere conquest of kingdoms.

The want of taste, of any sense of fitness, let alone poetry, is sufficiently illustrated in the examples above; but, from another point of view, something may be said for these changes as, to a certain degree, adjustments to the newer conditions of the stage. To anticipate slightly, when Cibber brought out his version of *Richard III* in 1700, showing a diffidence in offering it very different from the self-satisfied confidence of some of his predecessors, his effort was directed especially to an adaptation of the old chronicle play to the conditions of the stage of his time. Considered in the abstract, the epic succession of scenes, with their incessant change of place, their intermittent action and long conversations while the action halts, all of these characteristics of the chronicle play as a species, are wanting in that concentration, concreteness and unity that was becoming more and more the recognised ideal of dramatic construction. While Shakespeare's *Richard III,* from the unity which the grim protagonist gives to the play, is less open to this criticism than some other plays of its species, it is not to be questioned that its technique belongs to an earlier age than that of Cibber. With his practical experience of the theatre, Cibber discovered this and attempted by omission, condensation and readjustment to render the tragedy more actable on his stage. In this he succeeded measurably although at the cost of much of the poetry and fitness of personage and episode all of which Shakespeare had so subtly wrought into one that no hand save his own dare touch them. Unhappily too, Cibber, doubting his own powers (as well he might), to mould together the dissevered parts, interpolated bits derived from other plays of Shakespeare, thus decorating with flowers, hopelessly withered from their context, the havoc he had made. I have dwelt upon this the most favourable of these alterations of Shakespeare — one that has held the stage almost to the present day — in order that we might comprehend the nature of the gyves which time had put upon the old free drama. The change was a momentous one; from a great popular utterance, claiming for its constituency the whole English people, safe in a broad appeal to love of country, the spirit of fair play, domestic virtue and capable, from its hold upon the emotions, of almost any flight into the realms of poetry and the imagination, English drama had shrunk into a thing of precedent and convention, governed by the laws of the ancients, as they were misunderstood and supposed to be practised in the drama of a foreign country, or guided by the dissolute taste of a court, which had long since gone its way to dissolution, leaving only its heartlessness, its godlessness and libertinism to be mimicked by those who came after. The spirit of Shakespeare's drama was that of the people; the spirit of Dryden's drama that of the court; for faith in man we have cynical laughter and mistrust in goodness, for patriotism, as demonstrated in the old chronicle play, we have party politics with which not only comedy but serious drama is permeated, at times to its utter undoing. In our current criticism of the dramatic and literary technique of other times than our own, we are apt to judge too singly by our own standards. The model of old was to fill three hours' time with a varied entertainment, and fulness of illustration, even if some of it were irrelevant, was one of the conditions in which that particular form of art flourished. The drama of the seventeenth century was far from realising the modern ideal by which " the dramatist seizes upon a crisis in the lives of his characters, states its conditions and follows its evolutions to an end," regarding everything else a surplusage. Yet in Cibber, as earlier in Congreve, we recognise an ideal above the practice of the time and in the case of *Richard III* a struggle toward the realisation of that ideal.

With the heroic play dead and the artificial comedy of manners at its *ne plus ultra,* we may well inquire what it was that held over into the new century. We have first the continuance of this comedy in the hands of Vanbrugh, Farquhar and Cibber, with a suggestion of a reformation of its immorality, if not its frivolity, by the last, an attempt more seriously made a little later by Steele. And we have, in serious drama, a revulsion from the extravagances and unrealities of the heroic play and its like which begot an increasing interest in subjects historical and in those which, like Otway's two most famous plays and some of Southerne's, gave opportunity for a display of the tenderer domestic emotions. If we except the classical frigidities of dramas like Addison's *Cato,* the trend of both comedy and tragedy in the reign of Queen Anne was clearly towards the sentimental, and in Steele and Rowe, as we shall see, the transformation is already assured, if not complete. This topic for the moment we must defer to turn back to the three notable followers of Congreve, who began to write in the reign of King William and almost as early as he, but who carried their labours over into the next age.

Sir John Vanbrugh was of Flemish descent on his father's side and well connected in England on his mother's. He was born in 1664, in London, and appears to have entered the army, being known in his earlier days as Captain Vanbrugh. We have a glimpse of him in Paris in 1692, imprisoned in the Bastile under suspicion of being a spy. He is said to have employed his enforced leisure there in meditating the scenes of a comedy. He was soon liberated and we hear no more of him until he emerges as an author in 1696. In 1682 the two companies, originally constituted, it will be remembered, as the King's and the Duke of York's, united; and there succeeded a period of prosperity for all concerned. But disputes arising between the patentees and the actors, Betterton, as we have already seen, seceded, in 1695, and started his rival company in Lincoln's Inn Fields with the success of Congreve's *Love for Love.* This brought about evil days for the Royal company at Drury Lane, the actors' wages were reduced and the need of a rival success to make weight against Congreve became imperative. This rival play came from an unexpected quarter. Colley Cibber was a stage struck lad who had been haunting the theatres for five or six years, to be at last given small parts in which he had comported himself perhaps none too well. He was doing better however of late and when he submitted a comedy to the perusal of Southerne, entitled *Love's Last Shift,* Southerne advised its acceptance by the company and, being given the part of Sir Novelty Fashion, "an affected fop whose soul is everlastingly in pawn to his tailor," Cibber had the satisfaction of achieving at once the triumph of an actor and an author. *Love's Last Shift* is properly described as "a well constructed and effective comedy" and "deserving of the favour with which it was received." There was something novel as well as healthy in the subject, however its similitude of wit might fail before the sparkle of Congreve. But to return, it was the success of Cibber's first comedy that turned Vanbrugh to the making of plays. Struck with the concluding situation of *Love's Last Shift,* Amanda's recovery of her recreant and penniless husband Loveless, after an eight years' wandering in pursuit of unlawful pleasure, Vanbrugh furnished, in *The Relapse,* so far as such a personage as Loveless is concerned, the inevitable, if cynical, sequel. In the upshot the author contrives in his way to pay his tribute to virtue and constancy in the character of the wife, a tribute that Congreve would not even have thought of, and he elevates Cibber's Sir Novelty Fashion, which, with the author's clever acting, had caught the town, to a dramatic peerage as Lord Foppington, the very prince of his diverting kind. In *The Relapse* we have at once the vivacity, gaiety and levity which characterise the happy art of Vanbrugh. He is little more a satirist in his presentation of fashionable life than was Etherege or Congreve, for anything in the nature of a moral standard as a point of departure is almost as conspicuously absent in his work as in theirs. On the other hand, Vanbrugh's lightness of spirit relieves his comedy, even in its frequent lapses from decorum, of a certain repulsiveness, not absent from Congreve, and gives to his wit an effect less premeditated and artificial.

But Vanbrugh was already immersed in other affairs. He had become a member of the Greenwich Hospital Commission in association with Sir Christopher Wren as early as 1692 and, in 1702, his sudden leap to fame as architect of Castle Howard in Yorkshire suggests that he must have begun the practice of that profession far earlier. Among the many houses that he designed, the most famous is Blenheim which brought him endless trouble and the lasting enmity of the Duchess of Marlborough. In 1703, "Vanbrugh was created Clarenceux King at Arms, against the protest of the college and despite the facts that he knew nothing of heraldry and had openly ridiculed that grave science in one of his comedies." He held his post notwithstanding and acceptably fulfilled its duties. A few years later Vanbrugh became Controller of the Royal Works, which post he held until his death in 1726. In 1705 he designed a new theatre in the Haymarket and with Congreve who, really gave very little assistance, undertook the management of it. But what with the rural surroundings and the serious acoustic defects of the building, the venture proved a complete failure and Vanbrugh withdrew from his undertaking in a year's time, a heavy loser. To return to his comedies, in the same fruitful year, 1697, Vanbrugh brought out *The Provoked Wife* at the theatre in Lincoln's Inn Fields. With Betterton, Mrs. Barry and Mrs. Bracegirdle in the cast, the play was a complete success. Superior in construction, *The Provoked Wife* sustained the author's repute, although it lapses into the utter moral callousness and flippancy of its school, without even a suggestion of a serious motive to sustain it. This was one of the plays justly singled out by Collier for attack, a subject to which we need not return. Vanbrugh's part in the replies to Collier was clever, as might be expected, though he was as blind as his fellows to the reality of the issue involved. In 1700, he rewrote *The Pilgrim* of Fletcher in prose for the benefit of Dryden who contributed the prologue and epilogue, his last work for the stage. This performance is otherwise memorable as that in which the famous actress, Anne Oldfield, whose talents Farquhar had discovered in the previous year, made her début. Of Vanbrugh's translations, chiefly from Molière, the only one that deserved success, though it did not at once attain it, was *The Confederacy,* derived directly from d'Ancourt's comedy *Les Bourgeoises à la Mode*. It was acted in 1705 and with it Vanbrugh's labours as a dramatist conclude.

Almost precisely correspondent in point of time with the comedies of Vanbrugh were those of Farquhar who resembled his competitor further in being likewise in the military service. George Farquhar was born in Londonderry in 1678, the son of an Irish clergyman, who could do little more for his son than offer him a good education. This he pursued for a time at Trinity College, Dublin, only too soon to fall a victim, like Lee and Otway before him, to the fascinations of the stage. Notwithstanding a prepossessing personality, Farquhar does not appear to have succeeded as an actor at the Smock Alley Theatre in Dublin where he made his first appearance as Othello; and the accidental wounding of a fellow actor in one of Dryden's plays brought him to the determination to abandon the stage. At this juncture his friend, the actor Wilks, later to become famous, induced Farquhar to follow him to London and, encouraged by him he offered Rich, the manager of Drury Lane, his first comedy, *Love in a Bottle,* which was acted, late in 1698, and favourably received. Through the good offices of Orrery, it is said, the young dramatist received a lieutenancy, but save for a brief absence in Holland, which may have been with his regiment, and a recruiting trip to Shrewsbury, Farquhar's soldiering interfered very little with his play writing. In 1700, the acting of Wilks in the part of Sir Harry Wildair in Farquhar's second play, *The Constant Couple,* so took the town that the success was followed up by a sequel in which that " son of chaos," as the character has been well called, gives his name to the play. *The Inconstant,* an able adaptation of *The Wild Goose Chase* of Fletcher, was not received with the favour which its merits demanded, nor did a better fate attend *The Twin Rivals* acted in the same year. *The Recruiting Officer,* on the other hand, based on the author's actual experiences, however fancifully enlarged, enjoyed an extraordinary success in its performance in 1706, and long continued a favourite stock piece. Farquhar was possessed of the gay, irresponsible nature that is habitually associated with the Celt. No success could relieve him of his incurable impecuniosity, no failure entirely dash his buoyant spirits. With neither fortune nor position to back him, he lived the gay life of his time and, despite the successes of his comedies, fell heavily into debt. Two anecdotes are related concerning the later years of his life. The first tells how a lady, almost as needy as himself, fell so desperately in love with him, that she represented herself to the credulous poet as a wealthy heiress thereby to justify their otherwise imprudent marriage which actually took place; the other, how on the advice of the Duke of Ormond, Farquhar sold his commission to pay his debts, " his grace promising, should this course be adopted, to give Farquhar a captaincy in his own regiment," a promise that his grace forgot. Farquhar died in poverty when less than thirty years old, a month after the triumphant success of his *Beaux' Stratagem,* leaving a touching letter to his friend Wilks beseeching him to care for his two fatherless daughters.

In one of the ablest estimates we have of Farquhar as a dramatist, we are pertinently reminded of his youth and his promise; how the latest of the group — Vanbrugh, Congreve, Cibber and Steele — to write, he was the earliest to die, and how, therefore, the nature of his sins against decorum was somewhat different from theirs, Wycherley's or Dryden's. We are further reminded, and the case well made out, that Farquhar, save for his first imitative work, was really less coarse, and, what is more important, less morally callous, than his school and assured that he was actually " progressing towards a sane and humane form of comedy when the pen fell from his hand." [3] To some this may seem an endeavour to distinguish between a dose of poison that has been quite sufficient to kill the man and one that he might have taken, powerful enough to kill at least two. But Mr. Archer is within the truth when he states that Farquhar, in his last three comedies, " gives a general preponderance to kindness over cruelty and good over evil, which reverses the order of things prevailing in his contemporaries," and that Farquhar " may fairly share with Steele the credit of having set earnestly about the ventilation of English comedy." Possibly, in this necessary opening of the windows and getting out of doors, the most salient change is that which takes us, in these comedies, out of the narrow confines of the social life of a coterie wherein the conventions of etiquette have been substituted for the laws of nature, into a somewhat wider sphere of action, one at least in which the world of fashion and frivolity is viewed from without. *The Recruiting Officer* carries the scene to Shrewsbury and substitutes a novel group of characters, country justices and country clowns, the prey of the humorous wiles and devious subterfuges of three recruiting captains, actual folk in a larger contemporary life than that of the fops and gallants of Covent Garden; while the scene of *The Beaux' Stratagem* is Lichfield, wherein a sim-

[3] See William Archer, Introduction to *George Farquhar,* " Mermaid Series," 1903.

ilar use is made of the life of a country inn. This comedy is Farquhar's masterpiece and it adds to our wonder at its humour, ease and brightness to know that it was written almost literally on the author's deathbed. The plot is alike fresh, natural and original and better constructed than any comedy of Congreve. There is a humanity about the two scapegraces, who give title to the play, and their conduct, judged entire, is not unworthy their gentle blood. The ladies of their seeking, Dorinda and Mrs. Sullen, are real women and the plight of the latter, married to a drunken brute, justifies the unconventional conclusion whereby a separation is mutually agreed to. It has been well remarked that this honest questioning of an institution, which the drama of the time universally accepted only to cast ridicule upon it, was in itself a sign of an awakening moral consciousness. We can heartily agree with Mr. Archer in his belief that in the death of Farquhar English drama suffered a veritable misfortune. For this dramatist alone of the authors of his time appears to have been possessed of the true *vis comica* that translates actual life into an effective stage picture. Only such a one as he could have held the stage against the more diffusive influences of the essay that shortly carried Steele away from the theatre and Fielding, a little later, into the novel.

Of Colley Cibber's first comedy and its inspiration to Vanbrugh we have heard, and likewise of the adaptation of *Richard III*. Cibber became an actor of note and is recorded as particularly happy in eccentric parts, the fops of Etherege, Congreve and Vanbrugh; and Justice Shallow, Jaques and even Iago and Richard III were among his Shakespearean rôles. Cibber began acting in 1690 and retired in 1733, appearing occasionally even after; and he became, too, the most important manager of his time, conducting the affairs of Drury Lane with a success both histrionic and financial which it had never known before. With the delightful material that Cibber has left us in his naïve and fascinating *Apology,* it would be pleasant to digress here into the history of the stage as he knew it, but neither our space nor the plan of this book permits. Cibber was intimately associated with nearly every dramatist, actor and patron of the stage from the heyday of Otway and Dryden to the latter days of Steele; and, on the death of Eusden in 1730, Cibber was appointed poet laureate, an honour that his good sense rightly attributed entirely to his staunch Whig principles. The work of Cibber as a dramatist grew out of the exigencies of his career as an actor and manager. It included upwards of thirty plays, comedies of manners and intrigue, pastorals, a farce, a masque, tragedies, alterations and adaptations of Shakespeare, Fletcher, Dryden, Molière, Corneille and even of his minor contemporaries. There were many failures among them, but likewise a number of successes such as *She Would and She Would Not,* an excellent comedy of manners, and *The Careless Husband,* a really brilliant comedy of intrigue. Neither originality, literary quality, elevation of sentiment nor anything in the least degree smacking of poetry can be claimed for Cibber. But he could construct a play and people it with acceptable and entertaining personages. His work for the stage discloses a certain amelioration in decency and morals, as the years go by, in which he reflected the progress of his age; to speak of " the moralised comedies of Cibber " seems an overstatement. His *Apology* introduces us to a man of singularly good sense and modesty who appears to have rated his associates fairly and to have laboured under no false misappraisement of himself. It was the irony of fate that thrust Colley Cibber into the laureateship thereby making him the butt of the ridicule of stronger men than himself; but assuredly the wit of Pope has seldom been so perversely misled by his spleen as when he makes this shrewd and capable business man, this adaptable dramatist and clever actor the hero of *The Dunciad.*

Only one other dramatist who carried over the manner of the previous age need here concern us; and that is Mrs. Susanna Centlivre whose earliest play corresponds in point of date with the year of the death of Dryden. Before her marriage to Centlivre, chief cook in the royal household of Queen Anne and King George I, she signed herself variously Freeman and Caroll. Mrs. Centlivre was of humble origin and began life in a company of strolling players in the provinces but later established a permanent position in London. Her eighteen plays were written between 1700 and 1721, two years preceding her death, and there is scarcely one of them that is not possessed of merit for the stage. Her comedies, which form the bulk of her work, are alike lively and ingenious. Her greatest success was the creation of a new comedy figure in Marplot in *The Busy-Body,* 1709. Don Felix in *The Wonder or a Woman Keeps a Secret,* 1714, is hardly less amusing and original, however different in kind. Mrs. Centlivre is bright rather than witty, fluent and easy in dialogue and absolutely of the school of Congreve and Vanbrugh whom she equals in the ingenuity and in the want of the slightest sympathy with the moral ideals which were beginning to make their way towards realisation during the period of her writings. Several of her comedies, however, long held the stage to be revived by Garrick and even later.

Into the interesting details of the life of Sir Richard Steele, it is impossible here to enter. Playwriting to him was not much more than an episode of his youth, though one of importance to the history of the drama alike from the consciousness of his art and from his recognition of what he conceived to be the moral obligations of the stage. Like Farquhar, Steele was of Irish birth, born in Dublin in 1672 and some six years the former's senior; like Farquhar, too, Steele began life as a soldier and saw as little service. But Steele was of better station in life and a kind uncle, who was secretary to the Duke of Ormond, was able to give his nephew the advantages of an education first at the Charterhouse, where began his friendship with Addison, and later at Oxford. The associations of Steele's youth stood him in good stead later, for his frank and engaging personality made him many friends. A certain dualism — rather than call it inconsistency — in the temperament of Steele disclosed itself early. His life as a young officer and rising wit, only too prone to conviviality, "exposed" him, as he expressed it, "to much irregularity," and among other escapades, he fought his man like any other gallant of his time, only to be afflicted — very unlike that personage — with serious after-thoughts on "the barbarous custom of duelling." *The Christian Hero,* 1701, honestly avowed with his name on the title page, was a strange book for a scapegrace young captain to write; and, losing caste among his fellow officers of the regiment because of it, with characteristic volatility, Steele wrote his first comedy, *The Funeral,* to make weight against this prejudice. But *The Funeral or Grief à la Mode* is no swing back into comedy after the manner of Congreve and Vanbrugh. Steele had already declared himself "so far as I durst for witty men, . . . a great admirer" of Jeremy Collier and acknowledged with candour the need of a reform of the stage. It was certainly a departure from custom for the author to "hope" in his preface that his subject might prove "acceptable to all lovers of mankind," and it was almost equally without immediate precedent that he should have invented his plot entire. On its performance, at Drury Lane late in 1701, *The Funeral* was received with " more than expected success," its timely satire on the folly of current fashionable vanities in grief, its several natural and amiable personages and its sprightly dialogue carrying off the utter improbability of the plot and such enormities as a young man, estranged from his father, visiting the home in which his father's dead body lies, to carry on the lively courtship of one of his wards. *The Lying Lover,* Steele's next comedy acted in 1703, owes considerable to *Le Meteur* of Corneille, but the serious twist to the plot in the last act, by which the careless Oxford lad, come up to town to play the gallant, is turned from his follies while in prison, supposedly for the killing of a man in duel, reads much like a page from Steele's own life. This comedy was written with the avowed purpose of banishing " out of conversation all entertainment which does not proceed from simplicity of mind, good nature, friendship and honour." The author acknowledges in it " an honest ambition to attempt a comedy which might be no improper entertainment in a Christian commonwealth." Four acts of *The Lying Lover* are excellent; the hero, Bookwit, with his imaginative lies, has a gay charm which accounts for the havoc that he temporarily works in the hearts of the ladies whose position of ironical friendship and concealed rivalry is well sustained. But the fifth act falls into " a moral homily," and the attempted picture of young Bookwit's despair in Newgate is as much above Steele's power as a dramatist as the sentimental ending is perilously near to priggishness. *The Lying Lover* ran but six nights. *The Tender Husband* acted in 1705 is a much better play, though it had hardly a better fate. In point of fact its comparative failure may be attributed, not this time, to a sermonizing fifth act, but to the union of two plots, the one (derived from Molière) as excellent in its farcical capabilities as the other (which was original) is unwholesome and unnatural.

With *The Tender Husband,* Steele ceased, for many years, to write for the stage, although his association with the theatre continued close as critic, patron of the players and sharer in the business, if not in the actual management of Drury Lane. Into the vicissitudes of these theatrical matters we cannot venture here nor can we trace, even in outline, the active life of Steele as a politician, essayist and, party pamphleteer. Steele was always a careless financier; and his extravagance, generosity and sanguine miscalculations as to his business undertakings and the returns of his various offices kept him in continual trouble, notwithstanding that his income, at times, was large. There are several indications of an intention on his part to return to writing for the stage, but what with his preoccupation with *The Tatler* and *The Spectator* and the several less famous " papers " that followed year after year, it was not until 1722 that his last comedy, *The Conscious Lovers,* was acted. This time, with help of an excellent cast, in which Booth, Wilks and Mrs. Oldfield were foremost and Cibber directing and advising, the author achieved an unquestioned success and his comedy held the stage for a century. *The Conscious Lovers* is founded on the *Andria* of Terence, but by no means slavishly, for the scene and personages are thoroughly English. In his preface Steele declares once more his purpose, " an innocent performance," and that " the whole was writ for the sake of the scene of the fourth act, wherein Mr. Bevil evades a quarrel with his friend; and I hope," the author adds, " it may have some effect upon the Goths and Vandals that frequent the theatres, or a more polite audience supply their absence."

The comedies of Steele raise several questions. There is first the ever recurring difficulty regarding the relations of art to morals; then there is the doubt, raised in his own time, if material such as that constituting *The Conscious Lovers,* for example, falls properly within the limitations of comedy; and the query to what degree may a sentimental interest be reasonably substituted for that steady and concentrated picture of life that we habitually expect of the drama. That the drama of Steele's generation demanded moral stimulus need not be repeated and that he administered the dose is not to be denied. Possibly it was unavoidable, in view of the accepted conventions of the stage, to escape either the dose or the label. Steele labelled his medicine and frightened the patient; and the qualified success of his three earlier comedies is to be attributed as much to a certain shyness on the part of the public as to his purpose as to the departure of these comedies from the kind of thing that his audience was accustomed to expect. There are few things so difficult to accomplish as the surprise of a theatrical audience, and success is as likely as not to be resented. The novelty of Steele's plays, even more than their conscious moral tone and sentimentality, accounts for their qualified success. About the limitations of any form of art, we have ceased to argue much in these later days and we are nearly ready to acknowledge that such argument is scarcely more profitable than talk as to the correct size and colour of orchids. Even the matter of the intrusion — if it be such — of sentiment into places which we think otherwise better occupied, may be acknowledged to be largely a question of where to draw the line. Eighteenth century sentiment seems to us at times mawkish; will anything much better be said some day of our own? As to Steele, with a fine discernment and power of drawing character and ability to write lively, natural and diverting dialogue, with a charming command of humour and pathos at need, he fails as a writer of comedies because of diffuseness, because of an inability to concentrate and to construct with the precision that several playwrights, otherwise his inferiors, possessed. Unconsciously or not, Steele sought expression in the essay and left the inimitable figures of Sir Roger de Coverley, Will Honeycomb and Captain Sentry to a larger audience than Sabel, Bookwit or Bevil could ever reach. It is interesting to know that Goldsmith borrowed his Tony Lumpkin from Steele's Humphrey Gubbin, and that Sheridan had his Lydia Languish from Biddy Tipkin; that Steele had his part in the paternity of Fielding's old fashioned Squire Western as in his " perfect man " Squire Alworthy. Even Sir Charles Grandison is only Richardson's elaborate glorification of Steele's virtuous, priggish, impossible paragon, young Bevil. In a word, Steele was the earliest literary man to express the new sentimental ideal of manhood which, whatever its shortcomings, set a contrast between the weakness and brutality of the flesh and decent, honest clean living, and recognised a respectable, if somewhat conventional, standard of moral conduct, governed by kindness and humanity, while seeing the world none the less truly as it was. This was a great step in advance of the conventional immorality of the previous age, with its cynical denial of any standard. Unhappily, however, this was precisely the step which the drama could not stand; for the substitution of the sentimental ideal carried with it the reference of conduct, character and situation to the standard of morals in place of the standard of artistic truth and fitness. We may acknowledge *The Lying Lover,* then, as the first unmistakable example of the sentimental comedy and the as yet healthy parent of a long and increasing sickly progeny.

To appreciate to the full the nature and extent of the decline in the English drama, not from the pinnacles of Shakespeare, but from the lesser heights of Heywood, Massinger and Dryden, we need to consider, not the inferior products of this later age or those, which failing to fall in with the taste of the time (like Steele's) enjoyed only a qualified acceptance, but the dramas that were acclaimed and approved, plays which, like the tragedies of Southerne and Rowe, were hailed with enthusiasm and maintained their place on the stage for generations. In the case of Rowe it happens that such a comparison is easy as three of his most popular works, *Tamerlane, The Fair Penitent* and *Jane Shore,* are on themes already treated by Elizabethan dramatists and two at least are independent writings over or translations, so to speak, into the terms of Augustan ideals of the drama. Nicholas Rowe was two years Steele's and Addison's junior and, though educated for the law, developed early an unusually deep interest in the drama as distinguished from the stage. An indefatigable reader and appreciator of old poetry, Rowe is now best remembered as the earliest editor of Shakespeare, the first to attempt to compile a biography of that great poet from the fading traditions and perishing memorials accessible at the time. But Rowe, with all his appreciation of the past, was absolutely a man of his own age. He was born two generations too soon to feel the slightest stirring in him of the returning spring of the romantic revival and even Shakespeare editorship was to darken to the days of Pope before the dawn. Rowe is the author of eight dramas, one of them a comedy, altogether trivial. The rest, which are more or less tragic, range from *The Ambitious Stepmother* in 1700 to *Jane Shore,* fifteen years later; and they enjoyed, for their clearly defined and well conducted, if artificial, plots, their easy florid and declamatory blank verse and their consistent expression of accepted conventional emotion, altogether the greatest popularity of their time. In *Tamerlane,* acted in 1702, Rowe has reduced the titanic and barbarous conqueror of Asia to an enlightened modern potentate, intended to figure forth and compliment his majesty, William III, drawing in contrast the weak and passionate Bajazet, to typify correspondingly William's enemy, Louis XIV. These political similitudes, so fatal to literary longevity, assured to the piece a contemporary success and brought fame to the author. It is but fair to say that Rowe owes nothing to Marlowe, although the two dramas might be instructively contrasted by one who would know to the full the extravagance of authentic poetry o'erleaping itself and the atrophy of even the similitude of that divine art.

In the following year, Rowe achieved a lasting success in *The Fair Penitent,* which, like its even more successful successor, *Jane Shore,* 1714, held the stage in almost unchallenged acceptance for more than three generations. As we read these old plays, acknowledging their merits in clarity, directness, sentimental, perhaps even to their auditors emotional, interest, we cannot but wonder how their poverty of thought, their obvious rhetoric, want of poetry and characterisation could have satisfied those who had seen Shakespeare, acted by Betterton, Booth and Garrick. A comparison of *The Fair Penitent,* with its source, Massinger's splendid, vivid *Fatal Dowry* — a comparison by the way made as long ago as the time of Richard Cumberland — discloses on the part of Rowe much the same attitude of mind and the same narrow intent to unify and simplify at any cost that we have already found characteristic of Cibber's alterations of *Richard III;* and even a greater callousness to the touches of life, those flashes of poetry and realisations of character that give reality to the old play. Massinger had given to Charlois, the wronged husband, a personality and a dignity in his manly grief that the body of his noble father must lie unburied for want of money to satisfy his creditors. He had given to him, in pleading his cause, a pathetic eloquence that moves the reader as it moved the judges in the play and, thus prepared, we proceed to the story of his wrongs. All this Rowe reduces to a cold recital, leaving us without a grain of sympathy for his Altamont, the corresponding figure. Again, Massinger had given to his heroine Beaumelle, a levity of nature that accounts for her infidelity and, in the end, an awakening that causes her, in her contrition, to realise the nobility of the husband whom she had abused. Rowe's corresponding figure, Calista, is the victim of her own animal passion, marries her husband because she must and is sorrowful and pathetic that her wickedness has been discovered and that convention demands her suicide. The play is miscalled, for not for a minute is Calista truly penitent. Rowe destroyed the humanity of every figure that he touched, conventionalising the friend, Romont-Horatio and losing all the noble distraction of the father. In a word the living drama becomes under the hand of its renovator, a succession of sentimental scenes in which the personages concerned are merely the mouthpieces of an emotion, oratorically expressed.

Nor can anything better be said for Rowe's most celebrated play, *Jane Shore*, the story of the fall from greatness of a king's mistress where many charities, amiability of temper and generosity of heart in a measure palliate, especially to the sentimental mind, her wrong doings. The subject had already been treated diffusely, but with genuine command of the dramatic interest and pathos of the situation, by Heywood in his *Edward IV.* The title of *Jane Shore* discloses the words: "written in imitation of Shakespeare's style," an amazing statement from an editor of Shakespeare and in view of its unutterable unlikeness. Indeed nothing could more plainly declare the obsession of the age of Pope and Voltaire on this topic than such a declaration. *Jane Shore*, like *The Fair Penitent* reduces the dramatic personages to a minimum, rejects absolutely the element of comic relief and is as regular as it is simple in construction; but here too, the personages like the dialogue, tend to abstraction. Rowe has been praised for his women; he knows only one, the plaintive sufferer, bewailing her woman's weakness, defending herself against man's lustful advances, moaning, sorrowing, declaiming, dying. And even this figure he had in a measure from Southerne and Otway before him, as he had from these predecessors, his interest in domestic subjects. Whether for these, his more famous plays, already mentioned, for *Ulysses, The Royal Convert* or *Lady Jane Grey*, we must recognise in Rowe this paternity and succession. A candid reading of the three authors in juxtaposition makes clear the decline from Otway to Southerne and the greater drop in poetry and mastery over genuine emotion from Southerne to Rowe.

The touch of Joseph Addison with the stage was even less than that of Steele, although his three efforts cover a more varied ranged. His *Rosamond,* 1707, to which Clayton wrote rather inferior music, was an effort in the direction of the establishment of English opera. The libretto is both commonplace and inadequate. *The Drummer,* 1716, is a comedy written with William Harrison. Its deserved failure caused Addison not to own his part in its authorship. The celebrated tragedy of *Cato* involves one of the most interesting matters in connection with the history of English drama, however its extraordinary contemporary success must be referred to a happy concatenation of political affairs and the great reputation of

Addison in contemporary letters and society. The last number of *The Spectator* had appeared in December 1712 and Addison was seeking for new fields of literary effort, when his friends prevailed upon him to complete a tragedy on the subject of Cato at Utica, the first four acts of which he had written nearly ten years before. There is no reason to doubt that Addison's serious misgivings as to the production of his tragedy were sincere. It had not been originally written to be acted and Addison was too judicious a critic not to recognise its shortcomings. But the subject at the moment was peculiarly fitting; the Tories had just come back to power with the conclusion of the Treaty of Utrecht, the Whigs felt that the treaty was the loss of all that the victories of Marlborough had gained for England. *Cato* was the last of the Romans, as conservative as the veriest of Tories; but he was also the defeated, the heroically unsuccessful upholder of the greatness of Rome; and the Whigs were quite as certainly defeated and, in their own opinion, the upholders of the glory of England. In consequence, on the staging of *Cato,* in 1713, the house was packed by the adherents of both parties, each as determined as the other to read the drama into an allegory favourable to its own deservings, and Addison enjoyed a dramatic success in London, and later at Oxford, above that of any dramatist of his time. Like everything of Addison's, *Cato* is full of noble sentiments, beautifully written and with a complete realisation of that regularity that the age united so to praise. With this, all commendation ends. The plot is barren, ill conducted and full of absurdities, the characters frigid, lifeless and mere mouthpieces for fine declamations. Considering the humanity of *The Spectator,* and with every allowance for Steele's part in it and influence on his friend, the coldness of Addison's tragedy is surprising and the dignity of Cato added to the dignity and selfconsciousness of Addison produced a result which even the author's own complacent age found it difficult wholly to accept. *Cato* was vastly admired and theoretically approved, but it was also severely criticised, most incisively and wittily by Dennis, for the irrelevancy of its love scenes and for its slavish adherence to the unities; and after a few revivals, it ceased to hold the stage.

Cato has been called " the grave of English tragedy "; perhaps it is better denominated that tragedy's sculptured tomb, not even inhabited by that much abused victim of a thousand crimes. And it was what Voltaire delightedly designated its reasonableness that killed English tragedy in *Cato*. It is possible, if one so wills it, to view the entire history of English drama (or all literature and art for that matter) as one continued struggle between the sanction of precedent and the spirit of freedom. In wide considerations such as these many cant words have been invented and it is difficult to avoid them and their misleading connotations. It is possibly not too much an exaggeration to say that the literal reading of a disciple's report of the opinions and theories of a certain Greek philosopher, with little reference to his larger system, led two modern literatures astray in their conception and practice of tragedy and shackled the development and freedom of at least two others. *Cato* demonstrated to the world how " a classical drama " might be written; and it demonstrated, likewise, what an undesirable thing it was to do. None the less, in the years that followed Addison and Rowe, English tragedy became more and more a conventional following of what had gone before; and the strongest influence upon it, because the nearest, was that of France. In the hands of genius and with vastly contrasted antecedents, the classical ideal had reached there the grace, the dignity, the purity of diction and elevation of thought that distinguishes the works of Racine and Corneille. The story of classical drama in England is very different; for such way as it made at times in the early Senecans, in Jonson and his followers, was always by main force against the grain of English genius. In England those bugaboos, the unities, had frightened many a play out of its senses and into absurdity, however rational the underlying principles which the age devoutly believed made for the realisation of all the dramatic virtues. Again and again among the commendations bestowed by the critics on Shakespeare, we read how his " irregularities " were thrown into the balance against him. From Jonson and Dryden to Pope and Dr. Johnson, though the degree of accusation may vary, its major count is always the same. Now in the very triumph of the classical ideal, as the eighteenth century conceived it in England, lay one of the elements of its undoing, and that was this same sentimentality that insisted, for example, on love-making in the senate chamber at Utica at the very extremity of Cato's resistance to Rome. The age that preferred Otway's Monimia and Rowe's Calista, as tragic heroines, to Lady Macbeth, let us say, or even to Dryden's Cleopatra, was scarcely stern enough to uphold the rigours of Attic tragedy elsewhere than in academic discussion; and hence the general breakdown in English tragedy of that theoretical aloofness and decorum on which French classical tragedy prided itself so highly.

In the forgotten plays of Ambrose Philips, John Hughes, Charles Johnson, Elijah Fenton and their lesser kind, in those of Edward Young, familiar author of *Night Thoughts,* and James Thomson, ever memorable for *The Seasons,* English tragedy dragged its weary length, rattling its French fetters and be-speaking tears as well as admiration for a form more or less avowedly classic. None of the three dramas of Young, from *Busiris* in 1719 to *The Brothers* in 1753, was successful, save in attracting the satirical ridicule of Fielding's burlesque *Tom Thumb;* and the five "tremendous tragedies" of Thomson (most of them acted between 1730 and 1752), despite the friendship and the acting of Quin and Garrick, achieved only a temporary success. Thomson's *Sophonisba* is at best a poor following of Otway, his *Edward and Eleanora,* based on an apocryphal anecdote concerning King Edward I, achieved the extraordinary distinction of being praised by John Wesley; in his *Coriolanus,* Thomson disdained to borrow from Shake-speare, but wrote the drama over anew and at much greater length, making Volumnia, the wife of Coriolanus, and now no longer silent, like Virgilia, and, expunging both the person and the humour of excellent Menenius Agrippa from a drama on so serious a subject as the history of Rome. No contrast could better make clear the nature of the difference between the ideals of the stage in Shakespeare's time and those of Thomson's than a comparison of the scene, in the *Coriolanus* of each, in which that conqueror is won to spare his native city by the intercession of his wife and mother; and few could make clearer the declamation, mannerism and conventionality of situation and personage into which the drama of the whole age had fallen. In these dramatic productions of distinguished poets we recog-nise the commencement of that break between the play as a pro-duction for the stage and the dramatic form as an attractive mould for the expression of poetic thought and literary ideals. This created an ever widening breach between dramatic litera-ture and the stage and contributed to the further atrophy of the drama; so that through the time of Cibber, throughout that of Garrick and beyond, the period becomes more and more the age of the actor as distinguished from that of the dramatist.

But there was much to intervene before we reach this later

period. Of the vogue of "opera," after the manner of the French, in Dryden's time, and the plays, furnished with incidental music, which went by that name we have already heard. In 1710, the famous German composer, George Frederick Handel came over to England, after having made a reputation for himself as an impresario of Italian opera both in Italy and in his native country. Between his *Rinaldo,* 1711, for which Aaron Hill, later a voluminous playwright, wrote the libretto, and *Deidamia,* thirty years later, he composed and staged more than forty Italian operas which have been generically described as consisting each of "some twenty or thirty detached arias set in the action of a classical drama to which nobody paid the slightest attention." Nor was Handel alone in exploiting this popular rival of the drama, as his well known rivalry with Buononcici alone is sufficient to show. Another feature of the time was the rise, in the second decade of the century, of pantomime of which the inspiring spirit was John Rich. Rich opened, in 1714, a new and gorgeous theatre in Lincoln's Inn Fields, having inherited the property from his father, Christopher Rich, well known as a manager before him. It is reported that, having a talent for acting but an insufficient voice, Rich developed the pantomime in consequence. It is more likely that he found the source for his innovation in current Italian practices. At any rate he soon developed in his pantomimes, a species of dramatic entertainment "consisting of dancing, gesture and action intermingled with trick and show," which became a serious rival to Italian opera and the regular drama. Rich played the part of Harlequin himself and devised clever variations, not only on the theme set by that ubiquitous personage, but on current matters such as the South Sea Bubble, on Faustus and other subjects; and he followed up these successes with those of other kinds. It was at this point in his prosperity that John Gay, after suffering a refusal at Drury Lane, offered Rich his *Beggar's Opera.* Gay, who had already gained a deserved reputation for his *Fables* and *Shepherd's Week,* had been taken up by Pope and backed by that satirical marksman from ambush in one or two previous dramatic ventures. After one or two false starts, Gay had staged in 1715, a dramatic skit, entitled *What d'ye call It,* in which Pope helped to aim the arrows of their combined wit at the contemporary taste for sentimental tragedy, *Venice Preserved* in particular. Apparently nobody appreciated exactly its significance; and, two years later, a scandalous comedy by the same collaborators failed so signally that Pope was glad to disavow any part in it. Nor did Gay fare any better in 1724 with a tragedy.

With *The Beggar's Opera,* however, Gay's reputation and fortune was made. It ran, according to Pope, sixty-three nights, an unprecedented run in those days, and for a time literally drove Italian opera, against which its burlesque was levelled, off the stage. *The Beggar's Opera* belongs to a species known as ballad-opera and may claim a descent, more or less direct, from the English masque through the " heroic opera," as productions like Dryden's *Tempest* and Davenant's *Macbeth* have been somewhat loosely called. Gay's work is actually a prose farce in three acts, interspersed with some seventy little songs —" lyrics " (alas for the abuse of words!), we should now call them in the cant of the musical drama. The music was taken from popular airs of the day and arranged so as little to impede the action such as it is. The plot, so far as there is any, is well described in the term " a Newgate pastoral." Indeed the very bareness of the " fable "— the situation of Captain Macheath, the handsome dashing highwayman, betrayed to a merited hanging by the conspiracy of a turnkey and a receiver of stolen goods, but beloved by the daughter of each — is a mere take-off, in its lowness of subject, of the high dramatic altitudes of current opera and tragedy. And the whimsical conclusion that restores the captain, against all logic, to his two sorrowing wives is a further thrust at current operatic absurdity. *The Beggar's Opera* is intrinsically a trifle, and more distinguished by its inconsequence and good humour than by its wit or any serious effort at satire; but it accomplished with a laugh what twenty years of rival endeavour could not do, the discouragement of the bombast and absurdity of many of its serious performances. Gay followed up his success immediately by a second part, called *Polly,* which, although not allowed to be acted for personal reasons, brought him in, on publication, a handsome sum to add to the fortune that *The Beggar's Opera* had made him. Later, we find Gay supplying an English libretto for Handel. His other dramatic ventures are negligible.

Let us return to the sentimental drama to which the advancing century brought a new development in the form of a revival of the once popular Elizabethan bourgeois tragedy. In June 1731, *The London Merchant or the History of George Barnwell* was acted at Drury Lane, the author, George Lillo.

This tragedy was a departure in several particulars from the vogue of the time. It was founded avowedly on fact, the homely fact of every day life; and while the author did not go to the length of representing the life of his own time, the veil of the story of an Elizabethan apprentice on his road to ruin was transparent enough for all to descry the contemporaneous moral application. The form, too, was an innovation, for *Barnwell* is written in the homeliest and baldest prose, however it falls at times into a certain lilt of rhythm in passages of emotional excitement, like the well known cases in Dickens. Prose for tragedy, if not quite unknown before, was at least — like Lillo's descent into the affairs of tradesmen — a daring flaunt in the regal countenance of tragic decorum. Although acted in vacation, *Barnwell* scored an immediate success, running for twenty consecutive nights to crowded houses and gaining, in its repeated revivals, altogether the greatest success of any piece of its age. More, this bald and homespun dramatic version of an old ballad — for it is no more — void of the least trace of poetry and without a single literary grace to recommend it, gained a reputation and exerted an influence on literature, especially abroad, which is simply amazing. The direction that Lillo gave to the drama involved a deeper respect for religion and morals and a more rigorous regard as to conduct, especially in the relations of the sexes. This is equally the bias of Richardson's novels and of the " moralised " pictorial satire of Hogarth: and both, be it remembered, came after. Moreover the success of Lillo's play, on the stage, made it the pattern not only of imitation in England, but practically founded a school of domestic tragedy in France and in Germany as well. This latter, an interesting subject in itself, cannot be pursued in this place. Suffice it to recall, in the one country, Diderot, whose transformation of the *comedie larmoyante* into his own *tragedie domestique et bourgeoise* was effected by the direct influence of a French translation of *Barnwell* upon him, and Lessing, in the other, who translated Diderot in the first instance and imitated Lillo in his tragedy, *Miss Sara Sampson.*[4]

To return to *Barnwell,* as a work of dramatic art, no one could rate it intrinsically highly; however, Lillo is to be commended for his directness, his freedom from redundancy, his steady movement forward, to the gallows that takes his un-

[4] On this whole subject see the excellent edition of *Barnwell and The Fatal Curiosity* by A. W. Ward, 1906.

happy and repentant hero to his doom in the end. It is one thing to consider this simple old tragedy from our modern point of view and label it "execrable stuff"; it is another to try to understand its popularity and influence. Lillo, of whom little personally is known, was, it appears, of Flemish extraction and carried on the trade of jeweller in London. He was, on his own confession, a dissenter, and exhibits in his work the close knowledge of the bible, the strong religious convictions and the acute moral sense that was characteristic of the Protestant nonconformists of his time. His success with *Barnwell,* which was great pecuniarily, led him to the writing of other tragedies of which *The Fatal Curiosity* is alike the best known and the most powerful. Here, once more we have a murder play and one circumstantially told as an actual occurrence in the old pamphlet form from which the story was derived. Here, too, Lillo left his story in the Jacobean period in which his source had placed it; but he sought to dignify the theme by writing in verse and heightening his language, in neither of which can he be said to be successful. *The Fatal Curiosity* tells of the return of a son in disguise after long absence, and of his murder by his own parents whom continued want and misery had driven to the verge of madness. It is a terrible little play, compressing, as it does, the subject into three short acts; and, we may agree, that the manner in which this horrible deed is made to appear the inevitable consequence of fate rather than the result of character, declares its psychology to be transnormal. In a word, Lillo's *Fatal Curiosity* is the logical application of sentimentality to the murder play. It may be added that this tragedy, too, has an interesting foreign history, especially in its influence on minor German romantic drama. In two other tragedies, *The Christian Hero* and *Elmerick,* both readable and interesting, Lillo holds up his ideal of the just prince and the righteous man. The Christian hero is the famous Albanian prince, George Castriota; *Elmerick* is a supposedly historical leaf out of the annals of Hungary. Save for the prevalence of strong moral ideas in them and a somewhat abortive attempt to give to their halting blank verse a rather greater elevation of language than the prose of *Barnwell,* they are not distinctive. Lastly, Lillo left behind him an unacted rewriting of *Arden of Feversham* which may show the source of his inspiration for *Barnwell* or be no more than a subsequent discovery of this earlier work of kindred spirit.

Notwithstanding the success of *Barnwell* and such immediate followings of its domestic scenes as Charles Johnson's *Cælia,* the pathetic story of a wronged woman and *The Gamester* of Edward Moore, a prosaic but genuinely moving play, the influence of this attempted return to subjects of every day life was less efficient on the stage than in the novel that began now to draw off to its wider field the attention of those who might otherwise have written plays. As early as the time of Mrs. Behn and Mrs. Manly, we find this division of interest between the novel and the stage. Congreve, it is true, began in fiction and turned back into comedy. On the other hand, Steele and Addison (if we count the elements of the novel in their essays), Fielding most notably, Smollett, Brooke, Goldsmith and even Dr. Johnson, wrote in both kinds, Fielding discovering his forte in the one, Goldsmith in the other. The drama at large still continued its compromising allegiance to the theory of France and to home-made sentimentality; and in tragedy, the influence of Voltaire, whose criticism of the English stage was much read, if not wholly appreciated in England, became more and more apparent. Voltaire, after his sojourn in England, found himself divided between an admiration, which he could not withhold, for the freedom of English tragedy, especially Shakespeare, and that restraining sense of the *licet* and *decet* which is alike the strength and the weakness of the classical ideal. His *Mort de César* was avowedly an imitation of Shakespeare so far as French taste would permit such an imitation; his other tragedies of this period exhibit a similar compromise between a long tradition and a great example. Discussion, translation and imitation of the great French author in England was almost immediate. There was Duncombe's *Brutus* as early as 1732, Miller's *Mahomet,* and Murphy's *Orphan of China,* much later. In 1736, Aaron Hill's *Zara* gained a success scarcely warranted by its slender merits, to be followed by other adaptations, *Alzira, Merope,* and *The Roman Revenge* in which Hill endeavoured to improve as much upon Voltaire's conception of the tragedy of Cæsar as Voltaire esteemed himself to have improved upon Shakespeare. But even if habitually mutilated, Shakespeare was better known in England than in France; and Voltaire's English imitators and admirers fell out at last with his exasperating criticism and his disingenuousness if not with his example. " Can our contempt and resentment," says Foote, in 1747, " be too strongly expressed against that insolent French panegyrist who first denies Shakespeare almost every dramatic excellence, and then, in his next play, pilfers from him almost every capital scene?" But by no means were all the tragedies, that cluster about the middle of the century, mere imitations of contemporary French plays. Only a few months before the performance in 1749, of Hill's *Merope,* one of the last of his translations of Voltaire, Garrick had placed Dr. Johnson's portentous tragedy, *Mahomet and Irene,* on the stage and by sheer force of his personal influence and good will to an old friend compelled it to run nine nights that the needy scholar might put the products of three author's nights in his pocket. *Irene,* as it was called on publication, is as heavy and essentially undramatic as its famous author himself. There is something deliciously ludicrous in the Ottoman conqueror of Constantinople grandiloquently praising the British constitution in the year 1453, and courting his fair Greek captive in the ponderous eloquence that rolled its beneficent thunder at the Turk's Head and the Mitre.

Dr. Johnson's tragedy, a model of correctness and weighted with perfections, was never acted again. Very much in contrast was the fate of John Home's *Douglas,* a prime favourite on its first appearance in Edinburgh in 1756, at Covent Garden in the next year and, on repeated revivals, thereafter up to the days of Kean and Mrs. Siddons. Home was a Scottish clergyman and the scandal of one of his cloth having written a play caused his resignation from the pulpit. *Douglas* is based on one of the old ballads of his country and written, as it was, somewhat apart from the influences that conventionalize all literary efforts in the hands of lesser men who live at the centre of culture, is sustained by a genuine sincerity, simplicity and pathos that fully account for its popularity. The story, that of the restoration to his mother of a long lost son who is slain almost in the moment of their recognition, comported well with the sorrows and distresses of which the stage was so fond; but is conspicuous in substituting motherly affection for the mawkish love making that intrudes so commonly into contemporary comedy and tragedy alike. Dr. Johnson, who could not but feel somewhat piqued at the success of *Douglas,* with its inartificial plotting and inadequacy as to literary quality, consoled himself in declaring, "There is not, sir, a good line in *Douglas.*" *Irene* is stuffed with good lines, and yet *Irene* is no play.

It was well before this period of the controversy with Voltaire that burlesque had begun to shower the arrows of its ridicule upon the unoriginality, the grandiloquence and desperate prosaic level of English tragedy. Henry Fielding, the famous novelist, began his long literary career with the penning of a couple of comedies in the manner of Congreve, the first of which was eclipsed on its performance, in 1728, by the popularity of *The Beggar's Opera.* Thereafter Fielding wrote some twenty or more other pieces, comedies, short farces or burlesques; and in 1742, gave up the stage for the law and the writing of fiction. Scarcely one of Fielding's dramatic ventures is wanting in interest, though all were written carelessly and under pressure of the moment. The two or three adaptations from Molière succeeded best in their day and one of them, *The Miser,* long held the stage. The earlier comedies are as coarse as we might expect comedies written by the author of *Tom Jones* to be, however he made the characteristic plea that in so writing he intended " to make vice detestable." Fielding's real dramatic successes were his mock-heroic burlesques for which his vigorous satirical pen found ample scope. In *The Author's Farce* he attacked opera, the vacuity of the drama and the wretchedness of Grub Street hacks, of which fraternity he was perilously near being a member at the moment. *Covent Garden* is an onslaught on the sentimental drama, especially as represented in *The Distressed Mother,* a popular play of Philips; and in *Pasquin,* as in *The Historical Register,* another farce, Fielding lampooned the Cibbers, father and son, against whom he disclosed a continual enmity. The best of these short pieces is *Tom Thumb the Great,* a burlesque of the whole romantic, sentimental and bombastic drama from Dryden, Lee and Otway to Dennis, whose criticism receives many a delightful thrust, and Thomson against whose *Busiris* the satirist appears to have had an especial grudge. It is Fielding's cue not only to turn the entire species to ridicule in his absurd and plotless extravaganza of the little hero, Tom Thumb, at the court of King Arthur, but to parody lines, passages and similitudes from the tragedies that are his quarry, in the manner of *The Rehearsal,* but far more extravagantly. While much of this banter must be lost to us, despite the author's diverting parallels and references, enough remains to declare how justified was the attack, and we learn with interest that *Tom Thumb* long held the stage, surpassing alike its predecessors and the several followings in its kind that its wit and its success inspired. Fielding's earliest successors in burlesque, were Henry Carey, author of *Chrononhotonthologos,* and Samuel Foote, an actor, notorious for his powers of mimicry, who, after evading the law ingeniously for years, at length succeeded in obtaining a license for his little theatre in the Haymarket, where the lighter muse long maintained herself, in comedy and farce, against the tears and dignities that ruled at the other houses.

To recapitulate in even the briefest outline the intricate story of David Garrick's leadership of the English stage during a period of more than forty years, can form no part of the subject of this book. He was unequalled as an actor, successful in steering for the most part a steady course in the troubled waters of theatrical management, and an able guide of the taste of the time, somewhat, though not so much as has been supposed, to the appreciation of a wholesomer dramatic diet. Garrick's Gallic temper combined wit, vivacity and versatility with prudence and, his enemies said, a certain niggardliness. It was perhaps less this last (for there are many stories to disprove it) than a certain want of moral courage that caused him to temporise and compromise so commonly in his dealings with the drama of his time. Garrick is often extolled as the restorer of Shakespeare to the stage. As a matter of fact there never was a time from Elizabeth's day to Garrick's own (to say nothing of what came after), when Shakespeare had not held the English stage, his rôles the ambition of the greatest actors, his plays, when honestly and adequately given, the delight not only of the cultivated and judicious but of the masses who cared for the stage. In another sense, the restoration of Shakespeare has been claimed for Garrick and he rather boasted at times of his return to the original texts. But his famous *Richard III* was Cibber's version; and he never dared to act *King Lear* save with Tate's unhappy happy ending; while his "dramatic works" (collected after his death, it is fair to add), disclose in *The Fairies, Catherine and Petruchio* and *Florizel and Perdita,* titles which are scarcely more varied from the original designations of plays of Shakespeare's than the texts themselves are altered. In the matter of the fitting of dramas for revival on a later stage under new conditions, it is easy to fall into a condition of unwarranted conservatism. Indubitably so plastic a thing as a drama should be adaptable to the immediate purpose which it serves. And in view of the incessant review, rewriting and alteration of Elizabethan plays in their own age we may feel sure that Shakespeare would have been himself the first to recognise this necessity. But there is cutting and rearrangement that respects the spirit of the play, and there is meddling and rewriting that spoils whatever it touches. The fine taste of Garrick must have appreciated this difference, however a somewhat pusillanimous practice failed to realise it. Certainly Garrick was far from deserving the frank satire which his friend, Fielding, bestowed on his predecessor in Elizabethan adaptation when he made Cibber say: " No play though ever so good, would do without alteration "; and then added: " Shakespeare is already good enough for people of taste, he must be altered to the palates of those who have none." Garrick's actual contribution to English dramatic literature, despite his three volumes of adaptations and collaborations, is surprisingly inadequate in view of his lasting and deserved reputation on the boards. " He was perpetually producing various little things in a dramatic way," says his earliest biographer, " some of which are original." As a matter of fact, very few are original and his talents as a playwright begin and end in a practical knowledge of the stage and an appreciation of the value of lively dialogue and ready action.

There is a tradition that Oliver Goldsmith once consulted Richardson as to tragedy which he had written, that he read it aloud to another friend in Edinburgh, " hastily blotting everything to which his listener objected "; and then the tragedy disappears. It has been surmised that, as Voltaire was still in the ascendant and as Goldsmith was known to admire him, here was perhaps another contribution however much more able, to English Gallo-classical tragedy, begun, as we have seen, with Duncombe and Aaron Hill and concluded in the failures of Murphy's *Orphan of China* and Cradock's *Zobèide*. Goldsmith was forty years old in 1768 before his comedy, *The Good Natured Man* was acted; the performance of *She Stoops to Conquer* preceded his death, in 1774, by only one year. For Goldsmith the period of preparation, rather of blundering incertitude, was long, and his time of realisation disturbed by hack work and hurry. In the comedy of the sixties, some have found a reflex influence, back from France to England, of much the character of that which England had extended through *Barnwell* on France, some twenty years earlier. The comedies of Arthur Murphy, some of them borrowed directly from La

Chaussée, as he had borrowed from *Pamela* and *Clarissa* certainly appear to bear this out. But whether the author be Murphy, Colman, Macklin or even Garrick himself (as in *The Clandestine Marriage* which he wrote with Colman), this comedy was ever moralised in its genteel commonplace and becoming sentiment until all humour and merriment had been driven to such refuge, as we have seen, in farce and burlesque. As early as 1759, in his *Enquiry into the Present State of Polite Learning,* Goldsmith had defended the exaggerations of folly and the absurdities of the vulgar in comedy against those who "proscribed the comic or satirical muse from every walk but high life." He especially objected to the current word *low* as used thus to restrict the legitimate functions of comedy, as he later deplored the circumstance that humour seemed to be departing from the stage; wittily defining sentimental comedy as "a kind of mulish production with all the defects of its opposite parents, and marked with sterility," he argues that "if we are permitted to make comedy weep, we have an equal right to make tragedy laugh, and to set down in blank-verse the jests and repartees of all the attendants in a funeral procession." [5] It was with a full consciousness of just what he was doing, that Goldsmith sought a more legitimate way, than that of burlesque, of restoring English comedy to its power over laughter. *The Good Natured Man* was offered Garrick at Drury Lane early in 1767; but Garrick hesitated, mistrustful of the innovation like the safe man that he appears always to have been; and, after a quarrel over the matter, Goldsmith's comedy was brought out a year later by Colman at Covent Garden. This, Garrick resented, placing in deliberate competition, Hugh Kelly's *False Delicacy,* a piece of the washiest sentimentality which scored a signal success while that of *The Good Natured Man,* which followed a few days after, was more than qualified. Indeed Garrick's mistrust of so bold a return to the comedy of humours by a contemporary was warranted in the proof. The capital scene, in which Honeywood dresses up the bailiffs in pieces of his own wardrobe to masquerade as his friends, was voted "low" by Goldsmith's genteel auditors and withdrawn; and the poet had the mortification to learn that the contemptible Kelly had made nearly four times as much out of his rival comedy.

[5] Quoted by A. Dobson in his ed. of Goldsmith, 1905, p. xiv from the *Westminster Magazine,* December, 1772.

The Good Natured Man, however loose and faulty in construction, was a better comedy than the English stage had seen since Farquhar. The figures, such as Honeywood with his easy nature and willingness to serve everybody, Croaker, worrying out his troubles before they occur and then taking them amicably, and Lofty with his officious importance and insinuating mendacity, are excellent " humorous " figures in the old sense of the word, and yet so originally and happily drawn as to produce a higher sense of reality than is common in their kind. There is, too, a geniality, as opposed to mere gaiety, and a naturalness in the personages, their conduct and their admirably written parts that could have carried the town in almost any age except that of the dominion of sensibility and feeling. The time was not yet ripe; and it was nearly five years later that *She Stoops to Conquer* reversed this verdict and carried the town by sheer force of genius. Between Goldsmith's two comedies, a second play of Kelly's — quite as good (or, for that matter, quite as bad) as the first — met with an accidental failure; and *The West Indian* by Richard Cumberland and among the best of its species, gained another triumph for the sentimental school. Whether it was the success or the failure of his rivals that encouraged him, Goldsmith set to work, late in 1771, on his second comedy, offering it to Colman early in the next year. It is a commentary on managerial discernment that, after nearly a year, all that the author could get from Colman was the return of his manuscript, scribbled over with criticisms and suggestions. At last with the bullying intervention of Dr. Johnson, Colman was brought to start the still nameless play in rehearsal; but his indifference communicated itself to the actors, some of whom even threw up their parts; and it was not until March 1773 that *She Stoops to Conquer* was performed with a success alike complete, brilliant and lasting. Scattered were now the host of genteel comedy and the breath of fresh air was let into the playhouse. With the memory of the delightful, living personages of this celebrated comedy and its spontaneous humour, a part of our literary birthright, its laughable situations, engaging style and perfect acting quality, we cannot but deplore that a period should so soon have been set to the dramatic activity of Goldsmith. His comedy was like a tonic to the stage, and the stage needed many another like draught. But Goldsmith no longer stood alone. Just before the performance of *She Stoops to Conquer,* Foote had pro-

duced, at his little theatre in the Haymarket, what he called
"a primitive puppet show," burlesquing the sentimental drama
and called *The Handsome Housemaid or Piety in Pattens*.
Herein is set forth, in evident parody of such stories as Richardson's *Pamela,* how a maiden of low degree "by the mere
effect of morality and virtue, raised herself to riches and
honour"; and the auditors are assured that they will not discover in the work "much wit or humour" as "his brother
writers had all agreed that it was highly unpopular and beneath the dignity of a mixed assembly to show any signs of joy-
ful satisfaction." We may believe the report that, preceding
Goldsmith's comedy by a month or more, this burlesque of
Foote's helped to prepare the way for *She Stoops to Conquer*
with a public, weary of the insipid morality long preached from
the stage.

Everything about Richard Brinsley Sheridan reads like a
romance, and much has been perverted by those who spare
neither fact nor character in the process. In contrast with the
social and political eminence attained in a life crowded with
triumphs yet checkered with vicissitudes, the story of his comedies seems little more than an episode of his boyhood; yet Sheridan, the author of *The Rivals* and *The School for Scandal,* is
known to thousands to whom his famous parliamentary career,
his celebrated eloquence and even the numberless stories of his
wit and engaging personality are the shadow of a recollection.
Born in Dublin, his father a clever actor, manager and elocu-
tionist, his mother a playwright and novelist, what better par-
entage could be demanded for the writer of comedy? Add to
this a sanguine temper that courted adventure, an address and
readiness that made every event an experience and an easy power
of expression that rose, on occasion, to brilliancy and the equipment of the dramatist is complete. Sheridan's youth was spent
in Bath, then at its height as the capital of pleasure, and his
comedies, while not actually autobiographical, are coloured to
a degree with the reminiscence of personal incidents the like of
which he knew in the midst of what has been happily called
"the sham chivalry and the sham romance of which he made
such immortal fun." He had carried out, when less than
twenty years of age an elopement with the beautiful Elizabeth
Linley, who became his wife, precisely such as Lydia Languish
had dreamed for herself and her "Beverly." He had fought
two duels, when less than two and twenty, only a little more

formidable than the immortal meeting of Bob Acres with Sir Lucius O'Trigger; and the verses of his heroes, the raptures of his heroines, smacking both of them as yet of the age of sentiment, even the follies and the fopperies of the whole circle of his dramatis personæ, were things of which he was none the less observant in that he had shared in them all.

Sheridan had been ambitious to write for the stage almost as a boy, but it was not until his tumultuous courtship was over that he carried the epic of his life into his works. *The Rivals* was written in six weeks and staged in November 1774, only to come perilously near failure because of its length and a mistake in the assignment in the part of Sir Lucius. With perfect good humour and the utmost good sense, Sheridan cut down his play, leaving out everything that had displeased and recasting the offending part; and offered it, some ten days later once more, with the very best cast the theatre could muster, to gain a popularity that has never since paled. *The Rivals* has been criticised as " a young play " and even the author was accustomed to declare that it was " one of the worst comedies in the language." But it is in the very qualities of sustained buoyancy and the high animal spirits of youth that the enduring charm of the work consists and it is this especially that has insured its perennial popularity. *The Rivals* was followed speedily by *St. Patrick's Day,* a farce written to display the talents of Clinch, who had created the rôle of Sir Lucius; and it served very well its temporary purpose. *The Duenna,* a year later, was an opera in the manner of Gay and in success second only to *The Beggar's Opera.* Sheridan was now twenty-four and the darling of the playgoer, his wit and talent no less admired than his courage and the romance that had made him " the husband of the loveliest woman and the sweetest singer of her day." His future as a dramatist seemed cut out for him; but with a volatility and daring that was characteristic of him, he aspired to become the manager of Drury Lane Theatre and to the amazement of every one, despite his youth, his inexperience in business of any kind and lack of the command of capital, he actually became not only manager but the chief owner of that historic house over which Garrick had so long presided. Where Sheridan obtained the money and how Garrick could have been content to thrust the difficult guidance of his glittering theatrical car to hands so youthful and unsteady, are matters which may well have excited wonder. As to the first, it has been explained

that a share in Drury Lane was a share in a monopoly and therefore as good a security as freehold land on which any banker
would advance money; and, secondly, that by the help of others
and the mortgaged condition of the second moiety (not Garrick's), which was acquired a year or two after, the transaction
was completed with very little passing of actual money. "It
appears," says Professor Matthews, who first cleared up the
matter, "that Sheridan invested only £1,300 in cash when he
bought one seventh of Drury Lane Theatre, in 1776, and that
he received this back when he became possessed of one half of
Drury Lane Theatre, in 1778, then valued [entire] at £90,-
000." [6] As to Garrick's consent, he was ready and anxious
to retire; Sheridan was the first dramatist of his age, however
young and inexperienced, and of a dauntless courage and buoyant hopefulness. Garrick, like half the people of Sheridan's
time, yielded to his inevitable, personal charm.

After a revival of *The Rivals* and an adaptation of Vanbrugh's *Relapse,* the new manager staged, in May 1777, and
with the greatest care ever bestowed upon a cast (we are told),
his imperishable *School for Scandal.* Its success was absolute
and to this the sympathy, suggestion and actual training of
Garrick contributed in no small degree. The source of this
second great comedy of Sheridan is referable, like the first, to
a vivid recollection of certain of the author's own personal experiences. On his return to Bath, while he was recovering
from the wounds of his second encounter, Sheridan was much
exercised at the outrageous reports and scandals circulated
about his private adventures and sketched out the plot of a
comedy to be called *The Slanderers.* This he subsequently
united with another rough draught concerning the domestic
differences of the Teazle's and in this union *The School for
Scandal* was wrought. But the essential contrast of the comedy
— the contrast of Tom Jones and Bilfil — may have had an
origin even more intimate; for Charles Surface, however faithful to a long dramatic ancestry, by way of Congreve and Vanbrugh, is possessed, with all his carelessness and inconsequence,
of an essential soundness of heart and a personal charm that
was recognisably the author's, while Sheridan's elder brother,
Charles Francis, is described as "a plodding selfish man, who
never ran avoidable risks, who was an unfilial son and an un-
affectionate brother," in a word, potentially at least, a very

[6] See Brander Matthews, *Sheridan's Comedies,* 1885, p. 31.

Joseph Surface. This celebrated comedy is avowedly a picture of life observed from a satirical point of view. In such a picture, even of the frivolous society of Bath, no man looks for the accuracy of the chronicler, any more than for his dulness; although it may be questioned if even the satire of Sheridan could seriously misrepresent the actual malevolence of mendacious gossip or the extravagant lengths of fashionable folly. As already suggested, the dramatist owed much to a long tradition, but *The School for Scandal* did not follow *The Way of the World* by nearly three generations for nothing.

Congreve's brilliant soulless dramatic art, as we have seen, fails to be truly satirical for the want of any real moral standard by which to measure the conduct of his personages. Possibly only the malicious — though who of us is free from malice? — can enjoy to the full so complete an exposure of the detestable social world in which his comedies had their roots and their being: at least it is difficult for the man not of his time to reach the moral detachment necessary to an appraisement of the comedies of Congreve solely for their literary worth. Between Congreve and Sheridan, the sentimental comedy had intervened which, with all its platitudinous over-emphasis of the moral aspects in life, had at least established a standard of conduct and with it a fulcrum for the lever of satire. No one can mistake either of Sheridan's great comedies for a lecture on morals; for, without further stricture on this score, the scapegrace is forgiven as he has been time out of mind in comedy — and in life — and we are taught that verily does a good heart cover a multitude of follies. But if these comedies are not " the purest morals undefiled by wit," neither do they hold up to our admiration a mode of life at which good men revolt or, on the other hand substitute for a hearty laugh at the foolishness of mankind a mawkish sentimentalising over the distresses of virtue. In a word it is the wholesomeness of Sheridan's humour that has given his comedies their place with Goldsmith's; and the popularity of both authors is an evidence of a healthy dramatic taste. Sheridan's last original drama was *The Critic* performed in 1779, the year of Garrick's death. The sentimental drama, scotched by Goldsmith, was still living on to the evening of its day, more particularly in the dramas of Richard Cumberland, an abler man than either Murphy or Colman, active in public affairs, in many kinds of letters and the author of more than fifty plays, now totally forgotten. Moved by the welcome always accorded to *The Rehearsal* on revival, Sheridan conceived the idea of bringing this famous burlesque of the drama up to date and in the upshot wrote a mock play that surpassed his example. *The Critic,* like *The Rehearsal,* represents a play within a play; and from that famous piece Sheridan derived, too, the clever artifice by which an author is made to witness a performance of his own play and comment upon it to his friends. From *Tom Thumb,* Sheridan borrowed the idea of a parody on a supposed tragedy of English histori- cal subject, here the Spanish Armada. But Sheridan bettered all his models and devised, in the person of Sir Fretful Plagiary, a personal lampoon which surpassed the poet Bayes, alike as it represented Dryden and as afterwards adapted to the lesser laureate, Cibber. "There is perhaps no other example," says Mr. Gosse, "of the absolute destruction of a reputation by ridicule so complete as that of Cumberland by the picture of Sir Fretful Plagiary."

And now triumphant in comedy and satire, Sheridan turned from the stage to the almost equally theatrical field of politics. His achievements and vicissitudes there and his long struggle from the zenith of success as a playwright and manager to all but complete financial ruin, do not concern our story. In Sheridan the old drama that took its original impulse from Marlowe and Shakespeare expires. There is nothing that has followed in its kind, whether comedy or tragedy, that is not contained well within the ample superficies of the great drama that was. Time had gone on and even the genius of Gold- smith and Sheridan could not restore the past. Literature and the stage were thenceforth to be all but completely separated, as poetry had long been banished the drama; and their revival was to come independently and apart. Between *The Ring and the Book* or Swinburne's trilogy of *Mary Stuart* and a tragedy of Shakespeare there is as great a difference as between either and *Clarissa Harlowe;* and the accident that some of our poets have written for the stage, like artists seeking experiments in an alien material, does not account for the fact that, in the Eng- lish language at least, our playwrights — dare we say even until recently? — have not been our poets.

CHAPTER XII

ENGLISH DRAMA SINCE SHERIDAN

SAVE for Goldsmith and Sheridan, as we have seen, acting drama, during the reign of George III, scarcely deserves chronicling in the annals of literature. Imitators these masters of comedy had, but none of conspicuous talent; and as yet the drama, written only to be read, was as unreadable as it was unactable. However, it is not altogether fair to refer the increasing decrepitude of the drama solely to a want of talent on the part of the playwrights. The ancient challenge of Collier that the stage reform or be shunned by decent men, was re-echoed throughout the century and the strong religious movements and efforts, reformatory of manners, tended not only to restrain the license of the stage but restricted its patronage among honest and godfearing men. By the time that the regenerative influences of the Wesleys were making themselves felt, the licensing act of 1737 had already passed, restricting the performance of legitimate drama to the two licensed theatres and restoring the censorship of the government over plays. The feeble opposition against these measures is alone enough to declare how weakened was the influence of the stage. Under such conditions it was safer for managers to temporise with old and tried material than to risk the uncertainties of novelty. With the demand so limited and the necessity of making each new play a theatrical success, whatever else it might be, the breach between plays written to be acted and plays written to be read, which had been bridged over in comedy by Goldsmith and Sheridan and in tragedy not at all, became wider and wider, marking at first no more than the difference between Dr. Johnson and Home, it came in time to mark the disparity between Shelley and Sheridan Knowles, or between Browning and T. W. Robertson. We have thus as to drama on the stage, restriction by law, limiting the output of plays, and competition among playwrights, a limitation of the constituency supporting the theatre owing to the contemporary moral and religious attitude towards the stage, and the drawing off of the best literary and poetic talent to the safer returns of the novel or the ampler poetic possibilities of the closet play.[1]

Among the writers of comedy who immediately followed Goldsmith, O'Keeffe, Macklin, Reynolds and the younger Colman are perhaps the least forgotten. The first has the gaiety and natural flow of humour that has made his countrymen time out of mind the world's jesters. Macklin, notable as an actor, wrote a remarkable satiric comedy in his old age, *The Man of The World*, although of an older school and really prior to Sheridan. In Frederic Reynolds we have a typical prolific maker of plays to order, without the technical skill of a Scribe or even a Tom Taylor; while in Colman (famous in his day like Reynolds) as an improvisator, the representation of character was often reduced to an incessant repetition of some oddity or peculiarity of speech and manner that his auditors found excruciatingly comical while his sentiment is described by Leigh Hunt as "mouthed" and "overdone" "in the manner of a man who is telling a lie." To these may be added Mrs. Inchbald, Thomas Morton and Holcroft whose one great theatrical feat was the capture of *Le Marriage de Figaro* by Beaumarchais by memory and conveyance of it across the channel and into English in his *Follies of the Day*. Holcroft's most popular play, *The Road to Ruin*, holds the provincial stage even to-day. Still obstinate in the ways of the older comedy of manners as exhibited in *The Clandestine Marriage*, which he wrote in collaboration with Garrick, was the elder Colman who died in 1794 to be succeeded by the vivacious son whom we have just mentioned. Among the sentimentalists, Kelly dying in 1777, Cumberland "the Terence of England, the mender of hearts," as Goldsmith called him, continued his tearful way despite the satirical slings of Sheridan, a busy playwright, essayist and writer of general literature, confidently assured of his own enduring fame whatever might be true of his contemporaries. It has been pointed out that in Hannah More, the feminization of tragedy, begun in Otway and Southerne, continued in the "she-tragedies," of Rowe, as he himself dubbed them, to reach in Hill, Murphy and Cumberland its culmination. Her *Percy*, 1777, was a very successful play, and her

[1] On the later drama see the excellent chapter (ix) by T. Seccombe in *The Age of Johnson*, 1900, pp. 199 ff.

Fatal Falsehood, a drama of domestic sentiment, only less so.
Notwithstanding the attacks of *She Stoops to Conquer* and *The
Rivals* on the strongholds of sentiment, little more was actually
accomplished than the readmission into serious drama of a certain quantum of low comedy. This, Holcroft justifies, for
example, in the preface to his popular drama, *Duplicity,* though
here, as in others of his and in Cumberland's *Jew* and *Wheel
of Fortune,* the virtuous steadfastly suffer and the heavens
threaten to fall, tears furrow the countenance of comedy and
the cause of morality is vindicated and upheld. In short the
auditor of the late eighteenth century had long lost the robust-
ness of constitution necessary to the endurance of the rigours
of tragedy; and, while still willing to be harrowed and thrilled
by situations, at which good taste in any age must revolt, demanded that he be sent home satisfied that no real harm had
been done to any human creature, that morals had been upheld, the wicked reformed (rather than punished) and the good
substantially rewarded for being good.

If it could be in any wise necessary to appreciate to the full
the insignificance of the bulk of the eighteenth drama, we need
but compare it with the giant stature that the novel had reached
in Richardson, Fielding, Smollett, and Sterne, to be succeeded
in Fanny Burney, Mrs. Radcliffe and the following romanticists, in Maria Edgeworth and Jane Austen, to look no further
forward. The drama was the last form of literature to feel
the quickening approach of the romantic return of the year.
When at last the stage did awaken to the fact that the world
was changed about it, it was influenced only by the coarser
and more obvious elements in " the renascence of wonder," the
delicate and poetical finding a more congenial place almost anywhere else. If we look for " traces " and " premonitions,"
there is a touch of fatalism and an appreciation for natural
scene in *Douglas* which, with its indeterminate mediæval setting, derived from the ballad of *Childe Maurice,* dimly fore-
shadows the romantic manner. As much cannot be said for
Hannah More's *Percy,* despite a similar origin. To the elder
Colman has been ascribed a part in the reawakening interest in
Elizabethan drama, witnessed in the revival of plays of Fletcher
and Massinger as well as in a certain effort to imitate Elizabethan methods and diction. And before long the mediæval-
ism of the new contemporary fiction, its Gothic horrors, super-
naturalism and feeling for nature as accompanying and affecting

in its various aspects the affairs of men, begins to show its parallels on the stage. Walpole himself wrote an unacted play *The Mysterious Mother,* in 1768, which is not an unworthy companion of *The Castle of Otranto,* itself adapted for the stage and acted in 1781, as *The Count of Narbonne.* Other "Gothic tragedies" are Robert Jephson's *Braganza,* 1775, which boasts itself, in the prologue, as "warm from Shakespeare's school," his *Julia,* 1787, a very popular play, the scene of which is Elizabethan England, and Cumberland's *Carmelite,* 1784; and all preceded the German romantic influence. To these premonitions of romanticism may justly be added an effort to comprehend the older age of dramatic greatness and deprecate the use of its stately marble structures to build temporary dramatic hovels, noticeable more particularly in a gradual return to the acting of Shakespeare's plays in a state approximately that in which he left them, and even more in the honourable succession of editors of the great poet, each more circumspect than the last in taking liberties with the text. None the less, it remains a commentary on the stage of the time and the want of taste and discernment in the public, that it took the insight of an eminent actor, who had learned its insipid lines, and an exhaustive scholarly "enquiry" by an equally eminent Shakespearean to expose the impudent association of Shakespeare's name by Ireland with his worthless "ancient British" tragedy of *Vortigern.* Well has the history of the drama in the age of Wordsworth been summed up as "the impact of successive waves of romantic method and *motif* upon the solid intrenchments of theatrical tradition; with the result, that while the grosser and baser elements found ready entrance, the finer and more poetic were stubbornly beaten back, and only towards the close of the period began to filtrate perceptibly through." [2]

We found English drama when at its lowest ebb as literature most widely affecting the stages of France and Germany through the homely domestic tragedy of *Barnwell.* Similarly now, it was not the great romantic dramatists of Germany, Goethe, Schiller or Lessing, whose poetry and ideality was to reach and influence the English stage, but the more obvious, clever and adaptable theatrical qualities of the romantic dramas of Kotzebue. William Taylor of Norwich and Sir Walter Scott translated Goethe and Lessing, reaching those who read poetry

[2] C. H. Herford, *The Age of Wordsworth,* 1897, p. 135.

rather than the theatregoer; it was Benjamin Thompson and
Anne Plumptre who were chief among some thirty or more
English translators of a score of the two hundred dramatic
productions of Kotzebue; while Mrs. Inchbald, " Monk " Lewis
and others hastened to adapt the new German wonder to the
English stage. Between 1797 and 1801, Kotzebue had an
enormous vogue. The conquest was complete in *The Stranger*
(*Menschenhass und Reue*), acted at Drury Lane in 1798; and,
in the next year, even Sheridan lent his talents to the adaptation and staging, in *Pizarro* (*Die Spanier in Peru*), of much
that kind of fustian romantic history that he had covered with
ridicule in *The Critic*, to be rewarded by the issue within three
years of nearly thirty editions and translation back again into
German. The phenomenal fortune of Kotzebue in England
has been attributed to several causes. In the first place he is a
consummate master of stagecraft and often as witty as he is
clever. Secondly he appealed strongly to the prevailing love
of the sentimental from which English drama seems never to
have been able to shake itself free; and this appeal is given a
wider social and political character which fell in thoroughly
with the democratic and humanitarian temper of the moment.
Kotzebue received the extraordinary hearing, accorded to him
in the theatres of the civilised world, because of the paradoxical
attitude that he had caught from the new romanticism, more
particularly as promulgated by Rousseau, the type of romantic
sentimentality that sets up natural impulse against the customs
and the laws of man and, with greater magnanimity than justice,
extenuates great offences because of trivial virtues and trifling
good deeds. Like some of our own time, Kotzebue habitually
enforces the exception for the overthrow of the rule, gaining
assent to a partial truth to make a point against convention. He
is as capable, if not nearly so witty, as Mr. Shaw in exposing
the wrongs of society and he is utterly wanting — here most
unlike Mr. Shaw — in any sincere underlying ethical principle.
There is nothing new in the " problem," as we should call it, of
The Stranger which is the same with that of *A Woman Killed
With Kindness*. But the Elizabethan met his question frankly,
merely sketching the figure of the unfaithful wife and vindicating the superiority of the ethics of forgiveness over those of
revenge. Kotzebue sentimentalised the situation of separation
and estrangement, " compassionated an adulteress," as Mrs.

Inchbald puts it, in her prefatory " remarks " to Thompson's translation, allowing his " pity " to " deviate into vice by restoring this woman to her former rank in life under the roof of her injured husband." The age must have revelled in the tears, generosities and struggles for command over feeling of the stranger and his Adelaide, in the final parting, converted into reconciliation by the timely thrusting in of the long motherless children and the rest of the lachrymose claptrap that appears " to do the business " with impressionable humanity when better stuff fails. Kotzebue is largely the old sentimental drama in a new romantic masque. *Pizarro,* we might almost call a resuscitation of the old heroic drama in its repetitions of the rival lovers and the rival ladies in the atmosphere of a far away and delightfully unknown Peru; while in the matter of strained emotion, even the hero of honour, distracted and distorted, is surpassed in " the renunciatory lover," as he has been called, " who sacrifices all for the happiness of the angel who loves not himself but his friend." [3] There are always those who mistake acute cynicism as to present conditions for the revelation of a new gospel. A translation of Kotzebue's *Negersklaven* was dedicated to Wilberforce, strange irony as to an author, whose life was that of a political reactionary and whose death came to him in the guise of an enthusiast's stroke for liberty. Neither artistically nor for any serious " reading of life," could Kotzebue be taken into account. Nor could more be looked for from Lewis (also one of his translators), whose notorious novel, *The Monk* with its *diablerie* and rococo romanticism is of much the stuff of his plays, *Castle Spectre,* his *Adelgitha* and *Venoni* which came and went with the German revival. Grotesque caricatures of the imitators of Goethe's *Goetz von Berlichingen* as these productions of " Monk Lewis " are, they link on to the literary translations of that famous romantic play by Taylor and Scott, while the latter's tragedy, *The House of Aspen,* " actually taken up," we are informed by Lockhart, " and put in rehearsal for the stage," discloses the wider relations of this species of the drama to the romantic fiction and balladry that, beginning in Mrs. Radcliff and Bishop Percy's revival of old balladry, rose to *The Minstrelsy of the Scottish Border* and the *Waverley Novels.* The influence of Schiller was less efficient, however one of his gigantic figures of romance cast its

[3] A. H. Thorndike, *Tragedy,* p. 328.

shadow far before to modify in Maturin's *Bertram*, 1816, one of the latest outcomes of the Gothic school.

The larger issues of the romantic revival can little concern so brief a sketch as this of the form of literature that was least radically affected by it. Not only was Scott carried by the eddy of the moment into the writing of a tragedy under German inspiration; the same was true of Wordsworth and Coleridge, *The Borderers* of the one, *Osorio* of the other, respectively offered to the managers of Covent Garden and Drury Lane, were refused by both in 1798. And, indeed, neither could be conceived of as successful on the stage, however the latter, revised as *Remorse*, met with a qualified acceptance when acted. Both young authors were directly affected by the romantic spirit of contemporary German literature; but Schiller, not Kotzebue, stood for that inspiration; however conscious Coleridge might be of the apparatus of the school of terror or Wordsworth of Godwin's principles of *Political Justice*, neither was unmindful of the deeper and more powerful traditions of Shakespeare and the English past. Moreover, incident, even character itself, was not that in which they were primarily interested; it was rather " the power of passion to reveal the depths of human nature " that was their quest; and for the expression of this they found solution not in drama but in the lyric, raised to new and more significant uses in *Lyrical Ballads*.

This idea of making the drama the means of a delineation of the stronger passions of the mind was followed out with extraordinary diligence and completeness by Joanna Baillie in her *Plays of the Passions* that range, some twenty-eight in number, from 1798 to 1812. Her notion was to illustrate in each play a dominant human passion, traced from its beginning to its end in ruin or satisfaction. To this she concentrated attention on the origin of that passion within, not as stimulated by external circumstance or happening; and subordinated all incident, development of character, even poetry and its embellishments, to a rigorous search for passion in its isolation. Her medium is verse; one is surprised, with her theory, why not prose. She presents in these dramas, a variety of subjects, domestic and historical, and is far from unaffected by the outward implements of romance, knights, vaulted Gothic chambers, music by night, moonlight and witchcraft. Miss Baillie wrote ostentatiously for the stage, as her many elaborate stage directions go to show, yet her works are full of improbabilities and her ignorance of

any real stagecraft is patent. Several of these dramas were
acted in London and Edinburgh and one of her tragedies, *De
Montfort,* held the stage for a short time. Her comedies,
which professed to substitute character for incident and intrigue,
had even less chance for success on the stage. The extravagant
praise that Joanna Baillie's work received at the hands of the
most judicious of her contemporaries, Scott, Campbell and Byron
among them, must continue a matter of surprise to any who may
have attempted the reading of her dull, prolix and unilluminated scenes. But after all, she was merely trying to do for
the drama what Wordsworth, after a generation of abuse, accomplished for lyrical poetry, return it to the language of every-
day life and, in the fervour of an actual representation of a
single passion, raise the product into the region of poetry. Unhappily Miss Baillie was devoid of genius and her age appreciated her sincerity, her morality and clearly defined purpose
and humanitarian spirit as we, at this distance, can not.

To return to the popular stage, of the effect of the monopoly
of the two licensed theatres on the nature of the drama we have
already heard in these pages. This restriction, however broken
through at times, discouraged, as we have seen, original drama
of serious intent and encouraged, in the illegal houses, not only
evasions of the law but the upgrowth of innumerable dramatic
hybrids — the opera, operetta, farce, pantomime, burlesque, bur-
letta, melodrama at last — all of which conspired to lower the tone
of the stage and to substitute mere diversion and the charms of
novelty and surprise for the legitimate pleasure of true drama.
The enlargement of the licensed houses, in 1791 and 1794,
and again, on their burning and rebuilding, in 1808 and 1809,
brought, besides, another disadvantage. Not only were new
productions discouraged but the old must be now more than
ever adapted to auditoriums in which the spoken word was lost
in the large dimensions of the house; and the legitimate drama,
as well as the illegitimate, was bolstered perforce by spectacles,
machines and great effects, with songs, choruses and other musical additions. In this dilation and amplification of the drama,
so to call it, Colman the younger was a leader, as clever as he
was unabashed and daring. In the process he achieved a new
and preposterous species of dramatic entertainment made up of
tragedy, comedy, opera and farce: the tragedy is blank-verse of
a Shakespearean sound, whatever its sense, the rest concocted of
farce in prose, dance and song, effect of light, scene, concourse

on the stage and what not. *The Surrender of Calais* has for
its basis the story of Queen Philippa's ransom of that be-
leaguered town, *The Battle of Hexham* is a love story thrust
into a chronicle play and served with much extraneous sauce,
The Mountaineers borrows a story from *Don Quixote* and en-
livens the whole with a humorous Irishman, and *The Iron Chest*
dramatizes Godwin's story of remorse for murder, *Caleb Wil-
liams*. Colman's comedies, if less extravagant, are equally ingenious and his burlesque verses and unfailing wit made him a
favourite in the society of the Regency and led to his appointment, by King George IV, to the office of licenser of plays
which he exercised with unexpected rigour and ability.

It was in 1802 that Holcroft, Colman's most prolific competitor, added the new French entertainment, known as *mélo-
drame,* to the resources of the illegitimate drama, supplying much
the kind of thing that Colman had been giving, with a somewhat
greater infusion of incidental and descriptive music, reducing the
dialogue in part to dumb show and increasing the rapidity of the
action, the sensations, startling situations and mechanical tricks.
The Gothic tale and the contemporary romantic novel were the
natural quarry of material for such productions. Leaving Holcroft who is only typical of his kind, we read of a stage version
of *Rob Roy,* in 1818, in which the rôle of Diana Vernon becomes a singing part, but in which, none the less, Macready
gained one of his theatrical successes; and of *Don Sebastian,*
turned at once into a musical play and into prose, illustrating
a highly exciting action, combining " equestrian combats, real
water, cataracts and machinery for thrilling escapes." Melodrama, however it originally denoted a play involving music,
lost this as a feature before long, and came to be characterised
mainly by the rapidity and incessant quality of its action, its
startling situations aided by mechanical devices, its dumb shows,
vivid contrast of vice and virtue and an inevitably happy ending
for the good with a corresponding dealing out of appropriate
punishment for the wicked. It is noticeable that not a single
feature in this category is new; each had long existed and all
were degraded in the combination. Melodrama has not yet
become extinct nor is it likely to perish alone by the influence
of higher ideals or better art. It has now to reckon with something lower than itself; for, in comparison with the banalities of
the music hall and the " musical comedy " and the suggestiveness of much besides that masquerades under a better name,

melodrama is an honest, if a gross, art and better on that score than the frank immorality of our older comedy or the perverted outlook of the drama of sentiment. But what of any true drama in such an age? crowded by melodrama, farce, sentiment and nonsense, by the opera for lovers of music, by the novel among readers for story, by poetry for lovers of beauty. It is no wonder that the stage languished of a wasting illness from which recovery was more than doubtful and that the best intellects, after a failure or two should have turned to fields not so hopelessly barren.

But it is not to be supposed that the young and ardent poets who were carried away on the waves of the new romantic poetry were content to leave the stage to melodrama and its like. From Southey's somewhat abortive attempt to dramatize a recent event in *The Fall of Robespierre,* 1794, into the reign of Queen Victoria, there is scarcely a name of poetical or other literary prominence to which there is not attached some effort in the drama. Scott contented himself after the rejection of *The House of Aspen* with an occasional dramatic sketch such as *Macduff's Cross or Holidon Hill,* suggesting unrealised possibilities in the direction of romantic historical drama. Godwin transferred less of the revolutionary ideas of his novels than might have been expected to a couple of dramas, *Antonio* and *Faulkner,* which failed as signally as Charles Lamb's *John Woodvil,* born as it was of enthusiasm for Elizabethan poetry and a following of Joanna Baillie's idea of an exposition of the passions from within and mainly by soliloquy. A happier stage "imitation of the old dramatic writers" was Tobin's *Curfew* which enjoyed a run of twenty nights, in 1807, and is as far from poetry as Lamb was remote from drama. To the year 1812, belongs Landor's first and best tragedy, *Count Julian,* in which his success in portraying the character of the protagonist is proportionate to his revelations of the poet's self. Here, in the trilogy of the story of Giovanna of Naples, and *The Siege of Ancona* (all of which followed in publication long after in the forties), Landor maintains that literary isolation that is always his: these tragedies are splendid literary works, but their relation to the stage is scarcely greater than that of *The Imaginary Conversations.*

With Coleridge's revision of his *Osorio* and offer of it to the stage under the title *Remorse,* in 1817, the poets begin a new and determined effort to recover the stage for poetic and romantic tragedy. Coleridge owed the acceptance of *Remorse* to the good graces of Byron; and the novel beauty of its diction and a certain fervour sustained it for twenty nights and extorted from so tried a theatrical critic as Genest the words " a tolerable tragedy." It must have struck the average auditor of the day with disappointment, rather than with any sense of novelty, that Coleridge's avenger seeks not blood, but contrition, in the brother who has done him wrong; and all the intrigue, rebellion, the necromancy and madness of this beautifully written tragedy could little sustain a plot in which all is disclosed in the first two acts. Before the performance of *Remorse,* Coleridge had offered Drury Lane his *Zapolya, a Christmas Tale,* avowed " an humble imitation of *The Winter's Tale* of Shakespeare," but despite a romantic plot and an elaborate effort at action, variety and stage effect, the play was refused. *Remorse* reached a third edition in the year of its performance and was revived once in 1817, and with this ends Coleridge's association with the theatre. And now parallel with stage successes of Sheridan Knowles and Sheil's Elizabethan adaptations, Byron, Shelley, Milman and Procter and even Keats, turned their attention to the drama.

Byron's actual preoccupation with the drama is concentrated almost within the limits of the single year 1821, although early in 1816, while a member of the subcommittee of management at Drury Lane, he cast a German tale into dramatic form, in *Werner,* with the purpose of representation on the stage. *Werner* was rewritten in 1822, after the experience that his other plays brought him; and, acted (first in New York in 1826 and at Drury Lane in 1830), was one of the stage successes of its time. *Manfred,* begun later in 1816, is a very different production. Whether the poignant regret for the inevitable past that characterises this tragedy comes of a terrible page in the autobiography of the poet or not, this extraordinary dramatic poem owes its indirect inspiration to Goethe's *Faust* which Lewis had read and translated to Byron, howsoever it is likewise a lyrical expression of the poet's self, exalted and abased before the grandeur of Alpine scenery. In *Marino Faliero,* begun almost immediately after *Manfred,* Byron made a serious effort to transplant to the stage the poetry of rebellion that was his. But distractions intervened and other work and it was not until 1820 that he resumed the task. With a subject dealing with an historical conspiracy, not unlike *Venice Pre-*

served, one, moreover, in which an historic parallel is discernible to " the mischief now afoot " which he hoped " might send the barbarians of all nations back to their own dens," the author, with characteristic inconsistency, announces his determination to escape " the reproach of the English theatrical compositions " " by preserving a nearer approach to unity in substituting the regularity of French and Italian models for the barbarities of the Elizabethan dramatists and their successors." [4] Against his will and almost against his legal action, *Marino Faliero* was acted at Drury Lane early in 1821; and, although repeated seven times, was coldly received, as the author had predicted. Genest echoed the popular impression that " despite the beauty and spirit of [Byron's] dialogue and the just delineation of his characters . . . too much is said, and too little is done." But of the play, Goethe wrote: " We forget that Lord Byron or an Englishman wrote it. The personages speak quite for themselves and their own condition, without having any of the subjective feelings, thoughts and opinions of the poet." And indeed, it may be admitted that in this tragedy, more than any other, Byron achieved the detachment and objectivity essential to dramatic success. But Byron had passed for himself " a selfdenying ordinance to dramatize, like the Greeks . . . striking passages of history," and *Sardanapalus* and *The Two Foscari,* following close upon *Marino Faliero,* were acted by Macready after Byron's death and both achieved all the success that a great name and splendid powers sustaining noble theories, counter to contemporary practice, could give them. *The Two Foscari* is another Venetian play, of much the general nature of *Marino Faliero.* Both plots are romantically improbable, however faithfully founded on the authorities that the poet consulted; for the probabilities of life and the probabilities of the stage are two things; and this the romantic poets rarely discovered. *Sardanapalus* is different; for in the Assyrian voluptuary, suddenly transformed to a figure of chivalric glory, in his " remorseful recognition of the sanctity of wedlock," his easy, dissolute nature, even in his sly sarcasm of temper, we have one of those interesting and incessantly recurrent projections of the author's self into his work. *Sardanapalus* is thus transformed from its species, an eighteenth century tragedy of palace intrigue, into a romantic and poetic expression of the poet's

[4] *Byron,* ed. Coleridge, 1901, iv, 327.

own experience and passion. Save for *Heaven and Earth,* a mystery, and *The Deformed Transformed,* a recurrence to the Faust legend, which had an irresistible attraction for Byron, there remains *Cain,* a splendid dramatic discant on the text, " Man walketh in a vain shadow," a poem in which Byron dared to try conclusions with Milton himself and about as capable of presentation on the stage as *Paradise Lost.* It was an audacious thing to dare match Milton's Lucifer, " the abstraction of infernal pride," and Goethe's Mephistopheles, the universal mocker of good and evil, with his Satan, who is alike a spirit and a mortal, " the traducer," as Mr. Coleridge puts it, " because he has suffered for his sins, the deceiver, because he is self-deceived; the hoper against hope that there is a ransom for the soul in perfect self will and not in perfect self sacrifice." [5] It is a commentary on the weakness of the stage as well as a tribute to the superb genius that Byron's *Cain,* with its daring and subtle attack on the conventional theological opinions of its day should have created a sensation and exerted a power which no acted play could ever attain.

Equally typical of the romantic revolt against the shackles of creed and convention are the two fine dramas of Shelley. *The Cenci* was inspired by the current traditions of that terrible story of incest and parricide as a type of the eternal struggle of man for justice and his eternal defeat. The elements of contrast here, as in *Cain* and in Shelley's *Prometheus Unbound,* are the tyranny of fact and law over essential innocence, helpless and betrayed. And the clarity with which the theme is developed, the skill by which its personages are disclosed in their passions, and the naturalness and truth of its situations and climaxes are as admirable as the language is simple, direct and unclogged with the usual embellishments of romantic art. The romance here, as in the greater dramas of Byron, is in the heart of the subject. *The Cenci* is an amazing first play, and the more extraordinary coming from the hand of a poet so purely lyrical in his art as is Shelley. It was offered to Drury Lane and declined because of the subject, though with a recognition of its merits; and the author was invited to submit another play. In *Prometheus Unbound,* the lyrist in Shelley reasserted itself, though the poem is equally, if not in a loftier degree, a triumphant presentation of the same world conflict

[5] *Ibid.,* v. 201.

of the unconquerable individual will against the tyranny of constituted authority.   The range, when all has been said, of the
poetic genius of such men as Byron and Shelley, was infinitely
beyond the hackneyed conventionalities of the Georgian stage,
if such genius does not actually transcend the conceivable
limitations of acted drama in the abstract.   And yet the rebel
philosophy, the cry for enfranchisement, political, social and
artistic, the clarity of vision, the power to compel words and
to wing them with the spirit of poetry, all of which belonged to
these divine and great souled singers of the poetry of revolt,
in some other age and with fewer literary and other distractions, might have crystallised their work in imperishable dramatic
form.   Byron and Shelley both died before the time of fulfilment.   We feel, especially as to Shelley, of whose development almost anything might have been predicted, that, once
more, in his death, the drama suffered an irreparable loss.
As to the lesser men, their contemporaries in the literary drama,
even Keats, whose exquisite poetry is so essentially lyrical and
descriptive, was emulous of " the writing of a few fine plays,"
and actually submitted his *Otho the Great* (the plot of which
had been mapped out for him by another hand, he furnishing
only the language and imagery), to both the licensed theatres.
The tragedy got no further than a promised rehearsal.   A better
fate awaited Milman's *Fazio,* " an attempt," says the author,
" at reviving the old national drama with greater simplicity of
plot," and though by a young clergyman, " written with some
view to the stage."   After one or two unauthorised performances elsewhere, *Fazio* gained a metropolitan success in 1818
and continued in favour, with all its florid eighteenth century
diction, for the possibilities of its chief woman's part.   None
of the other somewhat more Byronic plays of this notable scholar
and historian are memorable.   A few years later, Miss Mitford,
the popular novelist, gained recognition as a tragic writer for
the stage in three or four productions, *Julian, Foscari* (written
she declared before Byron's), and, most successful of all, *Rienzi*
acted for more than a month in 1828.   Her friend, too, Thomas
Noon Talfourd, the biographer of Lamb, a leading critic of
his day and later a judge, achieved a somewhat unexpected success in his classical tragedy *Ion,* which he was unable to equal
in several later efforts.   Procter (the Barry Cornwall of song
and literary friendship), furnished the stage two or three
dramas, accepted in their day, most important among them,

Mirandola, acted as far back as 1821; and nearly twenty years later Leigh Hunt, who belongs in the impetus of his prose and poetry alike to this earlier period, staged with deserved recognition his poetical drama *The Legend of Florence.* Most of romantic drama that immediately follows his time fell under the spell of Byron. But there was a Wordsworthian poetic influence more calm, more meditative and, it may be added, more remote alike from the bustle of life and the stage. As to these plays, more strictly of the study, to mention only two of the more prominent, Sir Aubrey de Vere's *Julian the Apostate,* 1822, and his *Duke of Mercia,* of the next year, were separated both in time and degree of excellence from his *Mary Tudor,* 1847, which some have placed in comparison with Tennyson's drama on the same historic subject; and Sir Henry Taylor, despite his *Isaac Comnenus,* 1827, praised by Southey, and later tragedies and comedies as well, remains memorable for his much lauded *Philip van Artevelde* which absorbed, as it exhausted, his thoughtful, lucid and essentially undramatic genius.

Mr. Archer, in an excellent chapter on the drama during the reign of Queen Victoria, has told of the continued struggle of " the minor houses " against the intrenched patent theatres and how theatrical " free trade " was at last established to the benefit of all by the act of 1843. He has told there, also how the age of the Kemble's, coming to its close, was succeeded by that of Macready, a stern but conscientious helmsman of the dramatic bark in waters commonly stormy, and, what was far more, the friend and encourager, so far as he was able, of literary and poetic endeavour for the stage. As to the state of dramatic literature the critic draws a picture, discouraging enough,—— " the ghost of the romantic drama stalked the stage," he tells us, " decked out in threadbare frippery and gibbering blank-verse. No one had yet reflected that, though Shakespeare might be for all time, his forms and methods were evolved to suit the needs of an age quite different from ours." Showing how Shakespeare was misinterpreted and misunderstood, he concludes " laboured rhetoric, whether serious or comic, was held to be the only ' legitimate ' form of dramatic utterance. This was literature — all else was mere drama and farce." [6] The leading dramatist, at the accession of Queen Victoria, was Sheridan Knowles, an Irishman, a Sheridan on his mother's

[6] *The Reign of Victoria,* 1887, edited by T. H. Ward, ii, 565.

side, an actor since 1809, a playwright with a dozen years' experience behind him — what more could be wanted for dramatic success? Knowles was the author between 1815 and 1843 of sixteen plays, beginning with the tragedies, *Caius Gracchus* and *Virginius,* 1820, so famous for their vigorous declamatory possibilities in their day, and continuing — to name only a few — through *William Tell,* 1825, and the historical plays, *The Hunchback,* 1832, most popular of all, and comedies such as *The Love Chase* and *Old Maids,* both acted for the first time after the accession of the queen. The ideal of Knowles was the revival of romantic drama: this appears to be the ideal of most dramatists in most ages. On one side Knowles was well equipped. He was possessed of a skilful stagecraft, alike in the construction and conduct of plot. Beyond this, Knowles is almost the least of the romanticists. Not only does he fail in that touchstone of the romantic art, an ability to turn a lyric, but his imagination is commonplace, he is uninventive, his dialogue, while at times sprightly, seldom rises above mediocrity and his blank-verse, which he uses almost to the exclusion of prose, is stiff with dignity or slovenly with carelessness. Mr. Archer wickedly calls Knowles the Shakespeare of 1837; possibly Bulwer Lytton was its Fletcher. Lytton began in the manner of Byron; his early novels have been declared too close in this following to have suited the taste of the rising generation. After a preliminary failure in the drama, Lytton leaped to immediate reputation in *The Lady of Lyons,* 1838, which with his *Richelieu,* of the same year, have continued to keep the stage to the present time. If Knowles was commonplace he was at least safe: Lytton's plays — these and the two or three others that he wrote before 1851 — appear to the modern reader, false in sentiment and false in taste. They have the glitter and attraction to the eye of tinsel and its repulsiveness to the touch and understanding. The plot of *The Lady of Lyons* contemplated in quiet is absurd; its hero, Claude Melnotte, is quite pitifully unheroic, and there is not the ghost of the art of historical portraiture in Richelieu. Yet the things act; Lytton, too, had the precious secret of stagecraft which verily does cover a multitude of sins. Amongst other names, Mr. Archer gives us G. W. Lovell, Gerald Griffin, and Westland Marston, reminding us of the success of Talford's *Ion* and the failure of Robert Browning's *Strafford,* just before the beginning of the reign, and granting to Leigh Hunt's successful *Legend of Florence,* 1840, the palm as the drama of the period in which " dramatic and literary qualities are most happily blent." Into " the minor drama," with Knowles and Lytton for the majors, we need not descend. The amiable Planché wrote burlesque and extravaganza for fifty years, doing less harm thereby than some who have followed him, and Douglas Jerrold, famous wit and contributor to *Punch,* with a dozen names now less remembered, added their comedies, melodramas, farces and what not to divert the time.

No drama, with a past such as that of England, could be unconscious of what had gone before, and there has been no time since his own when Shakespeare has not been read, acted, admired and misunderstood in proportion to the degree in which he stands at variance with temporary standards of taste and manners. The growing respect for Shakespeare among scholars and the return of the stage to the presentation of his words, as nearly as possible as he wrote them, has already been mentioned. Before long other Elizabethans began to receive the editorial and critical attention that had so long been denied them; and Lamb's *Specimens of English Dramatic Poets,* Gifford's edition of *Jonson,* Coleridge's *Biographia Literaria* and the several books of Hazlitt, involving the discussion of dramatic literature, presented the whole subject to the reading public in a new and truer light. These works, coinciding as they did in point of time, with the vogue of Byron, whose plays, deny it as he might, owed much to this same dramatic past, begot in the years that followed a veritable Elizabethan revival. On the stage this influence was necessarily superficial, except in so far as it stimulated the staging of the old plays. Shakespeare became even more popular in the days of Macready than in those of Garrick or Kean. The two licensed houses vied with each other in the number of these " revivals " and in their appropriate setting and novelty, leaving only some few of the out of the way plays unacted. Other old authors were brought to light, though here the age preferred the Elizabethan veneer which Knowles, Sheil, and others were able to give to their own plays. From a literary point of view, by far the most interesting outcome of this rereading of our old drama was the series of fine poetic closet plays that came from the pens of Darley, Wade, Wells, Beddoes and Horne within little more than the decade, from 1825 onward. Darley's *Sylvia* is a lyrical fairy pastoral, reminiscent, in the best sense, alike of *A Midsummer Night's*

Dream and *The Faithful Shepherdess;* Wade and Wells fall
together in their discipleship to Marlowe, however immediately
both were influenced lyrically by Keats. Wade's two dramas
are *Woman's Love* and *The Jew of Arragon,* the latter a
failure, we are told, because it dared to champion the Jew much
as Shakespeare's *Merchant of Venice* has been contorted into
doing in our own day. Wells is practically the author of but
one work, *Joseph and his Brethren,* first published as early as 1823,
and absolutely unnoticed at the time; but finally revised, nearly
fifty years later, owing to the praise of Rossetti and Swinburne.
Joseph and his Brethren is a fine dramatic poem " writ dialogue wise "; it was never intended for the stage. Nor can
more be said, from this point of view, for the two extraordinary
dramas of Beddoes, *The Bride's Tragedy,* published in 1822,
when the author was a student at Oxford, and *Death's Jest-
Book,* complete four years later, but not printed until after the
author's death in 1851. Beddoes was a physician who passed
the greater part of his life in Germany and Switzerland. The
influences upon his work are, for the Elizabethans, Marlowe
and more particularly Webster, but both acting on the German
Gothic romance, derived less through its English imitations,
than direct. Beddoes was possessed of an extraordinary imagination and wealth of phrase and imagery, a spirit of daring
and metaphysical brooding, all of which recalls the spacious old
days of England's dramatic glory. But neither he, nor Wells,
nor Darley could have been, but for the more immediate influences, the speculative lyricism of Shelley, and the gorgeous
descriptive sensuousness of Keats.

Lastly of this group, Richard Hengist Horne is the author of
three tragedies *Cosmo de'Medici, The Death of Marlowe* and
Gregory VII. All partake, in notable degree, of the Elizabethan spirit, especially the play on Marlowe which has a fire,
directness and intensity that the subject and example should inspire. Horne's are the least inconceivable of the group on the
stage; but his dramas never reached it. " Pseudo-Shake-
spearean," I do not like to call these sincere and strong spirited
poets who found in the inspiration of a great age of the past
an impetus for expression which their own time could not give
them. But there is no better summary of the futility of all
such art than is to be found in the often quoted words of Beddoes himself: " These reanimations are vampire-cold. Such
ghosts as Marlowe, Webster, etc., are better dramatists, better

poets, I dare say, than any contemporary of ours, but they are ghosts — the worm is in their pages,— and we want to see something that our great-grandsires did not know. With the greatest reverence for all the antiquities of the drama, I still think that we had better beget than revive, attempt to give the literature of this age an idiosyncrasy and spirit of its own, and only raise a ghost to gaze on, not to live with." [7]

Browning's *Strafford* was actually performed a few weeks before the accession of Queen Victoria. The suggestion that the poet write for the stage came from Macready, who had ever an ambition to unite literature once more to the drama; the great actor even proposed the subject. But the play ran only five nights. For some eight years Browning continued largely preoccupied with the drama, *Pippa Passes, King Victor and King Charles, The Return of the Druses, The Blot on the 'Scutcheon, Colombe's Birthday, Luria* and *A Soul's Tragedy* following in almost an annual succession. *A Blot on the 'Scutcheon* was also inspired by Macready, but when it came to the stage, in 1843, he took no rôle in it; and, the play being "underacted," had only a short run. *Colombe's Birthday* was printed first and acted some nine years after; *Pippa Passes* was not staged until much later and then not professionally. These eight years of dramatic experimentation produced by far the bulkiest single part of Browning's work, a part, too, in which the powerful, original, eloquent and manly poet has left us some of the most beautiful and characteristic work. It is notable, however, that this work rises in poetic value in proportion as it departs from the conventions of accepted stagecraft, that the series, instead of exhibiting a rise in this respect, remains, from first to last, the individual expression of a powerful intellect forcing its art into an alien mould. However, by no means were all these works intended for the stage; but the distinction between those that were so intended and those that were not is unessential. Without renewing here a discussion that has been worn threadbare, it may be noted that in his dramas the two cardinal limitations of this great poet are his inability to escape from his own personality and, what may be called, the static quality of his art, as contrasted with that dynamic impulse which keeps things moving in drama that has

[7] Quoted by Mr. E. Gosse, *The Poetical Works of Beddoes,* Introduction, i, p. xxiv.

been successfully written for the stage. It is a commonplace that all the dramatic figures of Browning reason and argue — and how much they reason and argue! — with the intellectual brilliancy and address of their creator. If this is an overstatement of the truth, it must at least be admitted that he is likely to take one central figure and view the rest of his dramatis personæ from this acquired subjective position. There is little agility in Browning, to put himself dramatically in any other man's place, is to him next to an impossibility; and while we feel, how carefully he has studied his characters that we may superficially distinguish them, the distinctions are not radical and leave in us an impression that his shadows are too heavily weighted with their emotions, or perhaps more accurately, with their mental processes about their emotions. As to the want of dynamic impulse, not only are the plots of Browning far from well chosen or wrought out; they are sluggish and if they move at all, uncertain and discontinuous in their movement. Browning has achieved some great situations, most notable among them, the famous scene between Ottima and Sebald in *Pippa Passes;* but it is wholly static and affected altogether from without; it is in the nature of drama, it is not truly dramatic, for the extraneous influence is accidental, not essentially within, as are the promptings of the witches in *Macbeth,* a parallel often suggested. It is because of this immanence of self and immobility that Browning is not a dramatist, despite the supremacy of his poetry, his noble ethics and his compelling force of thought. Browning must have recognised his limitations, for while that surprising power of his to give vitality to a situation by an analysis of its component elements, delivered in flashes of insight, continues to animate his poetry to the end; he ceased writing dramas as such in 1846. Shall we say, to find a larger utterance in a poem such as *The Ring and the Book?* Or may we doubt whether this marvellous ability to focus the mental activity, so to speak, on the poetic analysis of a situation, viewed successively from half a dozen points, may not mean the individuality of a remarkable genius of a very exceptional kind, rather than mark any permanent step in an evolution away from the simpler, less perplexing art that is content with the interplay of incident and character illuminated by the light of poetry and unclogged with ratiocination.

Browning tried the drama early in his career; Tennyson waited until he had reached full recognition in his art, when

In Memoriam was nearly a generation old and the cycle of *The Idyls of the King* had reached its completeness. Tennyson is likewise the author of eight plays. *Queen Mary,* adapted to the stage by Henry Irving, was favourably received in 1876; three years later *The Falcon,* a poetical drama based on Boccaccio, ran sixty-seven nights; in 1881, *The Cup* was successfully acted; but, the next year, less applause was bestowed on a tragedy of village life, called *The Promise of May.* The poet had already published *Harold* and *Becket* which latter, abridged by Irving, was acted in 1893; and a little before this time a Robin Hood play, *The Foresters,* was presented first in America and later in London. Tennyson's trial of the stage was a more thorough one than Browning's. Though he came to it a far older man, there was an adaptability about his genius which, leaving out the lesser plays, shows itself in the improved technique and stagecraft of *Becket* as contrasted with the overcrowded scene of *Queen Mary.* Moreover, the association with Irving was happier than that of Browning and Macready, and his great fame, the accepted poet laureate, not only by royal patent but by the suffrage of the world of English speaking readers, gave to anything he might do a sanction and prestige that no other poet of the century could enjoy. Yet even Tennyson could not bridge the chasm between the stage and literature, and in his case for a different reason. Tennyson had long since reached an objectivity in his beautiful art that was never Browning's. But while his personages never represent Browning's masquerading projection of himself upon the canvas of his scene, save for the strong lines of *Becket* and possibly the fine original conception of *Harold,* distraught between two realms and two ages, Tennyson's characters have little individuality and, to some extent, even his poetry fails him in important moments. Mere cutting down will not convert a closet play, however poetic, into a drama for the stage; and neither Tennyson's nature nor his training gave him that sympathy with the auditors' point of view, that feeling for the word as spoken, that sense of reality in the unreal world of the stage, all of which are among the infinitude of things that go to make up that mystery, the successful dramatist. Moreover, Tennyson's greater dramas, far more than Browning's, are another renewal of the effort to rehabilitate the stage by following the Shakespearean tradition. And so, too, as to Swinburne we recognise that it was his passionate love for Elizabethan drama, which he knew so well and championed so enthusiastically, that begot the greater number of his nine memorable and beautiful poems in dramatic form. Especially is this true of his earliest play *Rosamund and the Queen Mother,* 1860, and his last, *Rosamund, Queen of the Lombards,* 1899, as of his version of the Marino Faliero story, already treated by Byron, and of the great trilogy of *Mary Stuart,* the enormous length and elaboration of which not only effectively defeats any possibility of stage representation but of a complete reading by any but the most valiant reader. Another influence in greater purity than ever before since Milton, has begotten in our age several exquisite imitations of Attic tragedy, among which Swinburne's beautiful *Atalanta in Calydon* is the most deservedly famous and his *Erechtheus* and Matthew Arnold's *Empedocles on Ætna,* which preceded them both, are the most important. But not only are these productions " Greek with a difference " quite as great, each in its kind, as was ever that difference in Keats, but all are essentially lyrical and in their thought expressive of the last great age that was but yesterday ours. There is no more salvation for the drama in infusing modern ideas into the myths of Æschylus and Sophocles, marble pure and marble cold, than there is for our religion in altars erected to the Diana of the Ephesians. Nor along the Tennysonian line of the following of the great example of Shakespeare can dramatic rehabilitation ever come. There will be no rejuvenation until we can escape from that great shadow and see anew the face of the sun.

As to Victorian writers for the stage, until we turn the new leaf of the present, into which we shall not look, the perversity of some malignant, or at least some mischievous, goddess, in charge of meting out the endowments of dramatic genius, appears to have pursued them. To T. W. Robertson, author of *Society, Caste, Ours* and other successes of monosyllabic title in the sixties and seventies, this fitful deity granted the actor's minute knowledge of the stage, a fresh humour and naturalness and a pervasive geniality that went far to account for his contemporary vogue; but she denied him originality, any genuine power to construct a plot or the least vestige of literary quality or distinction in what he wrote. On Tom Taylor, on the other hand,— remembered by the playgoers of a generation before the last for *The Fool's Revenge, The Ticket of Leave Man* and *Our American Cousin* — the jealous goddess bestowed a cultivated taste and no mean constructive ability, but she gave him only a commonplace imagination with which to employ these happier endowments. Still again, Charles Reade, the novelist, was an earnest, eager if difficult man, full of confidence in himself and possessed of a hectoring and controversial style. His best play is *Masks and Faces,* the stage version of his later story, *Peg Woffington,* an interesting comedy of intrigue, possessed of genuine wit and true feeling; and his version of Zola's *L'Assommoir, Drink,* is a drama of brutal reality and violence to move, disclosing, in its fidelity to the actual, the novelist's equally fatal limitation as a playwright, while the improbabilities of which he is readily convicted elsewhere, display a conflicting, if equally dangerous limitation. Lastly, there is Dion Boucicault, "the adaptive Mr. Boucicault," as Fitzgerald called him, who appropriated to his immediate dramatic uses whatever light article he might find, French or other, floating on the broad surface of the drama of the past or the present. Boucicault is responsible for two well-known dramas of the supernatural, "ghost plays," they are perhaps better called, *Rip van Winkle* (that has made more than one actor's reputation), and *The Corsican Brothers,* by no means dead yet in the purlieus of the theatrical world. But his great forte lay in the Irish play, *The Colleen Bawn, The Shaughraun, O'Dowd,* careless, "patriotic," unprincipled and impossible caricatures of his native country — or of any other country or society of men, for that matter — which somehow long continued to carry their loose joints through five acts of humorous improbability to the delight of their auditors. In the make-up of this last dramatist, our capricious goddess had forgotten not only literature, but responsible dealing with the wares that he handled.

Nor can much more be said for the names which Mr. Archer, that tried and outspoken critic of our late Victorian stage, chose to distinguish as "dramatists of to-day," in the year 1882, five years later picking out the following from among them: W. G. Wills, W. S. Gilbert, A. W. Pinero, J. Albery, S. Grundy, H. A. Jones, G. R. Sims and H. Merivale — the order is Mr. Archer's. With as great a delight as any of his contemporaries in Gilbert's humour of topsy-turvydom, and with respect for the fertility, thoughtfulness, industry and substantial success of all who, working in the drama, are still with us, it can not be said that in any of these names, or perhaps in those of our present moment,— even the keen, the trenchant, the irrepressible, the delightfully unexpected Mr. Shaw — is to be found that great regenerator of the stage who is to unite once more, in a dramatic picture of life, the quality of literature, whether poetic, satirical or realistic, with the histrionic art. One name that arose in the drama of the nineties, only too soon to be tragically eclipsed, seems to stand out in this respect above others. The name is that of Oscar Wilde; his comedies *Lady Windemere's Fan, A Woman of No Importance* and *The Importance of Being Ernest*. For the serious minded, who are unable to judge any work of art on its merits as such, but must always challenge the right of man to exist except as a machine for the solving of problems, the righting of wrongs, the active pursuit of all evils and anomalies to their utter undoing, there is nothing to say for these incomparable trifles. It takes an extraordinary amount and quality of thought to perpetrate trivialities such as these; and there is more beneath than appears in this dazzling swords' play of wit, this amazing ingenuity and endless resource. Moreover, here the literary quality, at least, is in no question, however we may pause at the want of any underlying ethical soundness, that greatest of the essentials to great drama. It is such glimpses as this of the promised land that forbid us to despair of drama in the English tongue for the future; such glimpses, too, as we are now getting of an indigenous drama, not nurtured to meet the cravings of a metropolitan audience, but arising out of local conditions, whether Irish, English or other, in which human nature is less sophisticated and abraided by the attrition of modern life. Least of all can we believe that the revolution effected in our manner of taking our serious theatrical amusements by the art, however great, of men of foreign birth and alien modes of thought, can ever restore to us the drama as a great national utterance.

INDEX

A

Abelard, 16
Addison, Joseph, 267, 276, 283, 287, 289–291, 297
Æschylus, 330
Albery, James, 331
Alençon, Duke d', 46
Alexander, Sir William, 142, 144
Alleyn, Edward, 51, 53, 105, 107, 204
—— John, 51
Ancourt, d', 278
Anne, Queen, 264, 282
—— Queen (of Denmark), 158, 159
Archer, Mr. W., 268, 280, 281, 323, 324, 331
Argenzola, 188
Aristophanes, 2, 153, 223, 224
Aristotle, 2, 6
Armin, Robert, 94, 110, 170

B

Bacon, Francis, 77, 118, 161, 176
—— Matthew, 77
Baillie, Joanna, 315, 318
Baines, Richard, 70
Bale, John, 28, 30, 69
Bandello, 190
Banks, John, 246, 265
Barclay, John, 219
Barnes, Barnabe, 139
Barrey, Lodowick, 170
Barry, Elizabeth, 237, 254, 259, 264, 274, 278
Bassano, 35
Beaumarchais, 310
Beaumont, Francis, 96, 117, 159–162, 174–184, 186–188, 196, 204, 206

Beaumont, Sir Francis, 175
Beddoes, Thomas Lovell, 325, 326
Beeston, Christopher, 209
Behn, Aphara, 257, 261, 262, 265, 297
Bellott, Stephen 76
Berkeley, Sir William, 231
Betterton, Mary Sanderson, 264
—— Thomas, 149, 238, 247, 249, 254, 264, 266, 272, 276, 278, 288
Blackmore, Sir Richard, 269
Boas, Mr. F. S., 71
Boccaccio, 171, 329
Booth, Barton, 285, 288
Boucicault, Dion, vi, 331
Boutel, Mrs., 274
Bower, Richard, 40, 41, 145
Boyle, Roger, see Orrery
Bracegirdle, Anne, 237, 264, 267, 278
Brandon, Samuel, 142, 143
Brend, Sir Nicholas, 51
Bridgewater, Earl of, 214
Bristol, Earl of, 256
Brome, Alexander, 231
—— Richard, 121, 170, 202, 205, 219–221, 261, 262, 272
Brooke, Arthur, 43, 81
—— Henry, 297
—— Lord, see Greville
—— Samuel, 193
Browne, William, 159, 162
Browning, Robert, vi, 99, 144, 309, 324, 327–329
Bruno, Giordano, 169
Bryan, George, 51
Brydges, John, 37
Buc, Sir George, 137, 201
Buchanan, George, 30, 38
Buckingham, first Duke of, 164

333